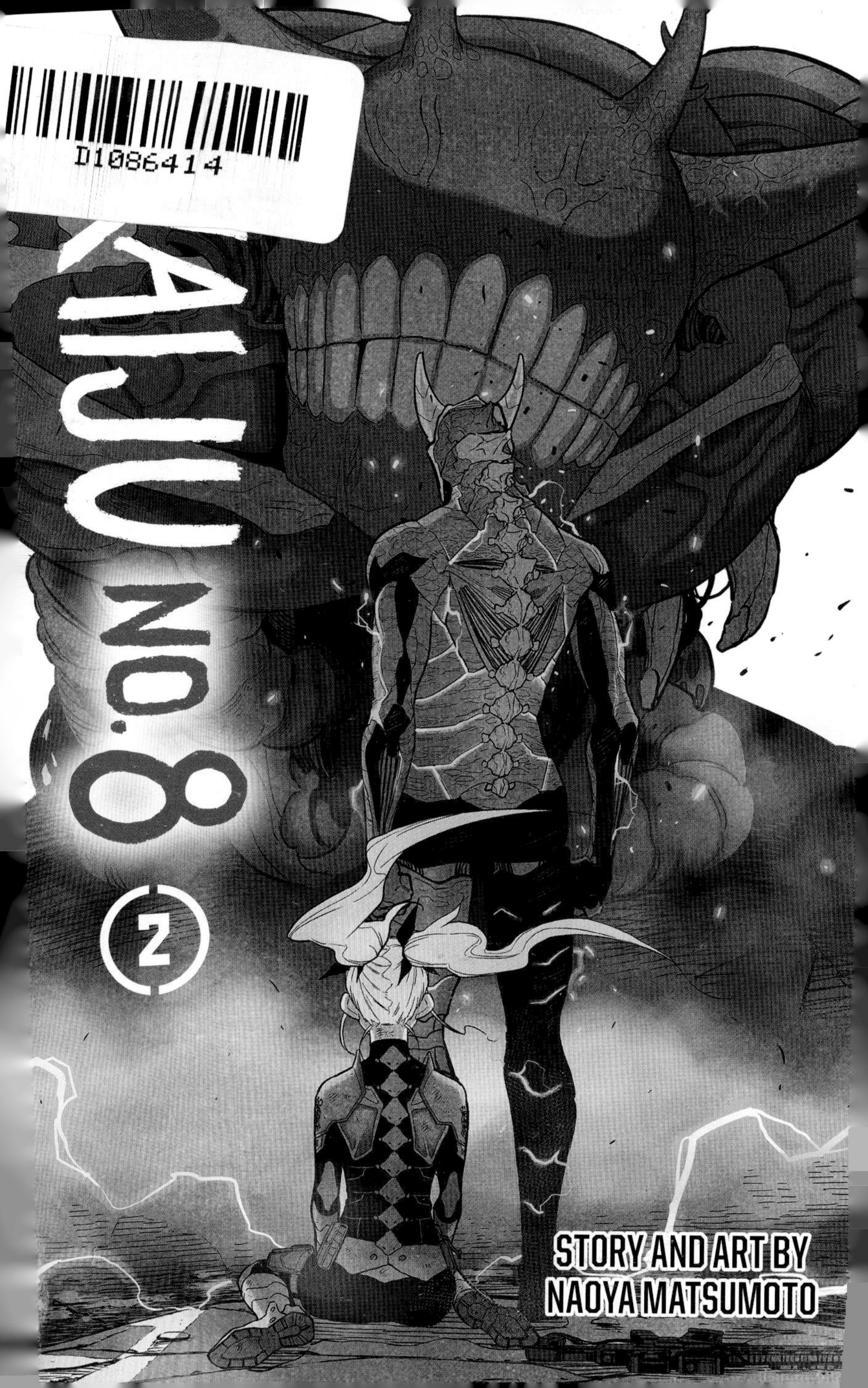
KAIJU NO.8
2
STORY AND ART BY
NAOYA MATSUMOTO

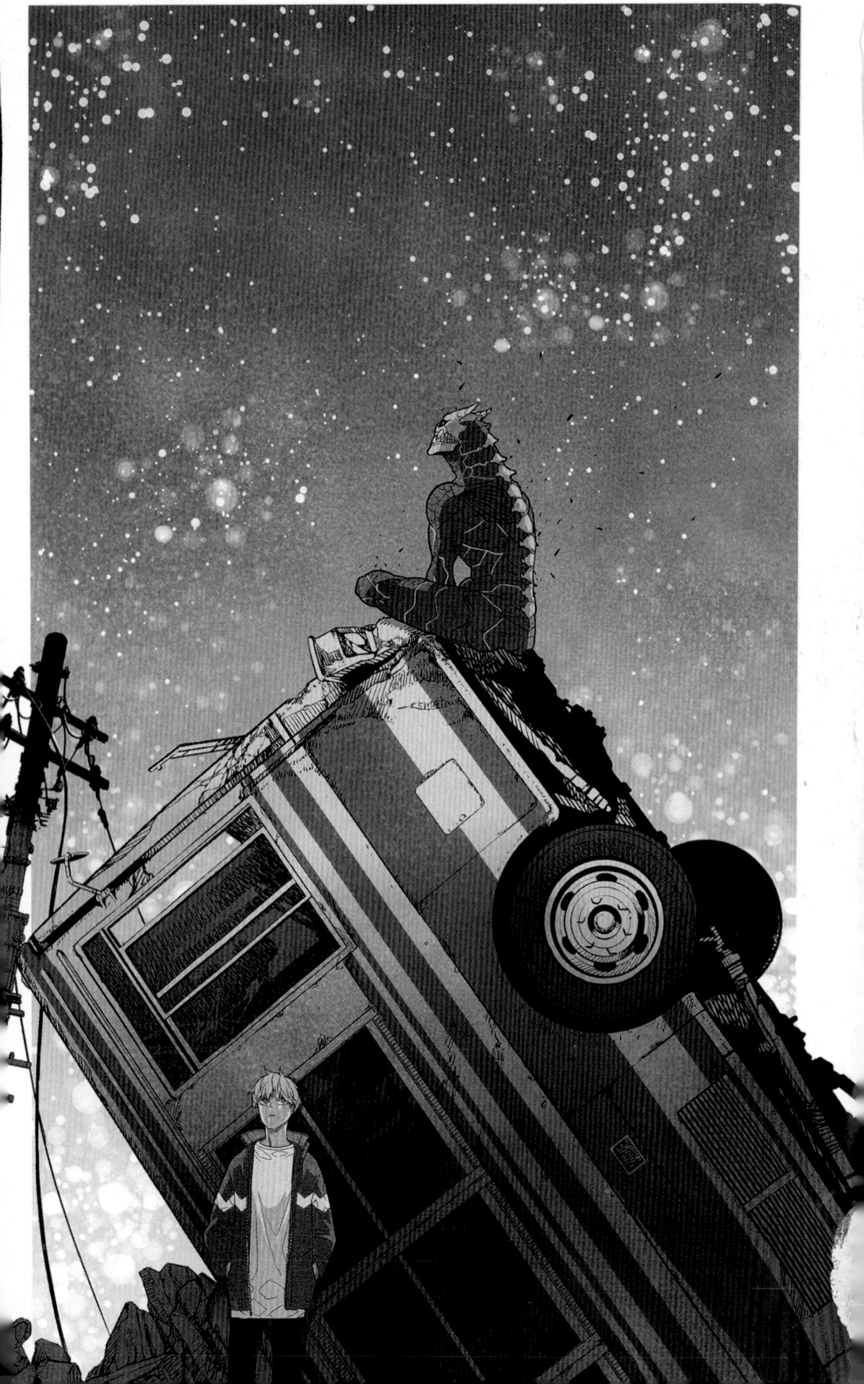

CONTENTS CONTENTS CONTENTS

KAIJU NO. 8

2

CONTENTS CONTENTS CONTENTS

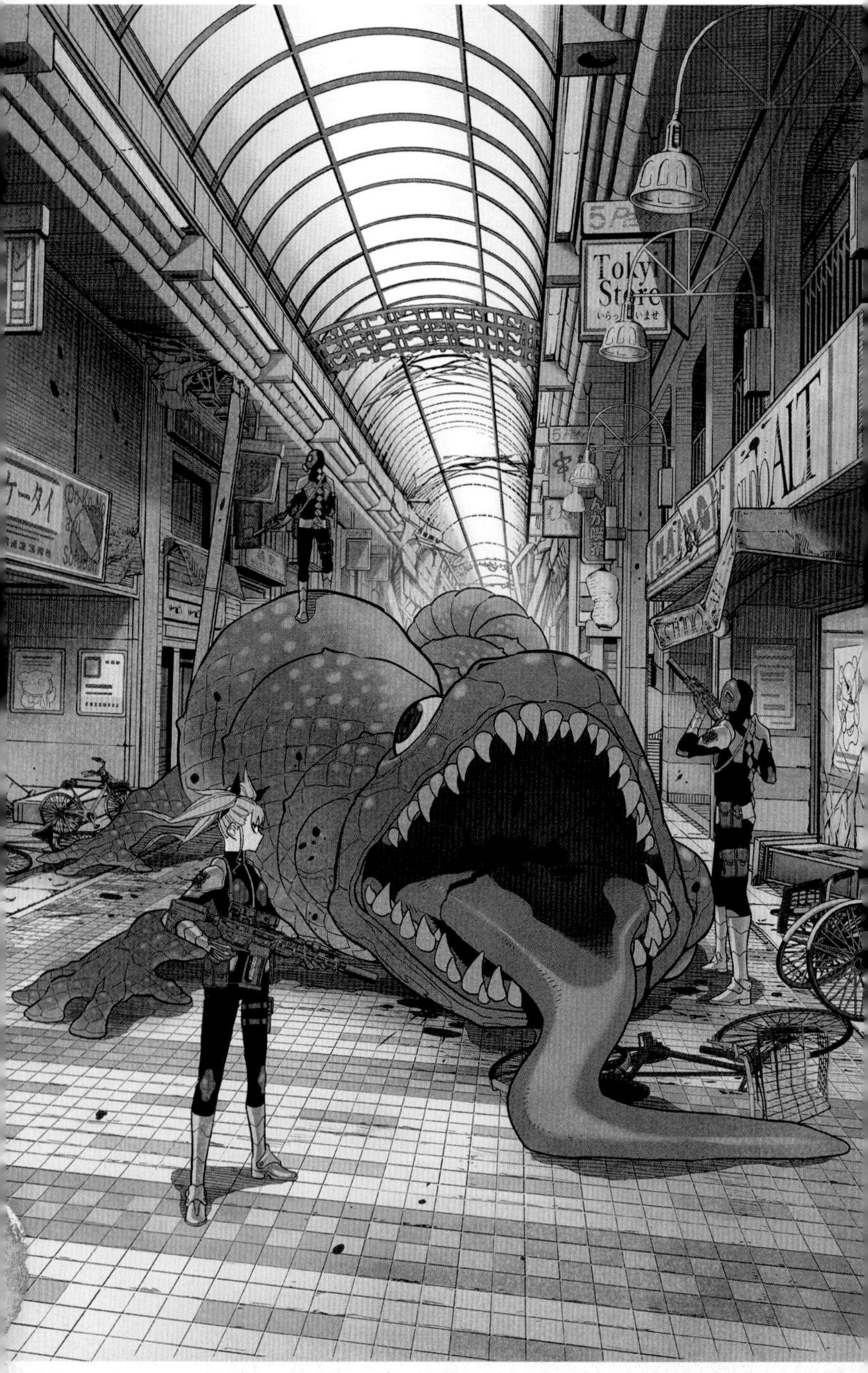
Store
ケータイ
ALT

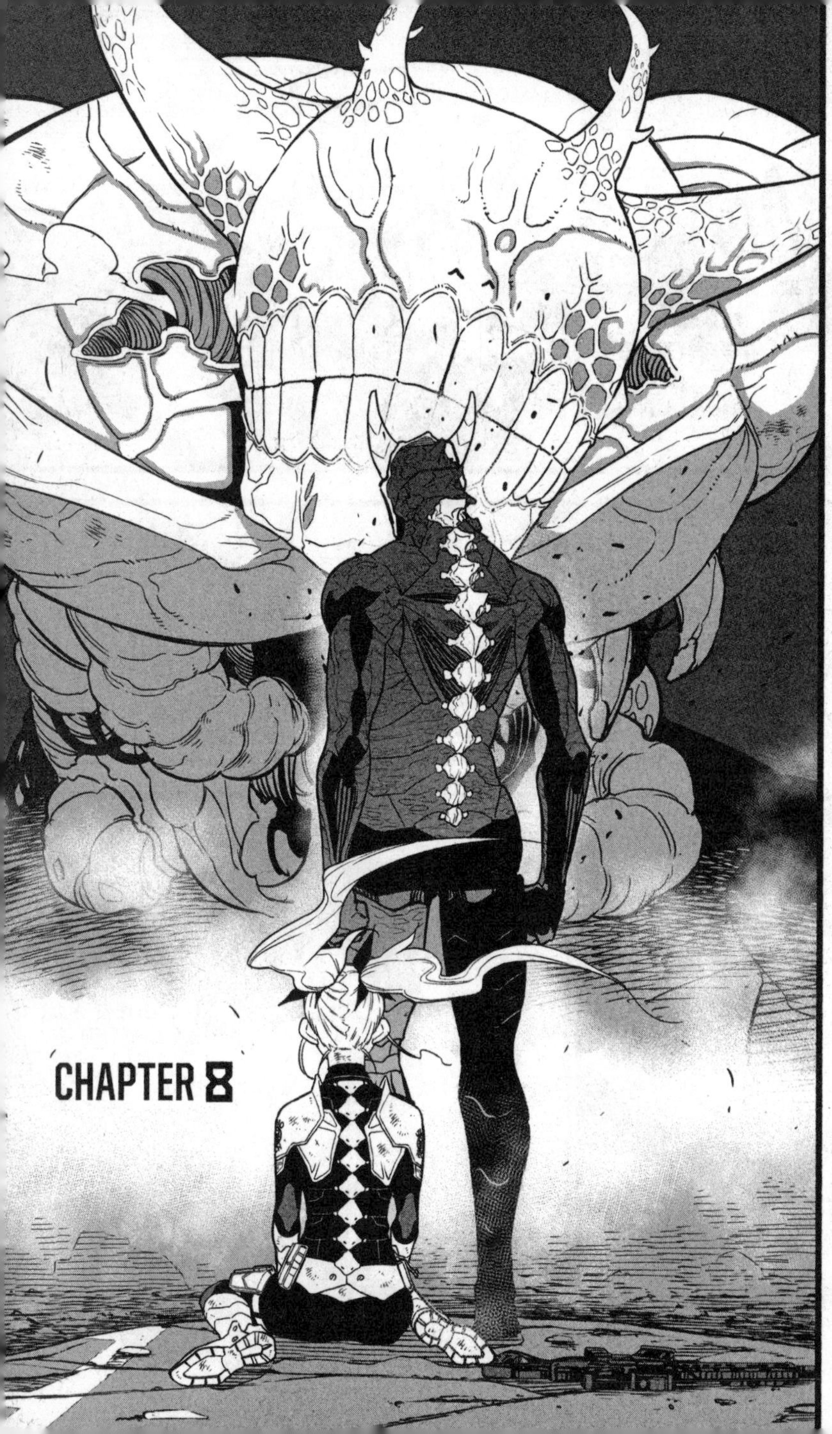
CHAPTER 8

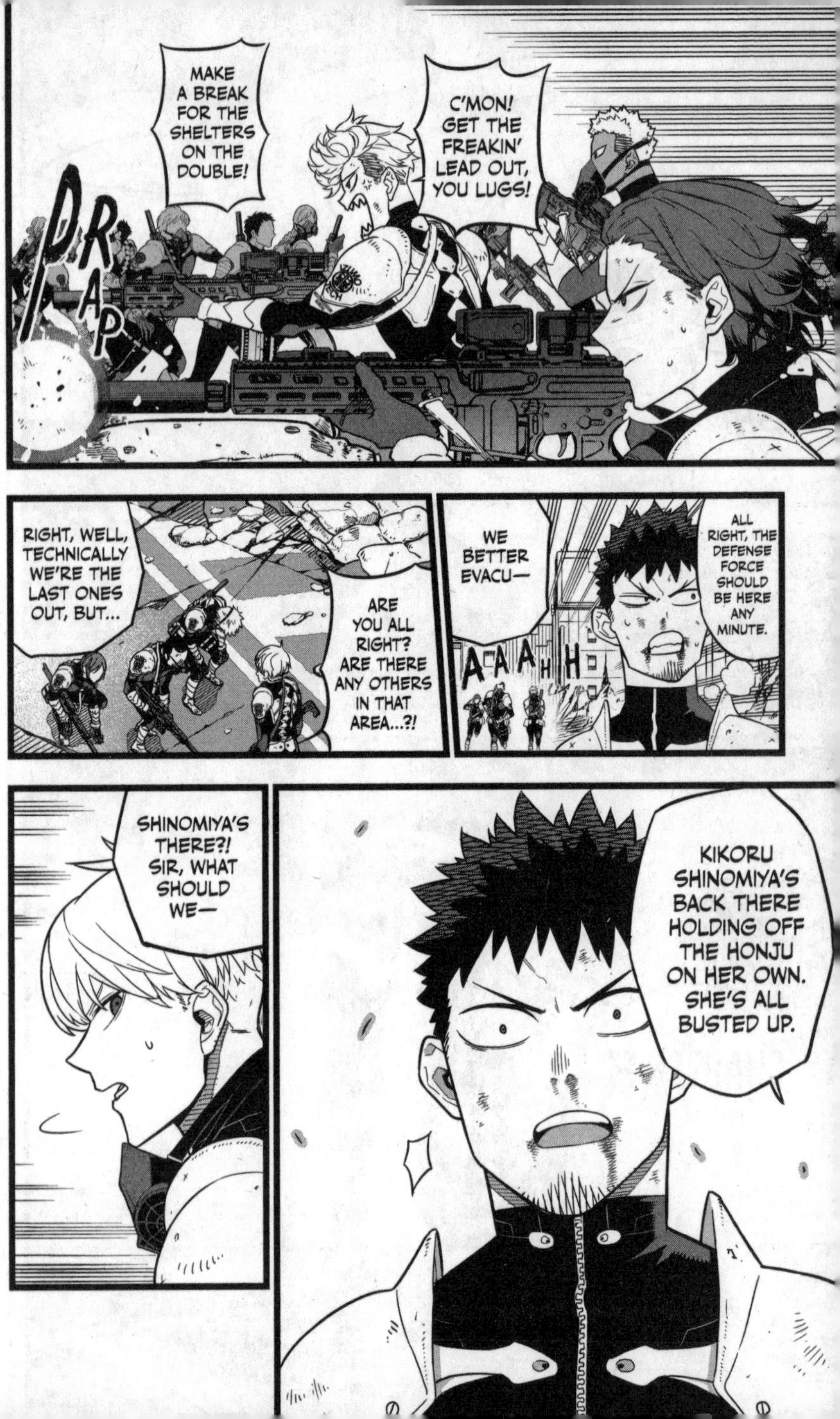
C'MON! GET THE FREAKIN' LEAD OUT, YOU LUGS!
MAKE A BREAK FOR THE SHELTERS ON THE DOUBLE!
DRAP
ALL RIGHT, THE DEFENSE FORCE SHOULD BE HERE ANY MINUTE.
WE BETTER EVACU—
AAAHH
ARE YOU ALL RIGHT? ARE THERE ANY OTHERS IN THAT AREA...?!
RIGHT, WELL, TECHNICALLY WE'RE THE LAST ONES OUT, BUT...
KIKORU SHINOMIYA'S BACK THERE HOLDING OFF THE HONJU ON HER OWN. SHE'S ALL BUSTED UP.
SHINOMIYA'S THERE?! SIR, WHAT SHOULD WE—

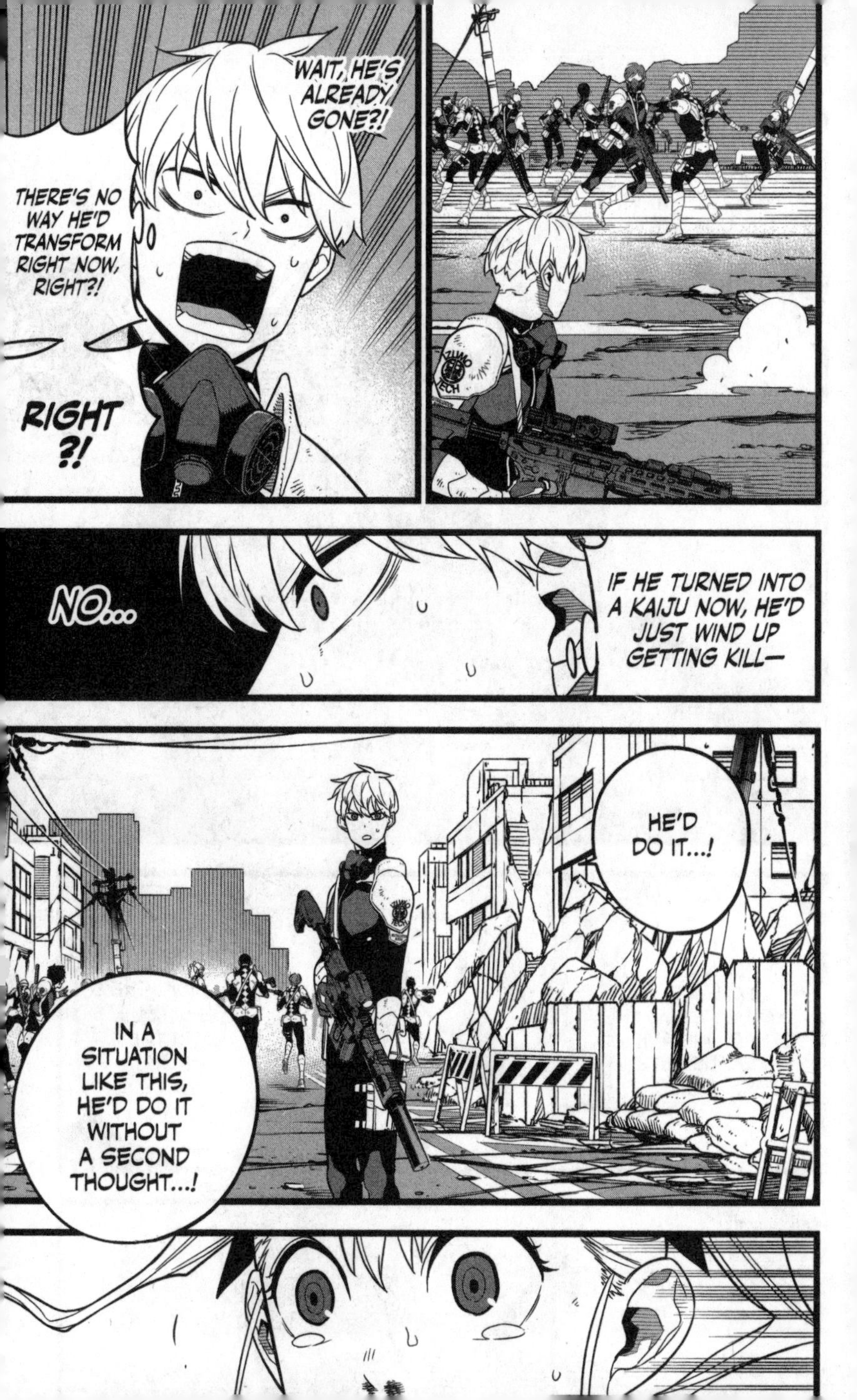
WAIT, HE'S ALREADY GONE?!
THERE'S NO WAY HE'D TRANSFORM RIGHT NOW, RIGHT?!
RIGHT ?!
IF HE TURNED INTO A KAIJU NOW, HE'D JUST WIND UP GETTING KILL—
NO...
HE'D DO IT...!
IN A SITUATION LIKE THIS, HE'D DO IT WITHOUT A SECOND THOUGHT...!

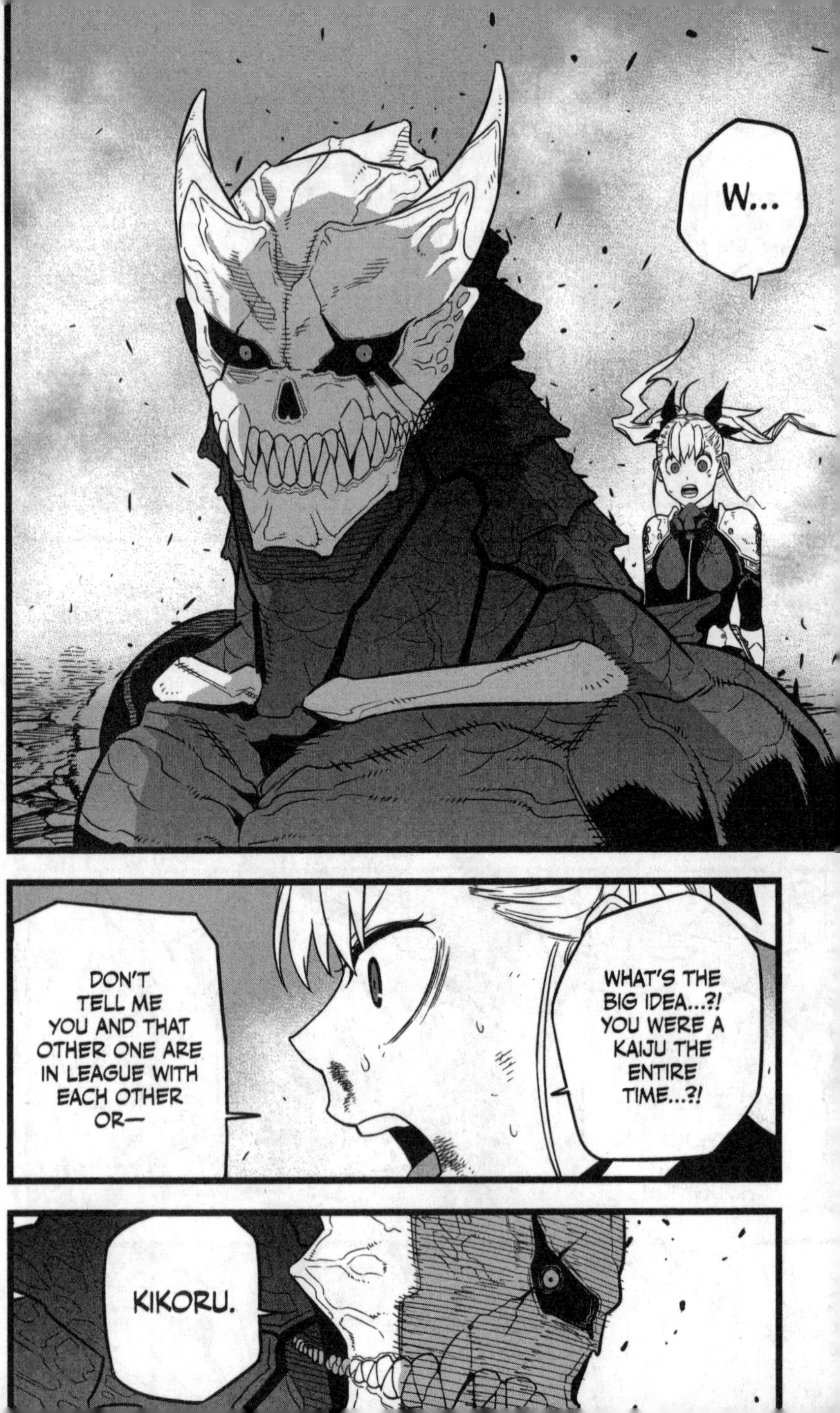
W...
WHAT'S THE BIG IDEA...?! YOU WERE A KAIJU THE ENTIRE TIME...?!
DON'T TELL ME YOU AND THAT OTHER ONE ARE IN LEAGUE WITH EACH OTHER OR—
KIKORU.

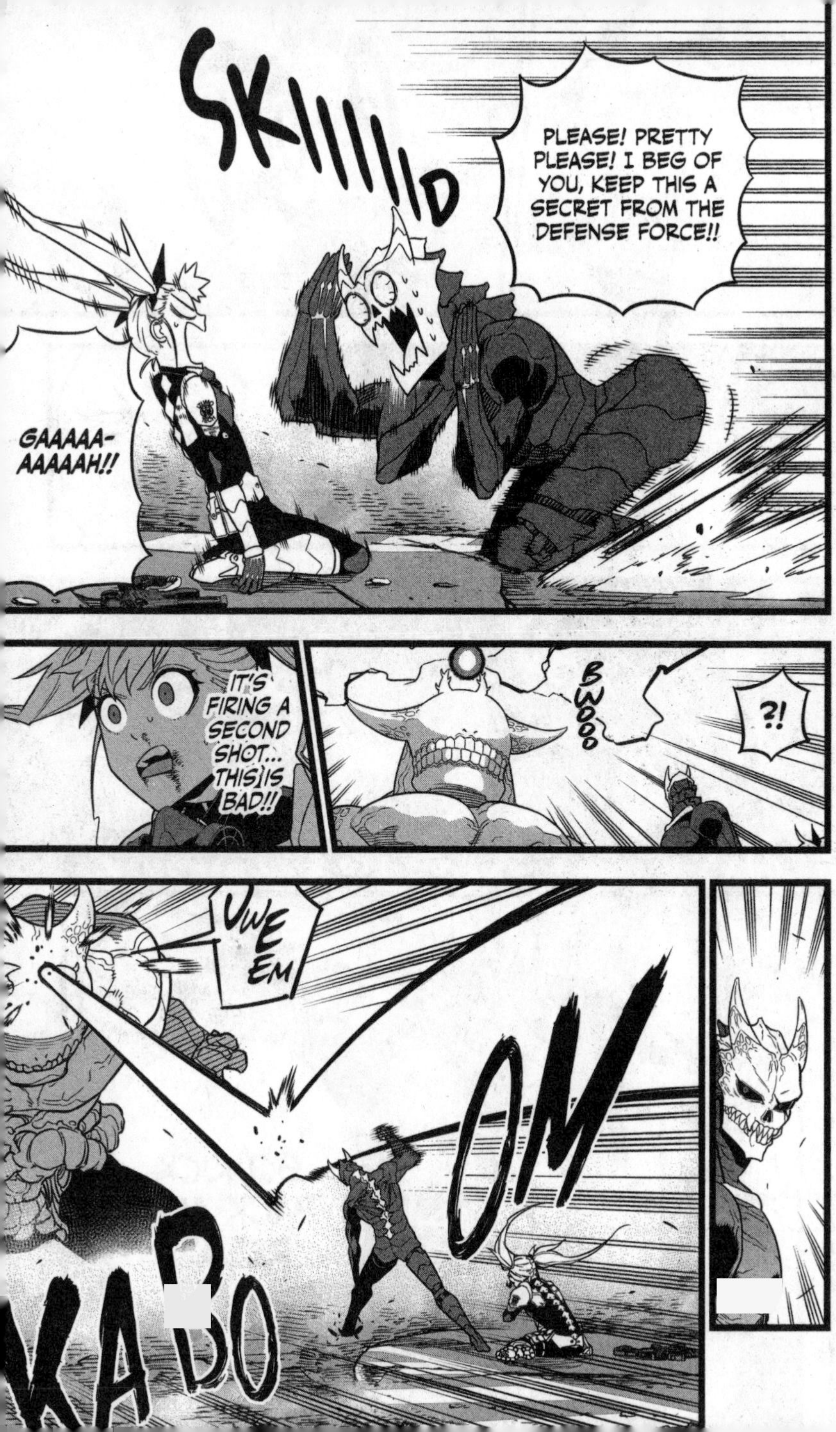

SKIIIIIID
PLEASE! PRETTY PLEASE! I BEG OF YOU, KEEP THIS A SECRET FROM THE DEFENSE FORCE!!
GAAAAA-AAAAAH!!
?!
BWOOO
IT'S FIRING A SECOND SHOT... THIS IS BAD!!
UWEEEM
KABO
OM

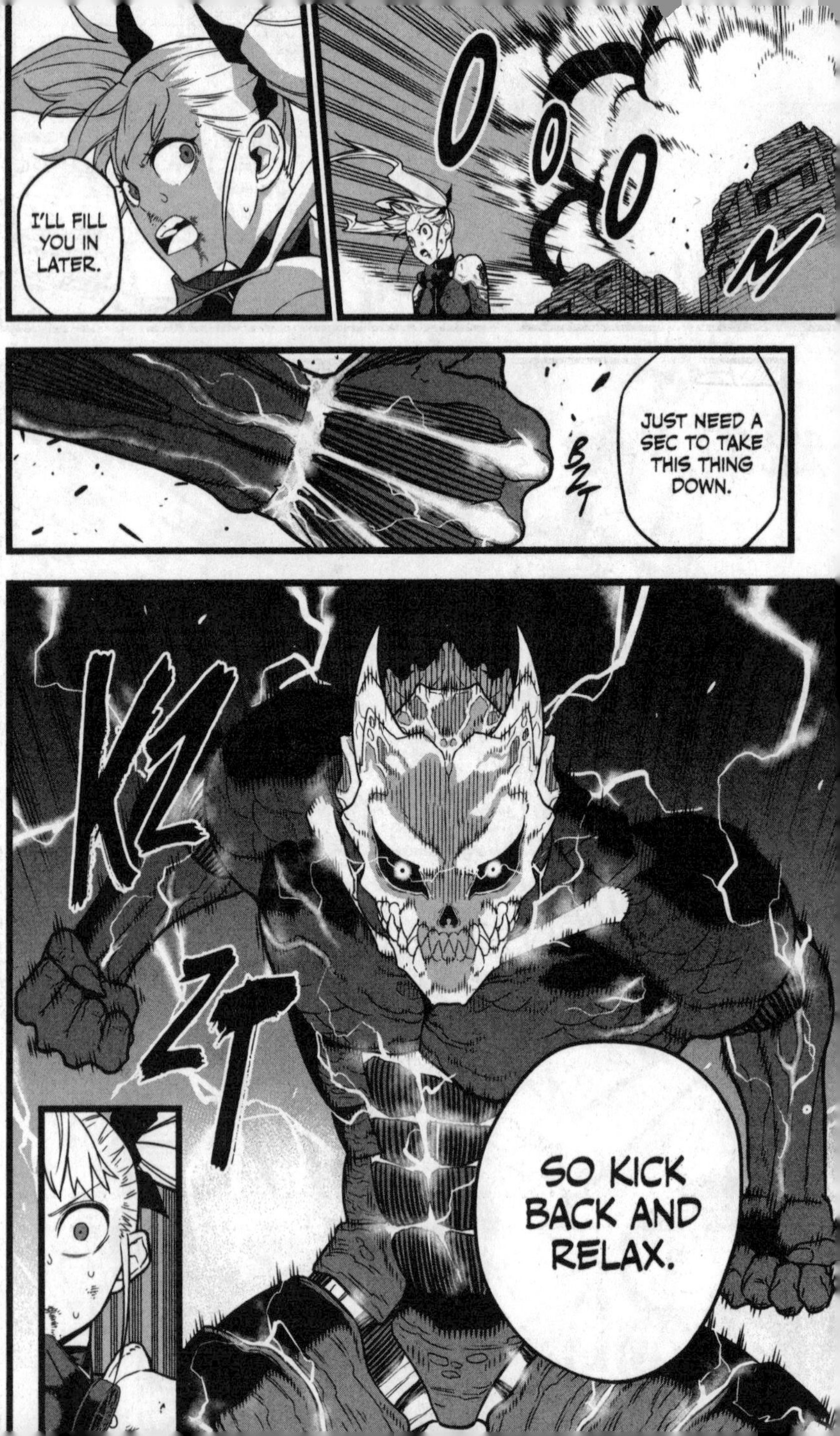
I'LL FILL YOU IN LATER.
JUST NEED A SEC TO TAKE THIS THING DOWN.
BZZT
KZZT
SO KICK BACK AND RELAX.

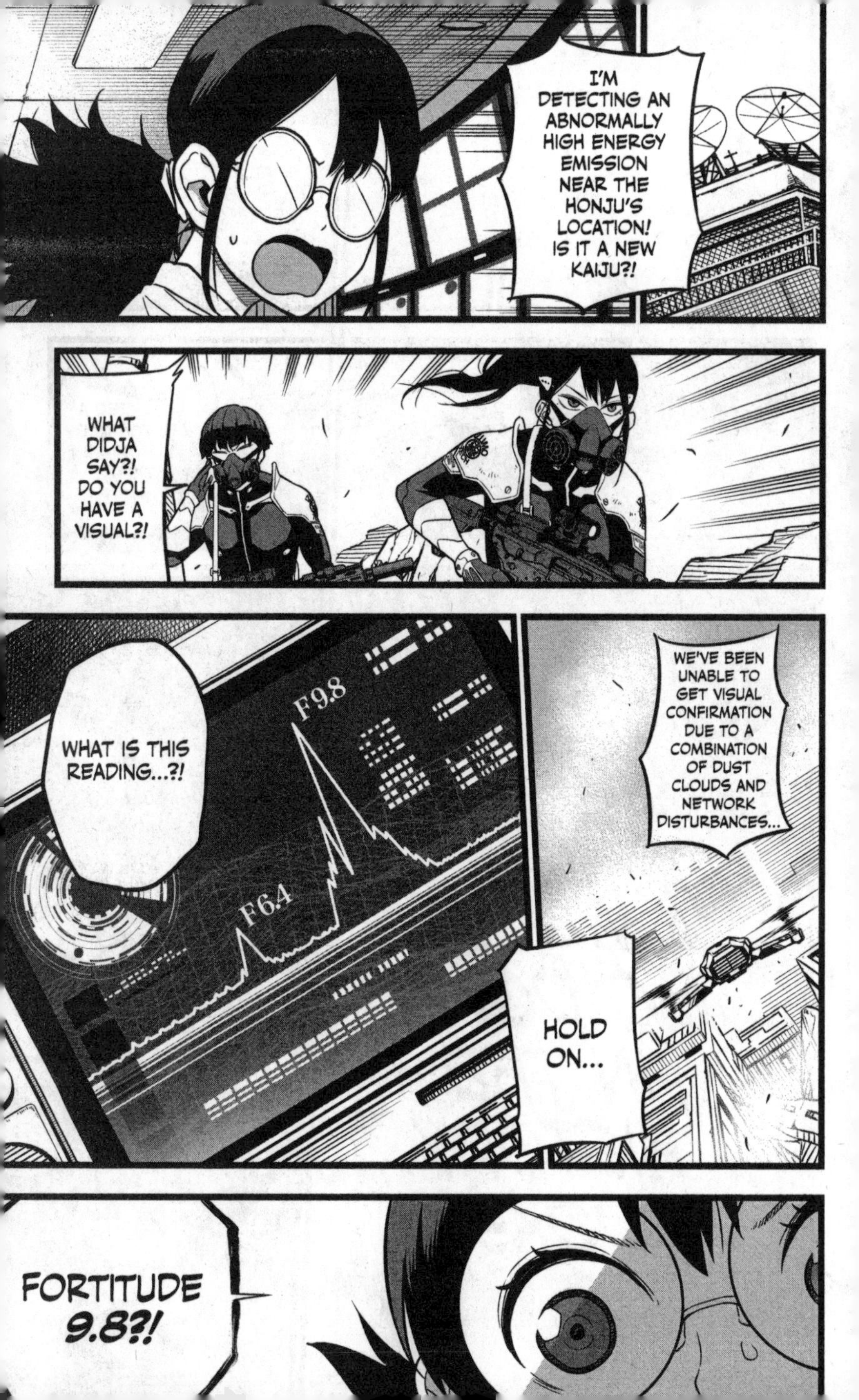
I'M DETECTING AN ABNORMALLY HIGH ENERGY EMISSION NEAR THE HONJU'S LOCATION! IS IT A NEW KAIJU?!
WHAT DIDJA SAY?! DO YOU HAVE A VISUAL?!
WE'VE BEEN UNABLE TO GET VISUAL CONFIRMATION DUE TO A COMBINATION OF DUST CLOUDS AND NETWORK DISTURBANCES...
HOLD ON...
WHAT IS THIS READING...?!
F9.8
F6.4
FORTITUDE 9.8?!

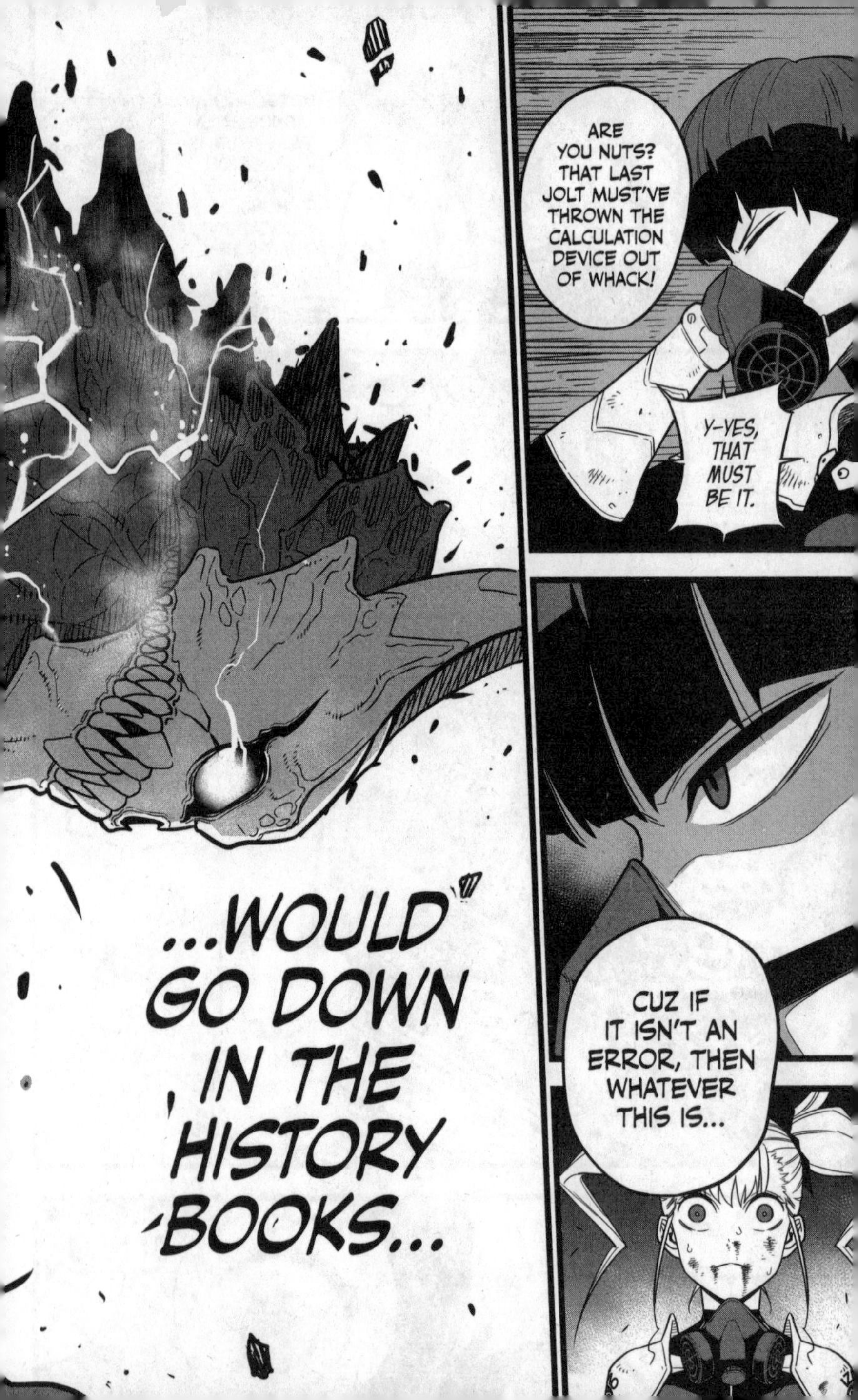
ARE YOU NUTS? THAT LAST JOLT MUST'VE THROWN THE CALCULATION DEVICE OUT OF WHACK!
Y-YES, THAT MUST BE IT.
CUZ IF IT ISN'T AN ERROR, THEN WHATEVER THIS IS...
...WOULD GO DOWN IN THE HISTORY BOOKS...

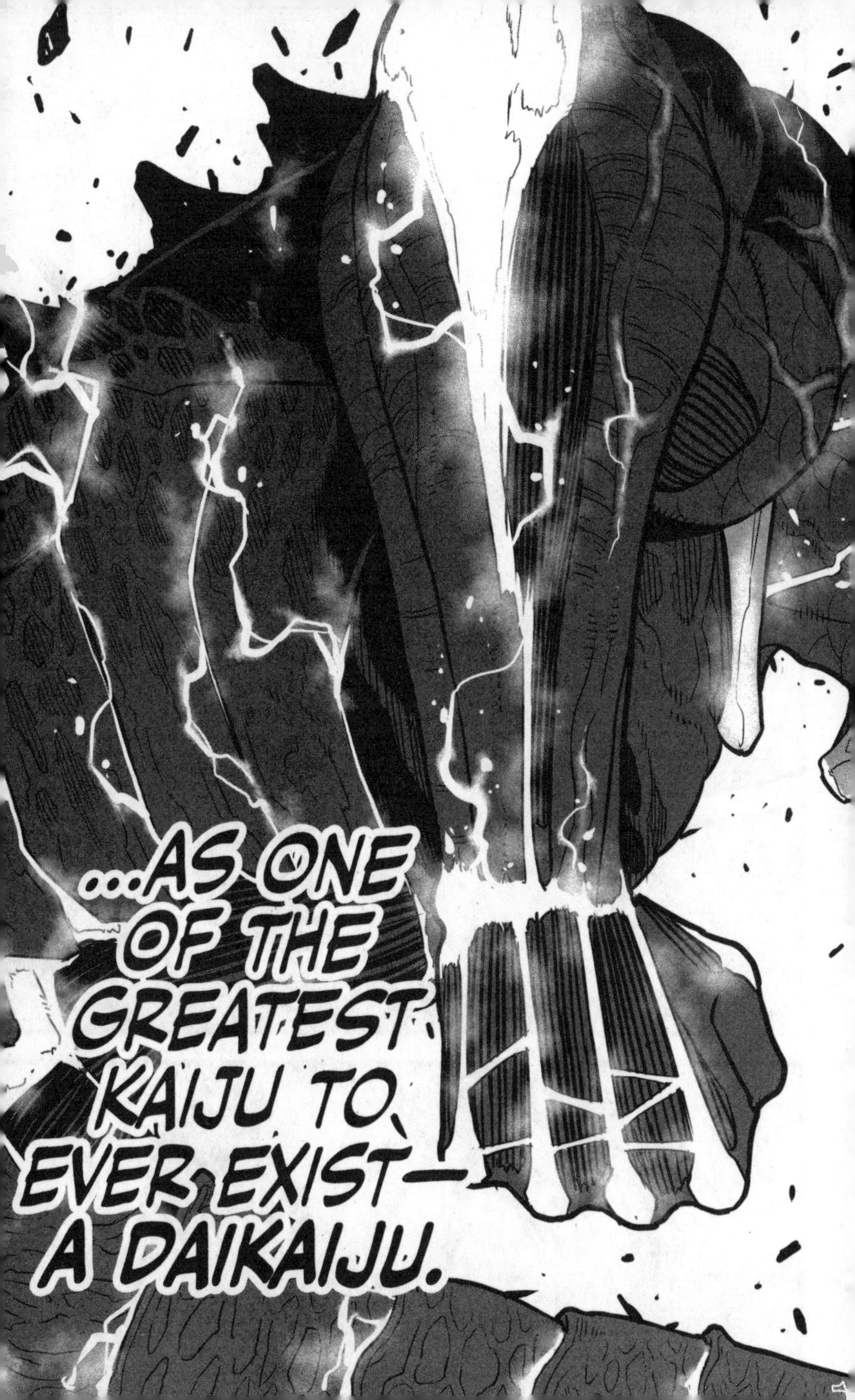
...AS ONE OF THE GREATEST KAIJU TO EVER EXIST—A DAIKAIJU.

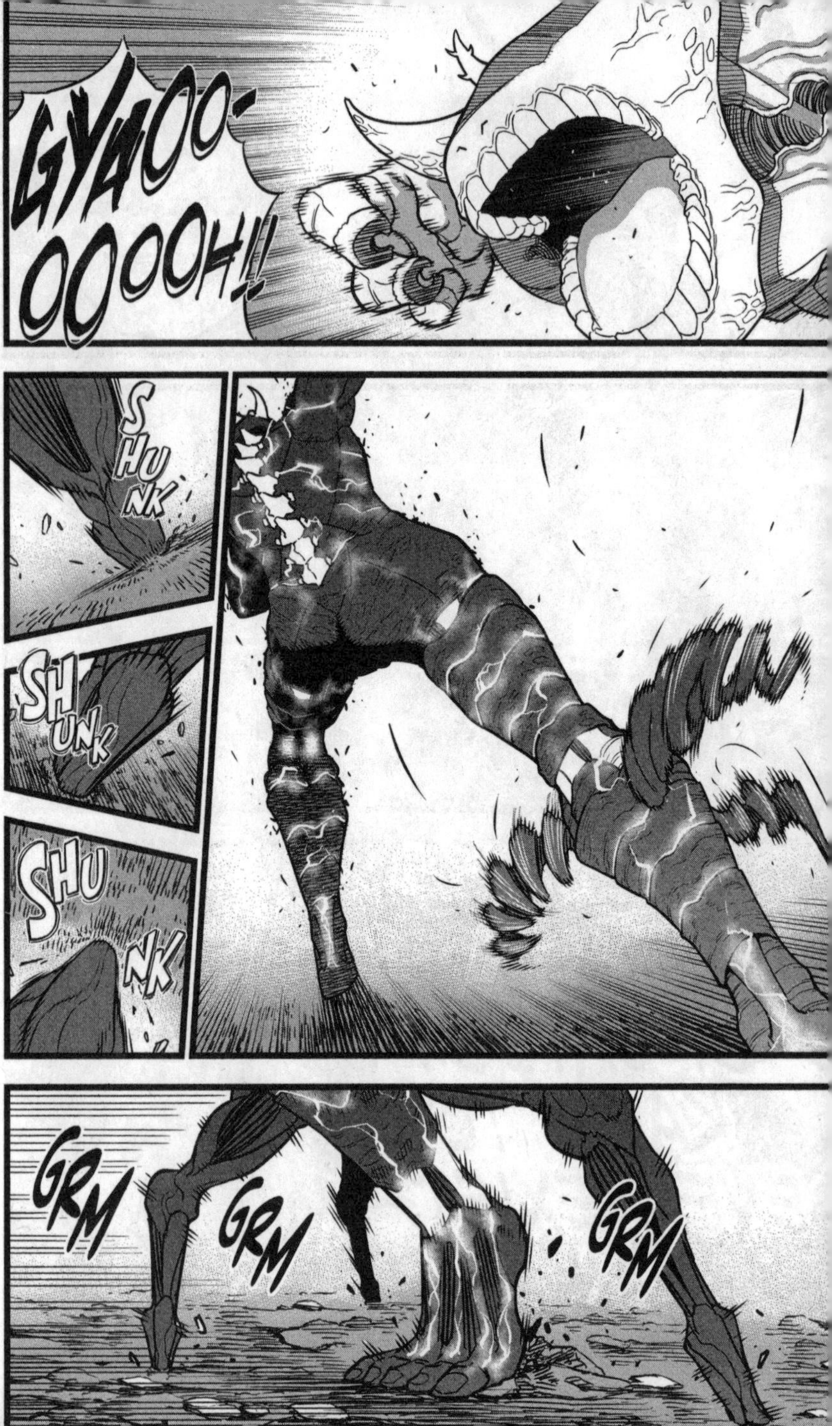
GYAOO-OOOOH!!
SHUNK
SHUNK
SHUNK
GRM
GRM
GRM

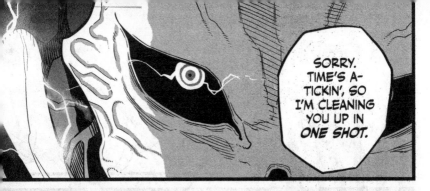

SORRY. TIME'S A-TICKIN', SO I'M CLEANING YOU UP IN *ONE SHOT.*

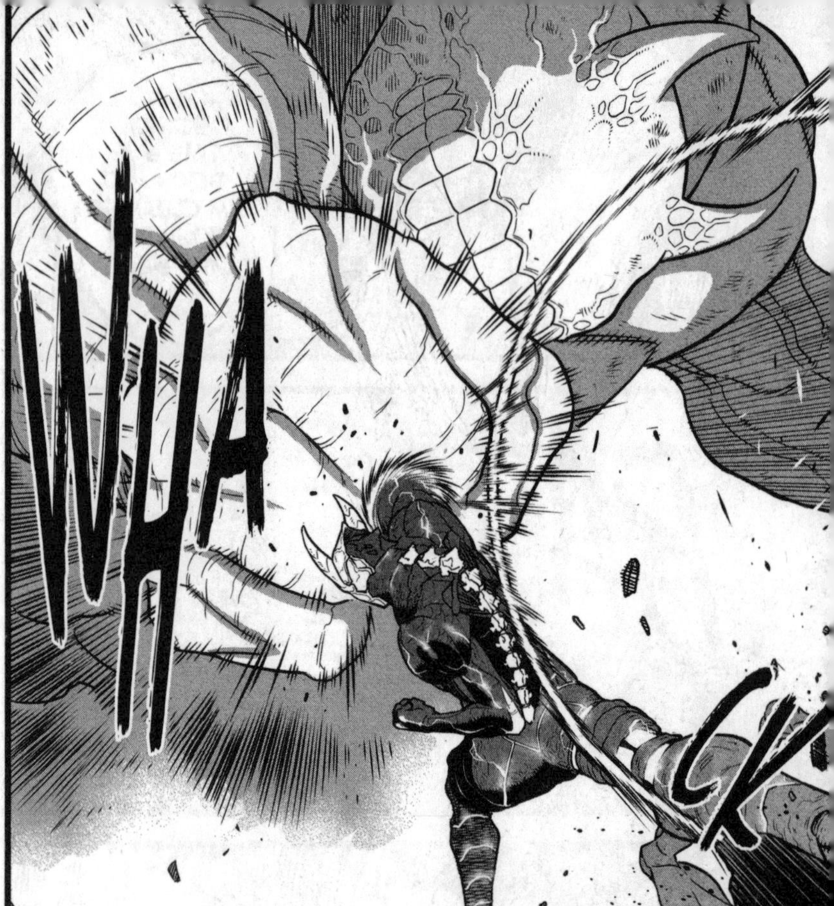
WHA
CK

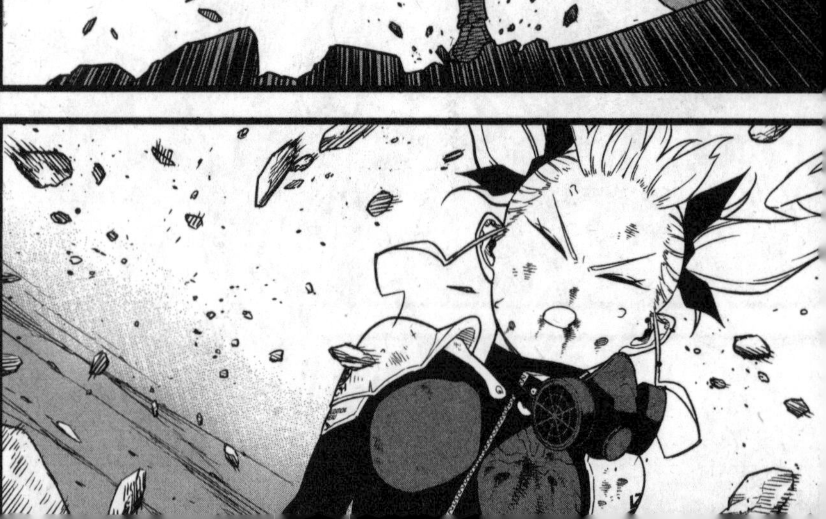

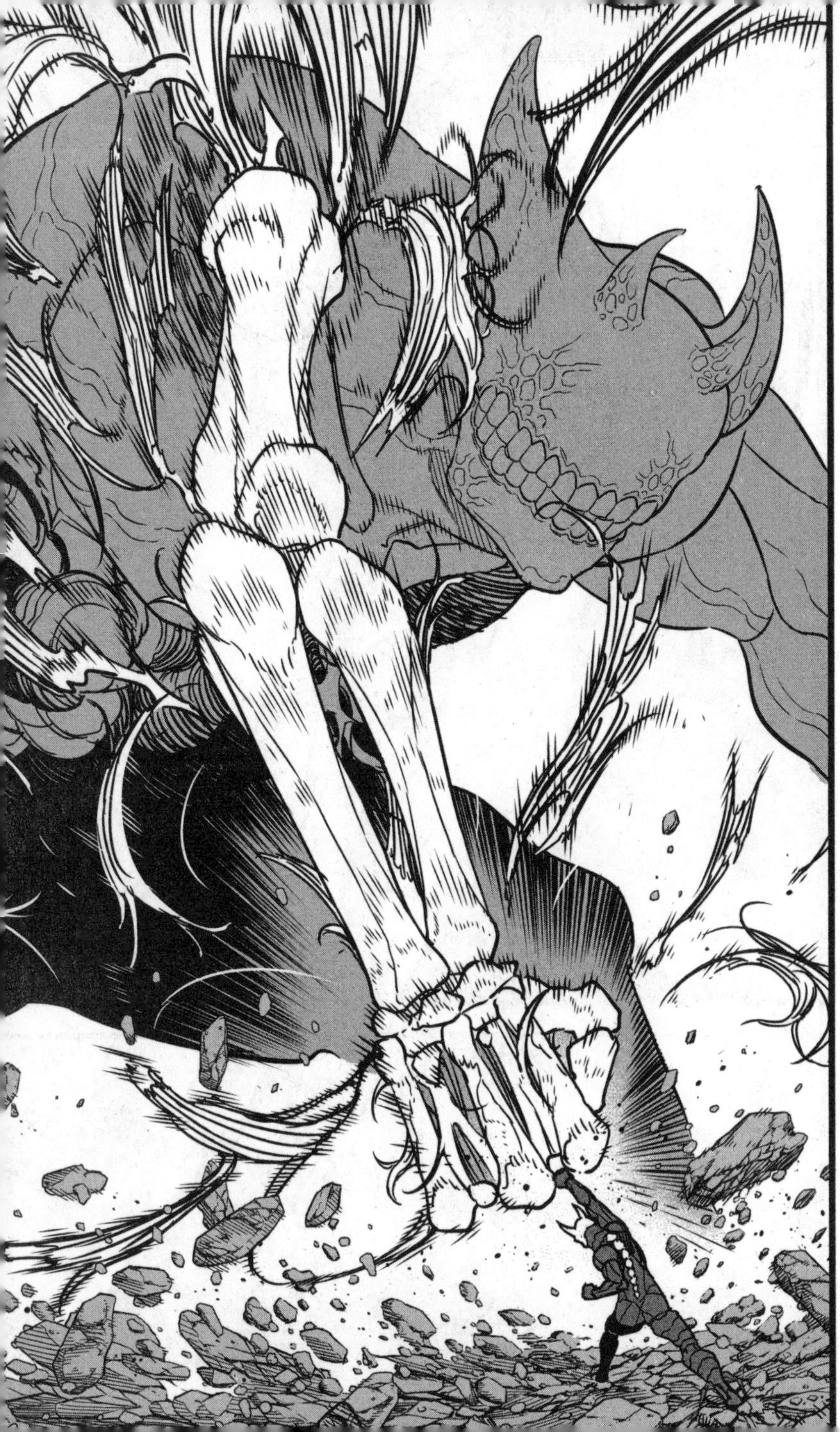

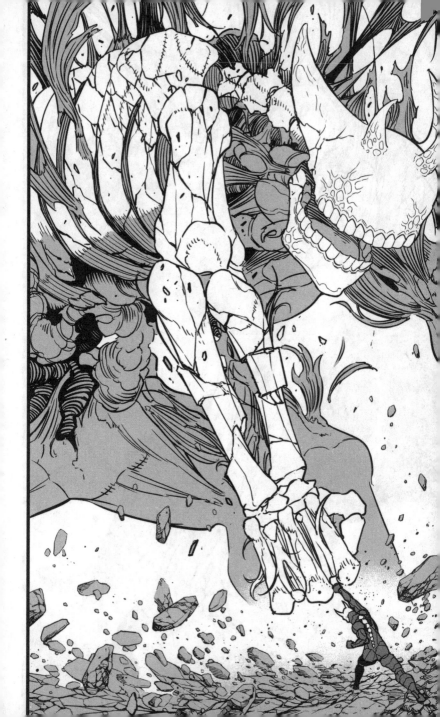

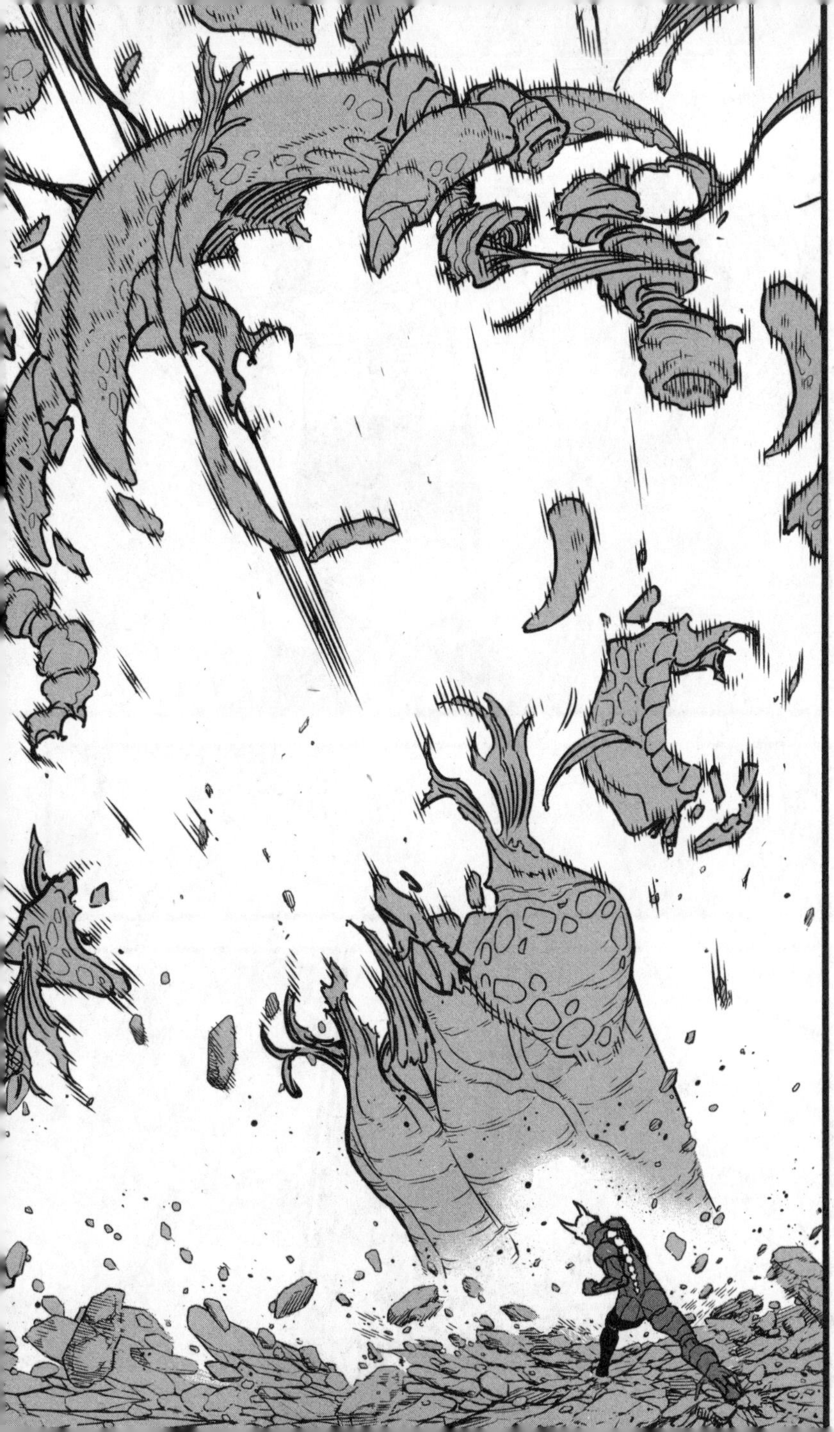

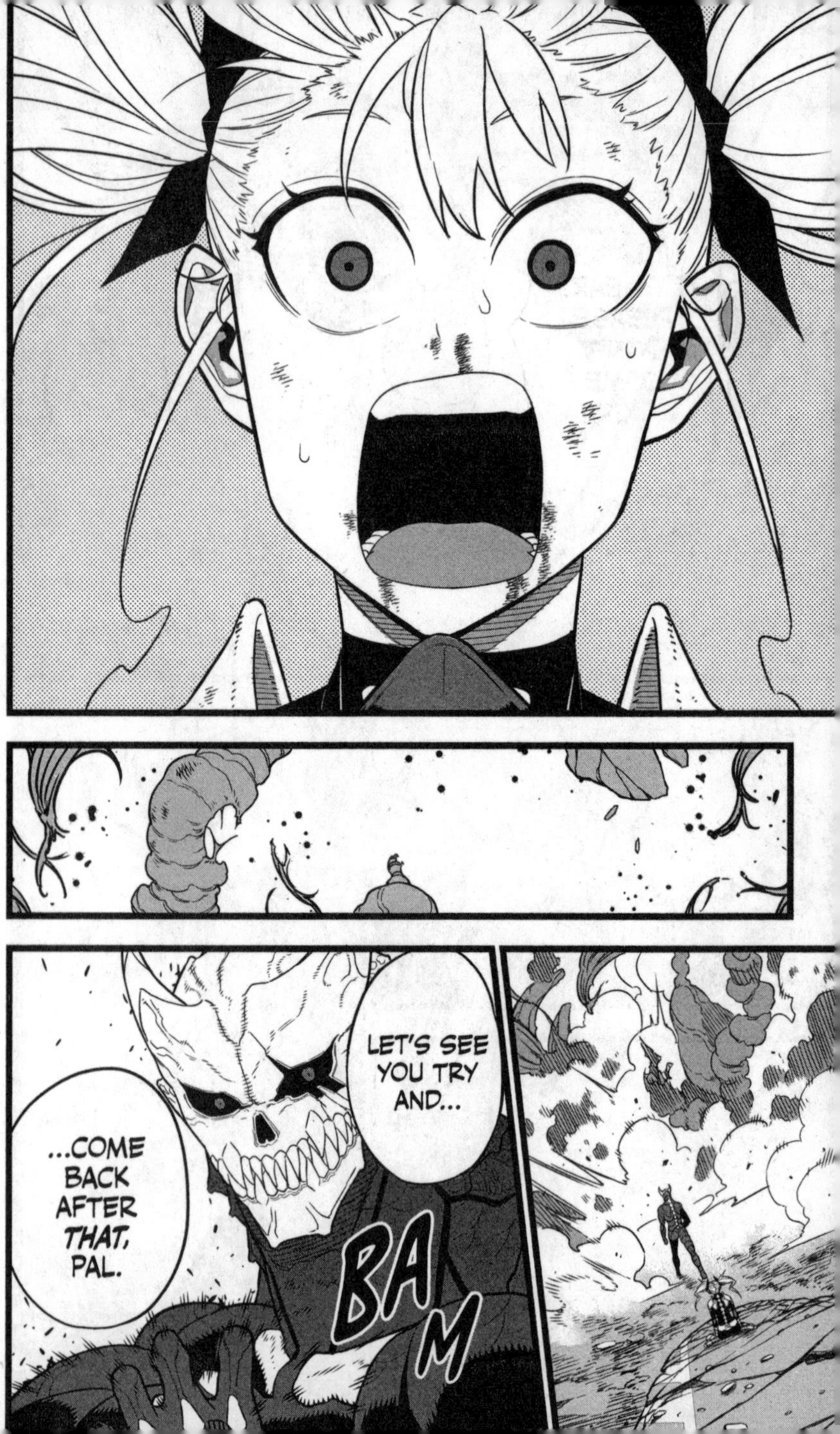
LET'S SEE YOU TRY AND...
...COME BACK AFTER THAT, PAL.
BAM

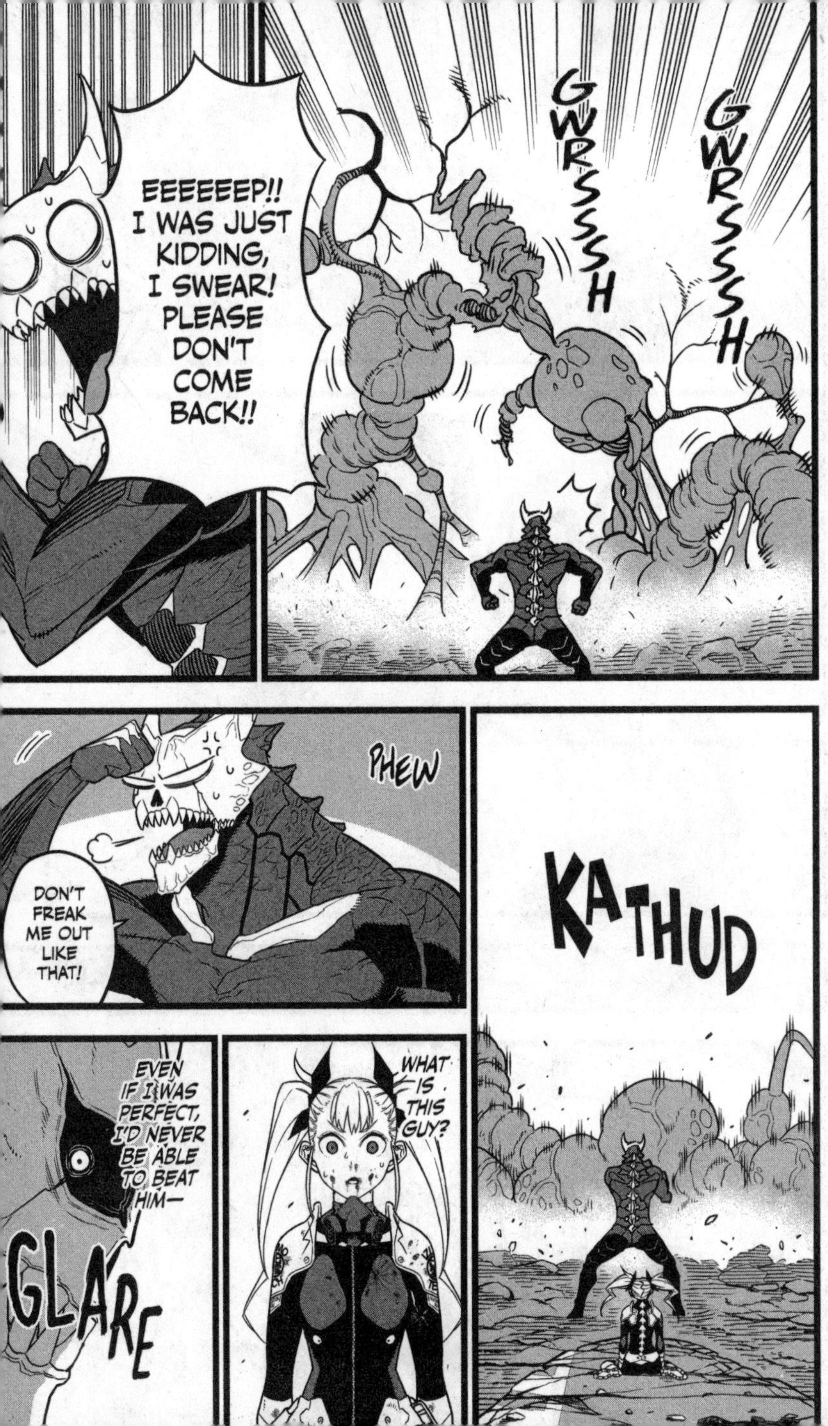
GWRSSSH
GWRSSSH
EEEEEEP!! I WAS JUST KIDDING, I SWEAR! PLEASE DON'T COME BACK!!
KATHUD
PHEW
DON'T FREAK ME OUT LIKE THAT!
WHAT IS THIS GUY?
EVEN IF I WAS PERFECT, I'D NEVER BE ABLE TO BEAT HIM—
GLARE

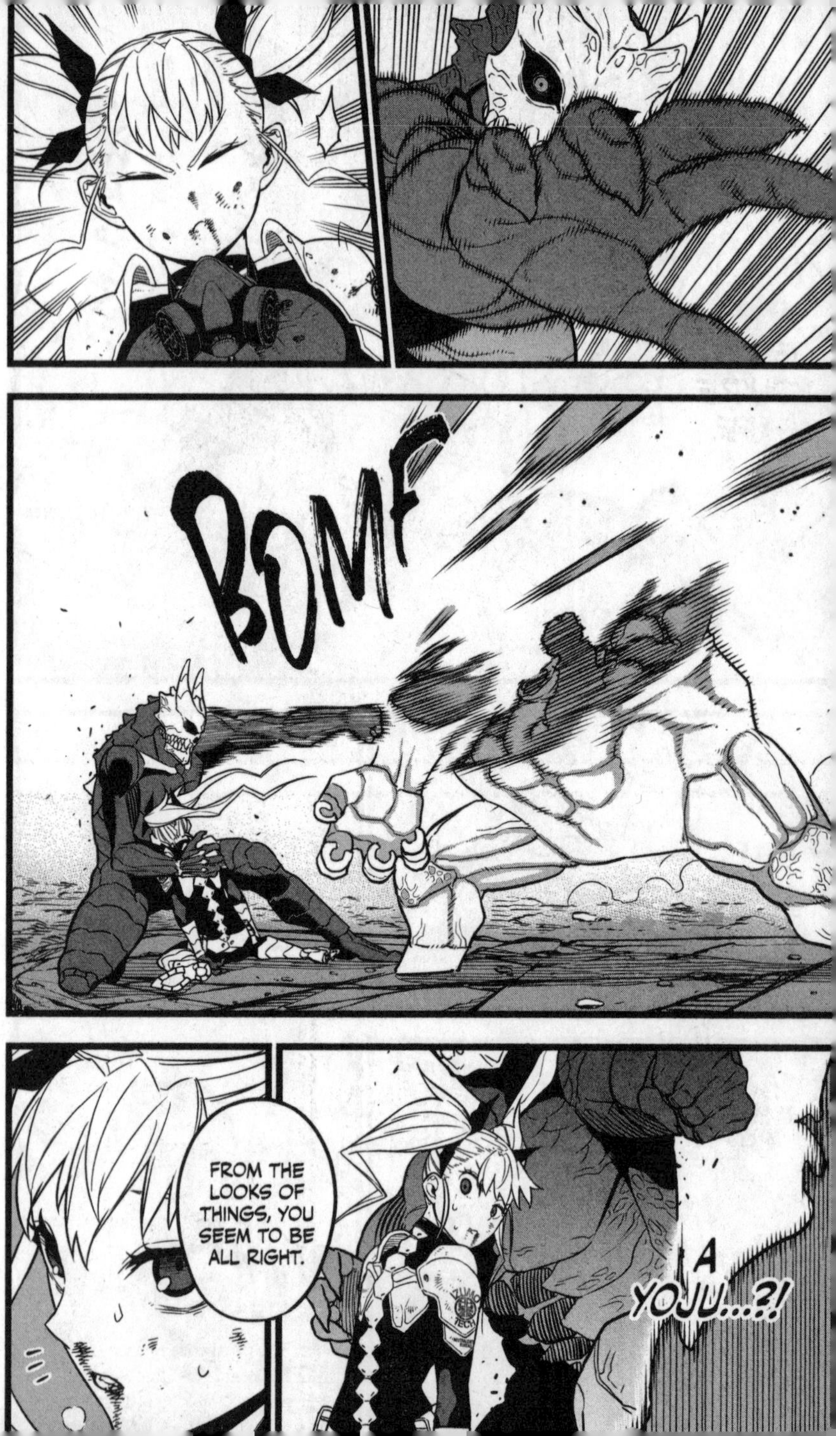
BOMF
A YOJU...?!
FROM THE LOOKS OF THINGS, YOU SEEM TO BE ALL RIGHT.

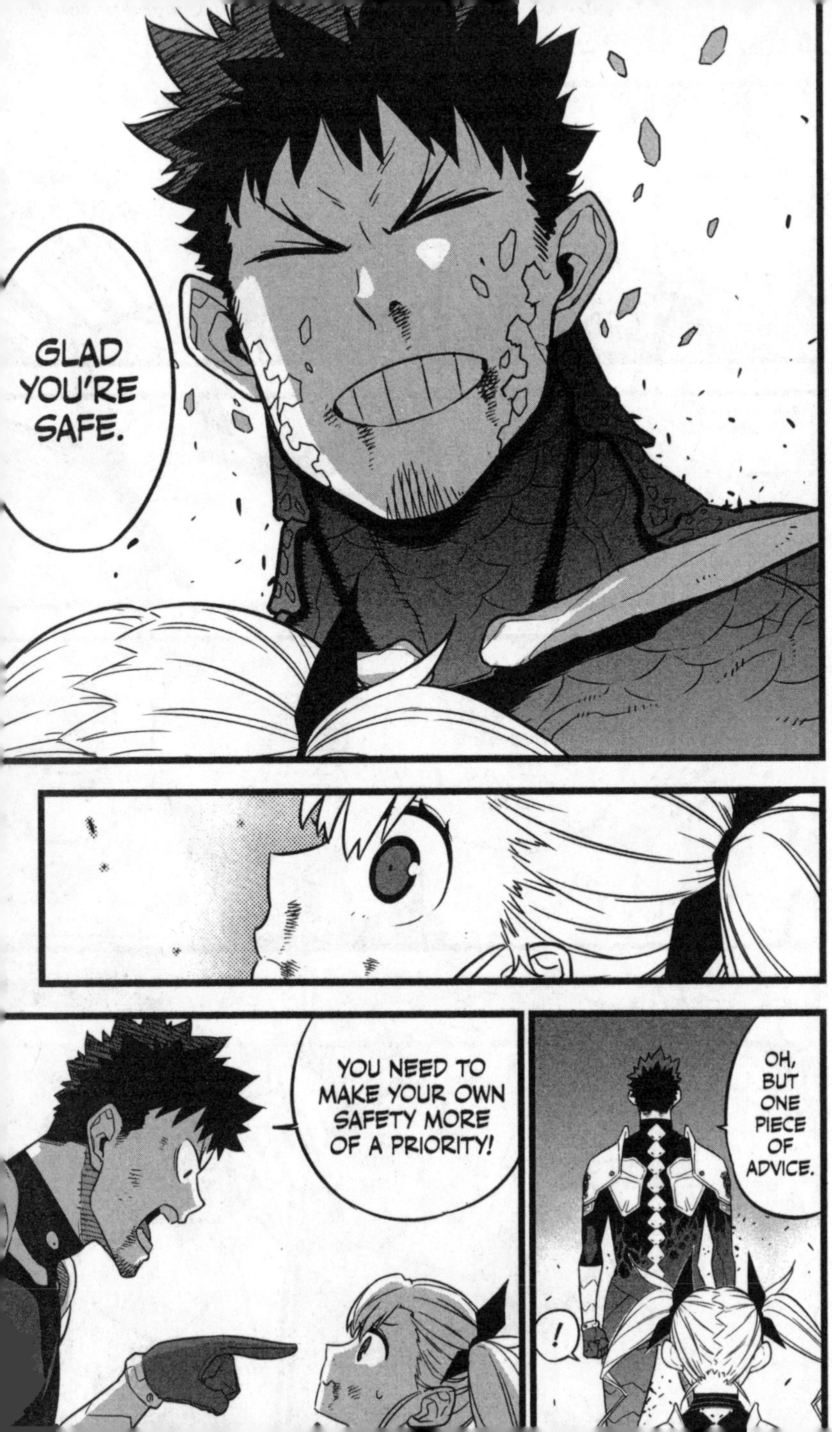
GLAD YOU'RE SAFE.
OH, BUT ONE PIECE OF ADVICE.
!
YOU NEED TO MAKE YOUR OWN SAFETY MORE OF A PRIORITY!

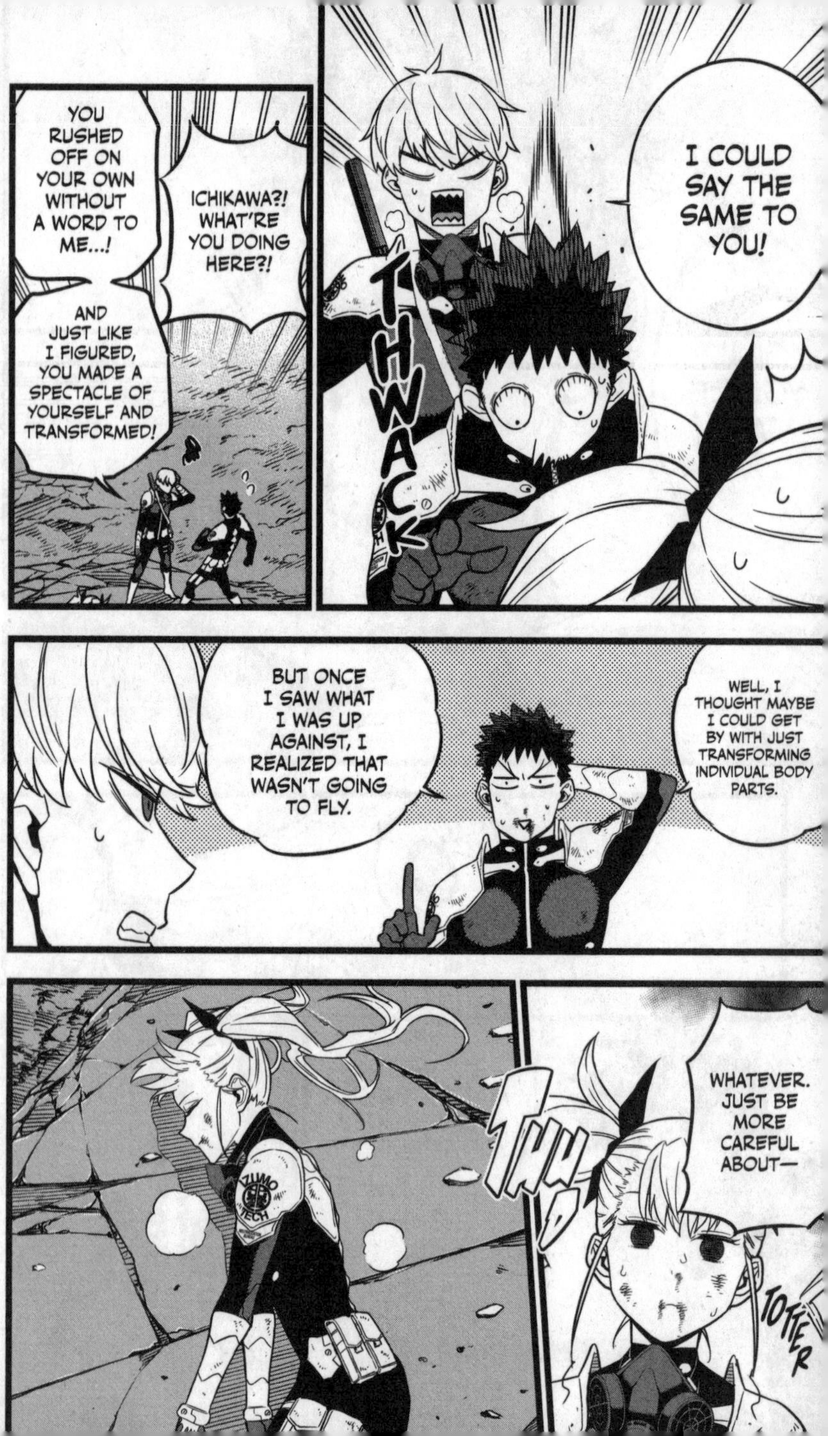
I COULD SAY THE SAME TO YOU!
THWACK
ICHIKAWA?! WHAT'RE YOU DOING HERE?!
YOU RUSHED OFF ON YOUR OWN WITHOUT A WORD TO ME...!
AND JUST LIKE I FIGURED, YOU MADE A SPECTACLE OF YOURSELF AND TRANSFORMED!
WELL, I THOUGHT MAYBE I COULD GET BY WITH JUST TRANSFORMING INDIVIDUAL BODY PARTS.
BUT ONCE I SAW WHAT I WAS UP AGAINST, I REALIZED THAT WASN'T GOING TO FLY.
WHATEVER. JUST BE MORE CAREFUL ABOUT—
THUD
TOTTER

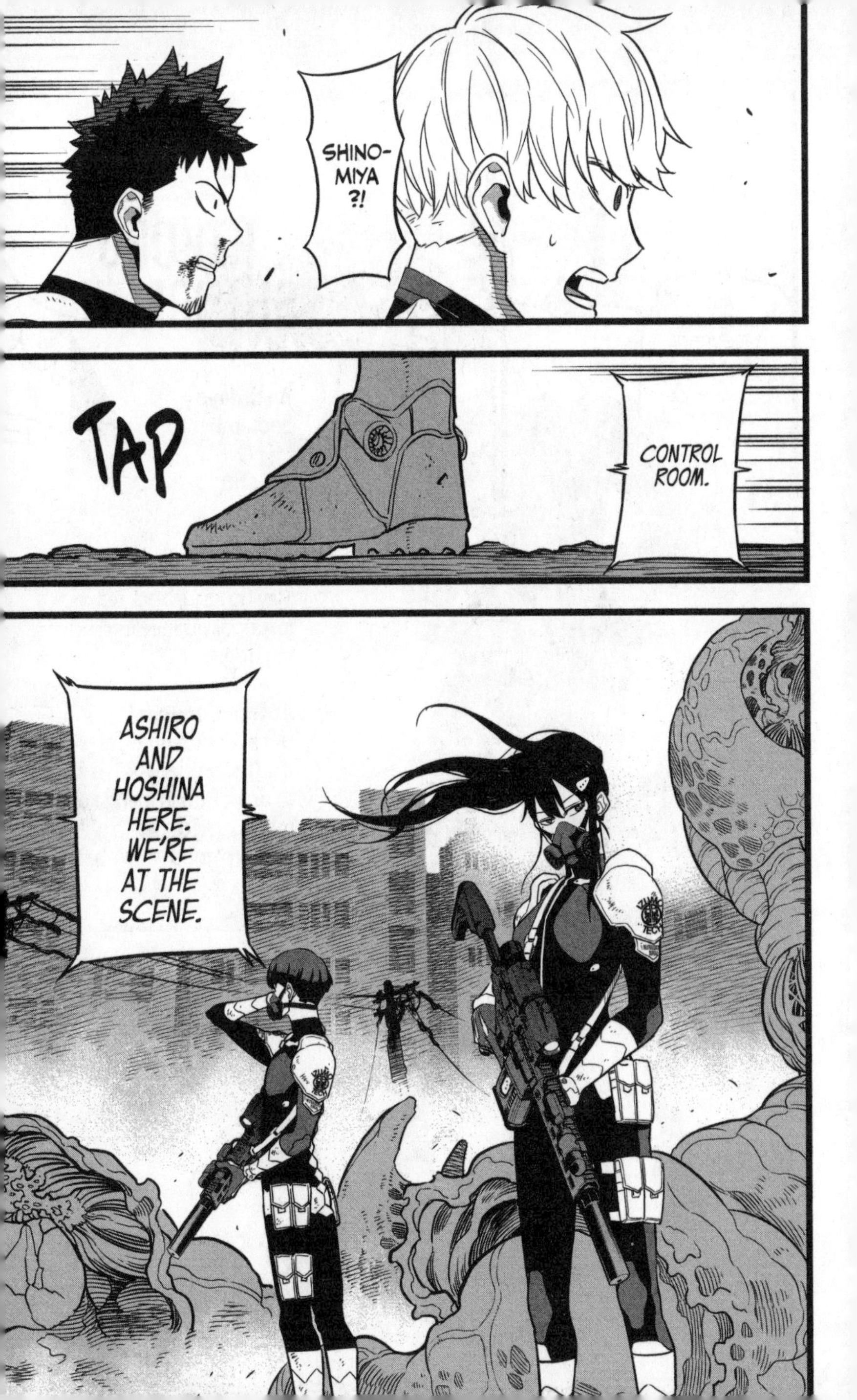
SHINO-MIYA?!
TAP
CONTROL ROOM.
ASHIRO AND HOSHINA HERE. WE'RE AT THE SCENE.

KIKORU
SHINOMIYA

Birthday:
September 7

Height:
157 cm

Likes:
Slaying kaiju, black tea
(especially Darjeeling),
big dogs

Author Comment:
Her actions tend to be on
the flashy side, which is fun
to draw. Be it in manga or
movies, I'm drawn to girls
who are good at combat.

CHAPTER 9

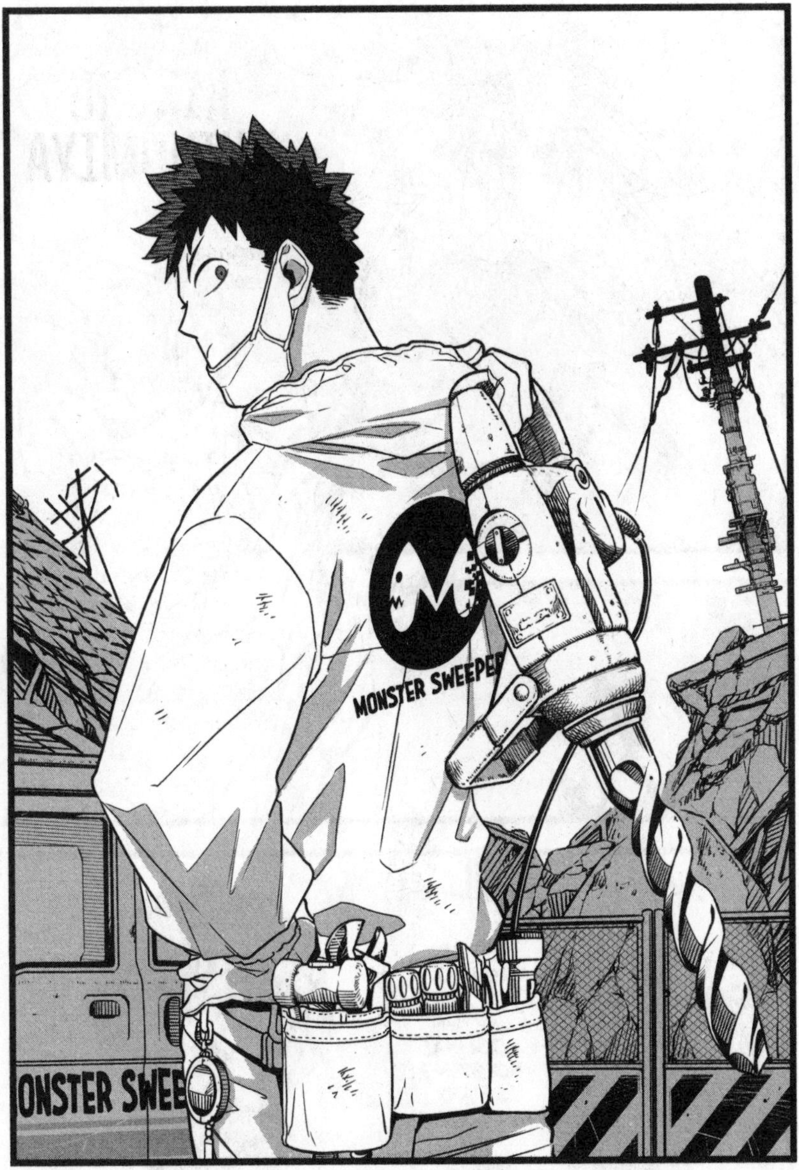
MONSTER SWEEPER
ONSTER SWEE

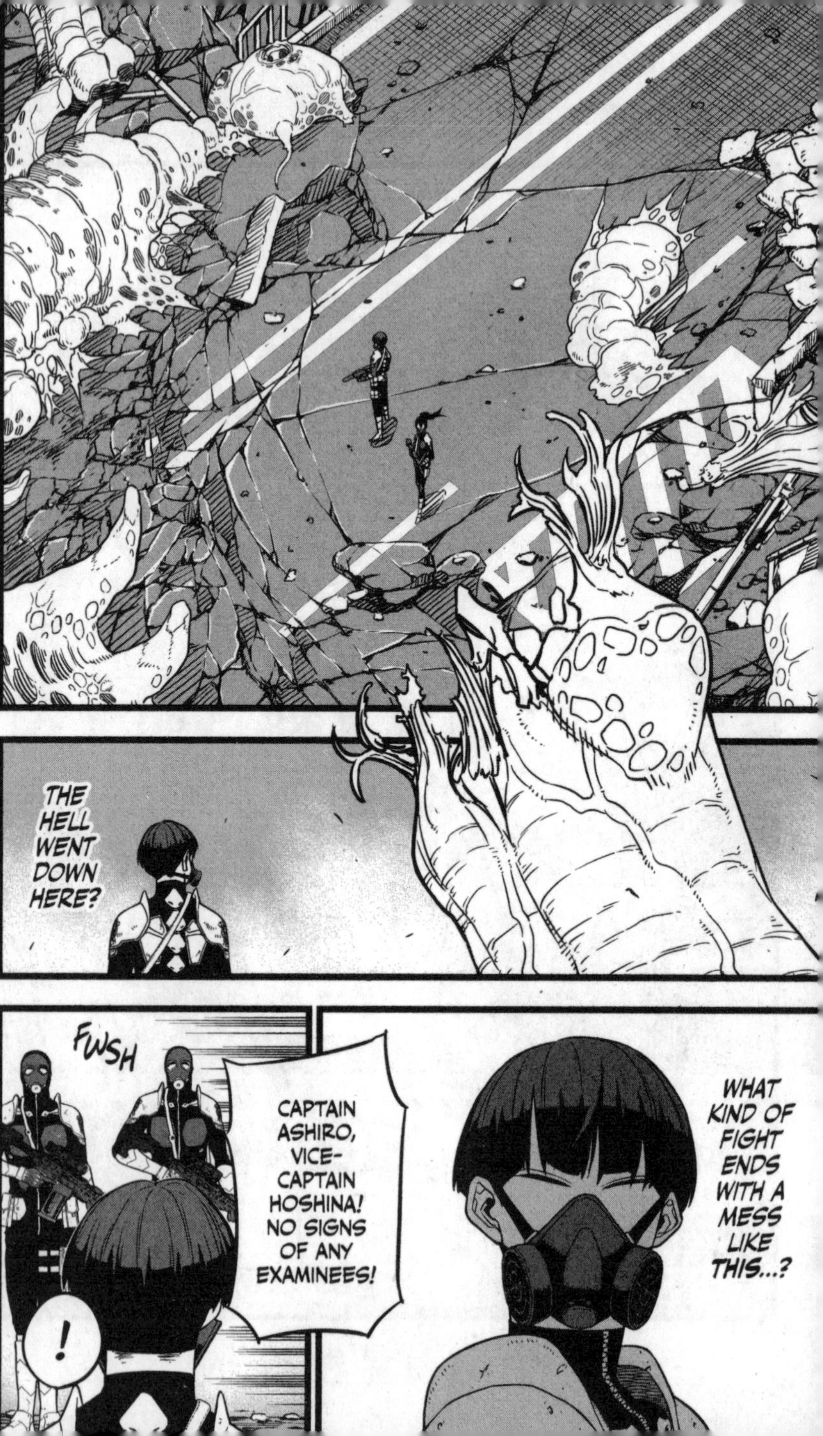
THE HELL WENT DOWN HERE?
WHAT KIND OF FIGHT ENDS WITH A MESS LIKE THIS...?
FWSH
CAPTAIN ASHIRO, VICE-CAPTAIN HOSHINA! NO SIGNS OF ANY EXAMINEES!
!

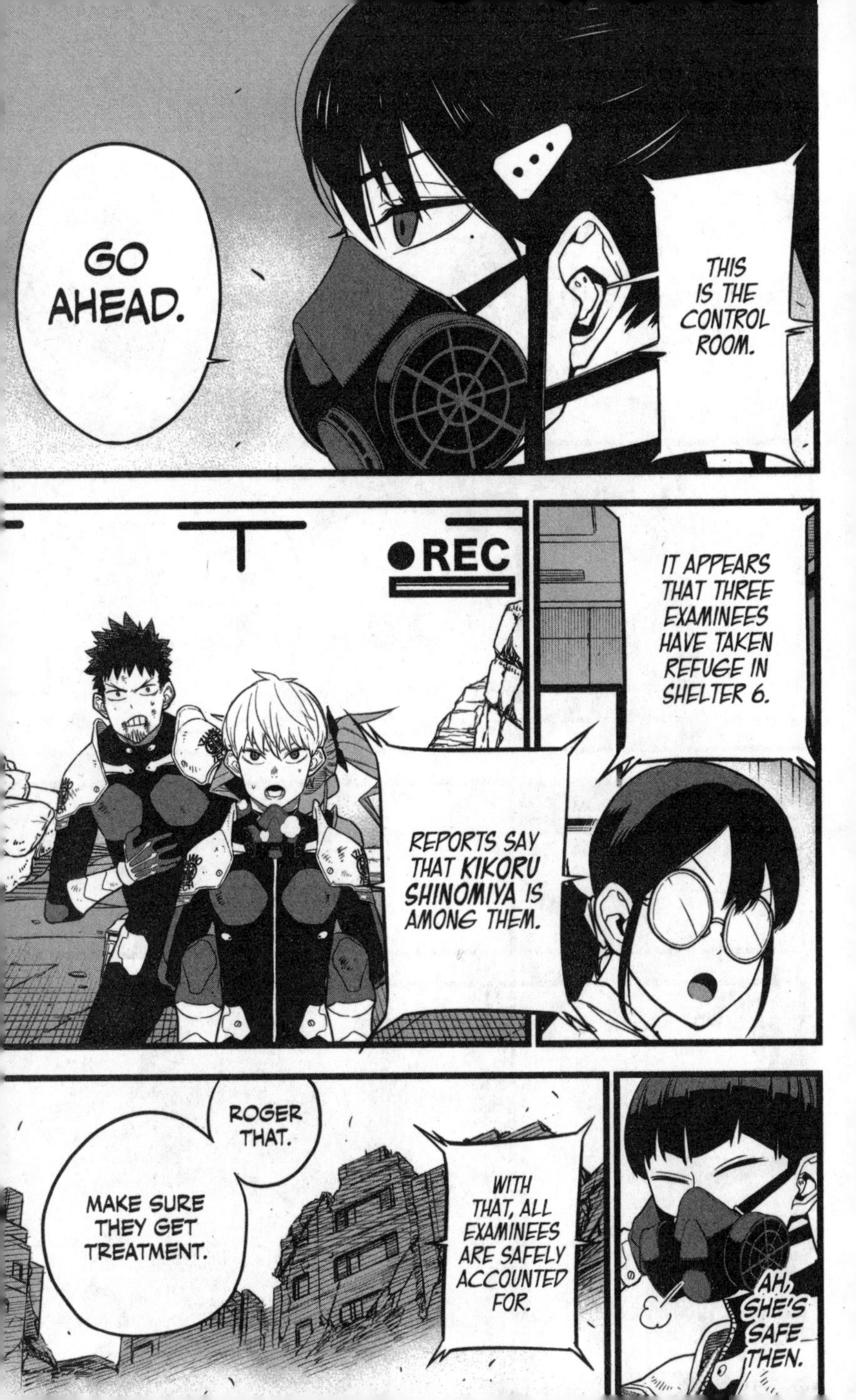
THIS IS THE CONTROL ROOM.
GO AHEAD.
IT APPEARS THAT THREE EXAMINEES HAVE TAKEN REFUGE IN SHELTER 6.
●REC
REPORTS SAY THAT KIKORU SHINOMIYA IS AMONG THEM.
AH, SHE'S SAFE THEN.
WITH THAT, ALL EXAMINEES ARE SAFELY ACCOUNTED FOR.
ROGER THAT.
MAKE SURE THEY GET TREATMENT.

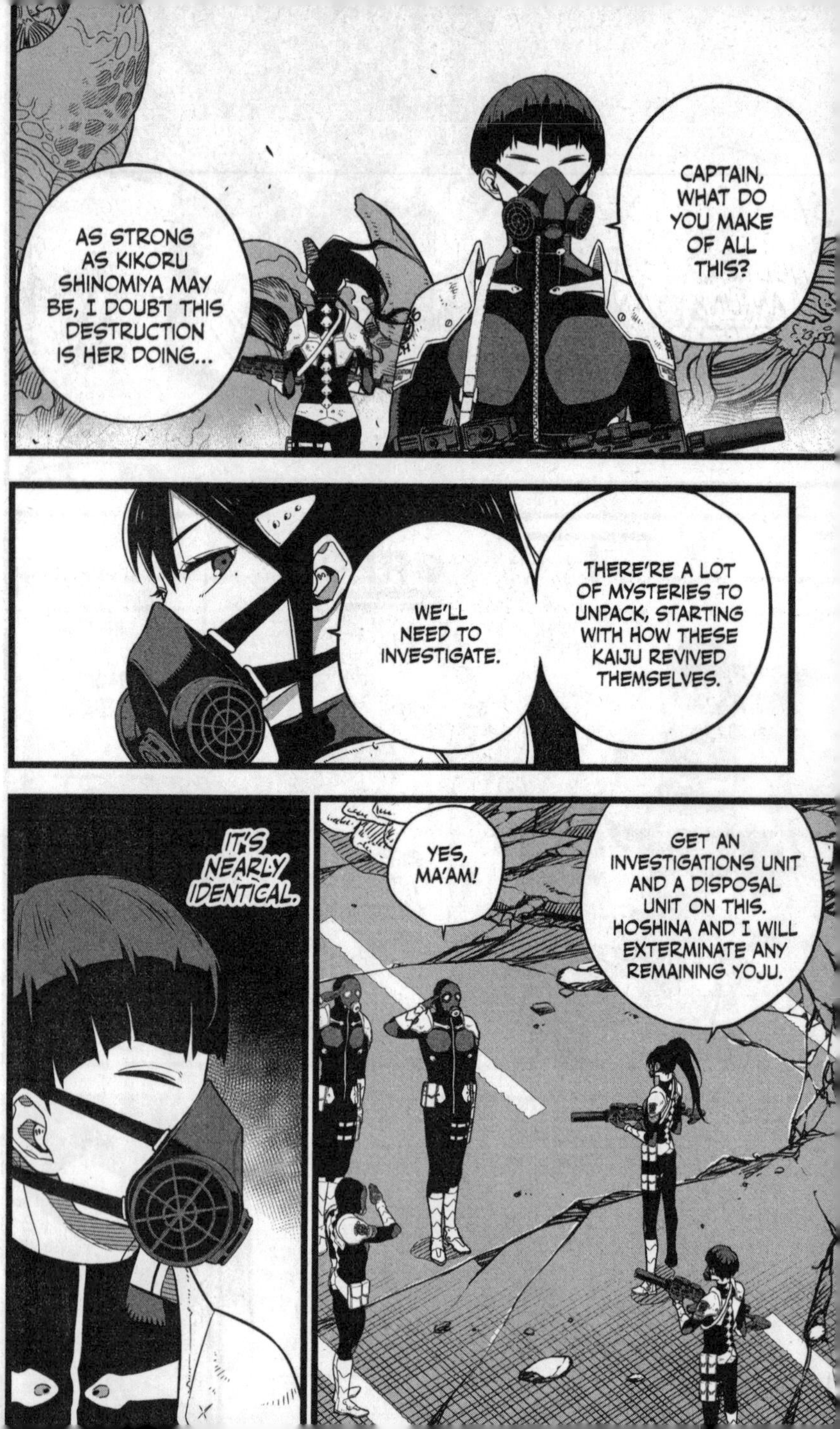
CAPTAIN, WHAT DO YOU MAKE OF ALL THIS?
AS STRONG AS KIKORU SHINOMIYA MAY BE, I DOUBT THIS DESTRUCTION IS HER DOING...
THERE'RE A LOT OF MYSTERIES TO UNPACK, STARTING WITH HOW THESE KAIJU REVIVED THEMSELVES.
WE'LL NEED TO INVESTIGATE.
GET AN INVESTIGATIONS UNIT AND A DISPOSAL UNIT ON THIS. HOSHINA AND I WILL EXTERMINATE ANY REMAINING YOJU.
YES, MA'AM!
IT'S NEARLY IDENTICAL.

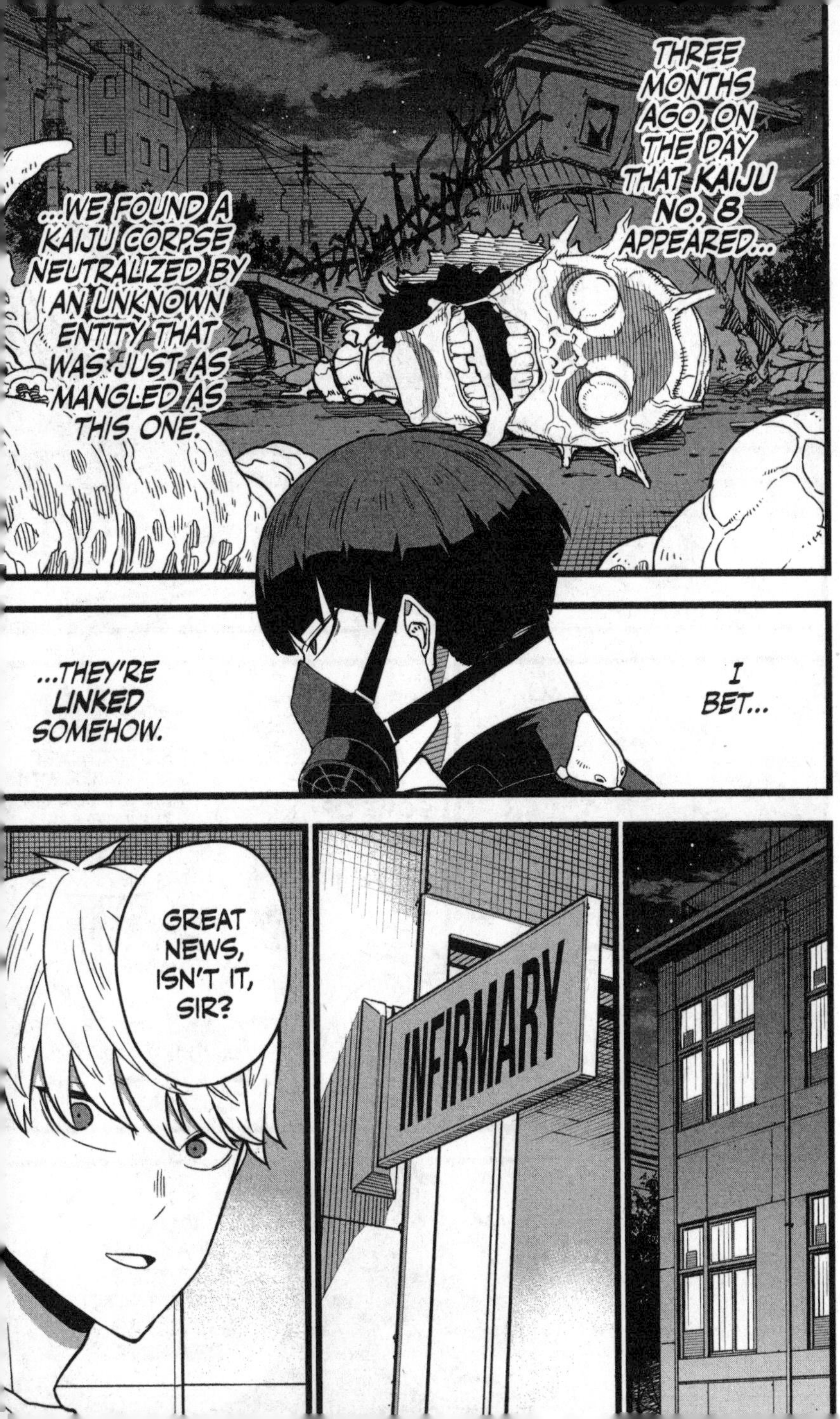
THREE MONTHS AGO, ON THE DAY THAT KAIJU NO. 8 APPEARED...
...WE FOUND A KAIJU CORPSE NEUTRALIZED BY AN UNKNOWN ENTITY THAT WAS JUST AS MANGLED AS THIS ONE.
I BET...
...THEY'RE LINKED SOMEHOW.
INFIRMARY
GREAT NEWS, ISN'T IT, SIR?

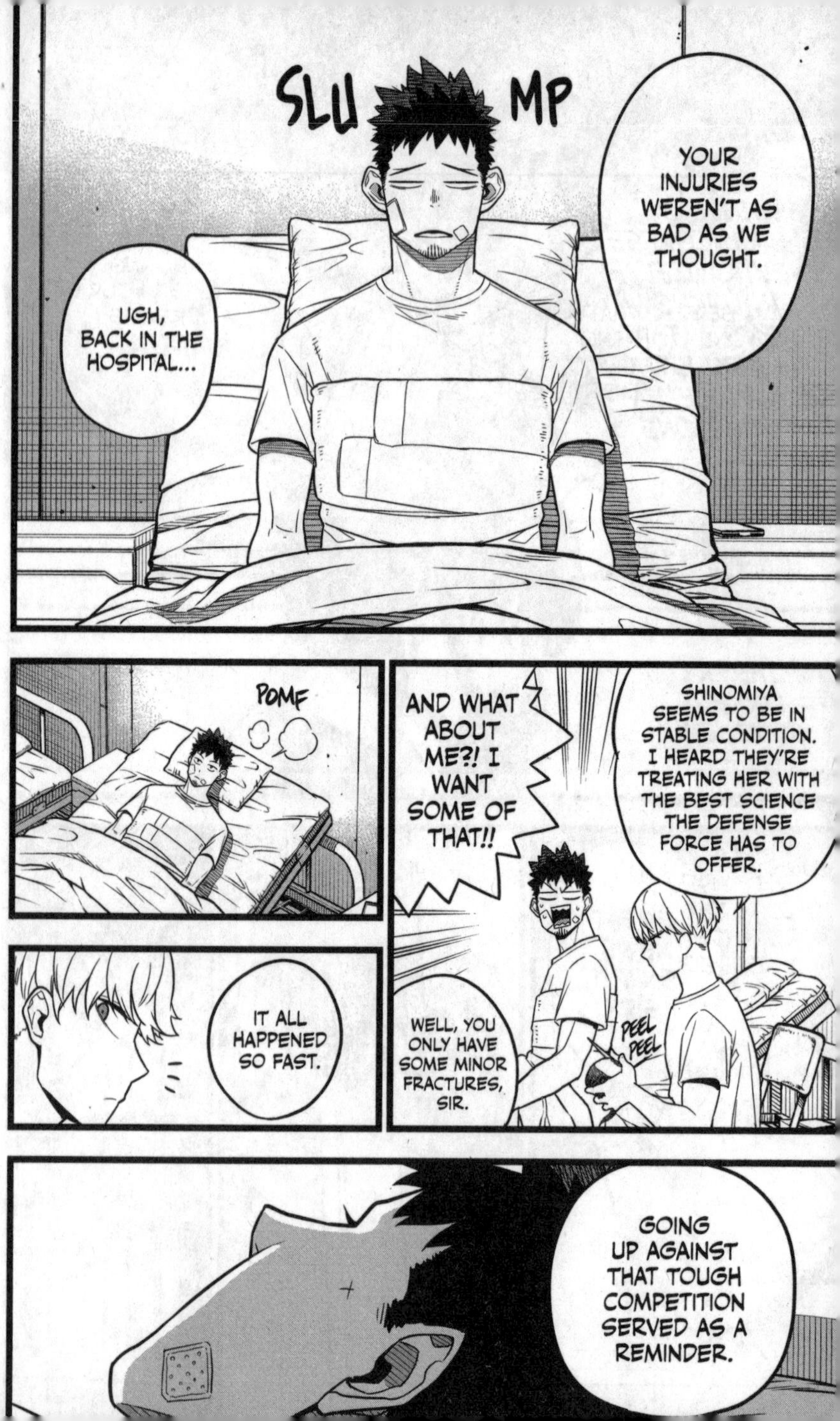
SLUMP
YOUR INJURIES WEREN'T AS BAD AS WE THOUGHT.
UGH, BACK IN THE HOSPITAL...
SHINOMIYA SEEMS TO BE IN STABLE CONDITION. I HEARD THEY'RE TREATING HER WITH THE BEST SCIENCE THE DEFENSE FORCE HAS TO OFFER.
AND WHAT ABOUT ME?! I WANT SOME OF THAT!!
PEEL PEEL
WELL, YOU ONLY HAVE SOME MINOR FRACTURES, SIR.
POMF
IT ALL HAPPENED SO FAST.
GOING UP AGAINST THAT TOUGH COMPETITION SERVED AS A REMINDER.

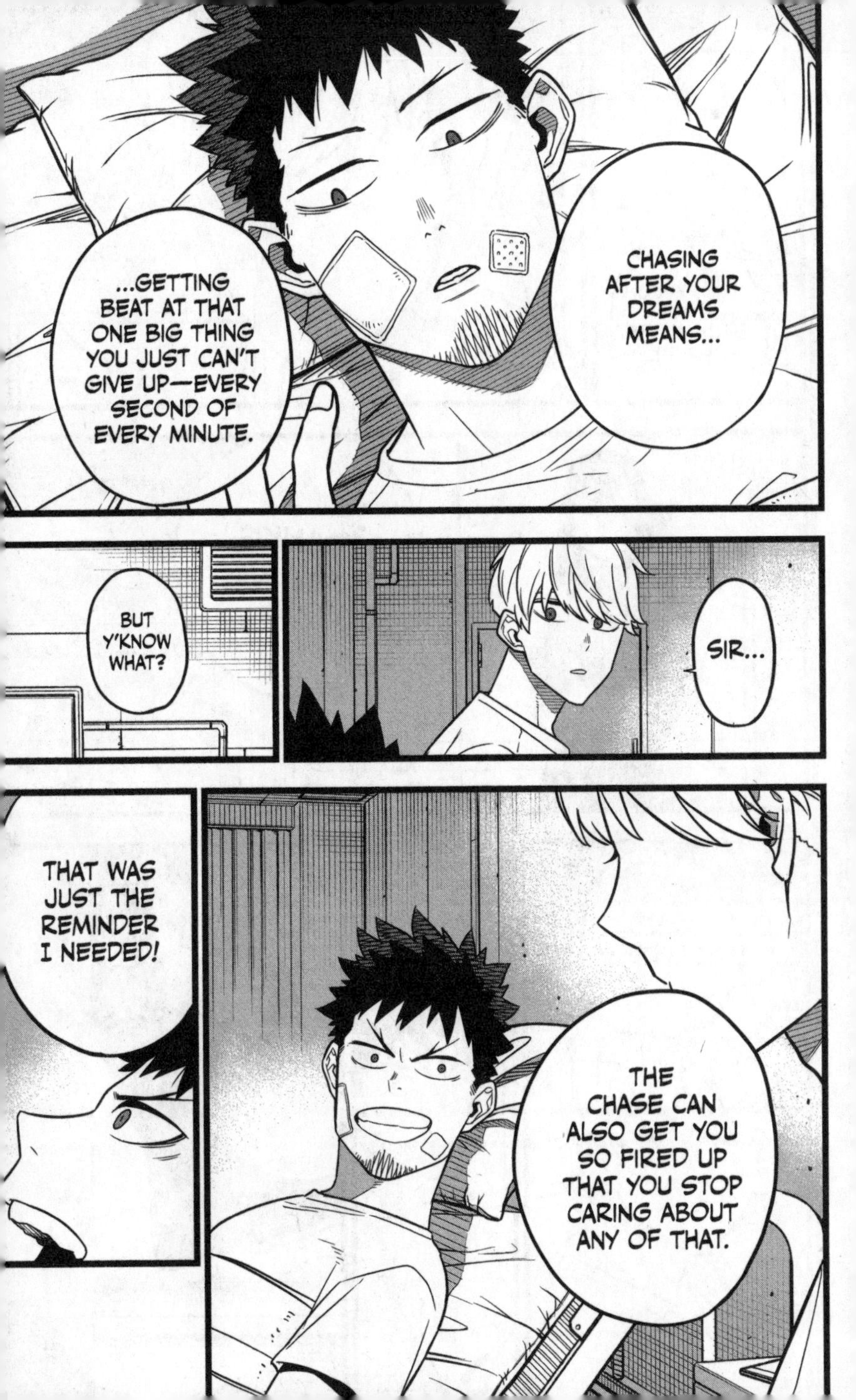
CHASING AFTER YOUR DREAMS MEANS...
...GETTING BEAT AT THAT ONE BIG THING YOU JUST CAN'T GIVE UP—EVERY SECOND OF EVERY MINUTE.
SIR...
BUT Y'KNOW WHAT?
THE CHASE CAN ALSO GET YOU SO FIRED UP THAT YOU STOP CARING ABOUT ANY OF THAT.
THAT WAS JUST THE REMINDER I NEEDED!

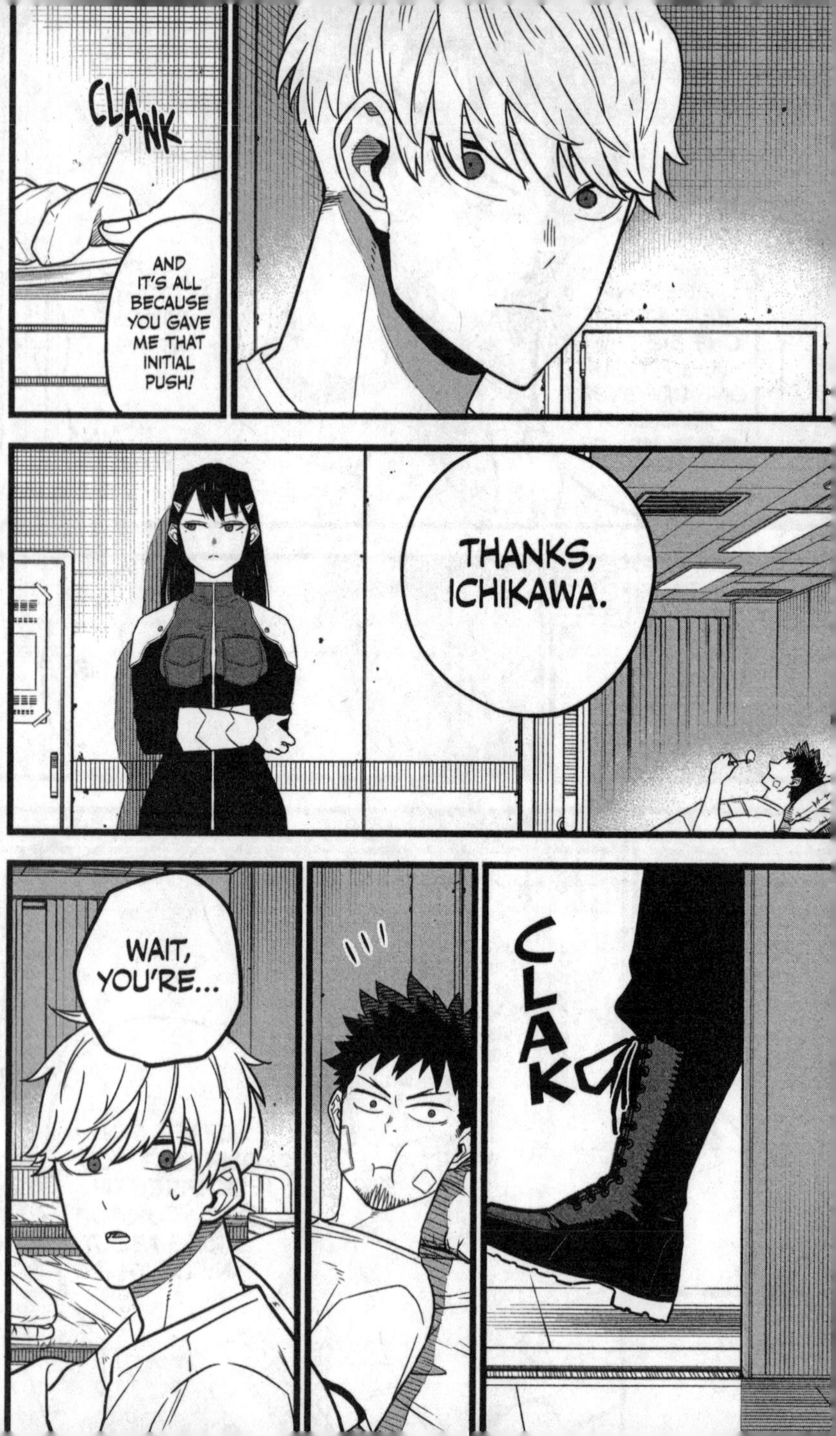
CLANK
AND IT'S ALL BECAUSE YOU GAVE ME THAT INITIAL PUSH!
THANKS, ICHIKAWA.
CLAK
WAIT, YOU'RE...

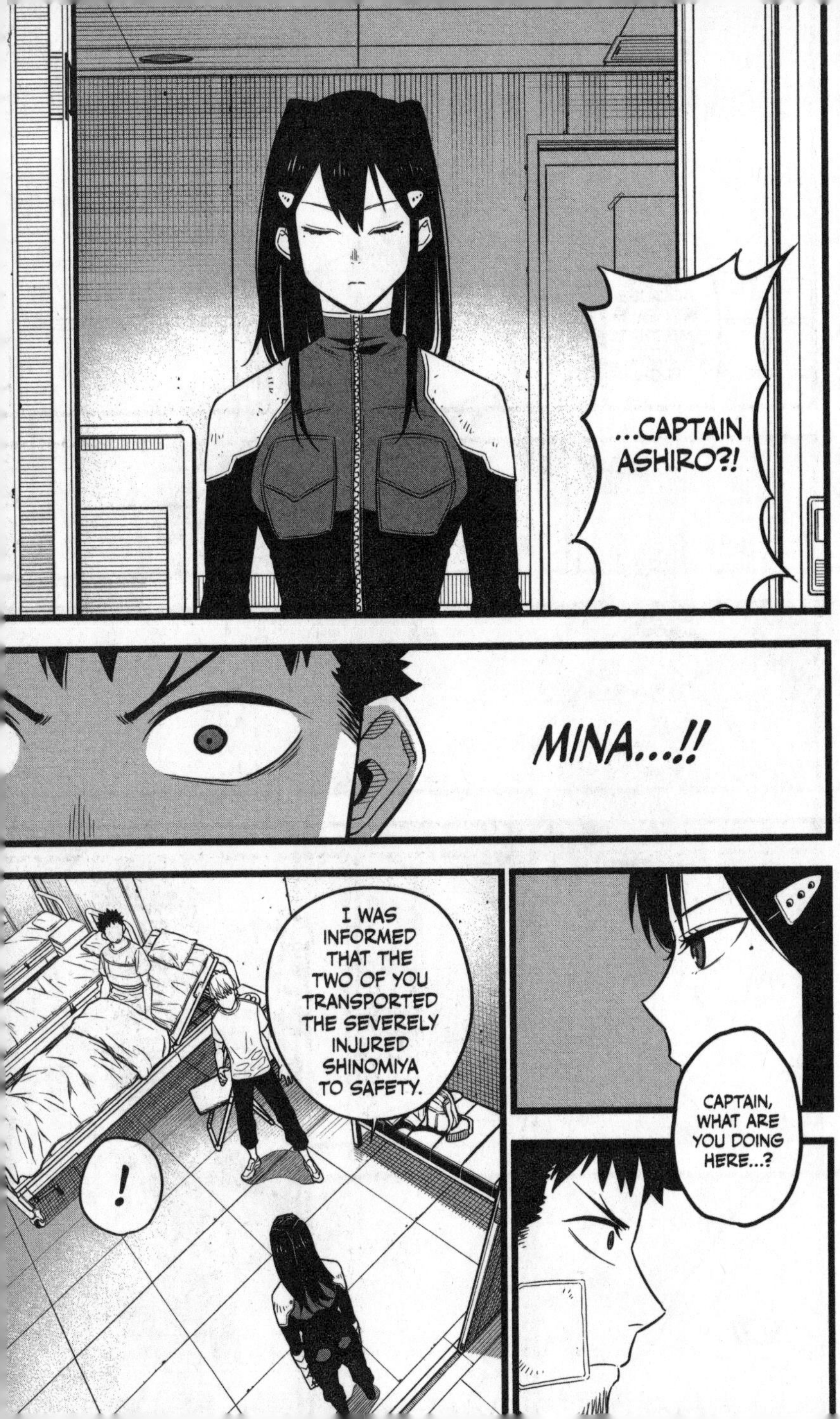
...CAPTAIN ASHIRO?!
MINA...!!
CAPTAIN, WHAT ARE YOU DOING HERE...?
I WAS INFORMED THAT THE TWO OF YOU TRANSPORTED THE SEVERELY INJURED SHINOMIYA TO SAFETY.
!

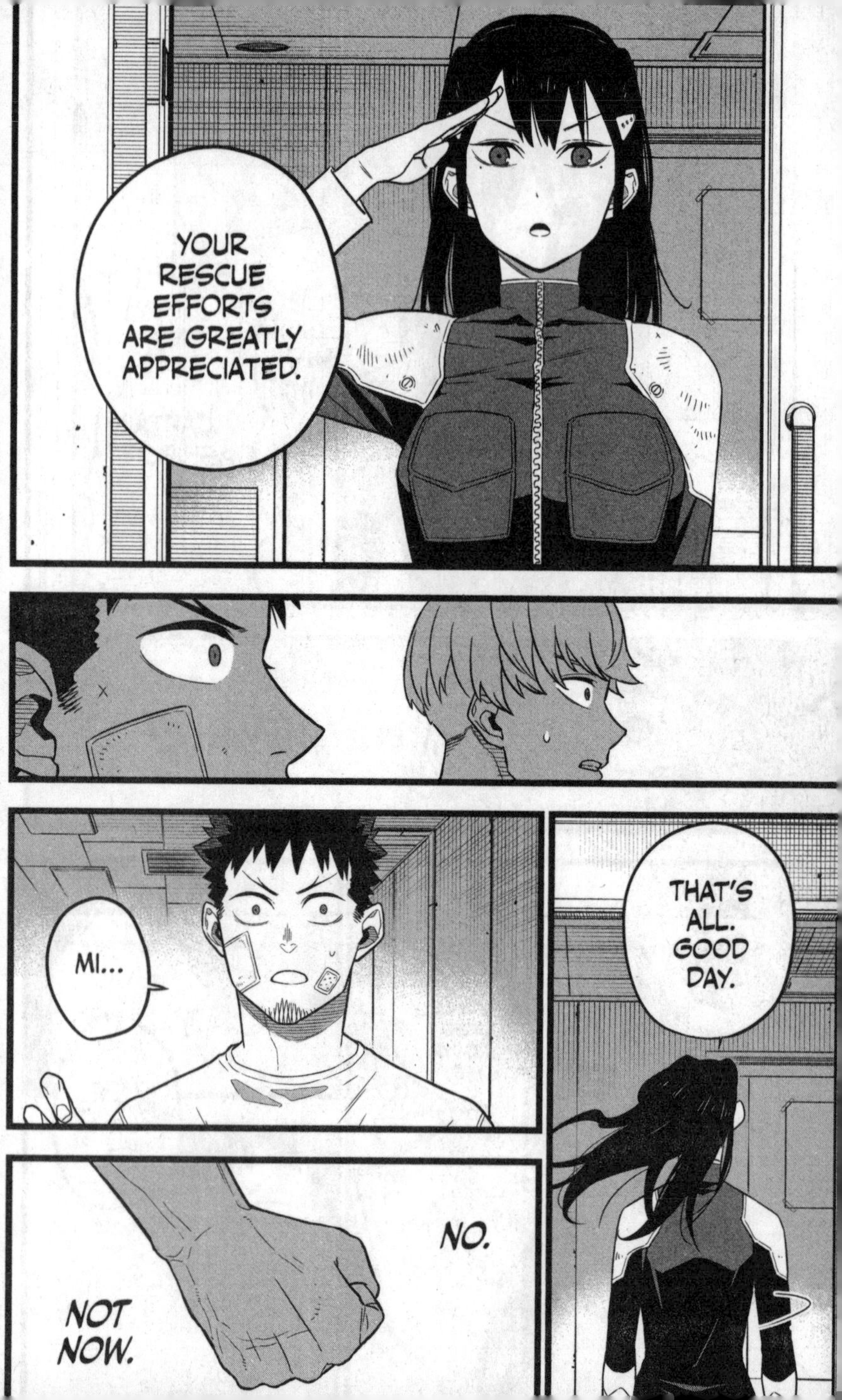
YOUR RESCUE EFFORTS ARE GREATLY APPRECIATED.
THAT'S ALL. GOOD DAY.
MI...
NO.
NOT NOW.

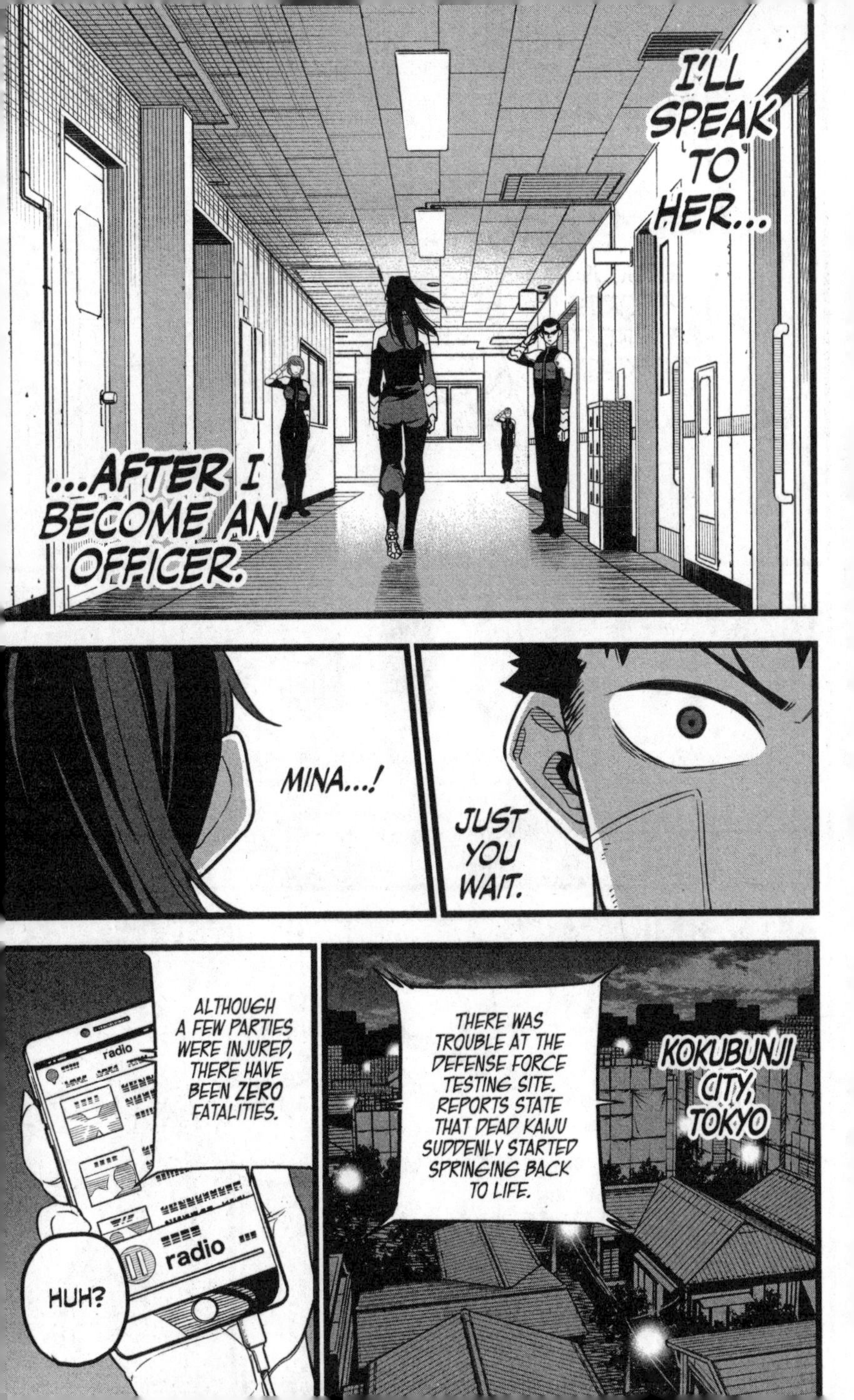
I'LL SPEAK TO HER...
...AFTER I BECOME AN OFFICER.
JUST YOU WAIT.
MINA...!
KOKUBUNJI CITY, TOKYO
THERE WAS TROUBLE AT THE DEFENSE FORCE TESTING SITE. REPORTS STATE THAT DEAD KAIJU SUDDENLY STARTED SPRINGING BACK TO LIFE.
ALTHOUGH A FEW PARTIES WERE INJURED, THERE HAVE BEEN ZERO FATALITIES.
radio
radio
HUH?

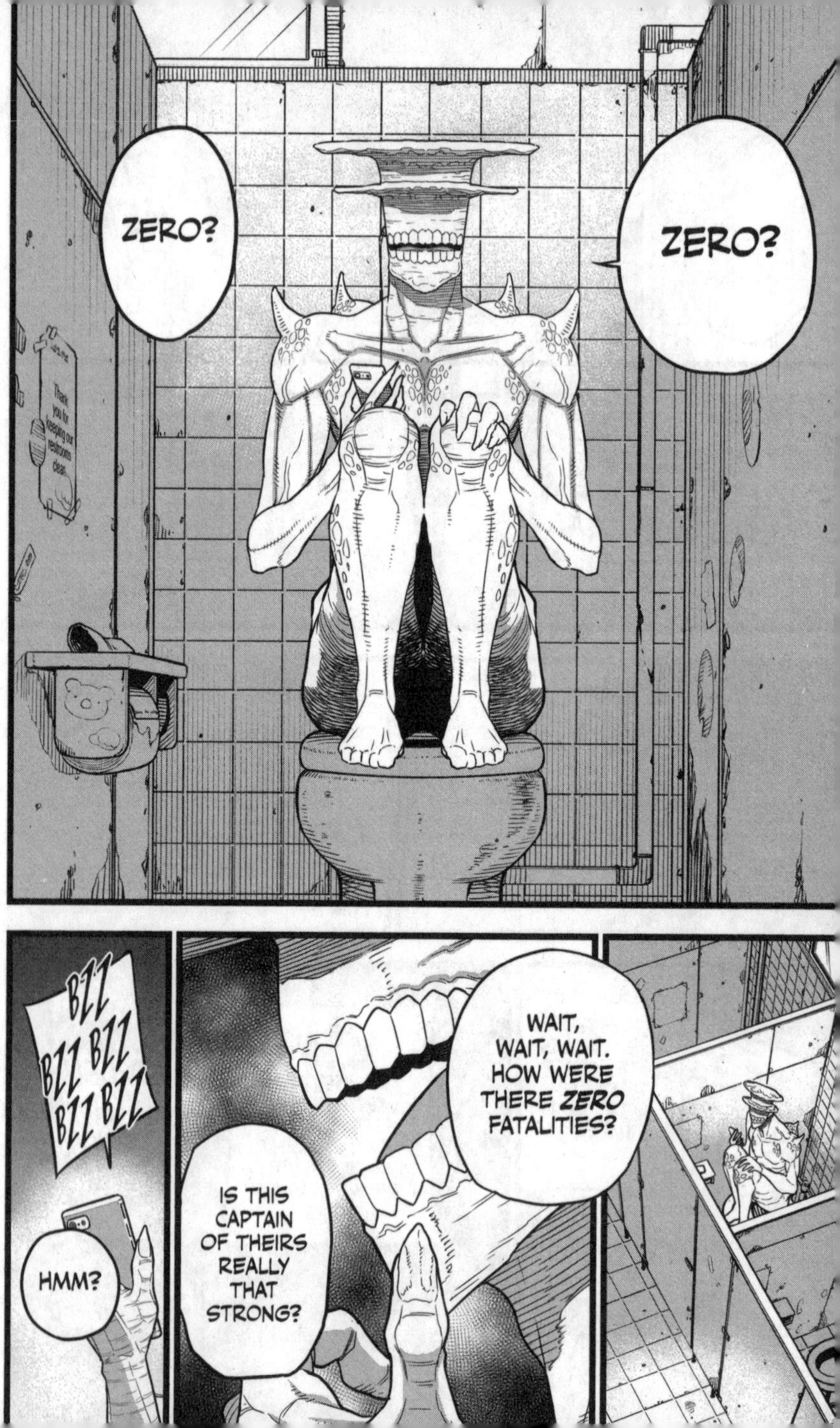
ZERO?
ZERO?
Thank you for keeping our restrooms clean.
WAIT, WAIT, WAIT. HOW WERE THERE *ZERO* FATALITIES?
IS THIS CAPTAIN OF THEIRS REALLY THAT STRONG?
BZZ BZZ BZZ BZZ BZZ
HMM?

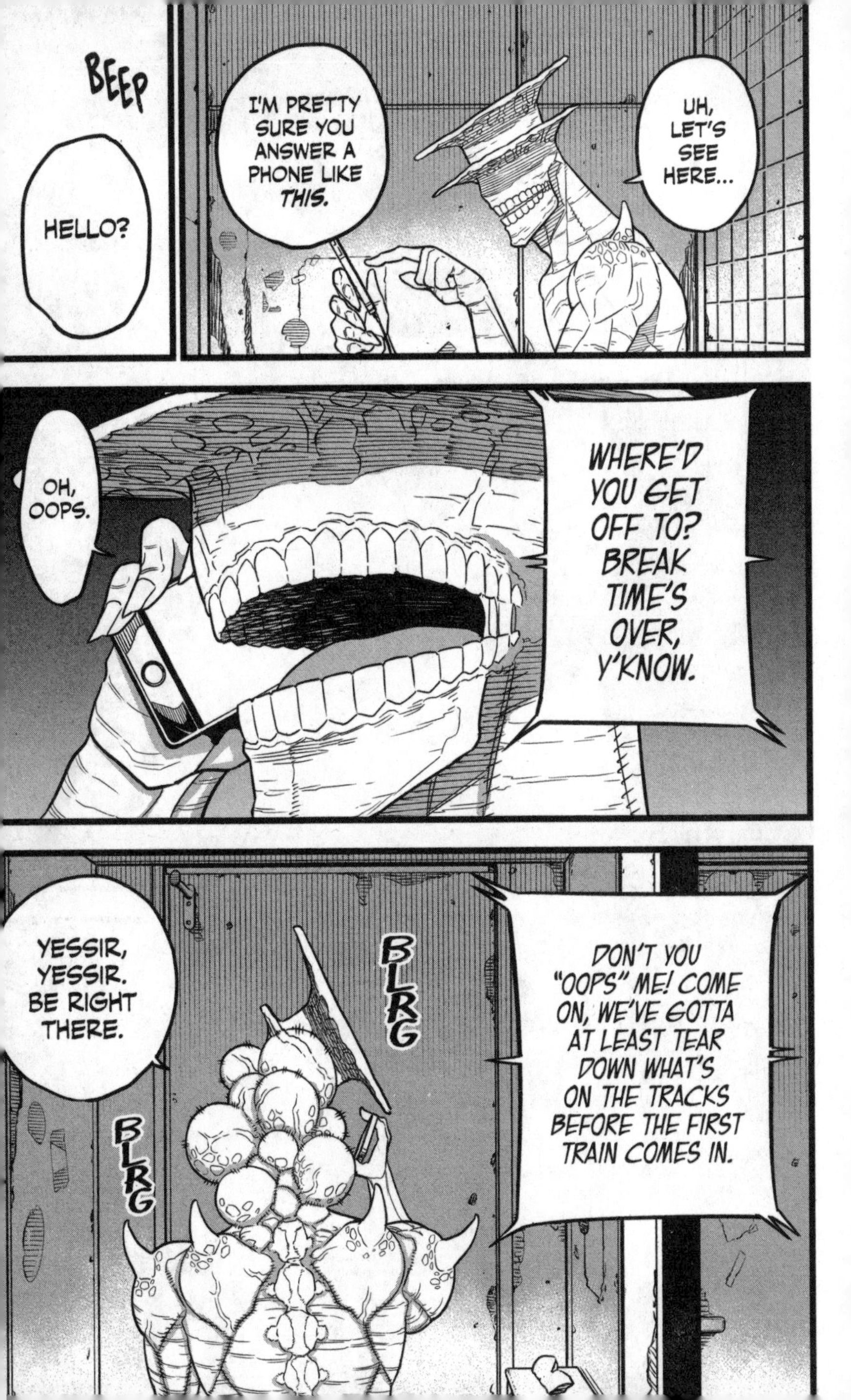
UH, LET'S SEE HERE...
I'M PRETTY SURE YOU ANSWER A PHONE LIKE *THIS.*
BEEP
HELLO?
WHERE'D YOU GET OFF TO? BREAK TIME'S OVER, Y'KNOW.
OH, OOPS.
DON'T YOU "OOPS" ME! COME ON, WE'VE GOTTA AT LEAST TEAR DOWN WHAT'S ON THE TRACKS BEFORE THE FIRST TRAIN COMES IN.
BLRG
BLRG
YESSIR, YESSIR. BE RIGHT THERE.

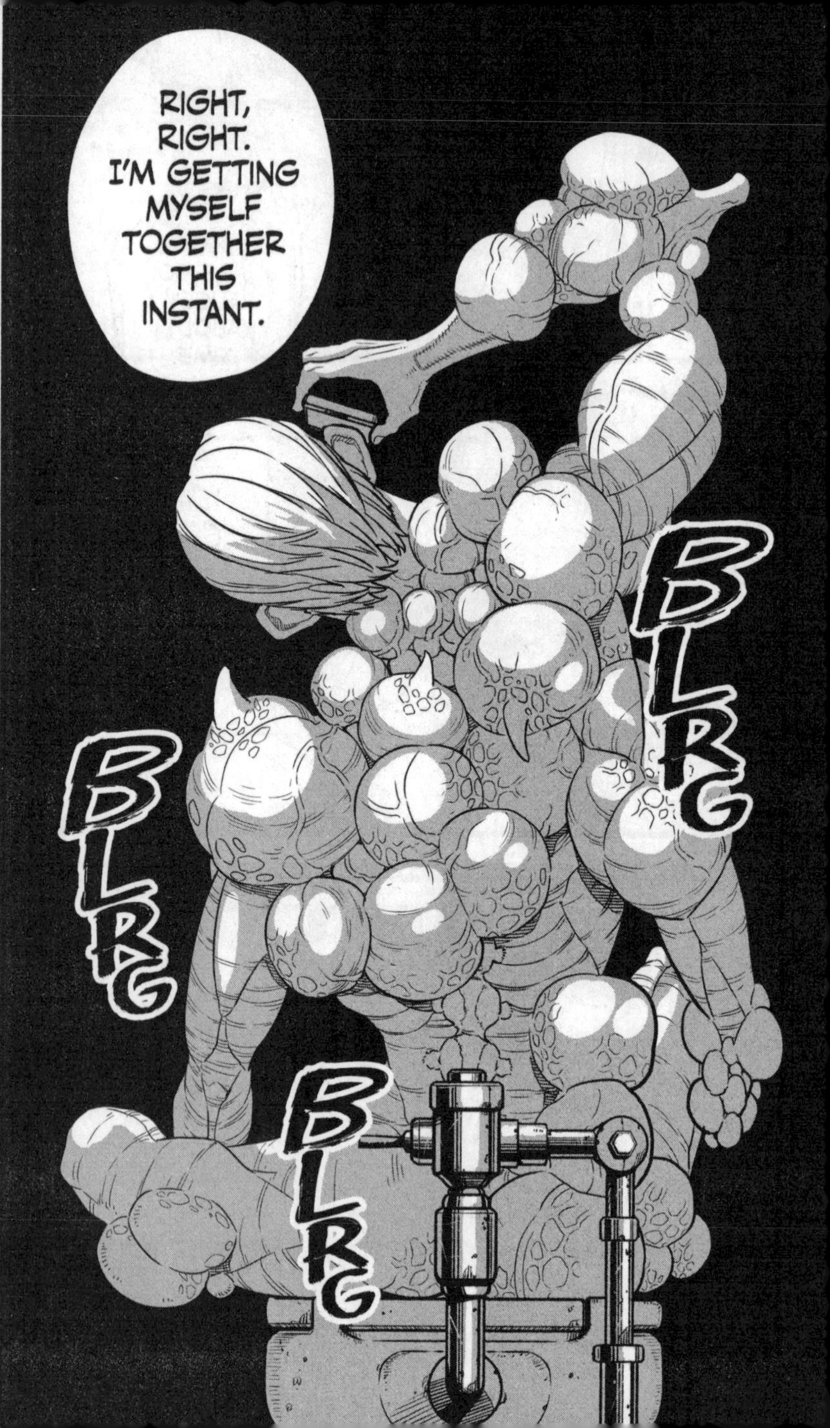
RIGHT, RIGHT. I'M GETTING MYSELF TOGETHER THIS INSTANT.
BLRG
BLRG
BLRG

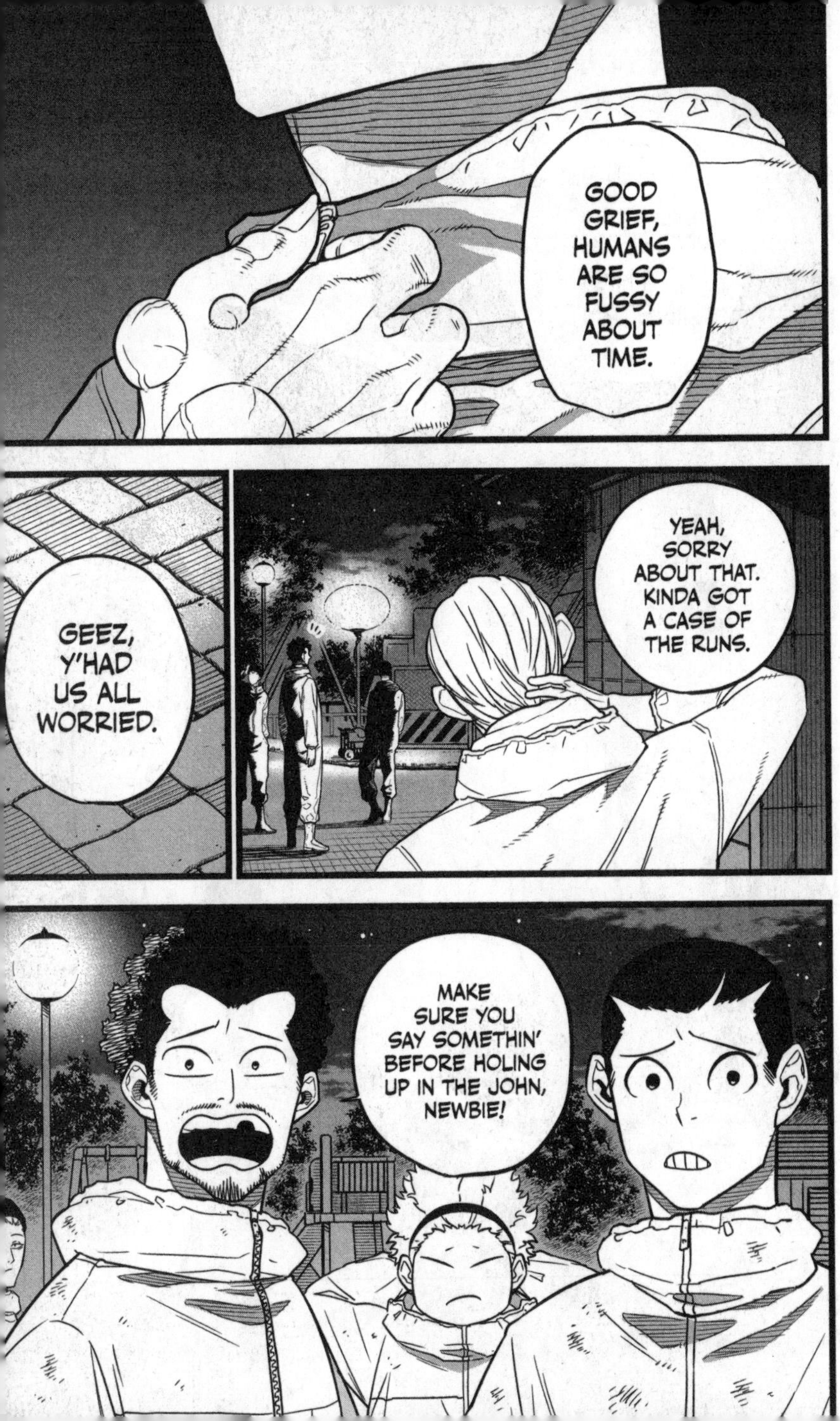
GOOD GRIEF, HUMANS ARE SO FUSSY ABOUT TIME.
YEAH, SORRY ABOUT THAT. KINDA GOT A CASE OF THE RUNS.
GEEZ, Y'HAD US ALL WORRIED.
MAKE SURE YOU SAY SOMETHIN' BEFORE HOLING UP IN THE JOHN, NEWBIE!

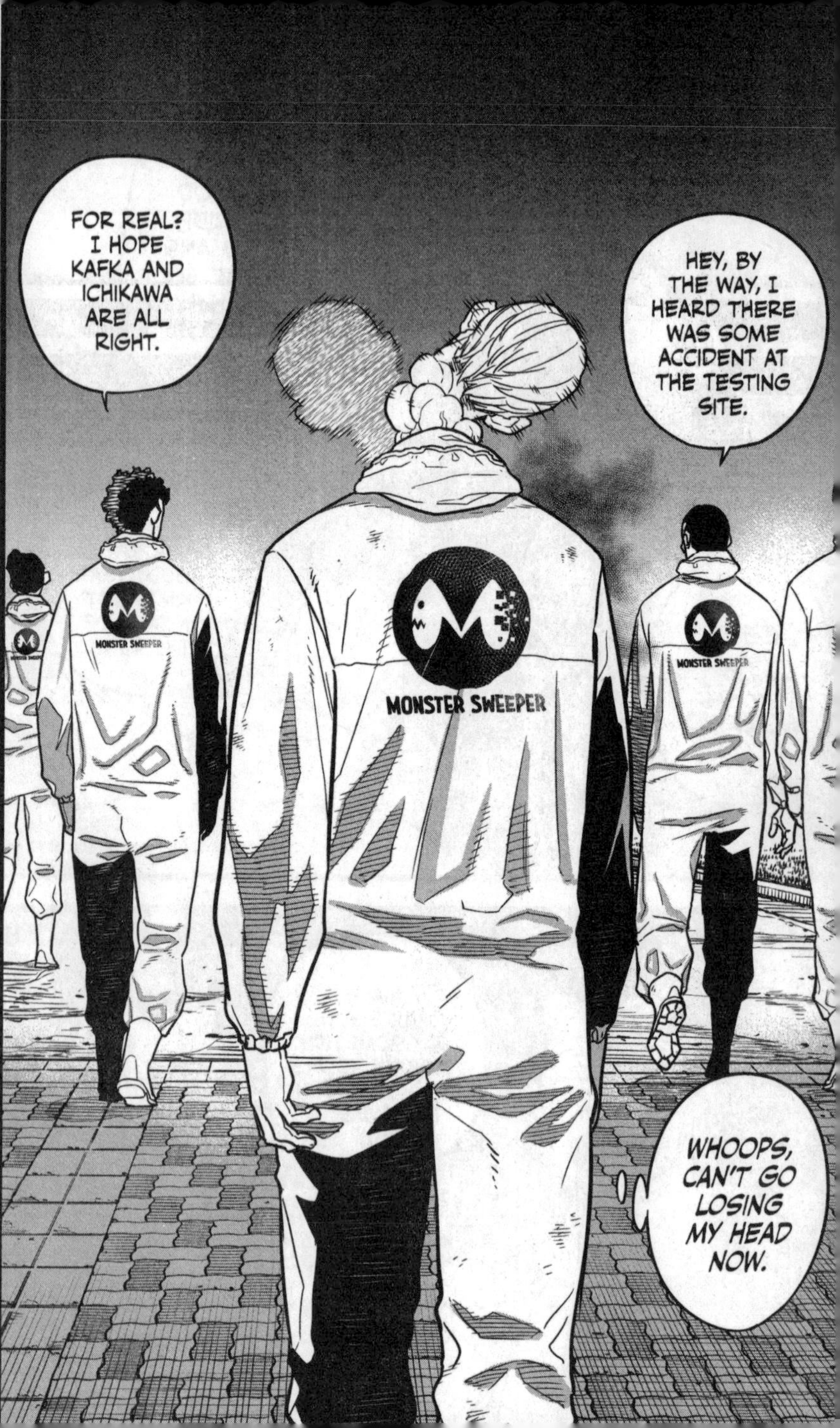
HEY, BY THE WAY, I HEARD THERE WAS SOME ACCIDENT AT THE TESTING SITE.
FOR REAL? I HOPE KAFKA AND ICHIKAWA ARE ALL RIGHT.
MONSTER SWEEPER
WHOOPS, CAN'T GO LOSING MY HEAD NOW.

CHAPTER 10

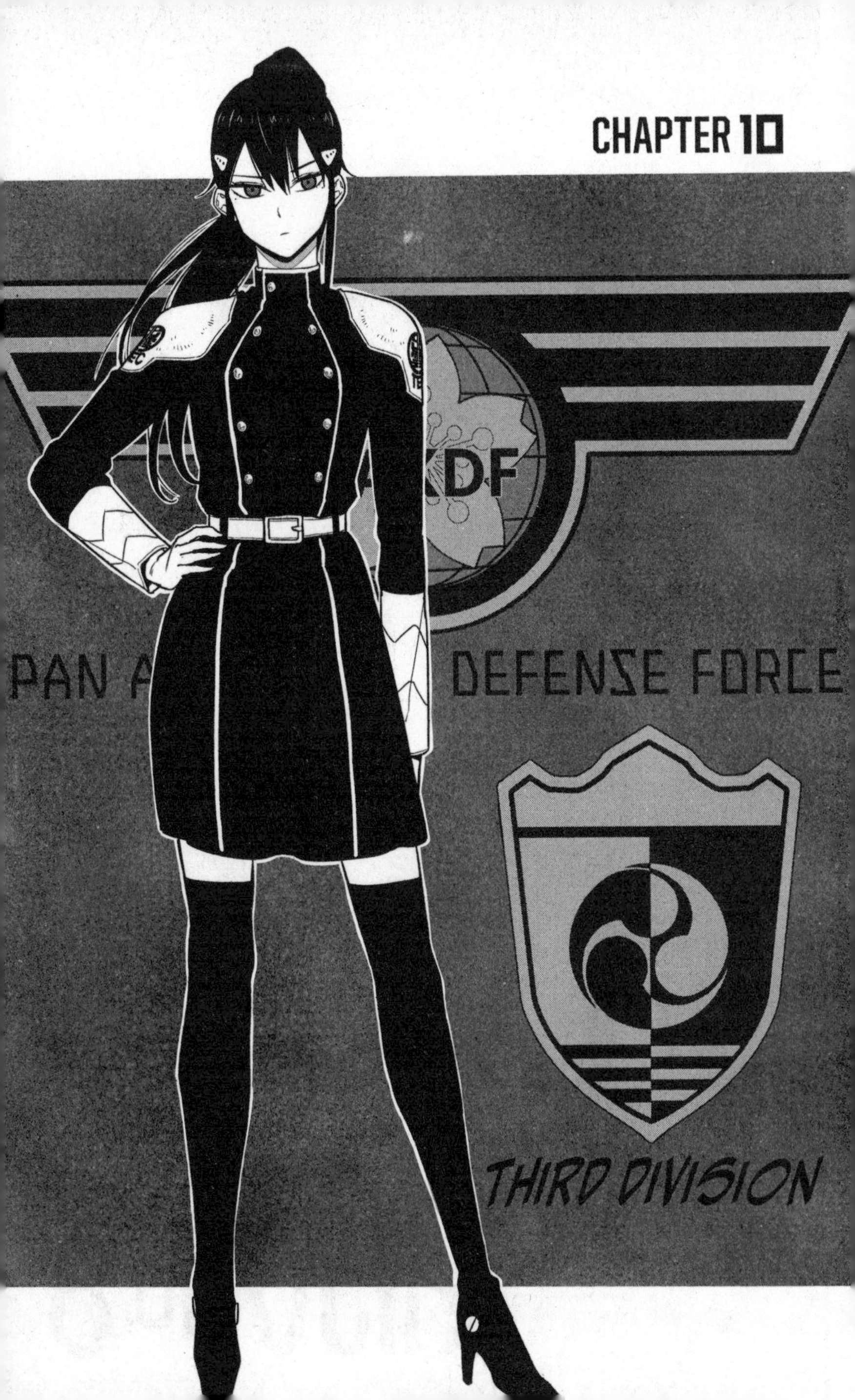
KDF
PAN A
DEFENSE FORCE
THIRD DIVISION

KAIJU NO.8

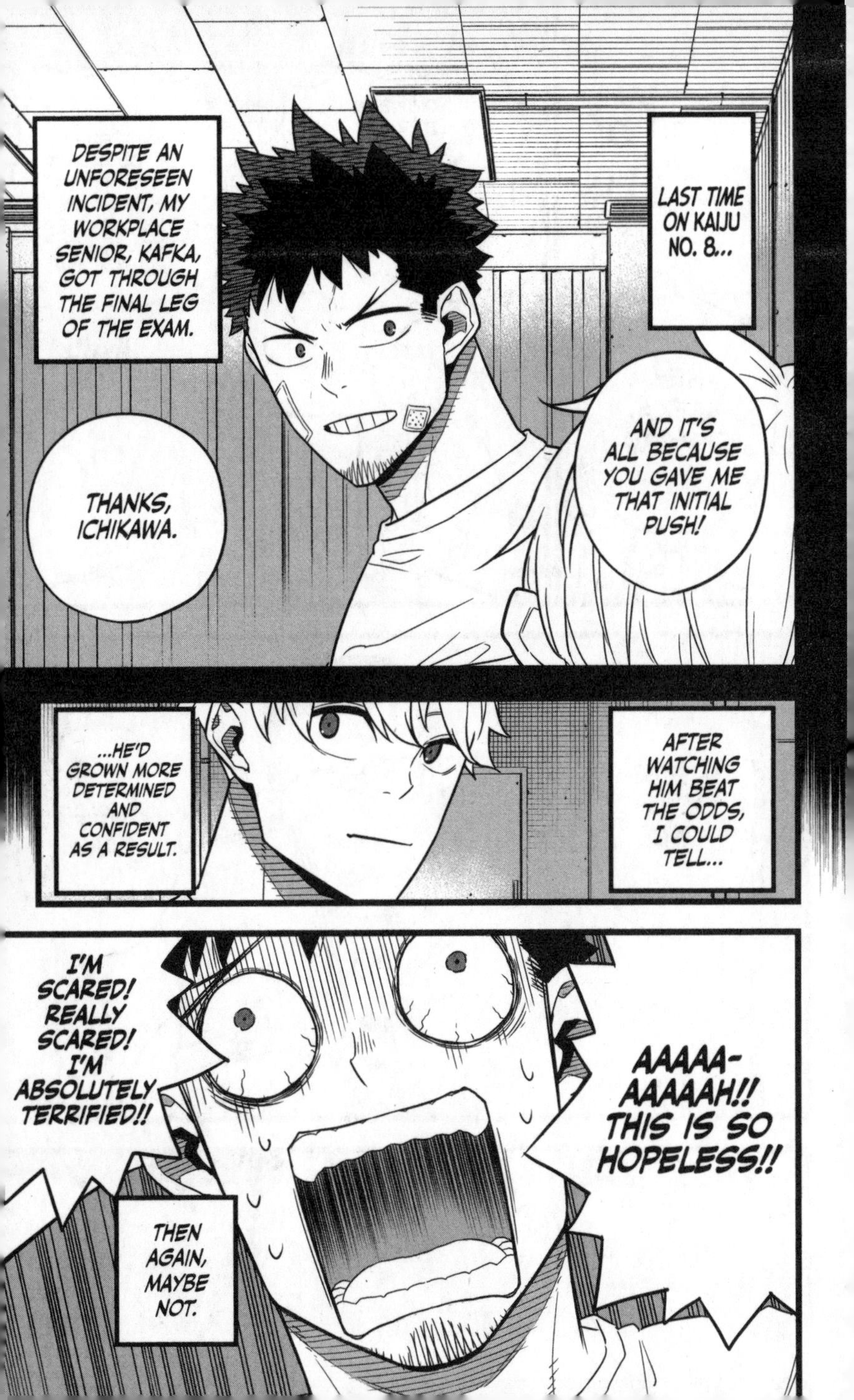
LAST TIME ON KAIJU NO. 8...
DESPITE AN UNFORESEEN INCIDENT, MY WORKPLACE SENIOR, KAFKA, GOT THROUGH THE FINAL LEG OF THE EXAM.
AND IT'S ALL BECAUSE YOU GAVE ME THAT INITIAL PUSH!
THANKS, ICHIKAWA.
AFTER WATCHING HIM BEAT THE ODDS, I COULD TELL...
...HE'D GROWN MORE DETERMINED AND CONFIDENT AS A RESULT.
AAAAA-AAAAAH!! THIS IS SO HOPELESS!!
I'M SCARED! REALLY SCARED! I'M ABSOLUTELY TERRIFIED!!
THEN AGAIN, MAYBE NOT.

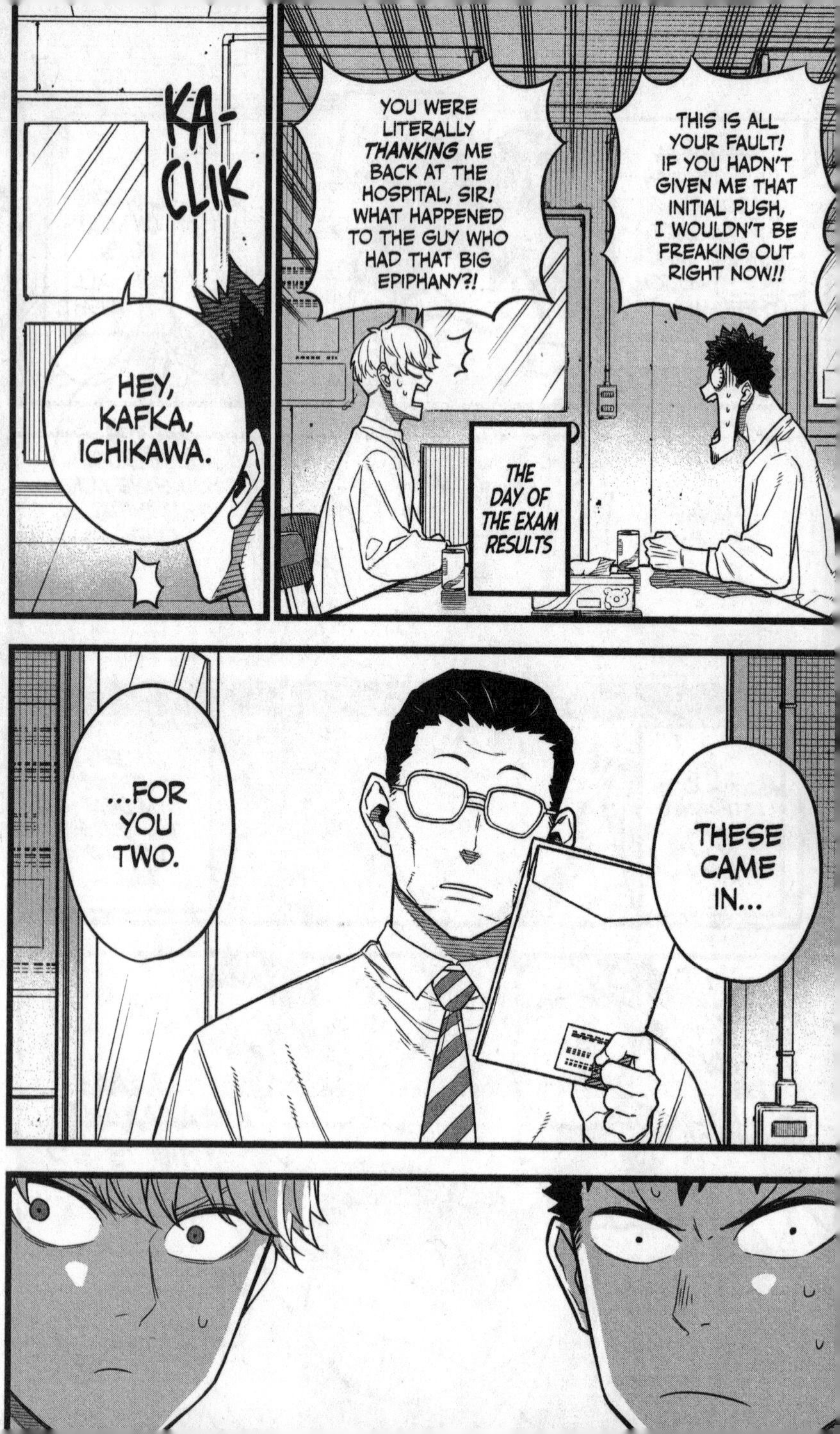
THIS IS ALL YOUR FAULT! IF YOU HADN'T GIVEN ME THAT INITIAL PUSH, I WOULDN'T BE FREAKING OUT RIGHT NOW!!
YOU WERE LITERALLY *THANKING* ME BACK AT THE HOSPITAL, SIR! WHAT HAPPENED TO THE GUY WHO HAD THAT BIG EPIPHANY?!
THE DAY OF THE EXAM RESULTS
KA-CLIK
HEY, KAFKA, ICHIKAWA.
THESE CAME IN...
...FOR YOU TWO.

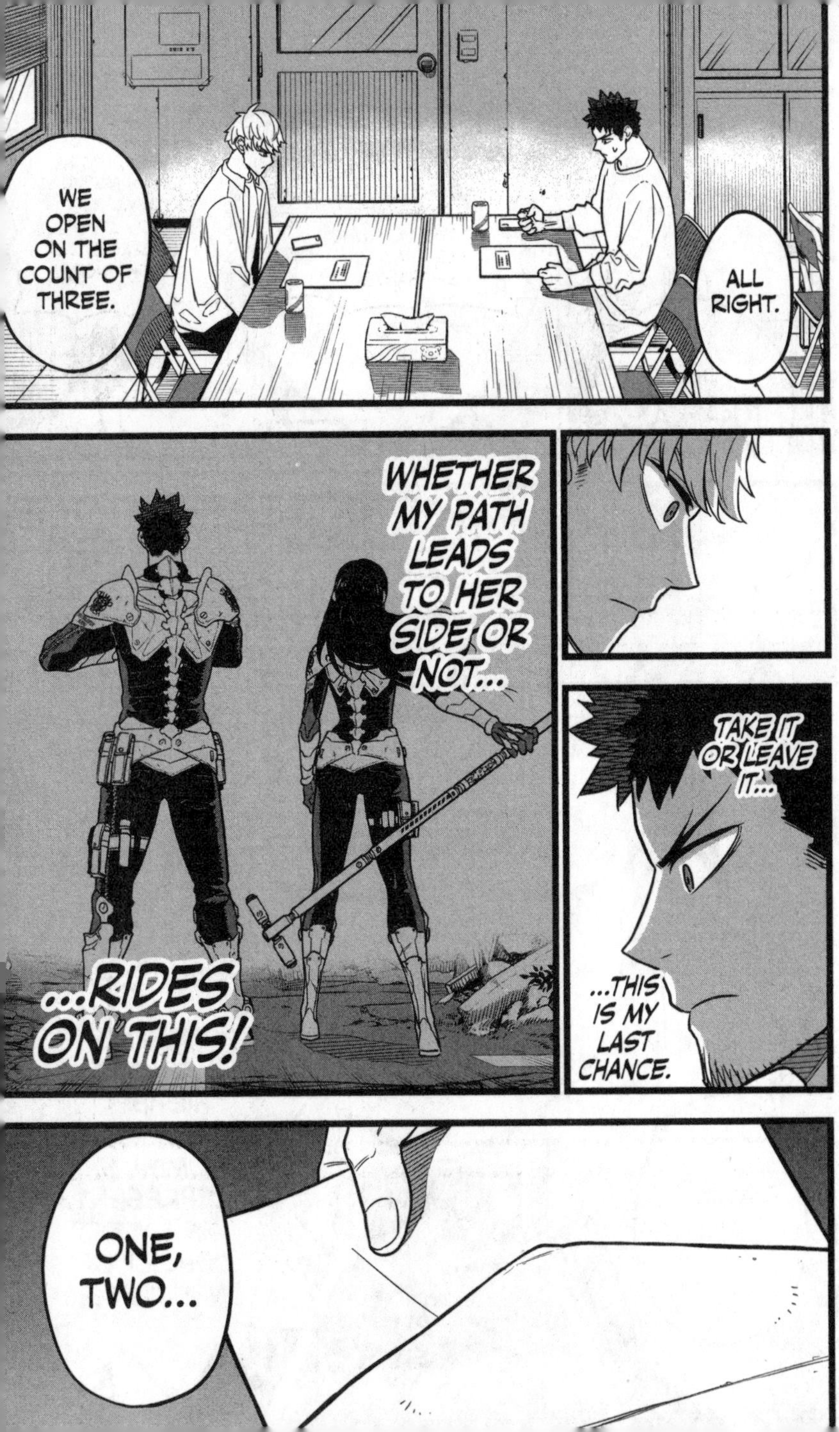
WE OPEN ON THE COUNT OF THREE.
ALL RIGHT.
TAKE IT OR LEAVE IT...
...THIS IS MY LAST CHANCE.
WHETHER MY PATH LEADS TO HER SIDE OR NOT...
...RIDES ON THIS!
ONE, TWO...

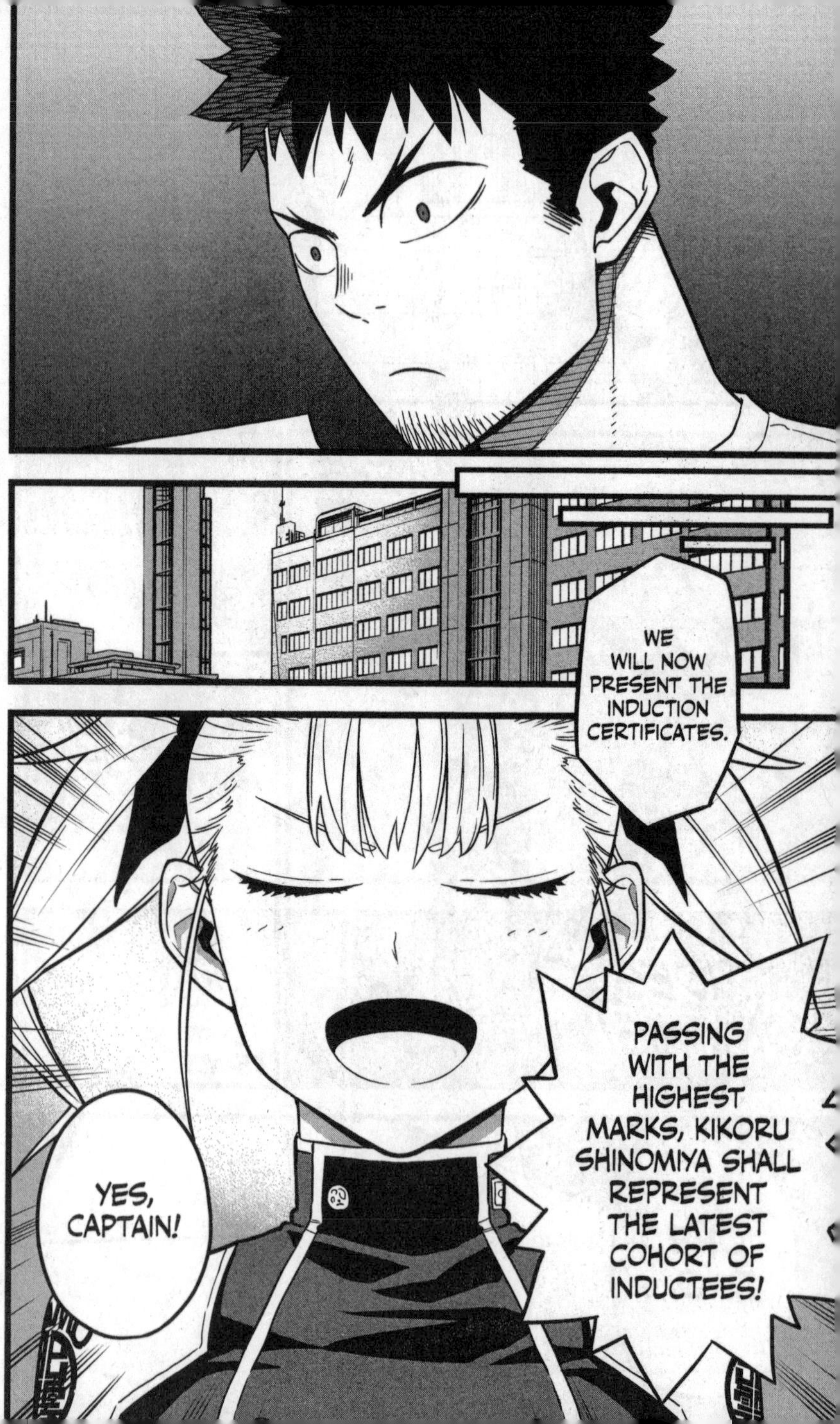
WE WILL NOW PRESENT THE INDUCTION CERTIFICATES.
PASSING WITH THE HIGHEST MARKS, KIKORU SHINOMIYA SHALL REPRESENT THE LATEST COHORT OF INDUCTEES!
YES, CAPTAIN!

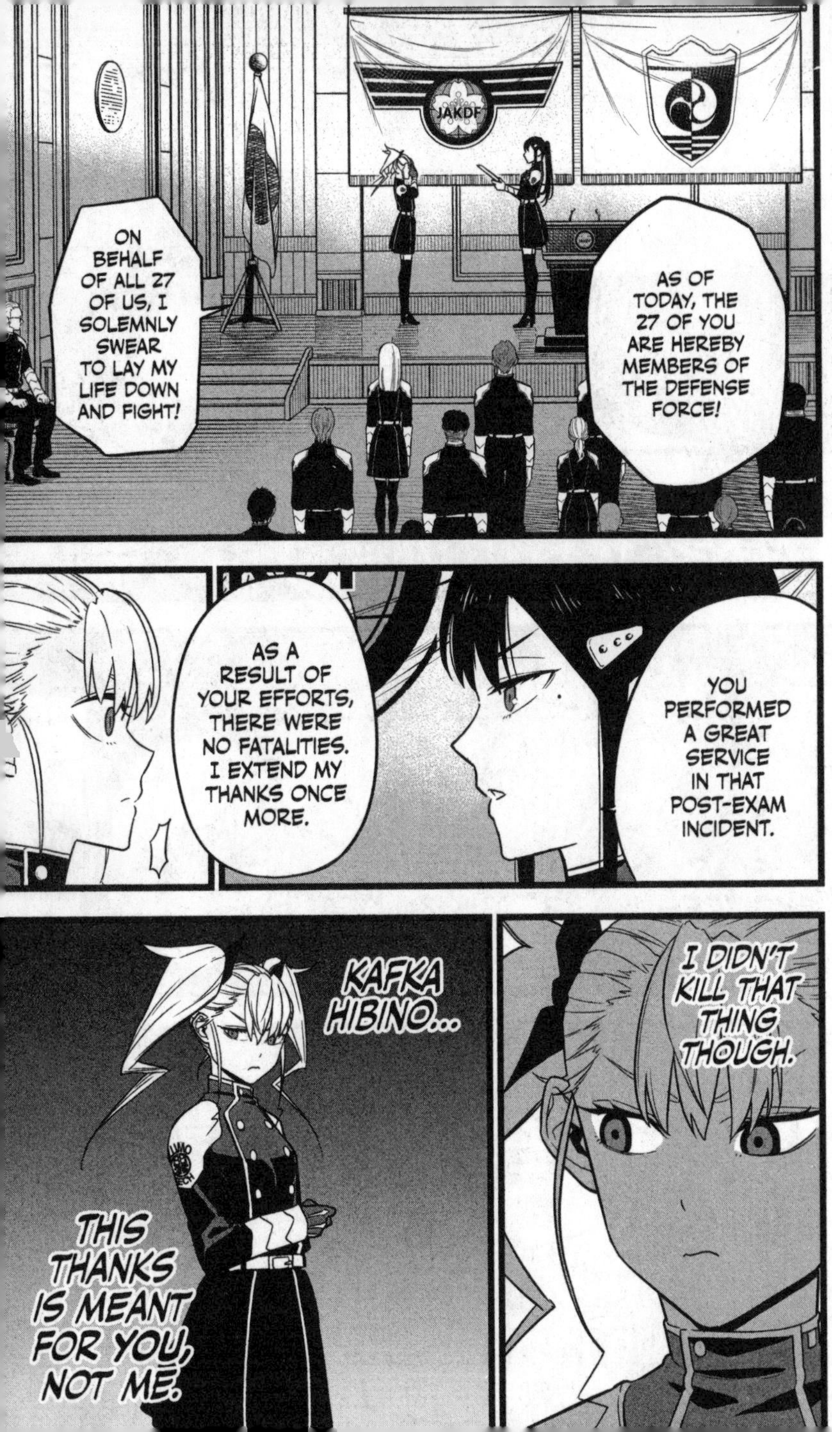
AS OF TODAY, THE 27 OF YOU ARE HEREBY MEMBERS OF THE DEFENSE FORCE!
ON BEHALF OF ALL 27 OF US, I SOLEMNLY SWEAR TO LAY MY LIFE DOWN AND FIGHT!
JAKDF
YOU PERFORMED A GREAT SERVICE IN THAT POST-EXAM INCIDENT.
AS A RESULT OF YOUR EFFORTS, THERE WERE NO FATALITIES. I EXTEND MY THANKS ONCE MORE.
I DIDN'T KILL THAT THING THOUGH.
KAFKA HIBINO...
THIS THANKS IS MEANT FOR YOU, NOT ME.

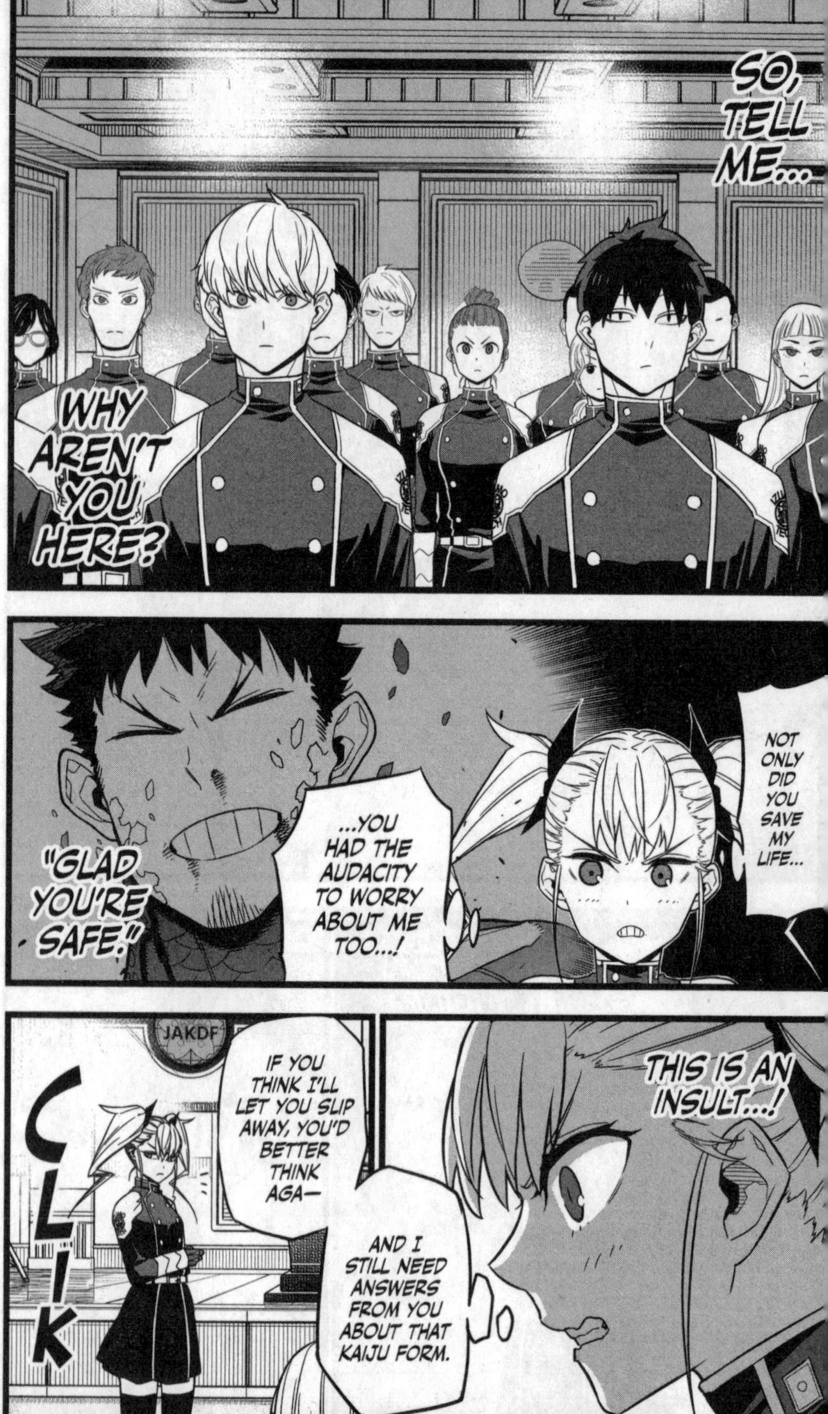
SO, TELL ME...
WHY AREN'T YOU HERE?
NOT ONLY DID YOU SAVE MY LIFE...
...YOU HAD THE AUDACITY TO WORRY ABOUT ME TOO...!
"GLAD YOU'RE SAFE."
THIS IS AN INSULT...!
AND I STILL NEED ANSWERS FROM YOU ABOUT THAT KAIJU FORM.
JAKDF
IF YOU THINK I'LL LET YOU SLIP AWAY, YOU'D BETTER THINK AGA—
CLIK

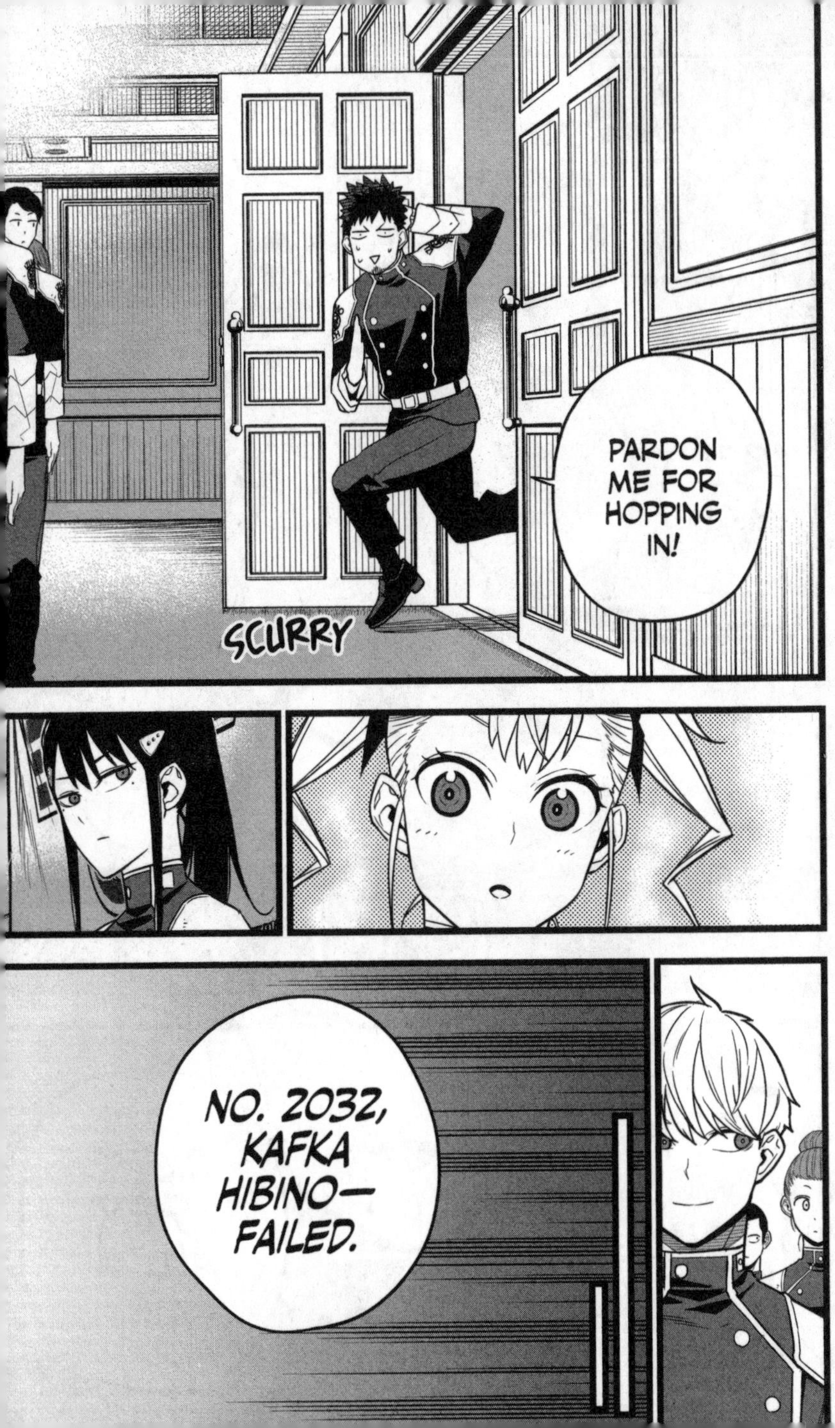
PARDON ME FOR HOPPING IN!
SCURRY
NO. 2032, KAFKA HIBINO—FAILED.

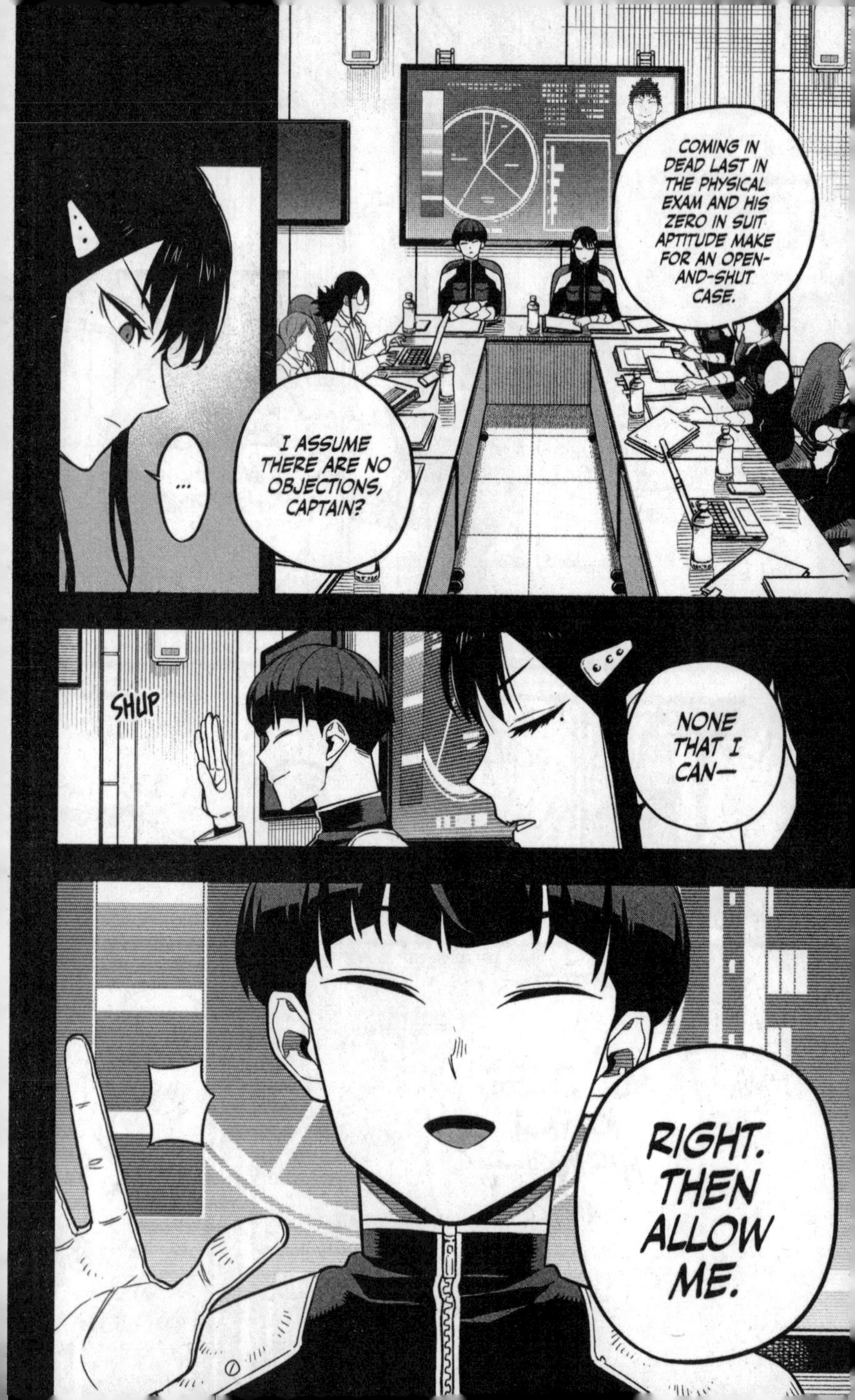
COMING IN DEAD LAST IN THE PHYSICAL EXAM AND HIS ZERO IN SUIT APTITUDE MAKE FOR AN OPEN-AND-SHUT CASE.
I ASSUME THERE ARE NO OBJECTIONS, CAPTAIN?
...
NONE THAT I CAN—
SHUP
RIGHT. THEN ALLOW ME.

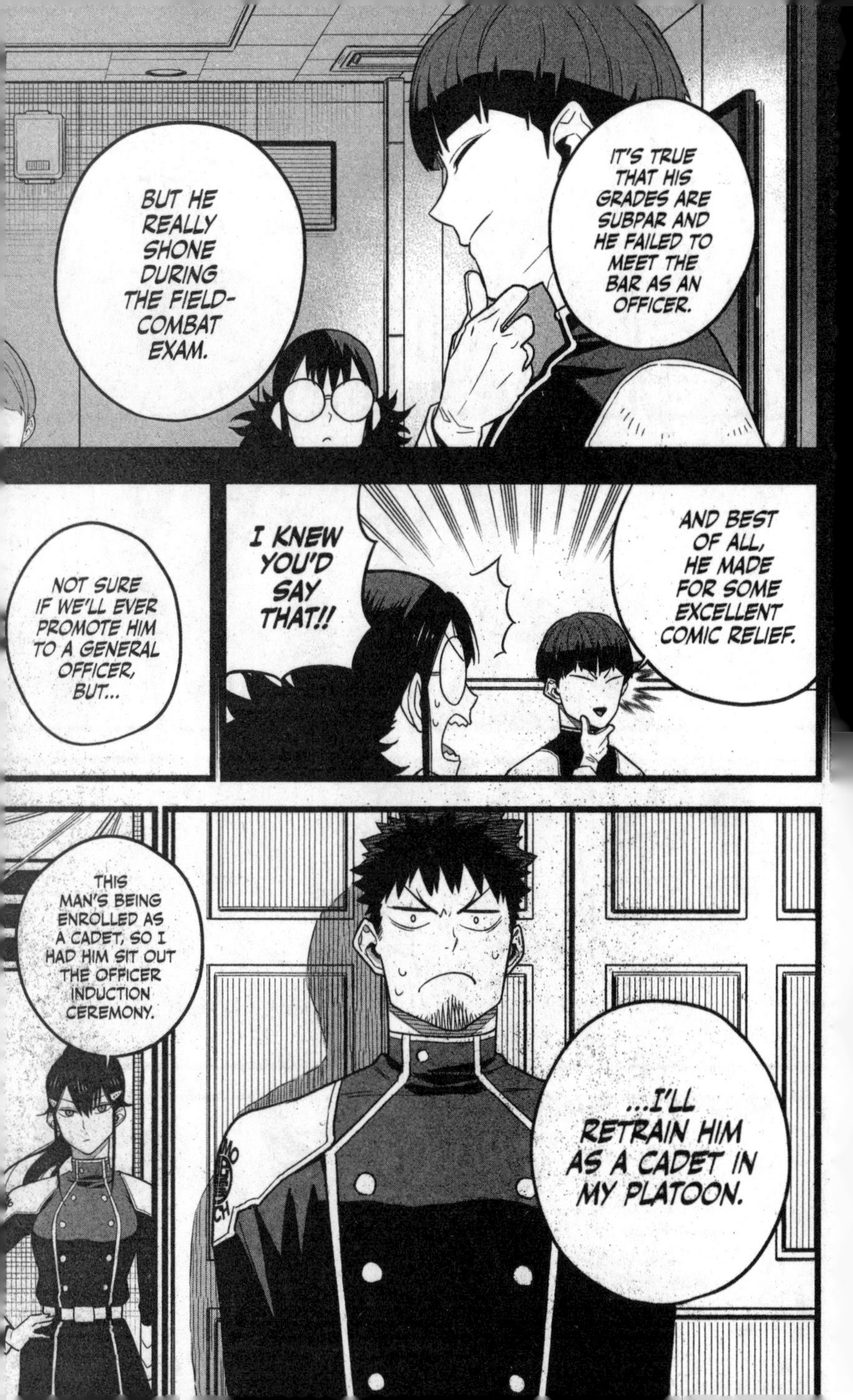
IT'S TRUE THAT HIS GRADES ARE SUBPAR AND HE FAILED TO MEET THE BAR AS AN OFFICER.
BUT HE REALLY SHONE DURING THE FIELD-COMBAT EXAM.
AND BEST OF ALL, HE MADE FOR SOME EXCELLENT COMIC RELIEF.
I KNEW YOU'D SAY THAT!!
NOT SURE IF WE'LL EVER PROMOTE HIM TO A GENERAL OFFICER, BUT...
...I'LL RETRAIN HIM AS A CADET IN MY PLATOON.
THIS MAN'S BEING ENROLLED AS A CADET, SO I HAD HIM SIT OUT THE OFFICER INDUCTION CEREMONY.

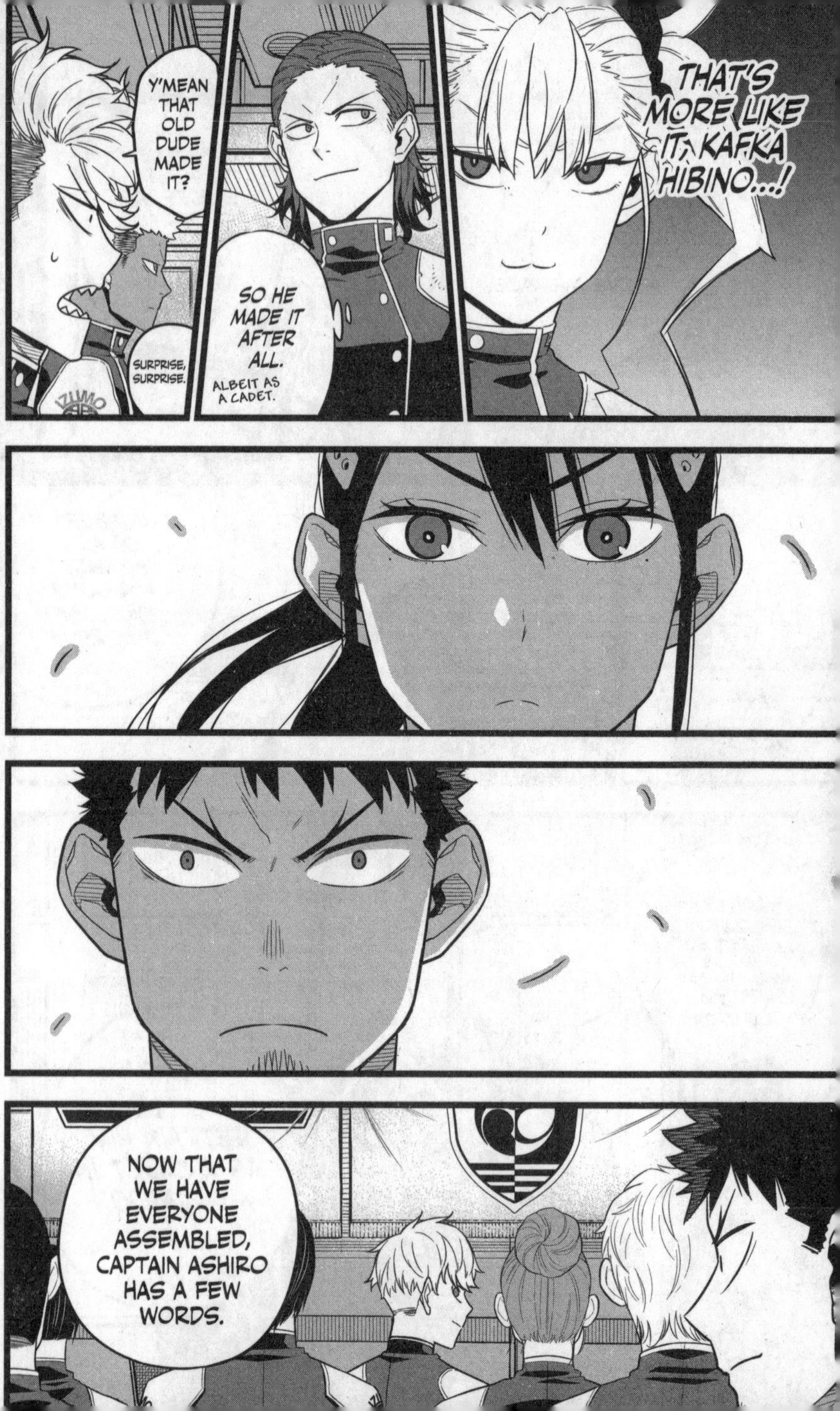
THAT'S MORE LIKE IT, KAFKA HIBINO...!
SO HE MADE IT AFTER ALL.
ALBEIT AS A CADET.
Y'MEAN THAT OLD DUDE MADE IT?
SURPRISE, SURPRISE.
IZUMO
NOW THAT WE HAVE EVERYONE ASSEMBLED, CAPTAIN ASHIRO HAS A FEW WORDS.

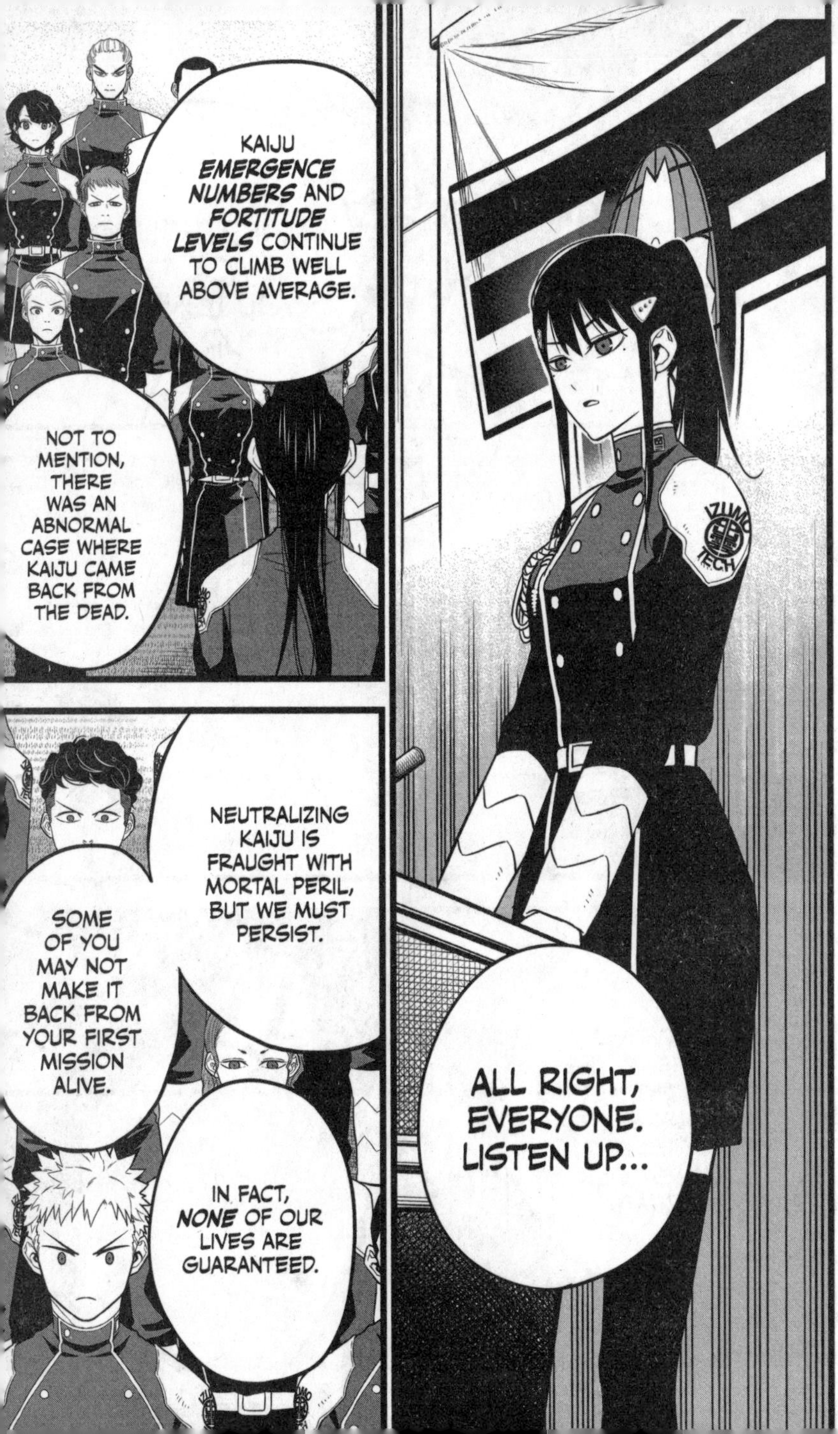
ALL RIGHT, EVERYONE. LISTEN UP...
KAIJU EMERGENCE NUMBERS AND FORTITUDE LEVELS CONTINUE TO CLIMB WELL ABOVE AVERAGE.
NOT TO MENTION, THERE WAS AN ABNORMAL CASE WHERE KAIJU CAME BACK FROM THE DEAD.
NEUTRALIZING KAIJU IS FRAUGHT WITH MORTAL PERIL, BUT WE MUST PERSIST.
SOME OF YOU MAY NOT MAKE IT BACK FROM YOUR FIRST MISSION ALIVE.
IN FACT, NONE OF OUR LIVES ARE GUARANTEED.
IZUMO TECH

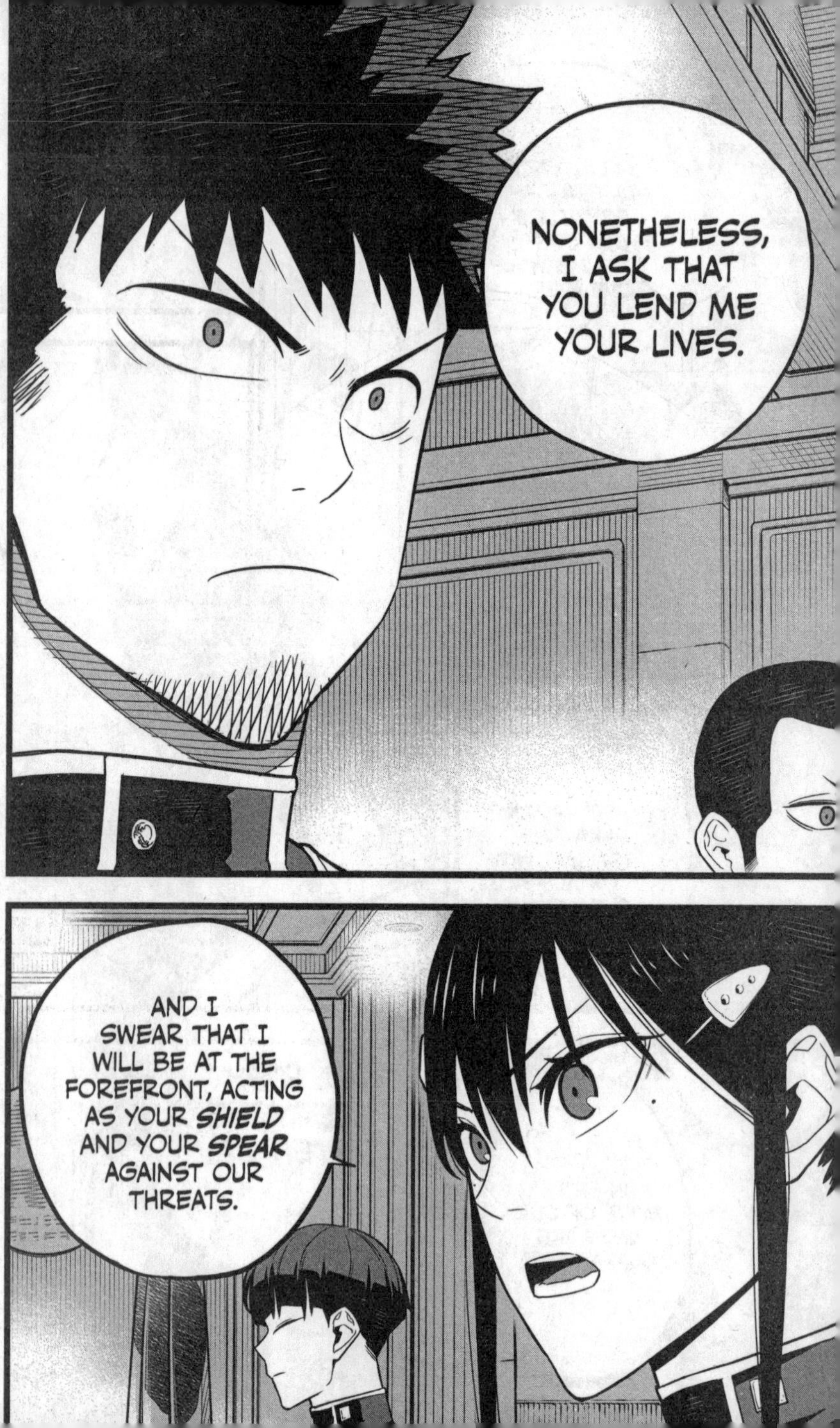
NONETHELESS, I ASK THAT YOU LEND ME YOUR LIVES.
AND I SWEAR THAT I WILL BE AT THE FOREFRONT, ACTING AS YOUR *SHIELD* AND YOUR *SPEAR* AGAINST OUR THREATS.

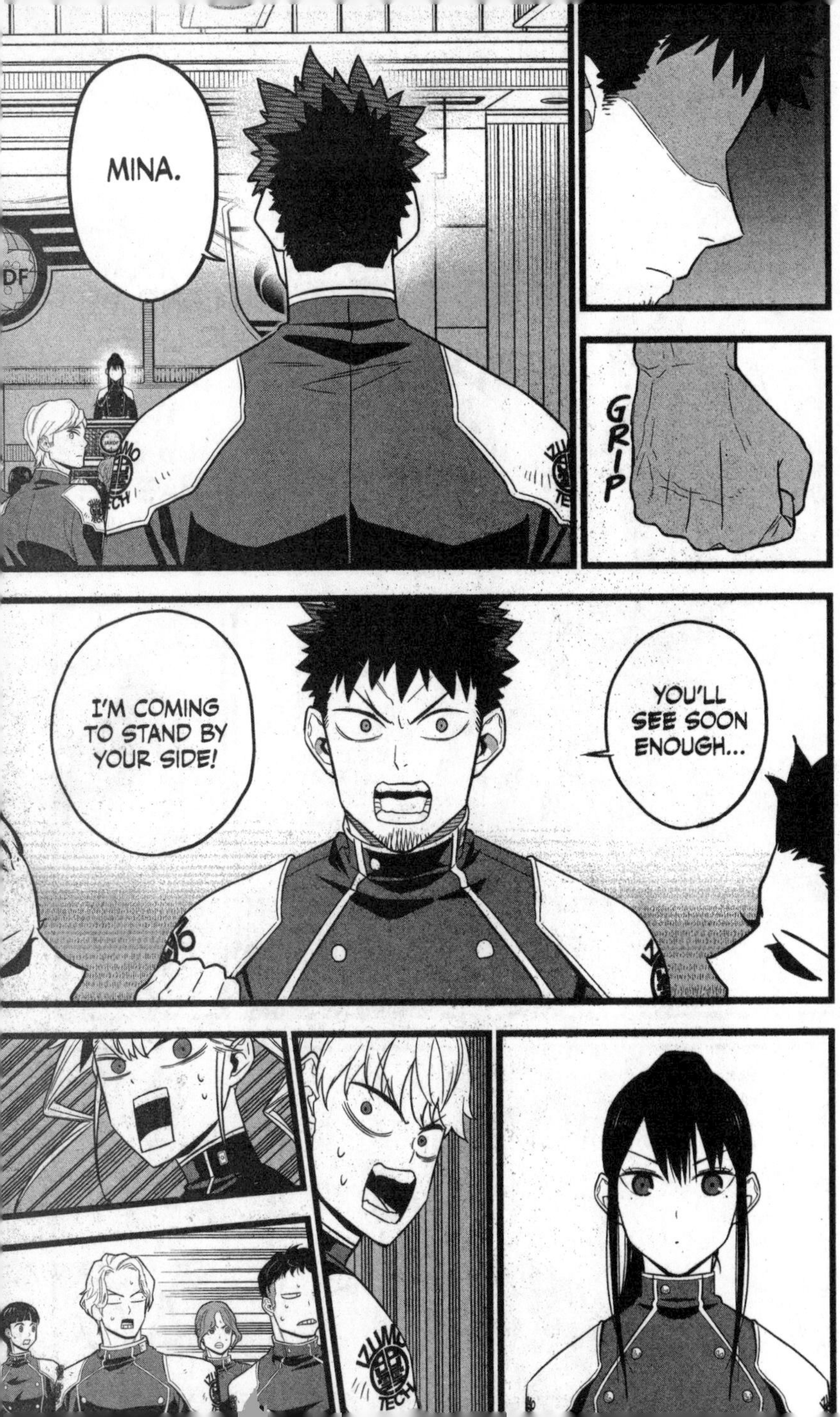
GRIP
MINA.
YOU'LL SEE SOON ENOUGH...
I'M COMING TO STAND BY YOUR SIDE!

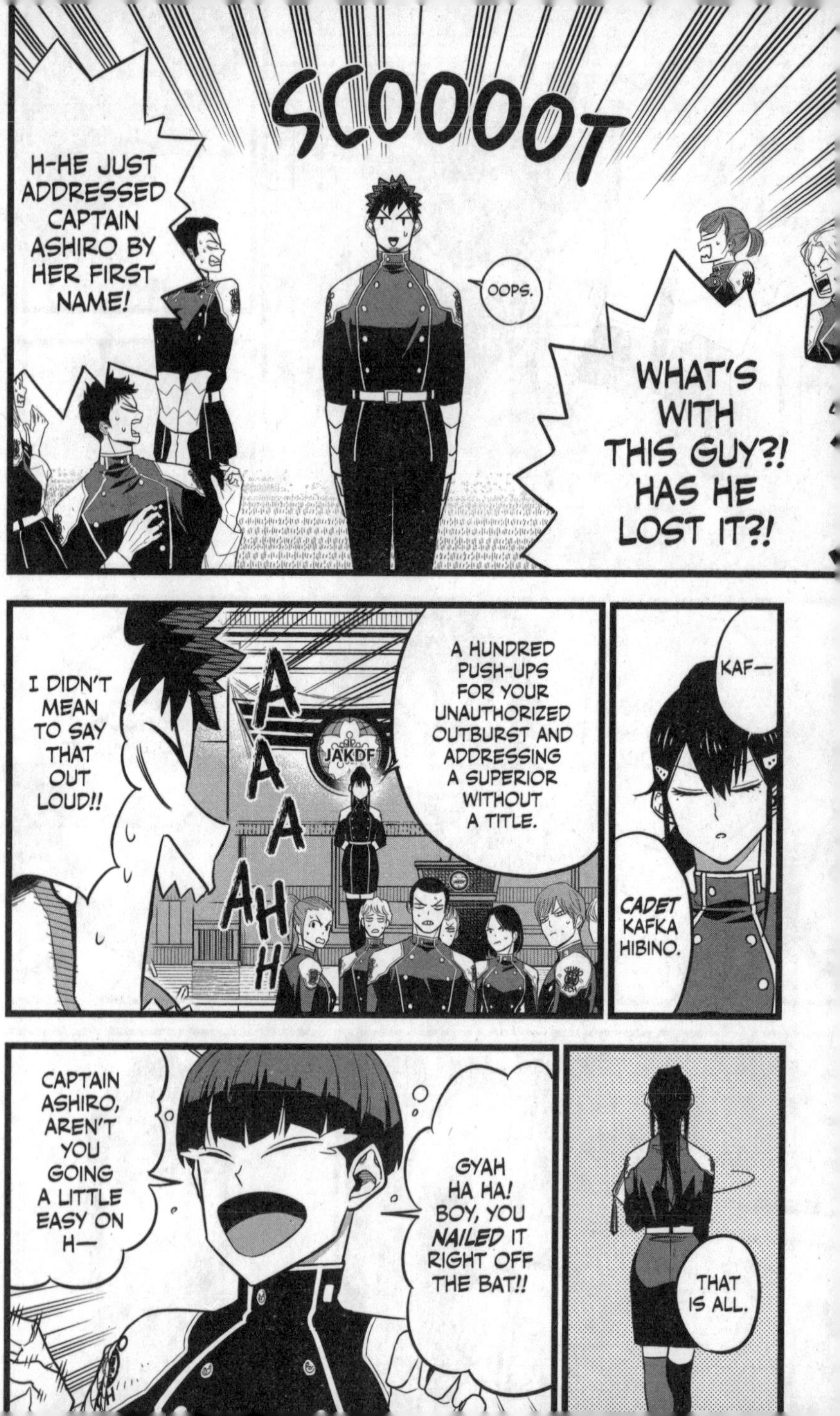

SCOOOOT
WHAT'S WITH THIS GUY?! HAS HE LOST IT?!
OOPS.
H-HE JUST ADDRESSED CAPTAIN ASHIRO BY HER FIRST NAME!
KAF—
CADET KAFKA HIBINO.
A HUNDRED PUSH-UPS FOR YOUR UNAUTHORIZED OUTBURST AND ADDRESSING A SUPERIOR WITHOUT A TITLE.
JAKDF
AAAAAHH
I DIDN'T MEAN TO SAY THAT OUT LOUD!!
THAT IS ALL.
GYAH HA HA! BOY, YOU *NAILED* IT RIGHT OFF THE BAT!!
CAPTAIN ASHIRO, AREN'T YOU GOING A LITTLE EASY ON H—

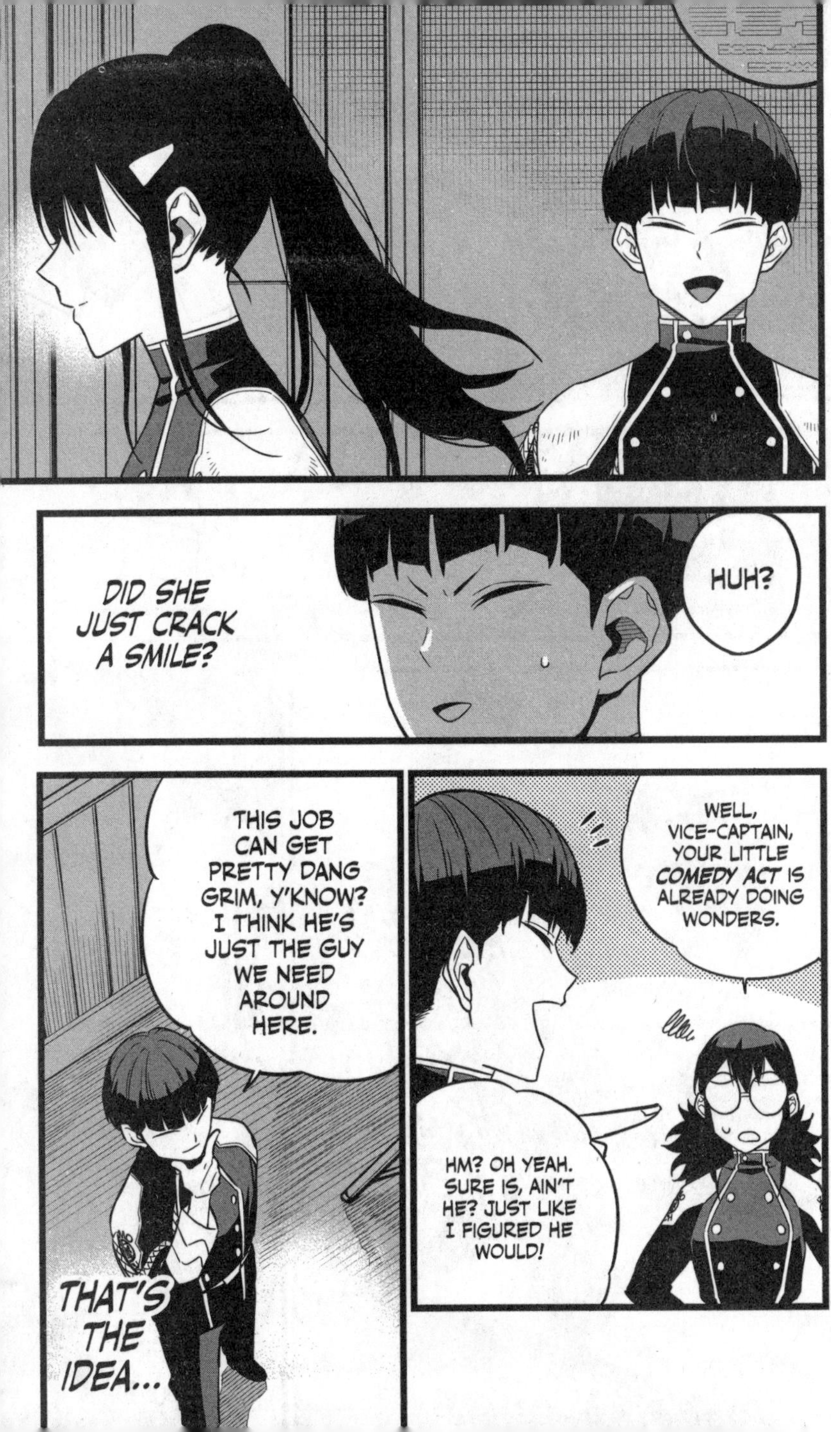
HUH?
DID SHE JUST CRACK A SMILE?
WELL, VICE-CAPTAIN, YOUR LITTLE *COMEDY ACT* IS ALREADY DOING WONDERS.
HM? OH YEAH. SURE IS, AIN'T HE? JUST LIKE I FIGURED HE WOULD!
THIS JOB CAN GET PRETTY DANG GRIM, Y'KNOW? I THINK HE'S JUST THE GUY WE NEED AROUND HERE.
THAT'S THE IDEA...

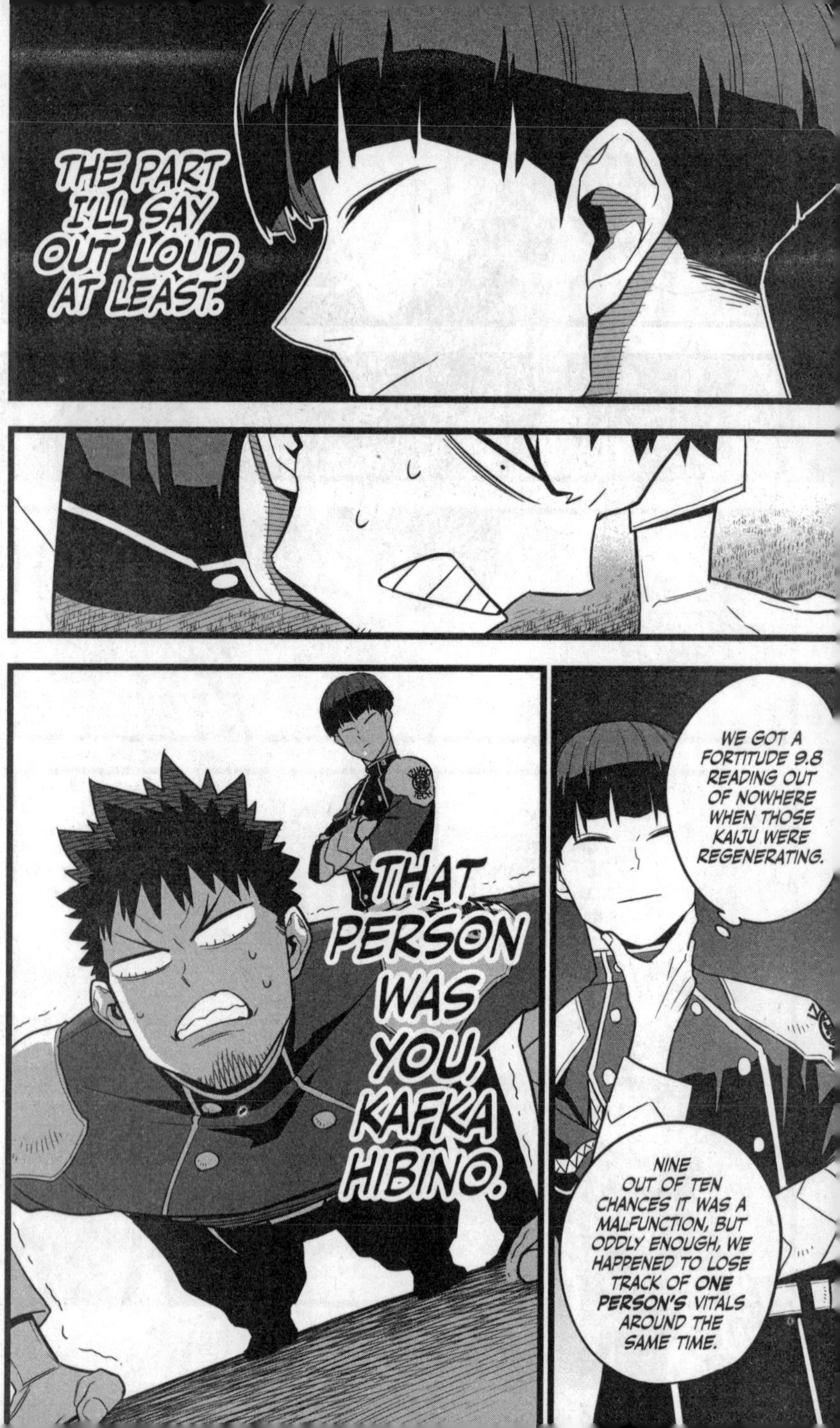
THE PART I'LL SAY OUT LOUD, AT LEAST.
WE GOT A FORTITUDE 9.8 READING OUT OF NOWHERE WHEN THOSE KAIJU WERE REGENERATING.
NINE OUT OF TEN CHANCES IT WAS A MALFUNCTION, BUT ODDLY ENOUGH, WE HAPPENED TO LOSE TRACK OF ONE PERSON'S VITALS AROUND THE SAME TIME.
THAT PERSON WAS YOU, KAFKA HIBINO.

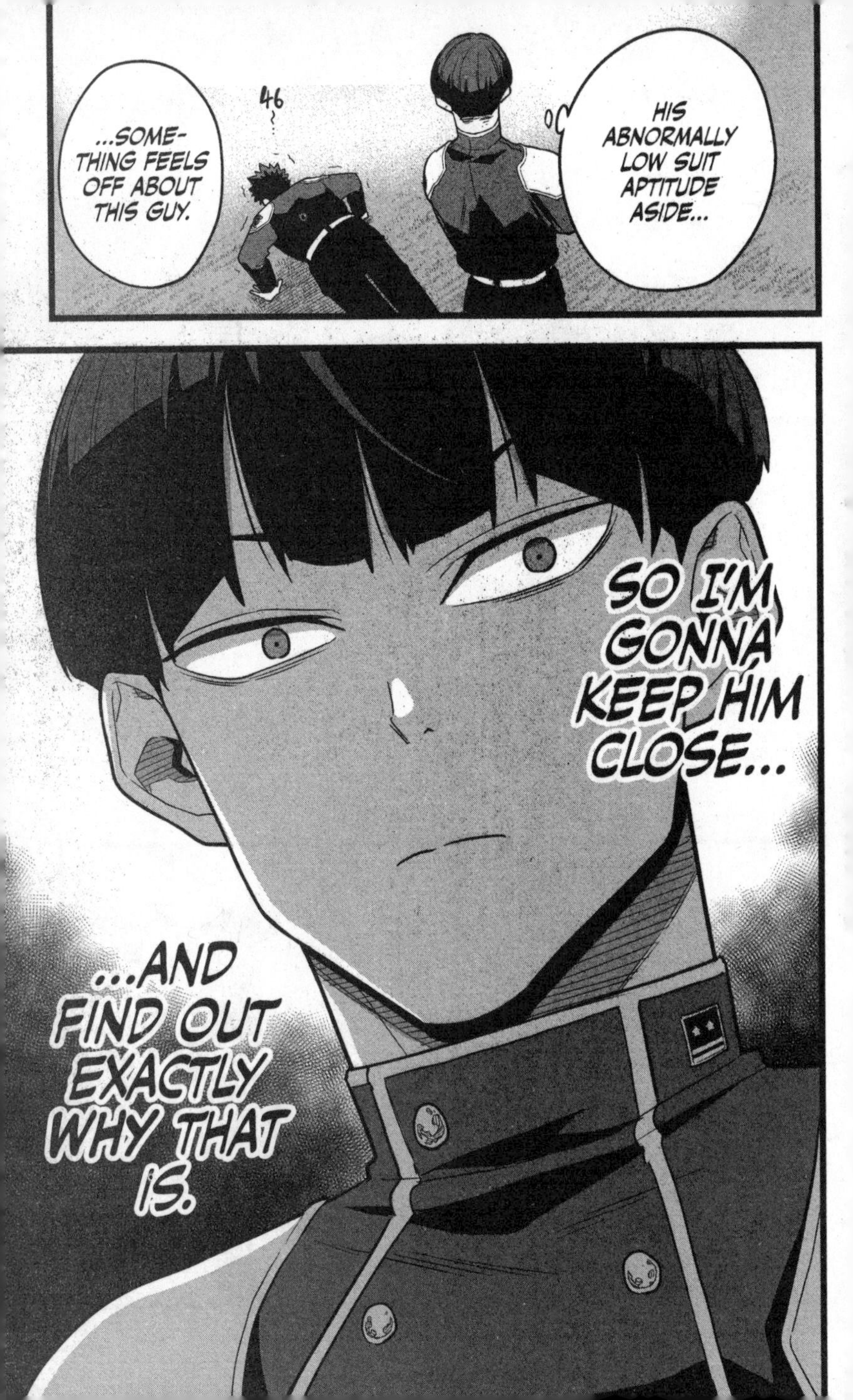
HIS ABNORMALLY LOW SUIT APTITUDE ASIDE...
...SOME-THING FEELS OFF ABOUT THIS GUY.
SO I'M GONNA KEEP HIM CLOSE...
...AND FIND OUT EXACTLY WHY THAT IS.

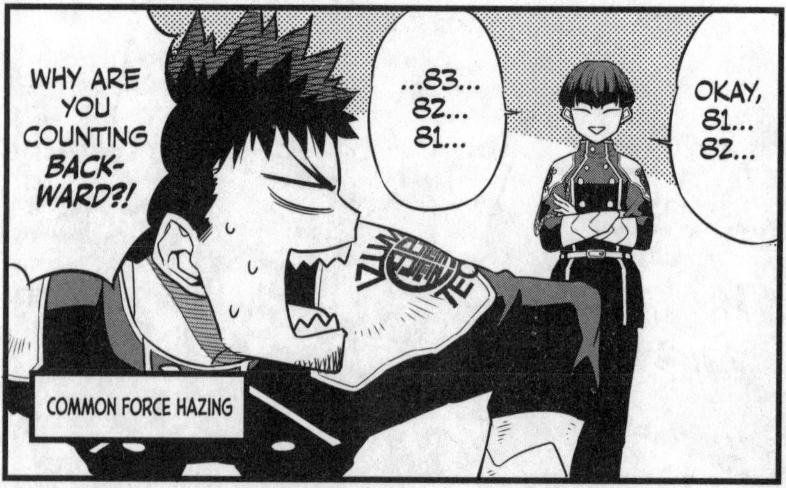
OKAY, 81... 82...
...83... 82... 81...
WHY ARE YOU COUNTING BACK-WARD?!
COMMON FORCE HAZING

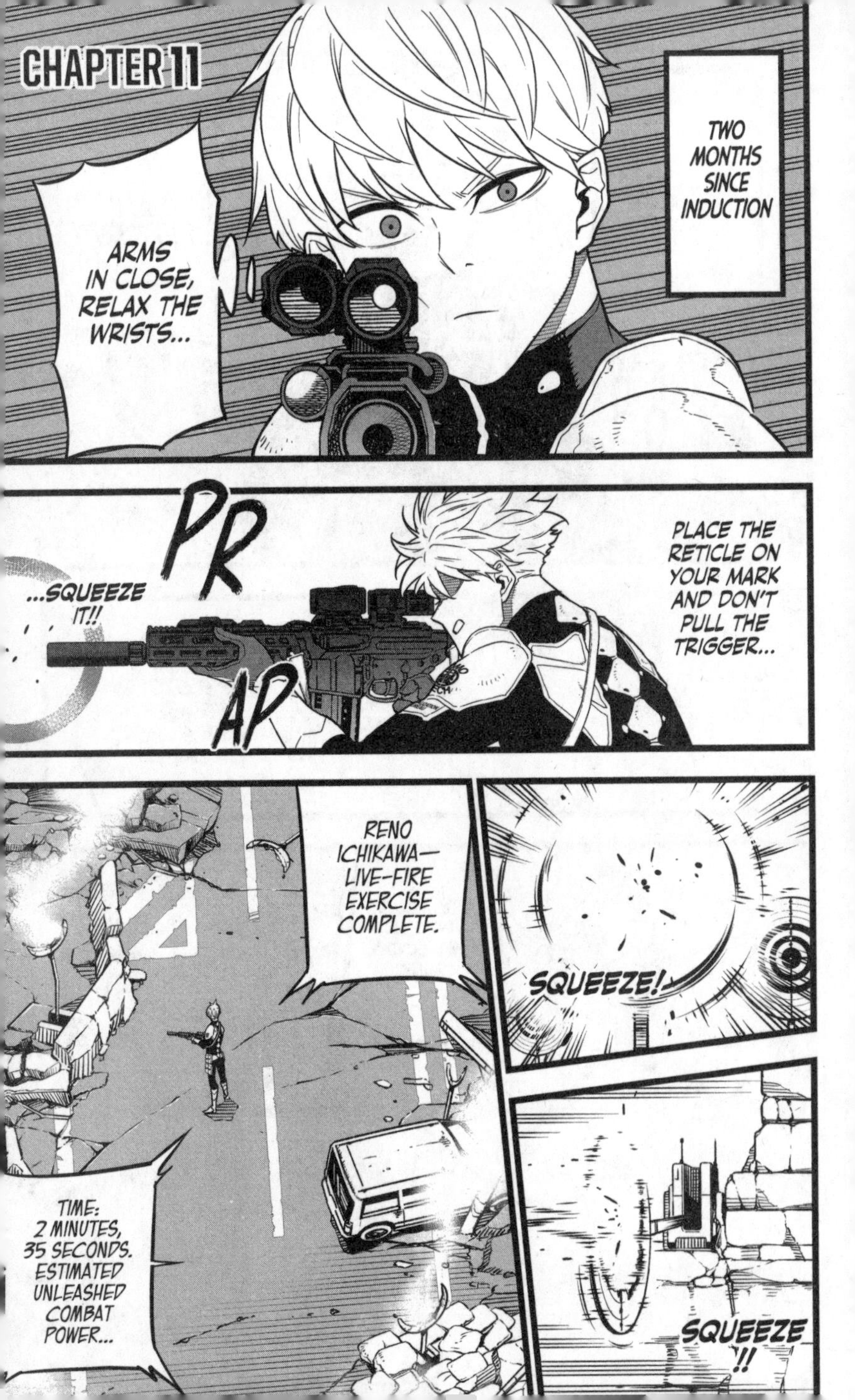
CHAPTER 11
TWO MONTHS SINCE INDUCTION
ARMS IN CLOSE, RELAX THE WRISTS...
PLACE THE RETICLE ON YOUR MARK AND DON'T PULL THE TRIGGER...
PRAP
...SQUEEZE IT!!
SQUEEZE!
SQUEEZE !!
RENO ICHIKAWA— LIVE-FIRE EXERCISE COMPLETE.
TIME: 2 MINUTES, 35 SECONDS. ESTIMATED UNLEASHED COMBAT POWER...

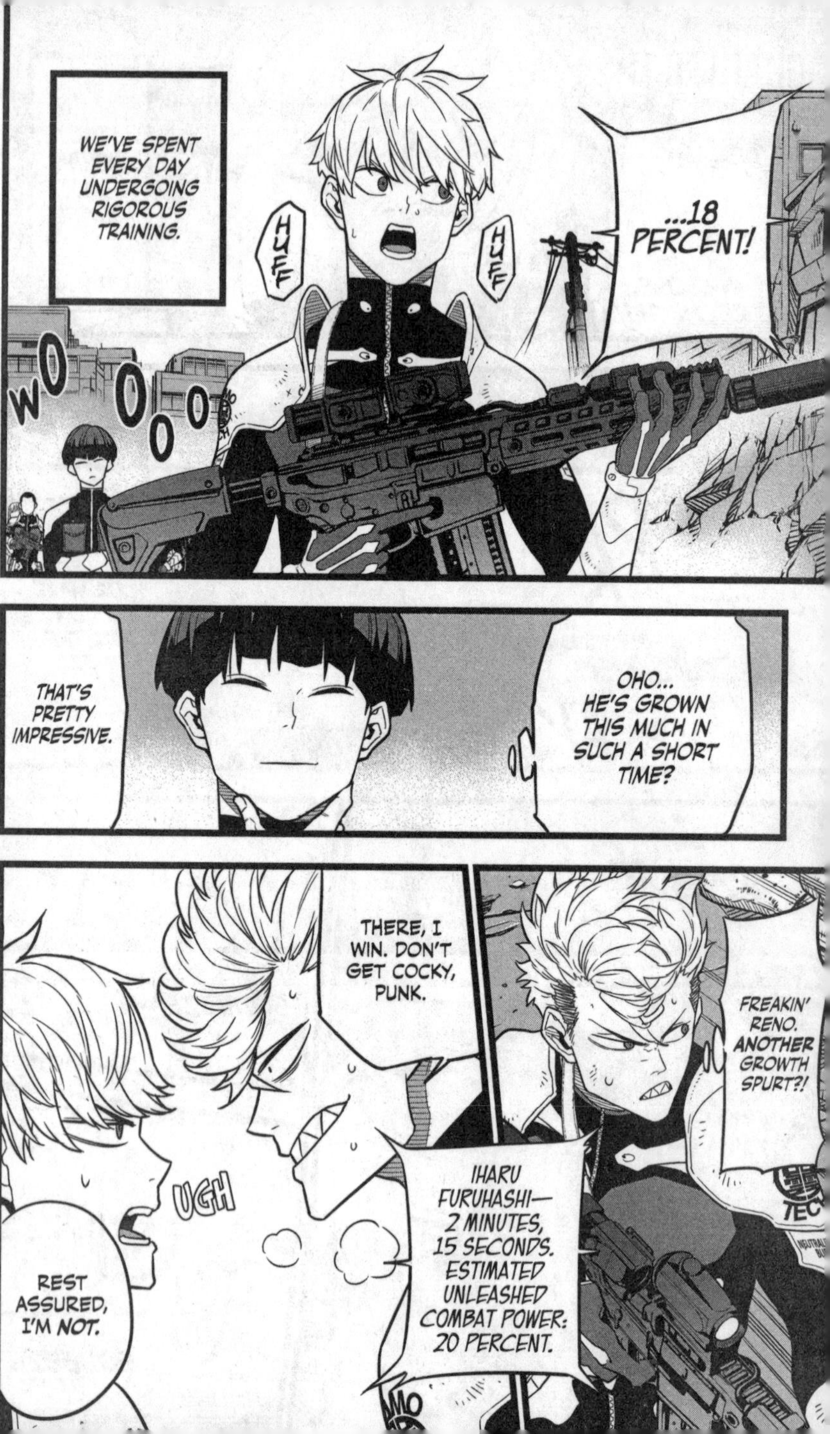
...18 PERCENT!
HUFF
HUFF
WE'VE SPENT EVERY DAY UNDERGOING RIGOROUS TRAINING.
WOOOO
OHO... HE'S GROWN THIS MUCH IN SUCH A SHORT TIME?
THAT'S PRETTY IMPRESSIVE.
FREAKIN' RENO. ANOTHER GROWTH SPURT?!
THERE, I WIN. DON'T GET COCKY, PUNK.
IHARU FURUHASHI— 2 MINUTES, 15 SECONDS. ESTIMATED UNLEASHED COMBAT POWER: 20 PERCENT.
UGH
REST ASSURED, I'M NOT.

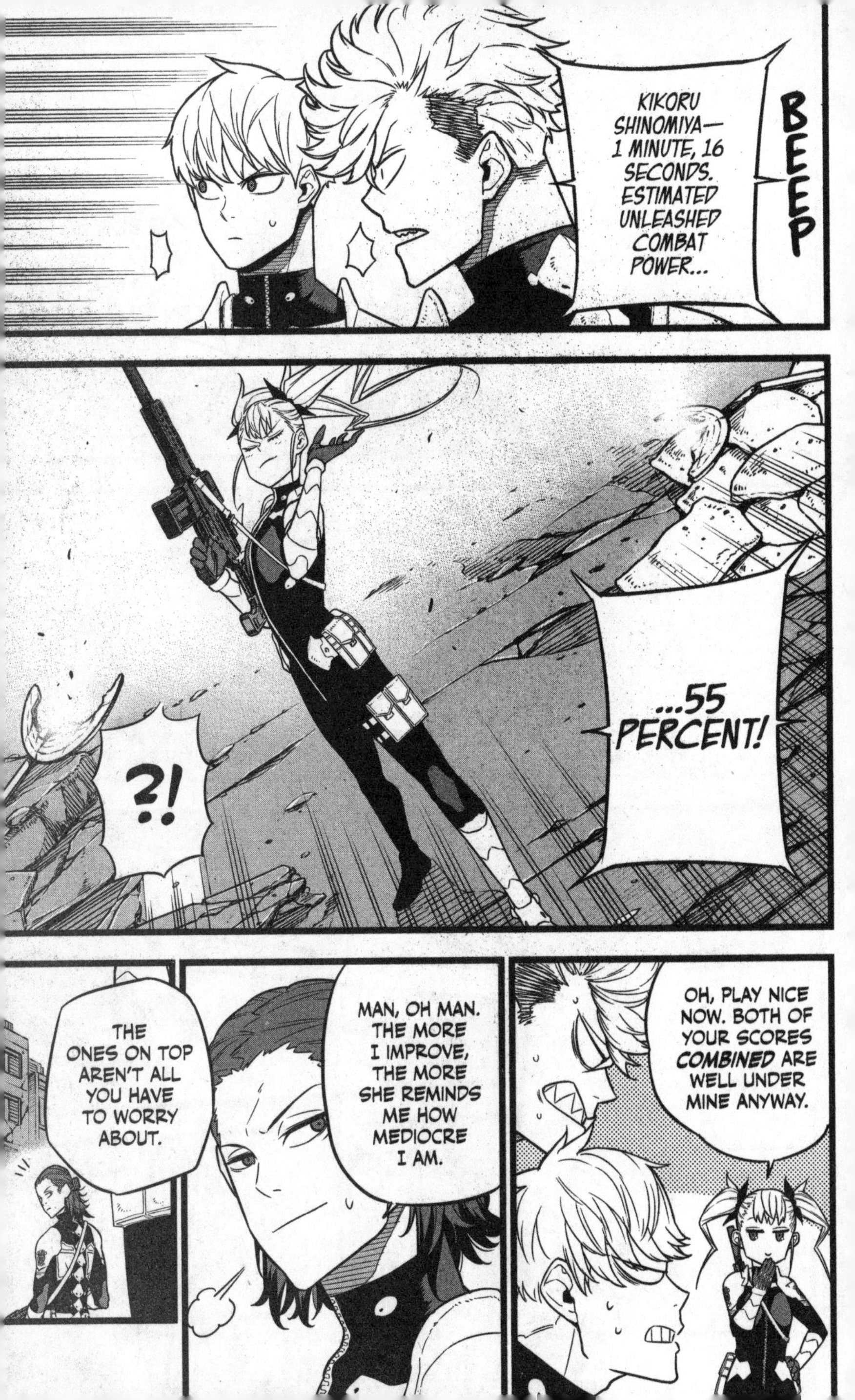
BEEP
KIKORU SHINOMIYA—1 MINUTE, 16 SECONDS. ESTIMATED UNLEASHED COMBAT POWER...
...55 PERCENT!
?!
OH, PLAY NICE NOW. BOTH OF YOUR SCORES COMBINED ARE WELL UNDER MINE ANYWAY.
MAN, OH MAN. THE MORE I IMPROVE, THE MORE SHE REMINDS ME HOW MEDIOCRE I AM.
THE ONES ON TOP AREN'T ALL YOU HAVE TO WORRY ABOUT.

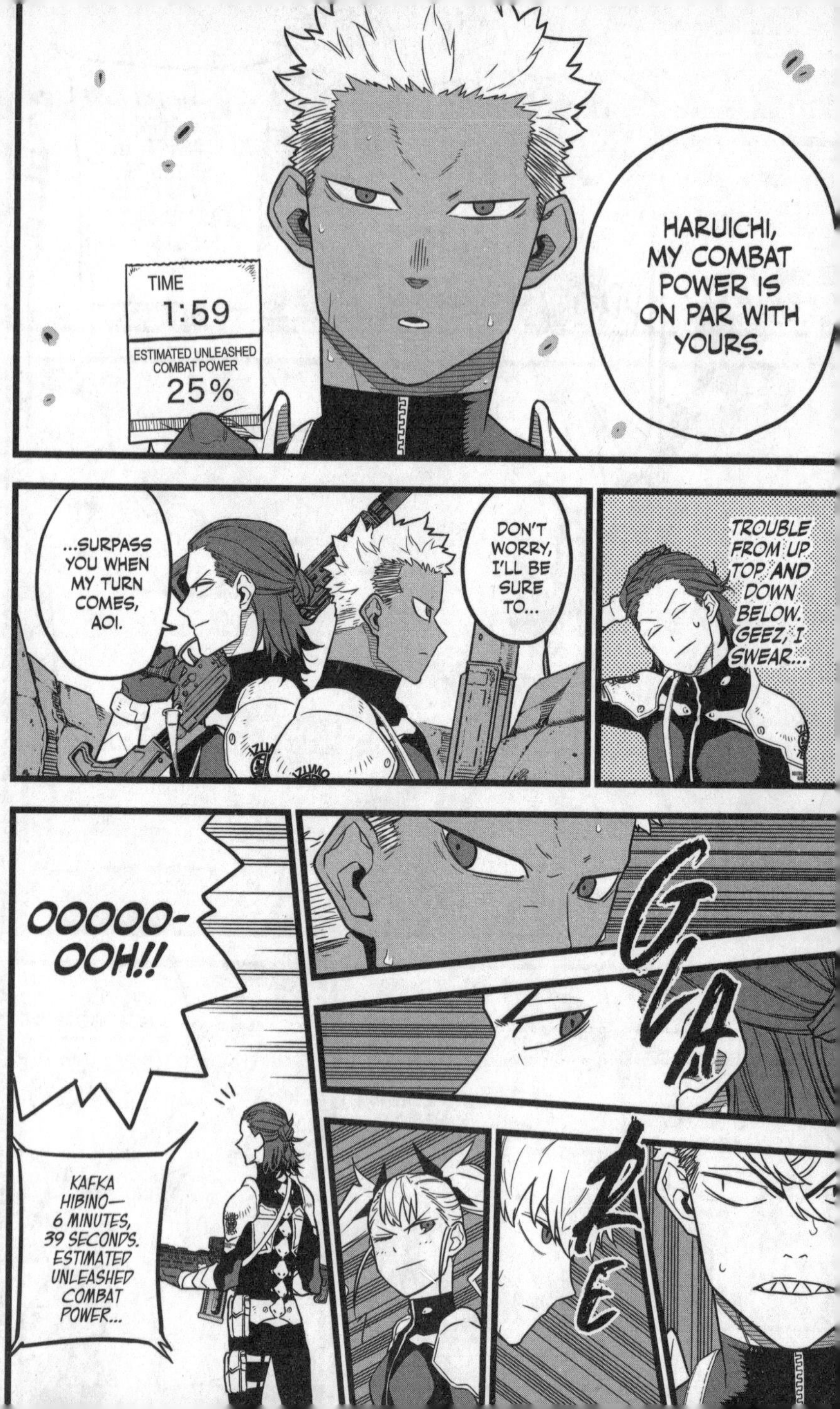
HARUICHI, MY COMBAT POWER IS ON PAR WITH YOURS.
TIME
1:59
ESTIMATED UNLEASHED COMBAT POWER
25%
TROUBLE FROM UP TOP AND DOWN BELOW. GEEZ, I SWEAR...
DON'T WORRY, I'LL BE SURE TO...
...SURPASS YOU WHEN MY TURN COMES, AOI.
GLA
ZE
OOOOO-OOH!!
KAFKA HIBINO— 6 MINUTES, 39 SECONDS. ESTIMATED UNLEASHED COMBAT POWER...

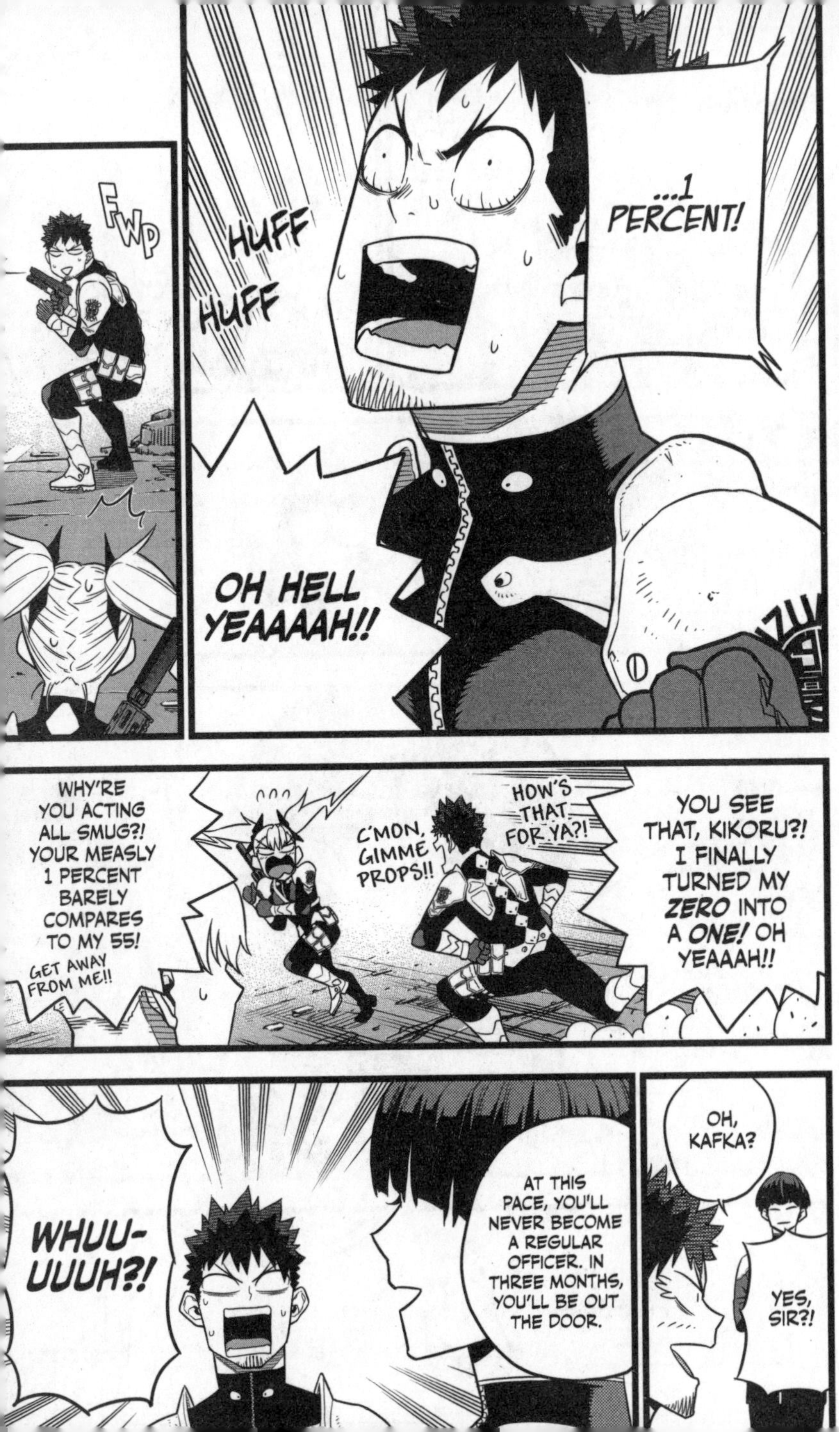
...1 PERCENT!
HUFF
HUFF
OH HELL YEAAAAH!!
FWP
YOU SEE THAT, KIKORU?! I FINALLY TURNED MY *ZERO* INTO A *ONE!* OH YEAAAH!!
HOW'S THAT FOR YA?!
C'MON, GIMME PROPS!!
WHY'RE YOU ACTING ALL SMUG?! YOUR MEASLY 1 PERCENT BARELY COMPARES TO MY 55!
GET AWAY FROM ME!!
OH, KAFKA?
YES, SIR?!
AT THIS PACE, YOU'LL NEVER BECOME A REGULAR OFFICER. IN THREE MONTHS, YOU'LL BE OUT THE DOOR.
WHUU-UUUH?!

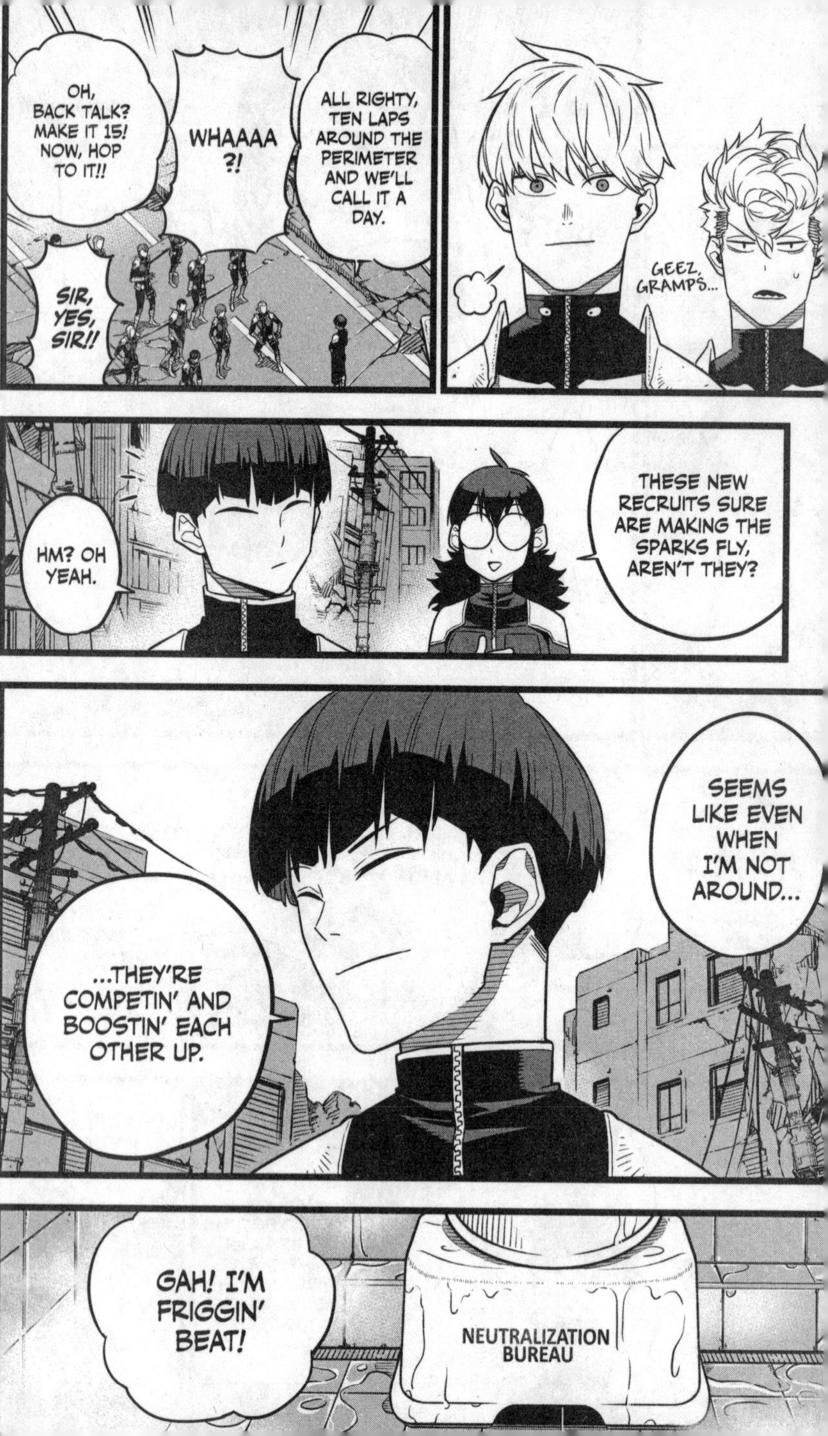
GEEZ, GRAMPS...
ALL RIGHTY, TEN LAPS AROUND THE PERIMETER AND WE'LL CALL IT A DAY.
WHAAAA ?!
OH, BACK TALK? MAKE IT 15! NOW, HOP TO IT!!
SIR, YES, SIR!!
THESE NEW RECRUITS SURE ARE MAKING THE SPARKS FLY, AREN'T THEY?
HM? OH YEAH.
SEEMS LIKE EVEN WHEN I'M NOT AROUND...
...THEY'RE COMPETIN' AND BOOSTIN' EACH OTHER UP.
GAH! I'M FRIGGIN' BEAT!
NEUTRALIZATION BUREAU

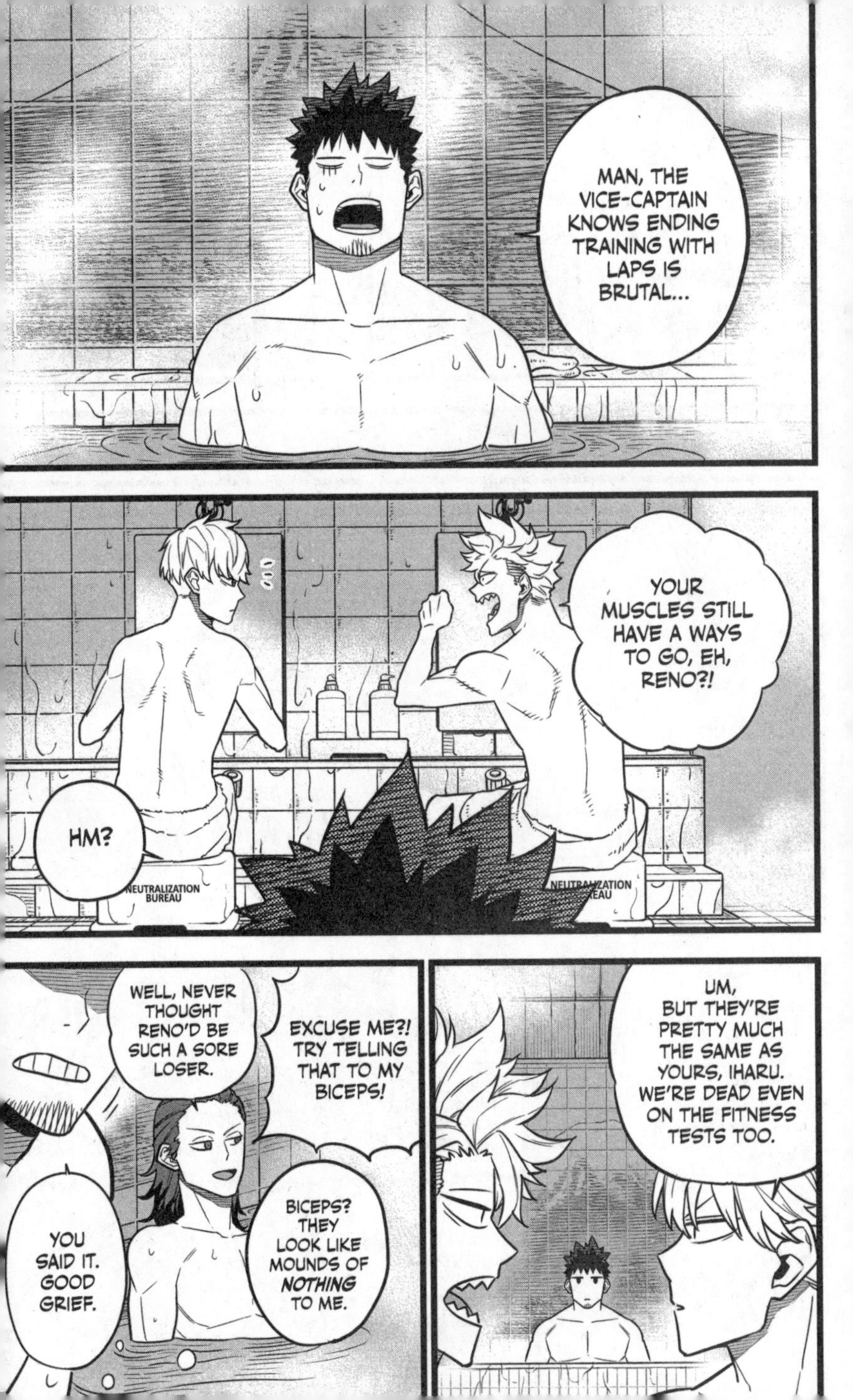
MAN, THE VICE-CAPTAIN KNOWS ENDING TRAINING WITH LAPS IS BRUTAL...
YOUR MUSCLES STILL HAVE A WAYS TO GO, EH, RENO?!
HM?
NEUTRALIZATION BUREAU
UM, BUT THEY'RE PRETTY MUCH THE SAME AS YOURS, IHARU. WE'RE DEAD EVEN ON THE FITNESS TESTS TOO.
EXCUSE ME?! TRY TELLING THAT TO MY BICEPS!
WELL, NEVER THOUGHT RENO'D BE SUCH A SORE LOSER.
BICEPS? THEY LOOK LIKE MOUNDS OF *NOTHING* TO ME.
YOU SAID IT. GOOD GRIEF.

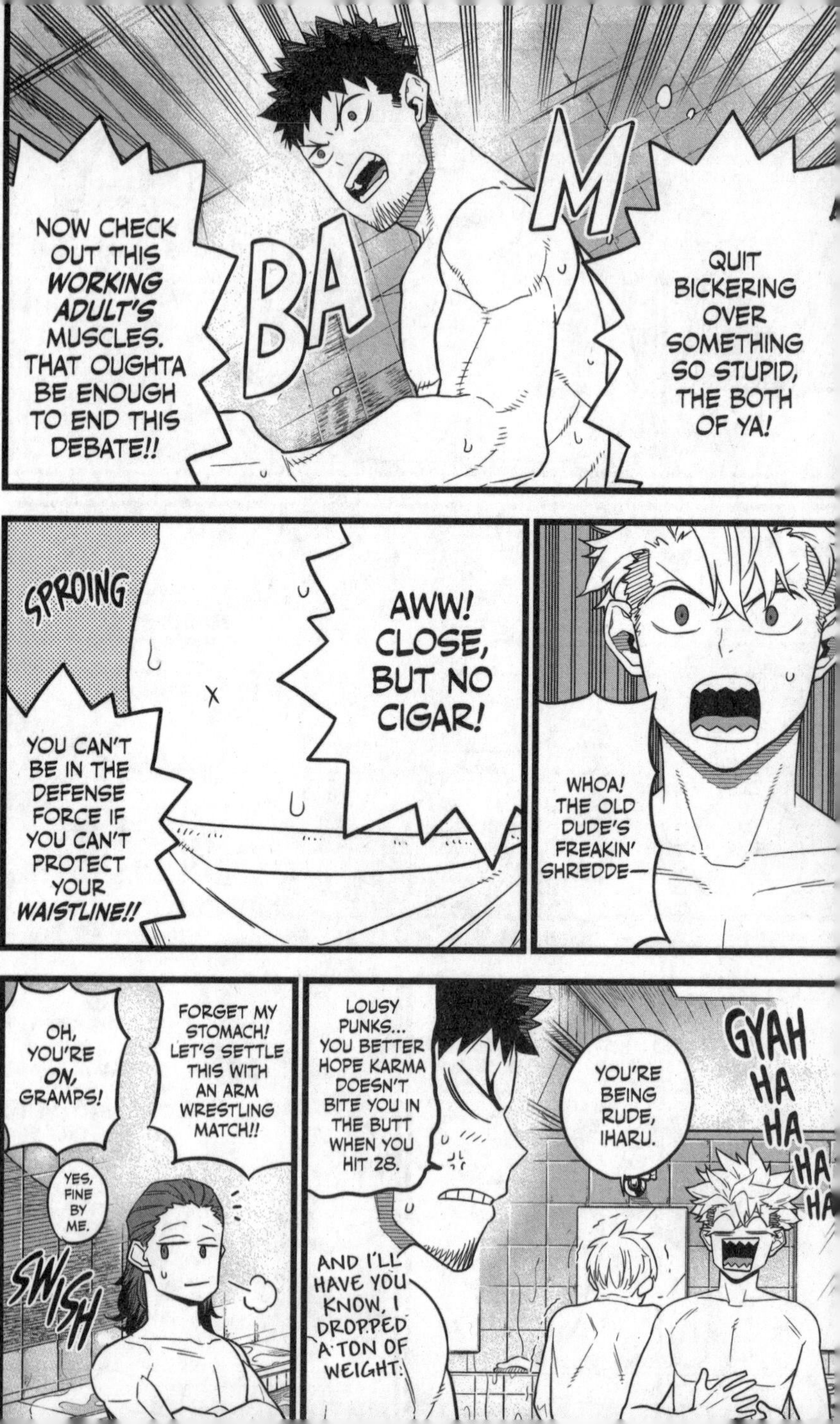
QUIT BICKERING OVER SOMETHING SO STUPID, THE BOTH OF YA!
BAM
NOW CHECK OUT THIS *WORKING ADULT'S* MUSCLES. THAT OUGHTA BE ENOUGH TO END THIS DEBATE!!
WHOA! THE OLD DUDE'S FREAKIN' SHREDDE—
AWW! CLOSE, BUT NO CIGAR!
SPROING
YOU CAN'T BE IN THE DEFENSE FORCE IF YOU CAN'T PROTECT YOUR *WAISTLINE!!*
GYAH HA HA HA HA
YOU'RE BEING RUDE, IHARU.
LOUSY PUNKS... YOU BETTER HOPE KARMA DOESN'T BITE YOU IN THE BUTT WHEN YOU HIT 28.
AND I'LL HAVE YOU KNOW, I DROPPED A TON OF WEIGHT.
FORGET MY STOMACH! LET'S SETTLE THIS WITH AN ARM WRESTLING MATCH!!
OH, YOU'RE *ON,* GRAMPS!
YES, FINE BY ME.
SWISH

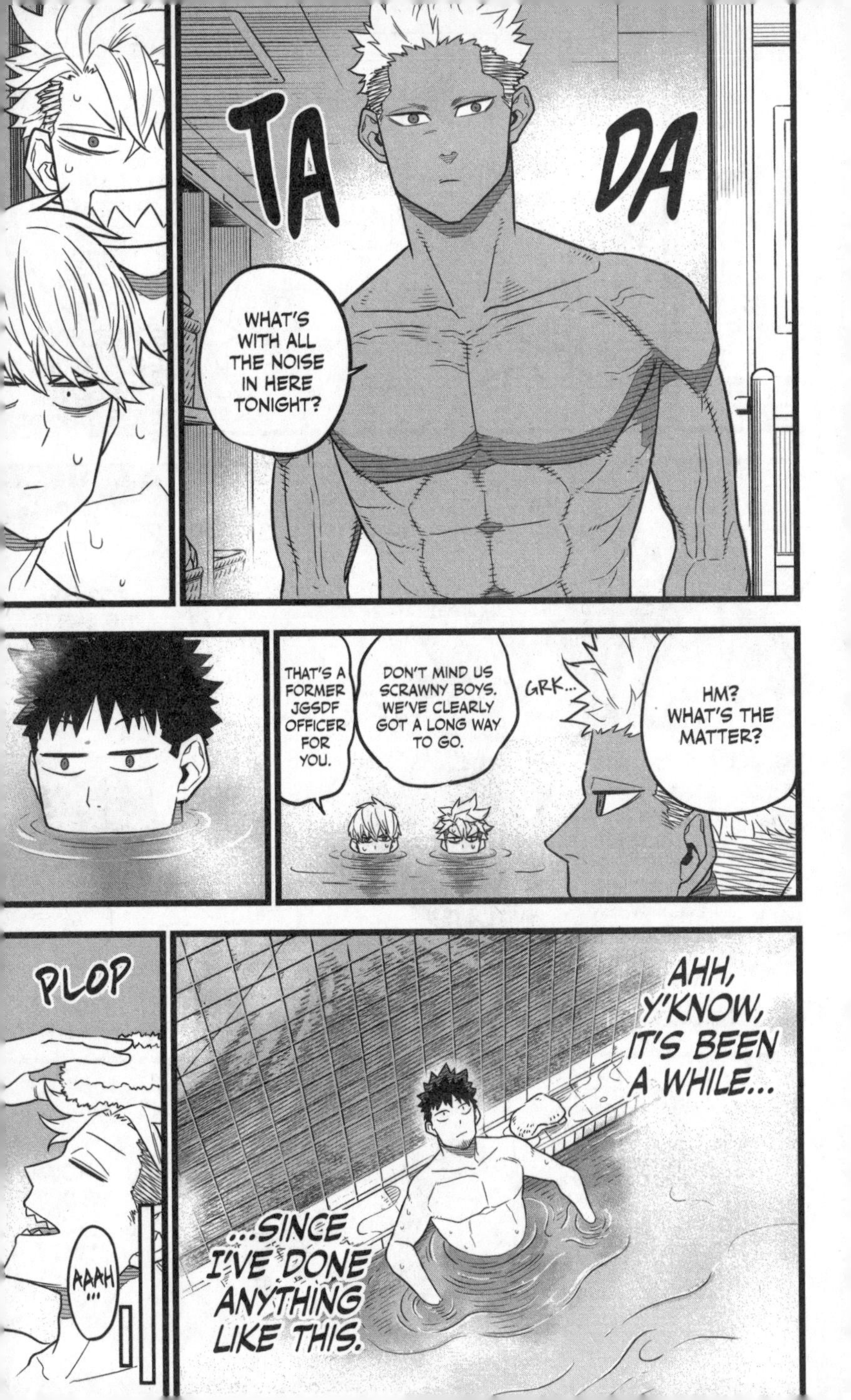
TA
DA
WHAT'S WITH ALL THE NOISE IN HERE TONIGHT?
HM? WHAT'S THE MATTER?
GRK...
DON'T MIND US SCRAWNY BOYS. WE'VE CLEARLY GOT A LONG WAY TO GO.
THAT'S A FORMER JGSDF OFFICER FOR YOU.
AHH, Y'KNOW, IT'S BEEN A WHILE...
...SINCE I'VE DONE ANYTHING LIKE THIS.
PLOP
AAAH...

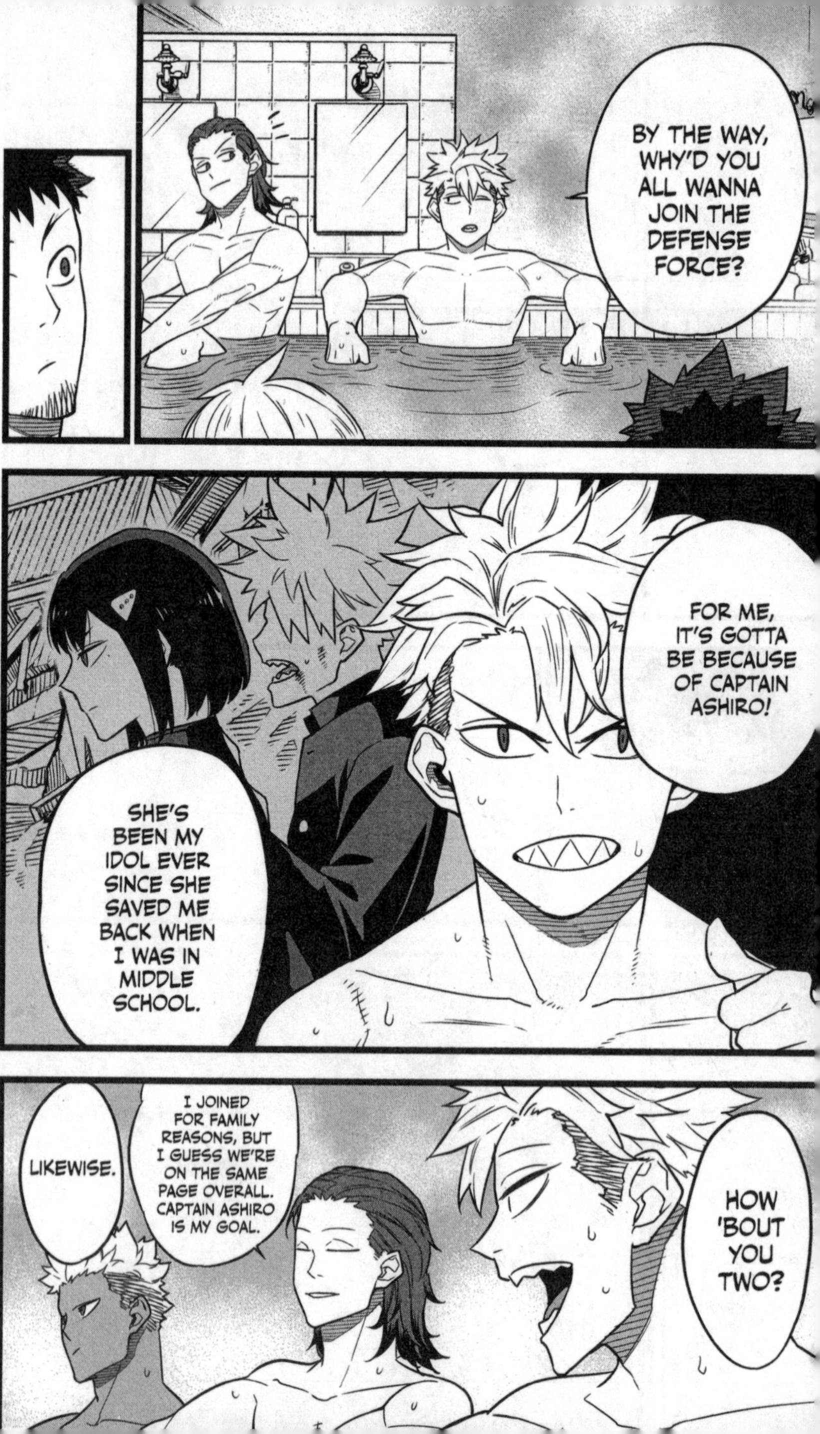
BY THE WAY, WHY'D YOU ALL WANNA JOIN THE DEFENSE FORCE?
FOR ME, IT'S GOTTA BE BECAUSE OF CAPTAIN ASHIRO!
SHE'S BEEN MY IDOL EVER SINCE SHE SAVED ME BACK WHEN I WAS IN MIDDLE SCHOOL.
HOW 'BOUT YOU TWO?
I JOINED FOR FAMILY REASONS, BUT I GUESS WE'RE ON THE SAME PAGE OVERALL. CAPTAIN ASHIRO IS MY GOAL.
LIKEWISE.

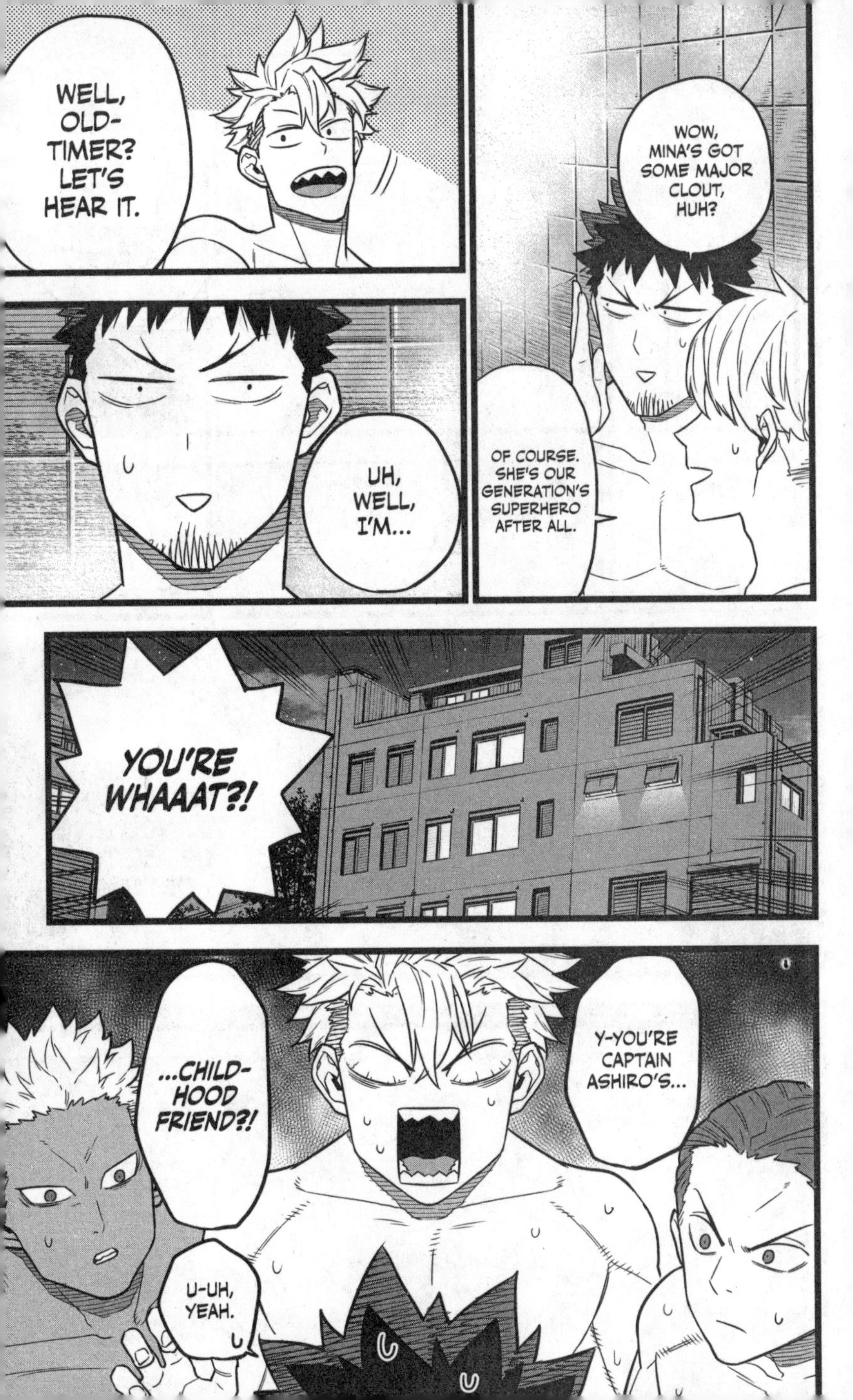
WOW, MINA'S GOT SOME MAJOR CLOUT, HUH?
OF COURSE. SHE'S OUR GENERATION'S SUPERHERO AFTER ALL.
WELL, OLD-TIMER? LET'S HEAR IT.
UH, WELL, I'M...
YOU'RE WHAAAT?!
Y-YOU'RE CAPTAIN ASHIRO'S...
...CHILD-HOOD FRIEND?!
U-UH, YEAH.

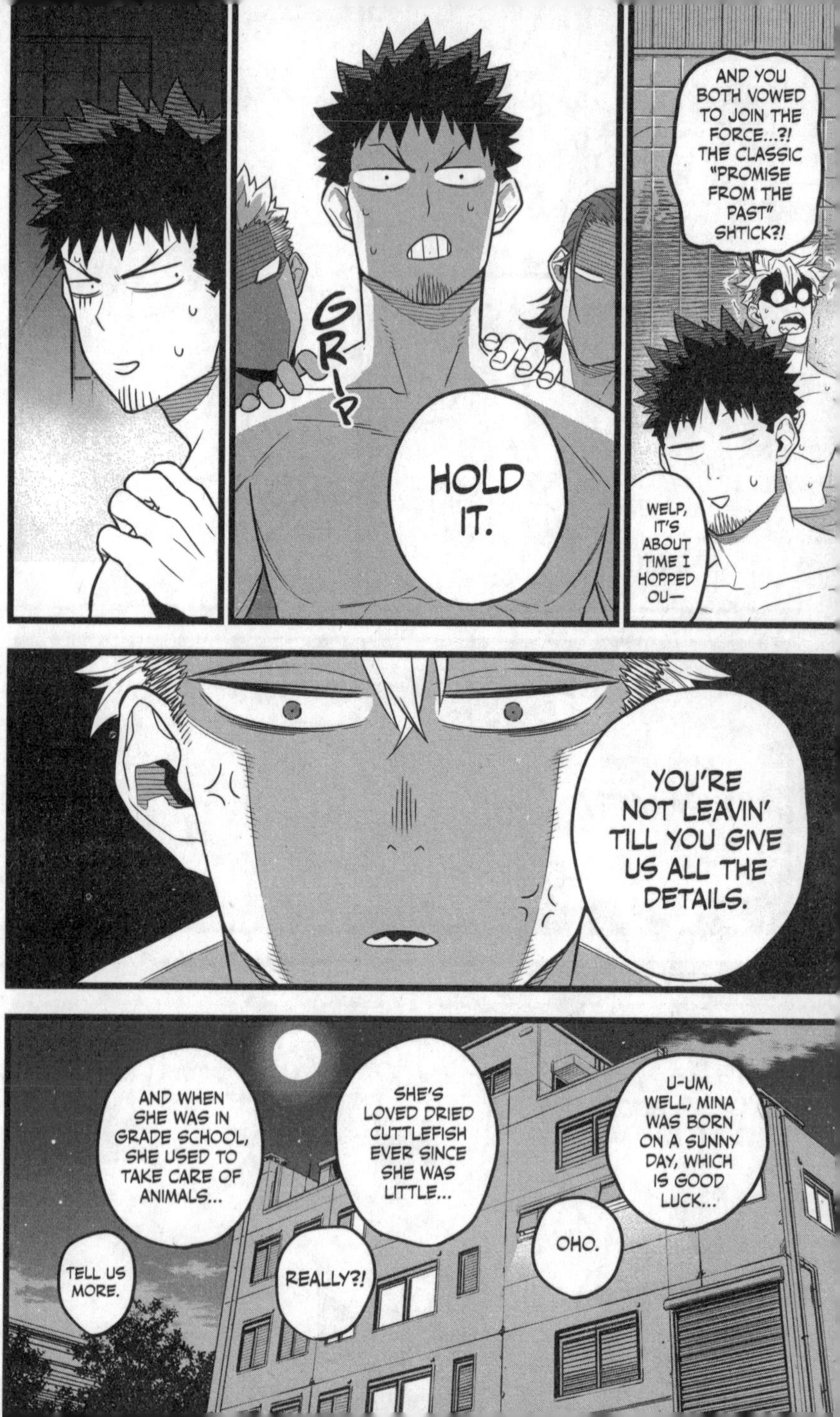
AND YOU BOTH VOWED TO JOIN THE FORCE...?! THE CLASSIC "PROMISE FROM THE PAST" SHTICK?!
WELP, IT'S ABOUT TIME I HOPPED OU—
GRIP
HOLD IT.
YOU'RE NOT LEAVIN' TILL YOU GIVE US ALL THE DETAILS.
U-UM, WELL, MINA WAS BORN ON A SUNNY DAY, WHICH IS GOOD LUCK...
OHO.
SHE'S LOVED DRIED CUTTLEFISH EVER SINCE SHE WAS LITTLE...
REALLY?!
AND WHEN SHE WAS IN GRADE SCHOOL, SHE USED TO TAKE CARE OF ANIMALS...
TELL US MORE.

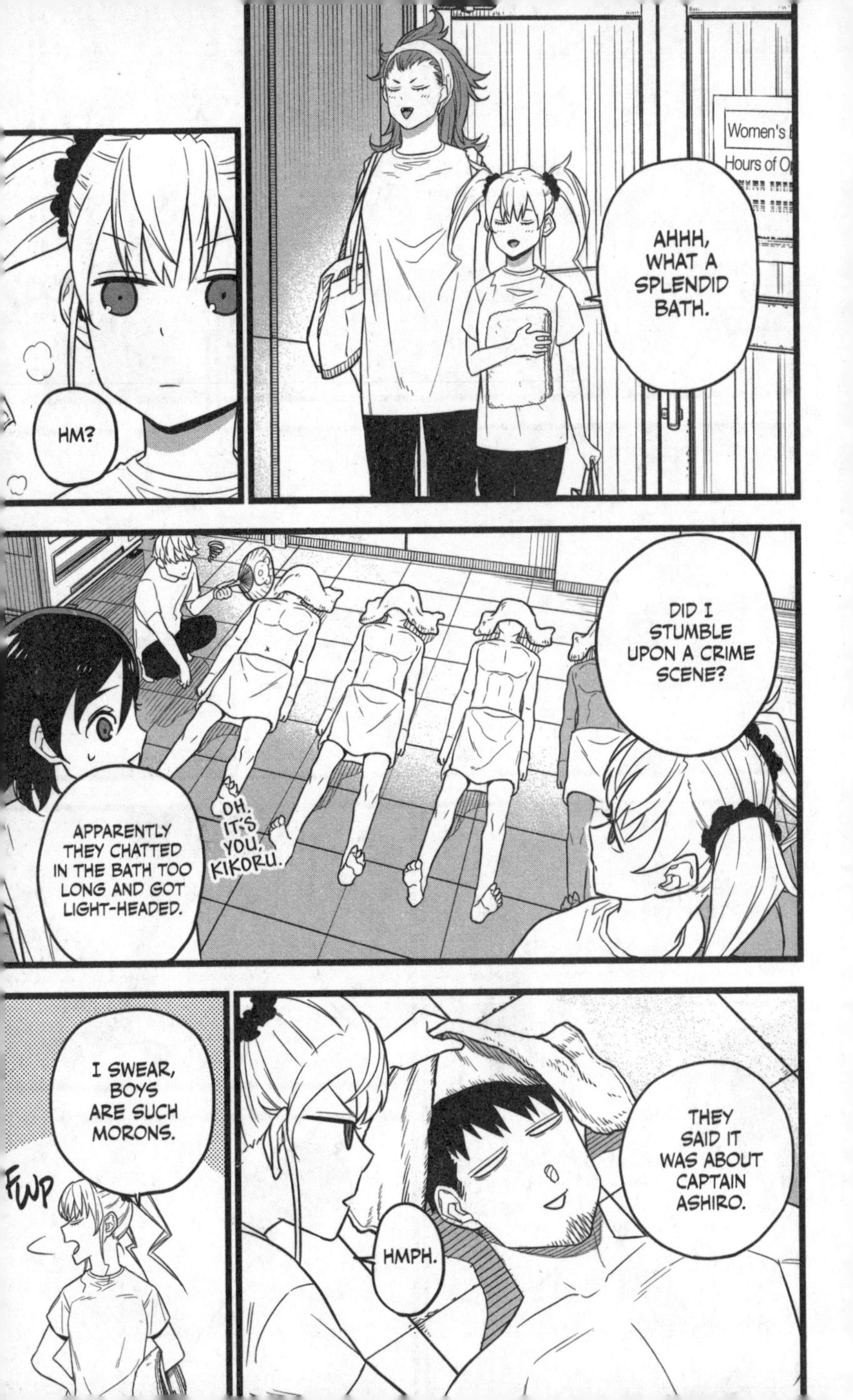
AHHH, WHAT A SPLENDID BATH.
HM?
DID I STUMBLE UPON A CRIME SCENE?
OH. IT'S YOU, KIKORU.
APPARENTLY THEY CHATTED IN THE BATH TOO LONG AND GOT LIGHT-HEADED.
THEY SAID IT WAS ABOUT CAPTAIN ASHIRO.
HMPH.
I SWEAR, BOYS ARE SUCH MORONS.
FWP

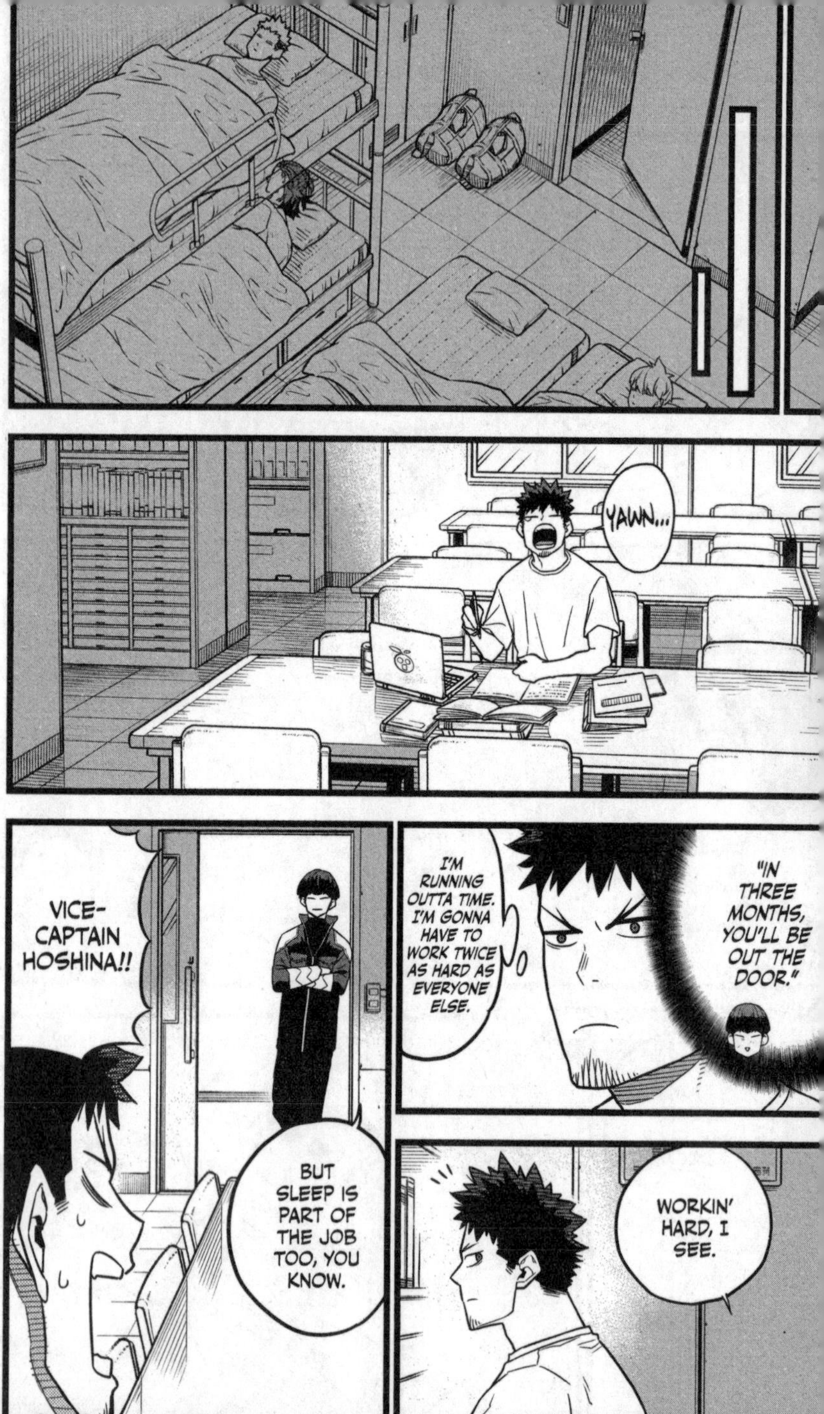
YAWN...
"IN THREE MONTHS, YOU'LL BE OUT THE DOOR."
I'M RUNNING OUTTA TIME. I'M GONNA HAVE TO WORK TWICE AS HARD AS EVERYONE ELSE.
WORKIN' HARD, I SEE.
VICE-CAPTAIN HOSHINA!!
BUT SLEEP IS PART OF THE JOB TOO, YOU KNOW.

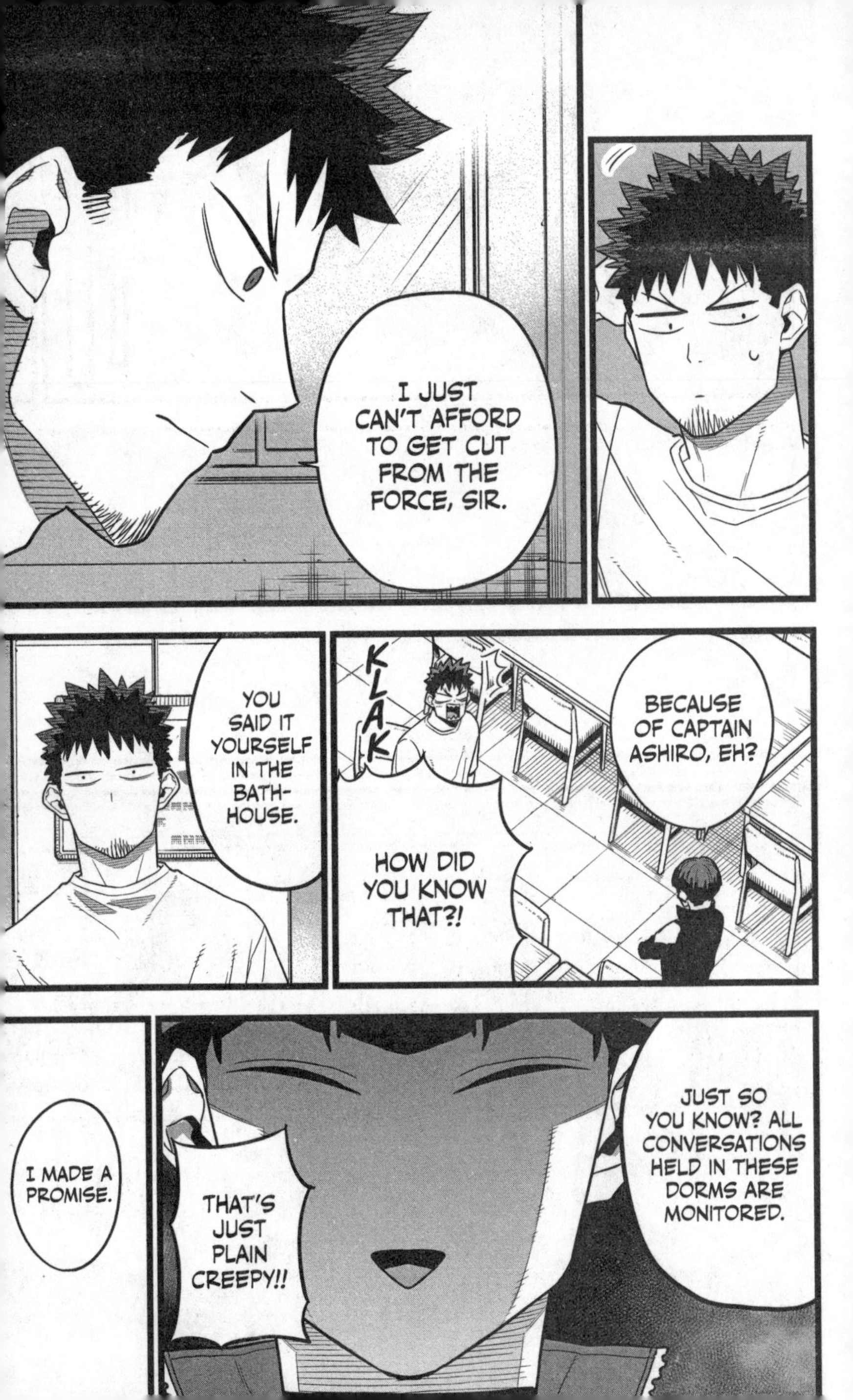
I JUST CAN'T AFFORD TO GET CUT FROM THE FORCE, SIR.
BECAUSE OF CAPTAIN ASHIRO, EH?
KLAK
HOW DID YOU KNOW THAT?!
YOU SAID IT YOURSELF IN THE BATH-HOUSE.
JUST SO YOU KNOW? ALL CONVERSATIONS HELD IN THESE DORMS ARE MONITORED.
THAT'S JUST PLAIN CREEPY!!
I MADE A PROMISE.

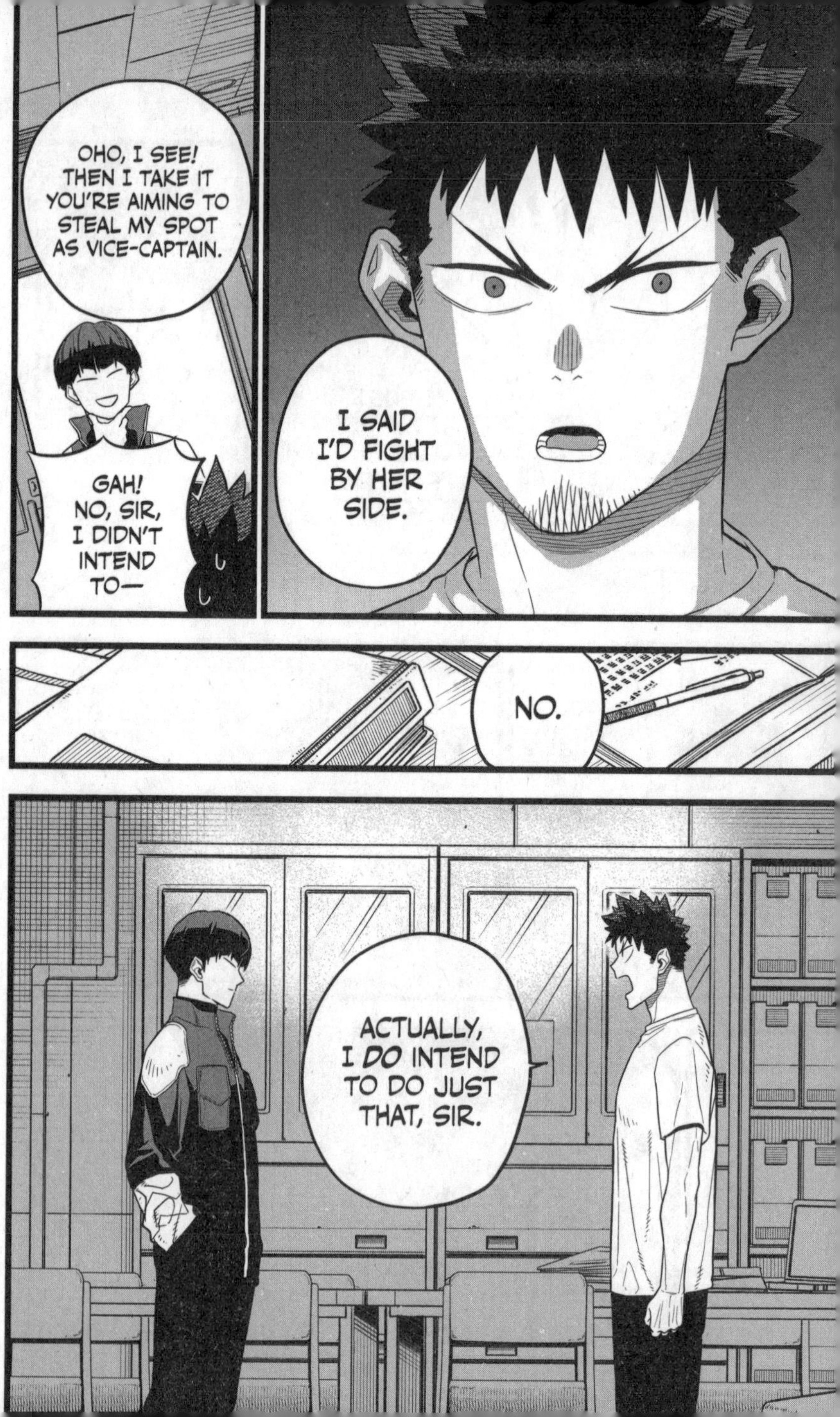
I SAID I'D FIGHT BY HER SIDE.
OHO, I SEE! THEN I TAKE IT YOU'RE AIMING TO STEAL MY SPOT AS VICE-CAPTAIN.
GAH! NO, SIR, I DIDN'T INTEND TO—
NO.
ACTUALLY, I *DO* INTEND TO DO JUST THAT, SIR.

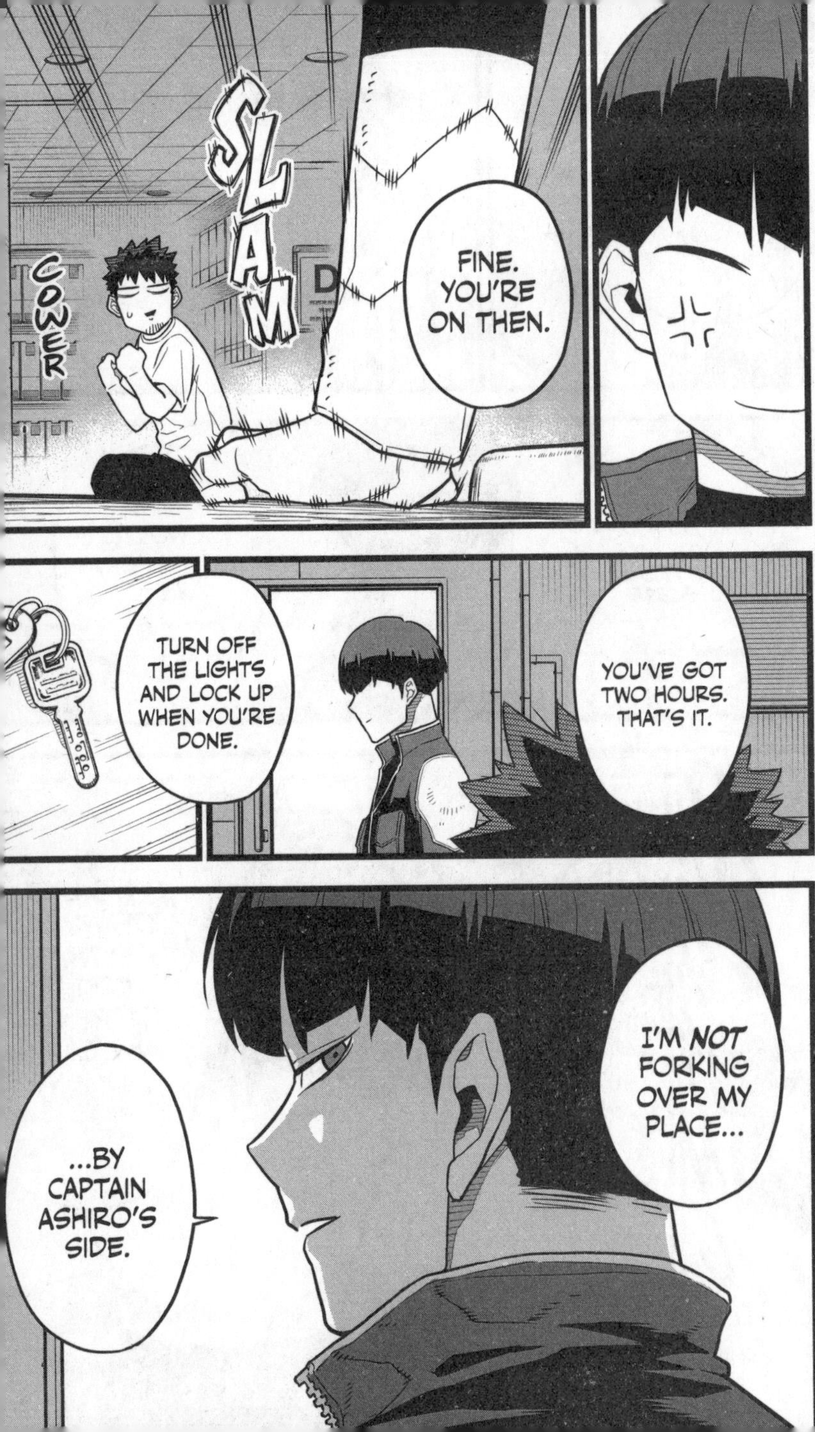
FINE. YOU'RE ON THEN.
SLAM
COWER
YOU'VE GOT TWO HOURS. THAT'S IT.
TURN OFF THE LIGHTS AND LOCK UP WHEN YOU'RE DONE.
I'M *NOT* FORKING OVER MY PLACE...
...BY CAPTAIN ASHIRO'S SIDE.

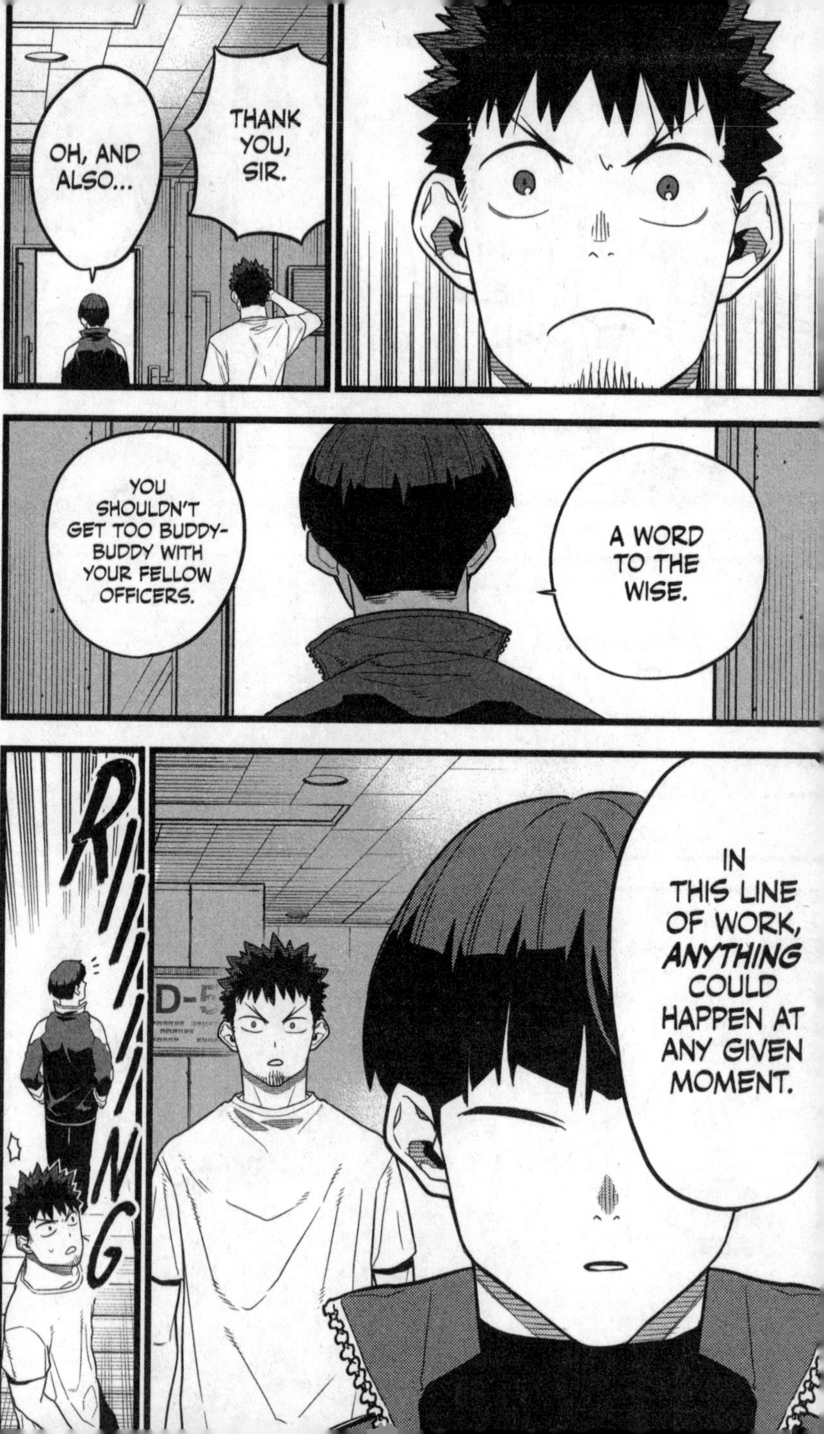
THANK YOU, SIR.
OH, AND ALSO...
A WORD TO THE WISE.
YOU SHOULDN'T GET TOO BUDDY-BUDDY WITH YOUR FELLOW OFFICERS.
IN THIS LINE OF WORK, *ANYTHING* COULD HAPPEN AT ANY GIVEN MOMENT.
RIIIING

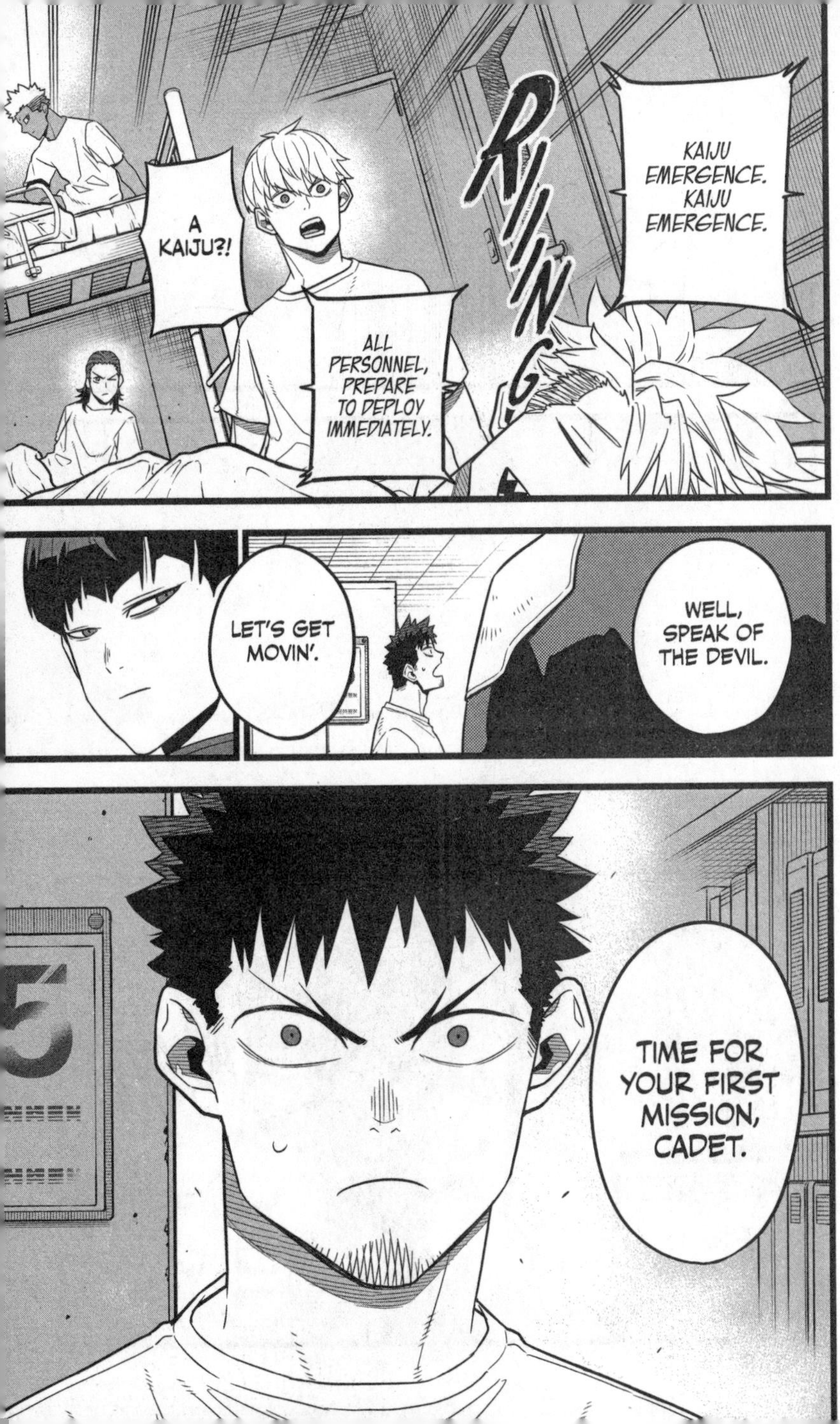
KAIJU EMERGENCE. KAIJU EMERGENCE.
RIIING
ALL PERSONNEL, PREPARE TO DEPLOY IMMEDIATELY.
A KAIJU?!
WELL, SPEAK OF THE DEVIL.
LET'S GET MOVIN'.
TIME FOR YOUR FIRST MISSION, CADET.

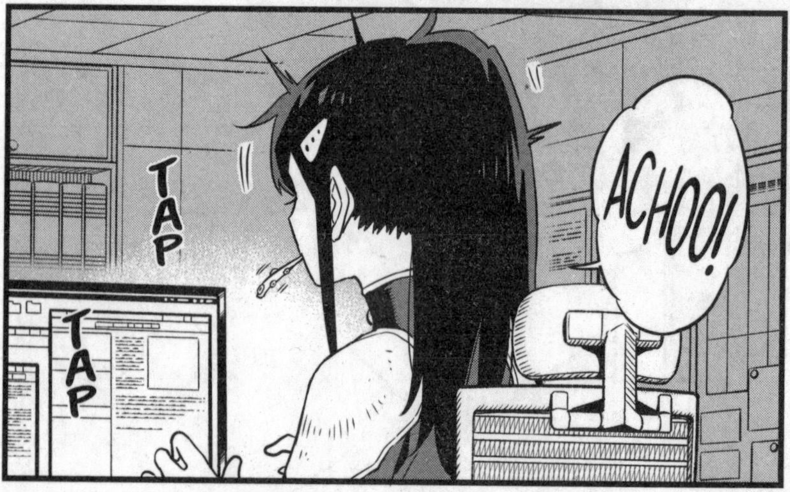
ACHOO!
TAP
TAP

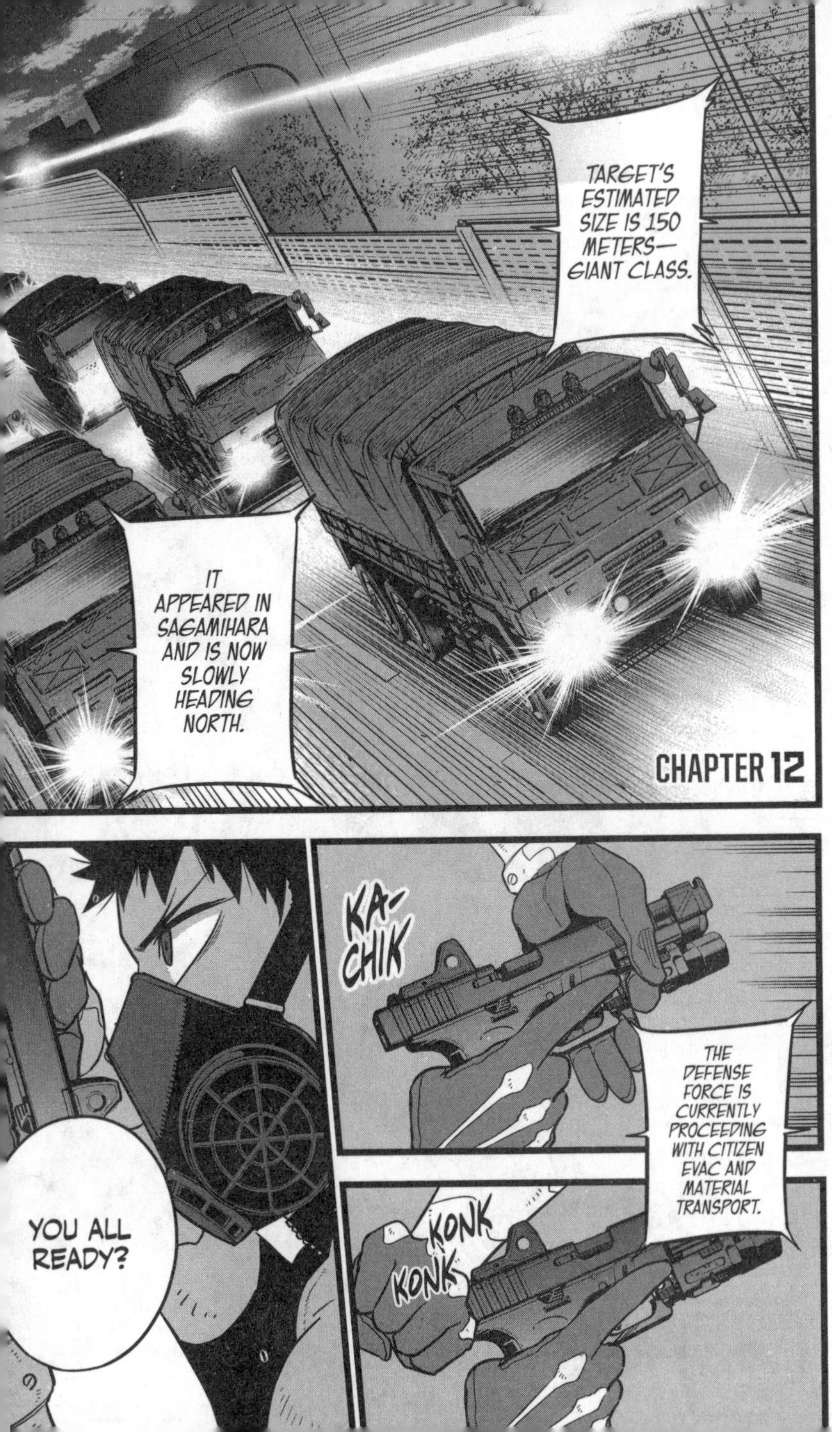
TARGET'S ESTIMATED SIZE IS 150 METERS—GIANT CLASS.
IT APPEARED IN SAGAMIHARA AND IS NOW SLOWLY HEADING NORTH.
CHAPTER 12
KA-CHIK
THE DEFENSE FORCE IS CURRENTLY PROCEEDING WITH CITIZEN EVAC AND MATERIAL TRANSPORT.
KONK
KONK
YOU ALL READY?

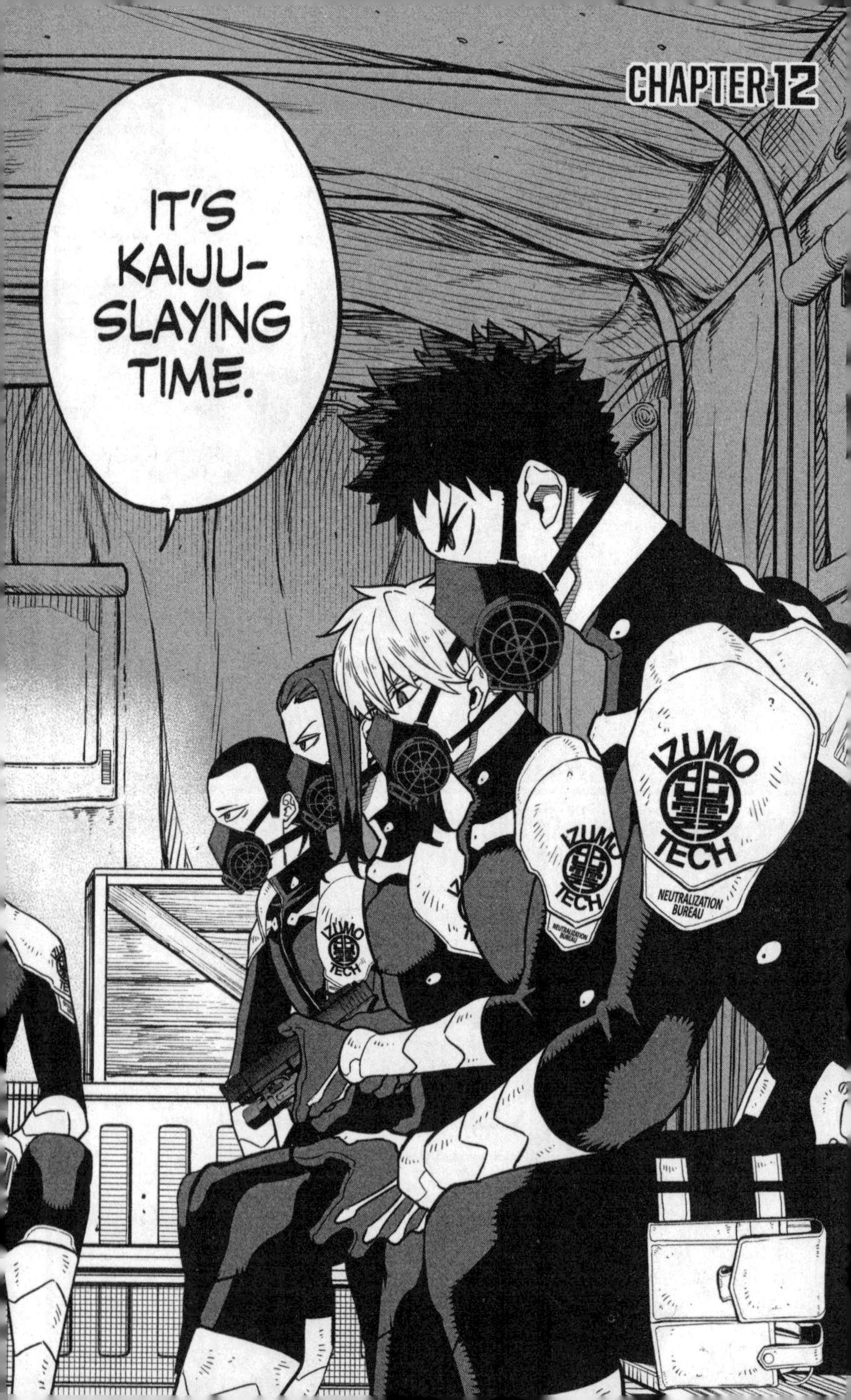
CHAPTER 12
IT'S KAIJU-SLAYING TIME.
IZUMO TECH NEUTRALIZATION BUREAU
IZUMO TECH NEUTRALIZATION BUREAU
IZUMO TECH

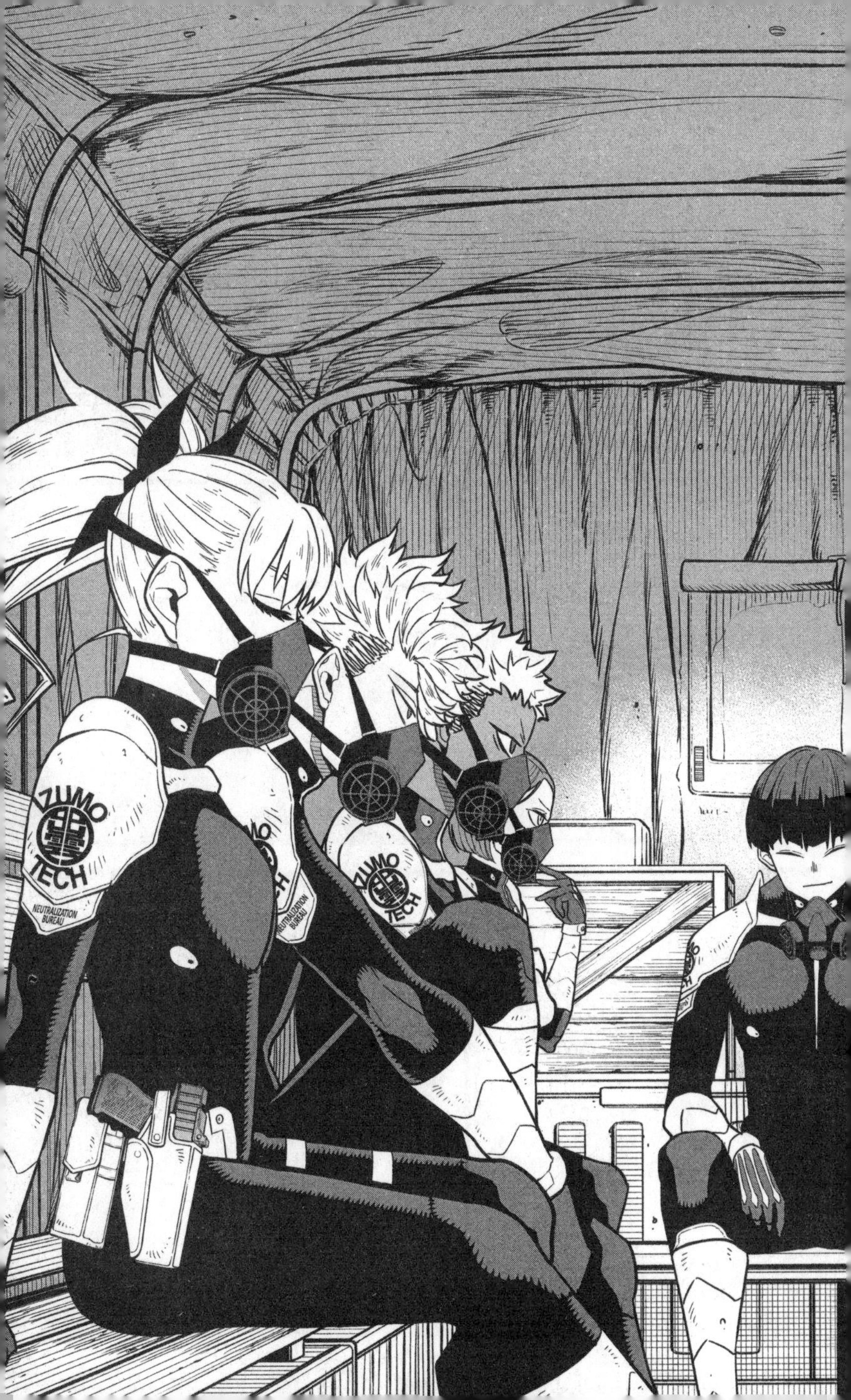
ZUMO
TECH
NEUTRALIZATION BUREAU

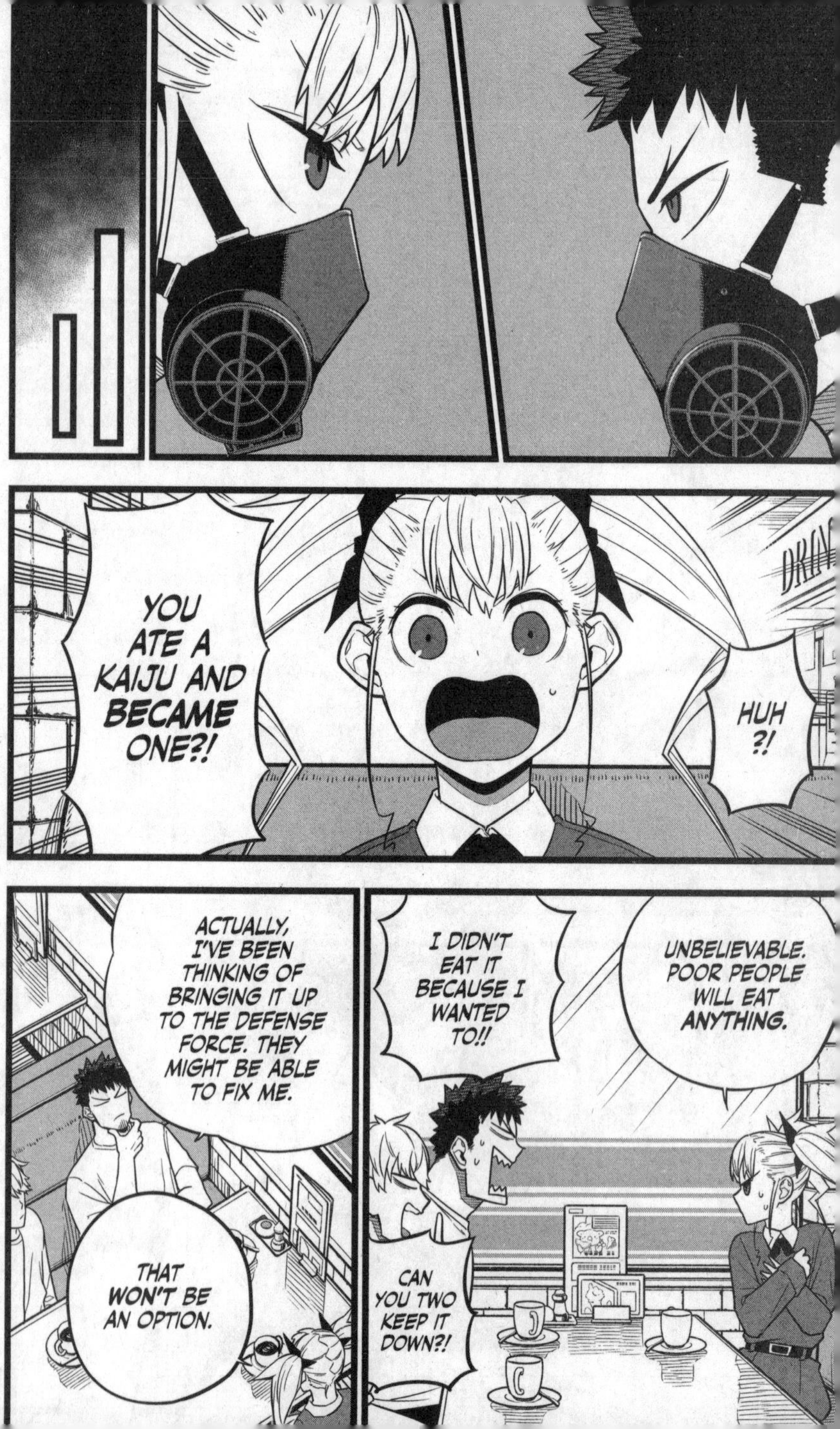
HUH ?!
YOU ATE A KAIJU AND BECAME ONE?!
UNBELIEVABLE. POOR PEOPLE WILL EAT ANYTHING.
I DIDN'T EAT IT BECAUSE I WANTED TO!!
CAN YOU TWO KEEP IT DOWN?!
ACTUALLY, I'VE BEEN THINKING OF BRINGING IT UP TO THE DEFENSE FORCE. THEY MIGHT BE ABLE TO FIX ME.
THAT WON'T BE AN OPTION.

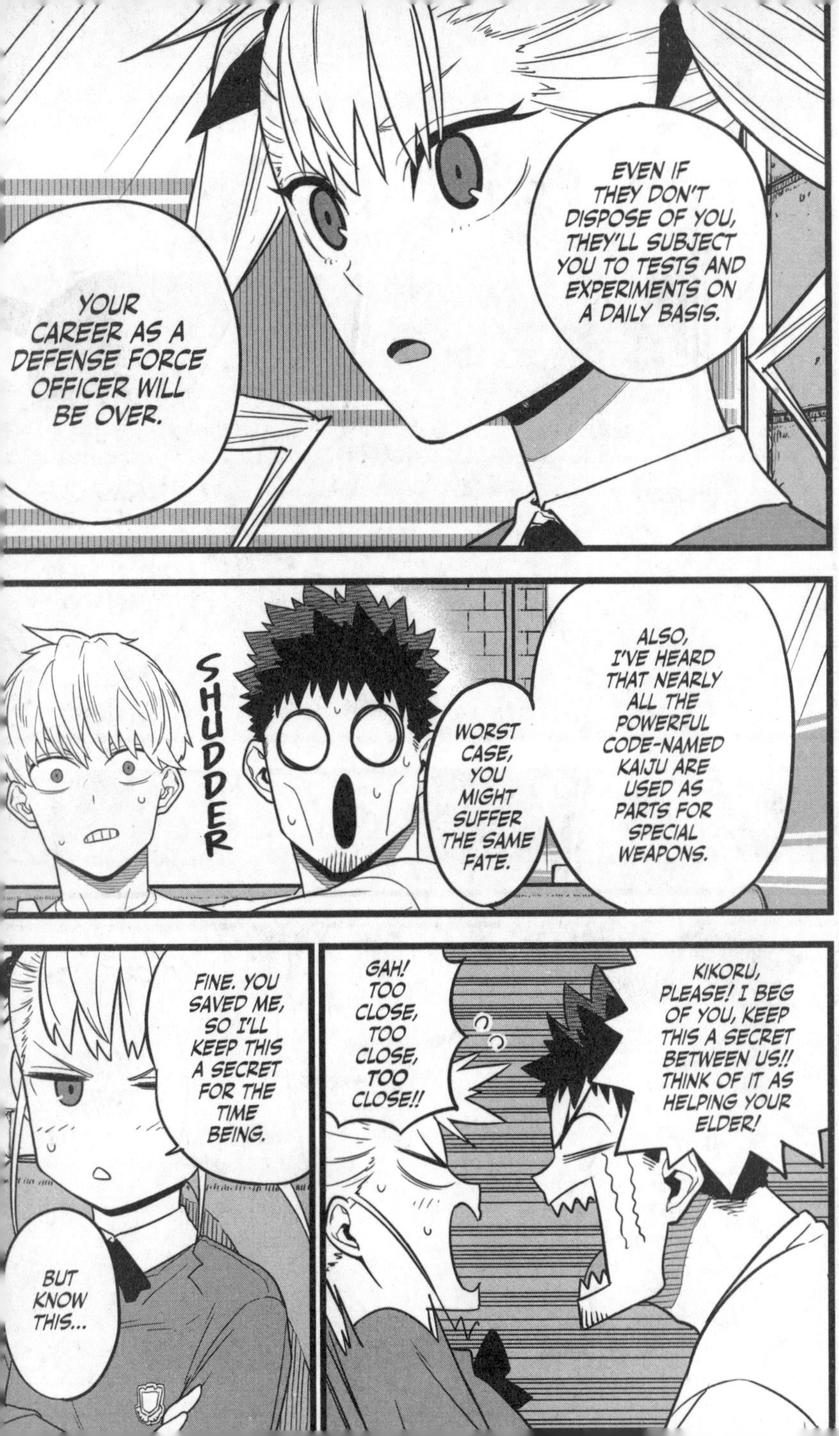
EVEN IF THEY DON'T DISPOSE OF YOU, THEY'LL SUBJECT YOU TO TESTS AND EXPERIMENTS ON A DAILY BASIS.
YOUR CAREER AS A DEFENSE FORCE OFFICER WILL BE OVER.
ALSO, I'VE HEARD THAT NEARLY ALL THE POWERFUL CODE-NAMED KAIJU ARE USED AS PARTS FOR SPECIAL WEAPONS.
WORST CASE, YOU MIGHT SUFFER THE SAME FATE.
SHUDDER
KIKORU, PLEASE! I BEG OF YOU, KEEP THIS A SECRET BETWEEN US!! THINK OF IT AS HELPING YOUR ELDER!
GAH! TOO CLOSE, TOO CLOSE, TOO CLOSE!!
FINE. YOU SAVED ME, SO I'LL KEEP THIS A SECRET FOR THE TIME BEING.
BUT KNOW THIS...

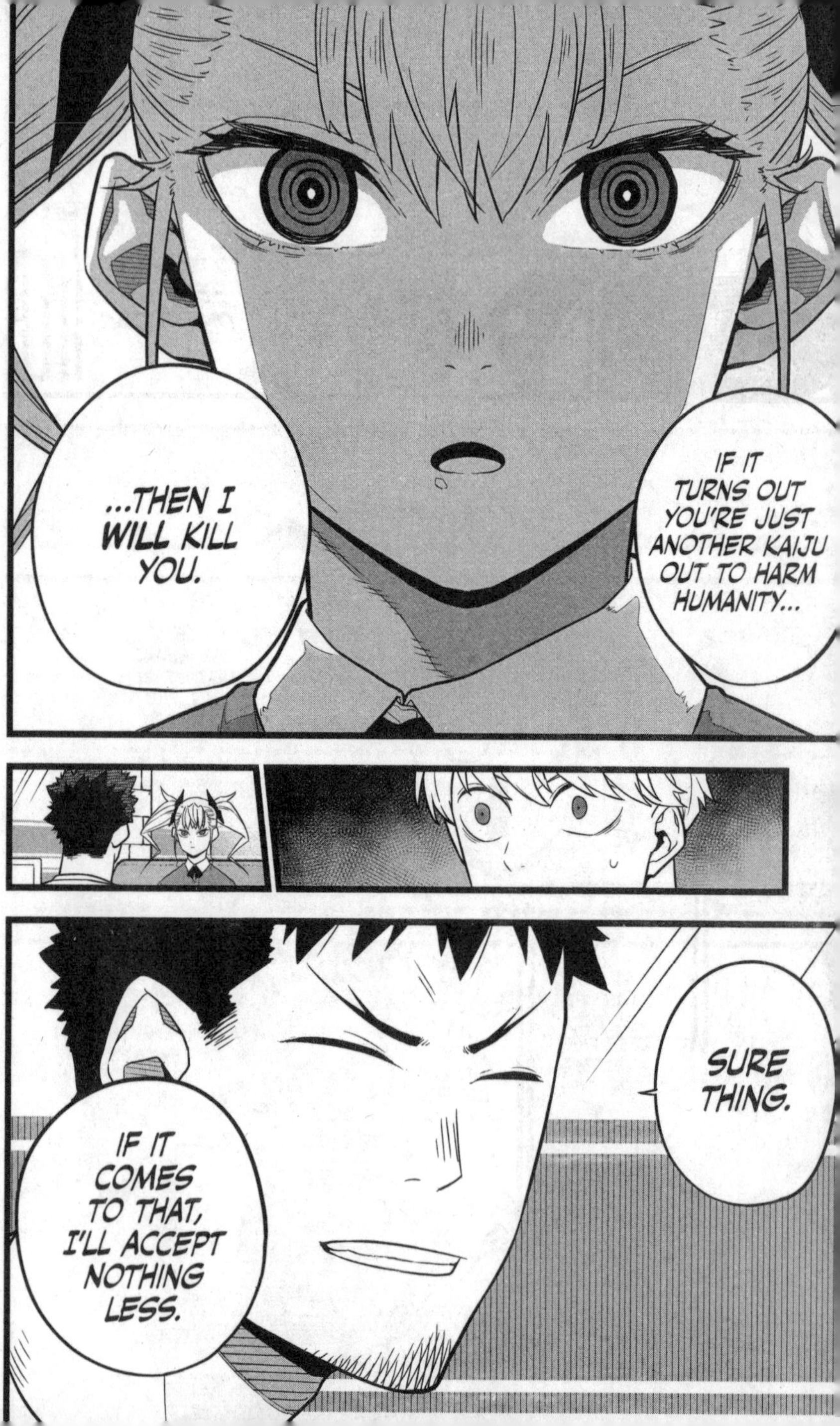
IF IT TURNS OUT YOU'RE JUST ANOTHER KAIJU OUT TO HARM HUMANITY...
...THEN I WILL KILL YOU.
SURE THING.
IF IT COMES TO THAT, I'LL ACCEPT NOTHING LESS.

...KAFKA HIBINO.

YOU'D BEST NOT DISAPPOINT ME...

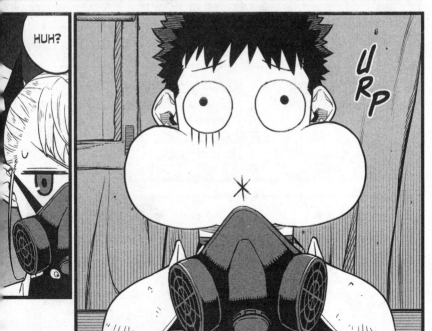

HUH?

URP

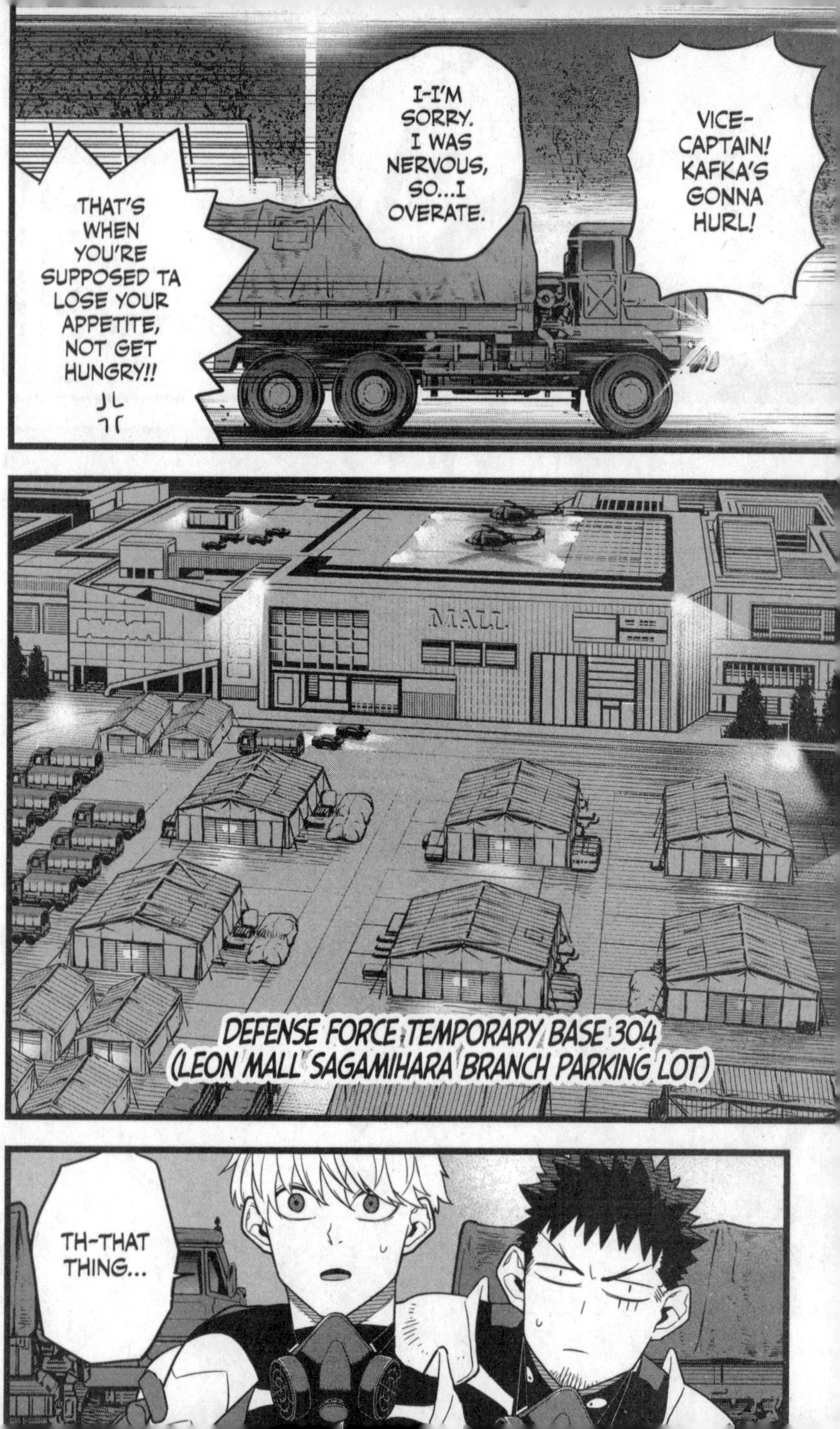
VICE-CAPTAIN! KAFKA'S GONNA HURL!
I-I'M SORRY. I WAS NERVOUS, SO...I OVERATE.
THAT'S WHEN YOU'RE SUPPOSED TA LOSE YOUR APPETITE, NOT GET HUNGRY!!
MALL
DEFENSE FORCE TEMPORARY BASE 304 (LEON MALL SAGAMIHARA BRANCH PARKING LOT)
TH-THAT THING...

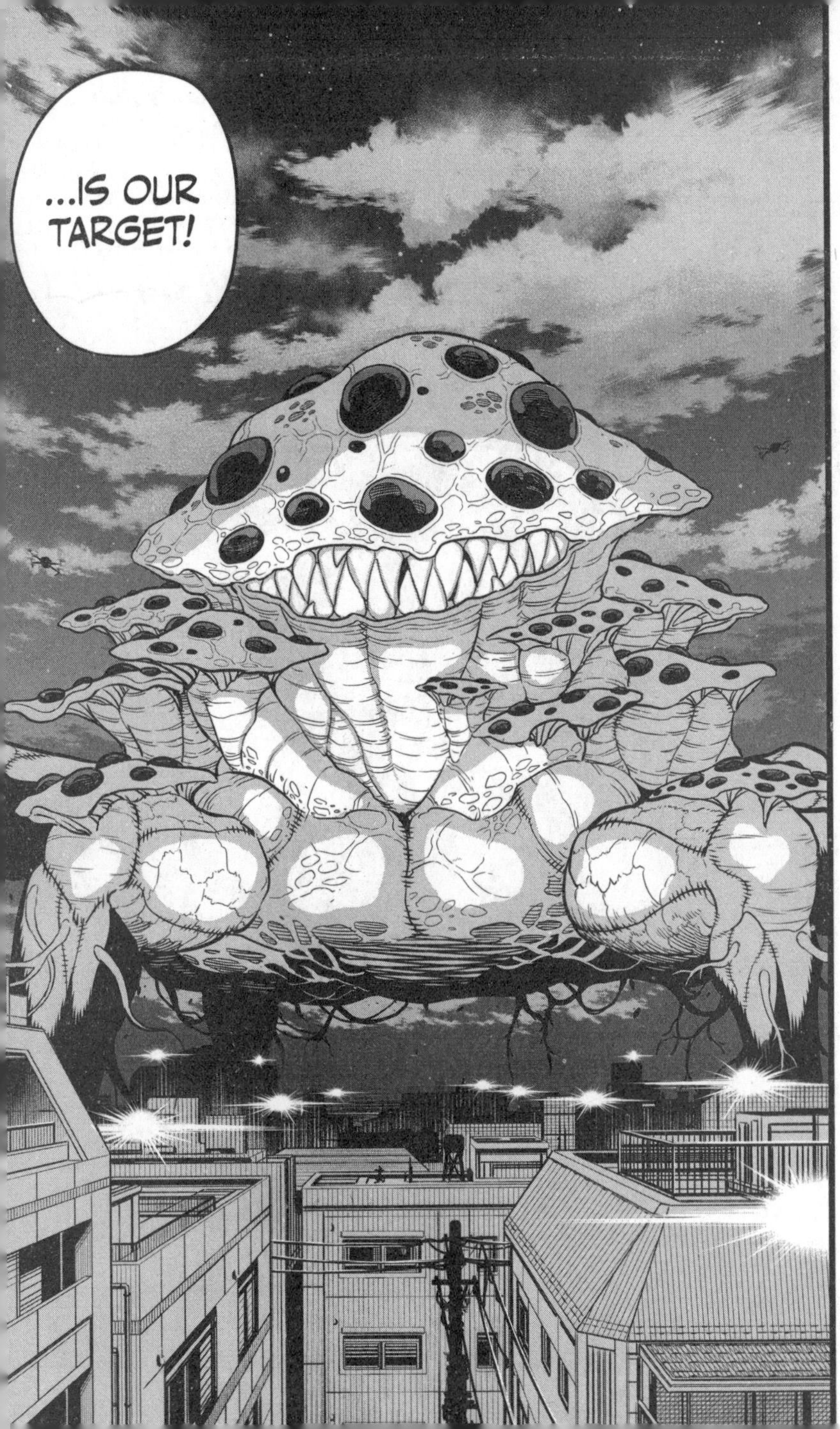
...IS OUR TARGET!

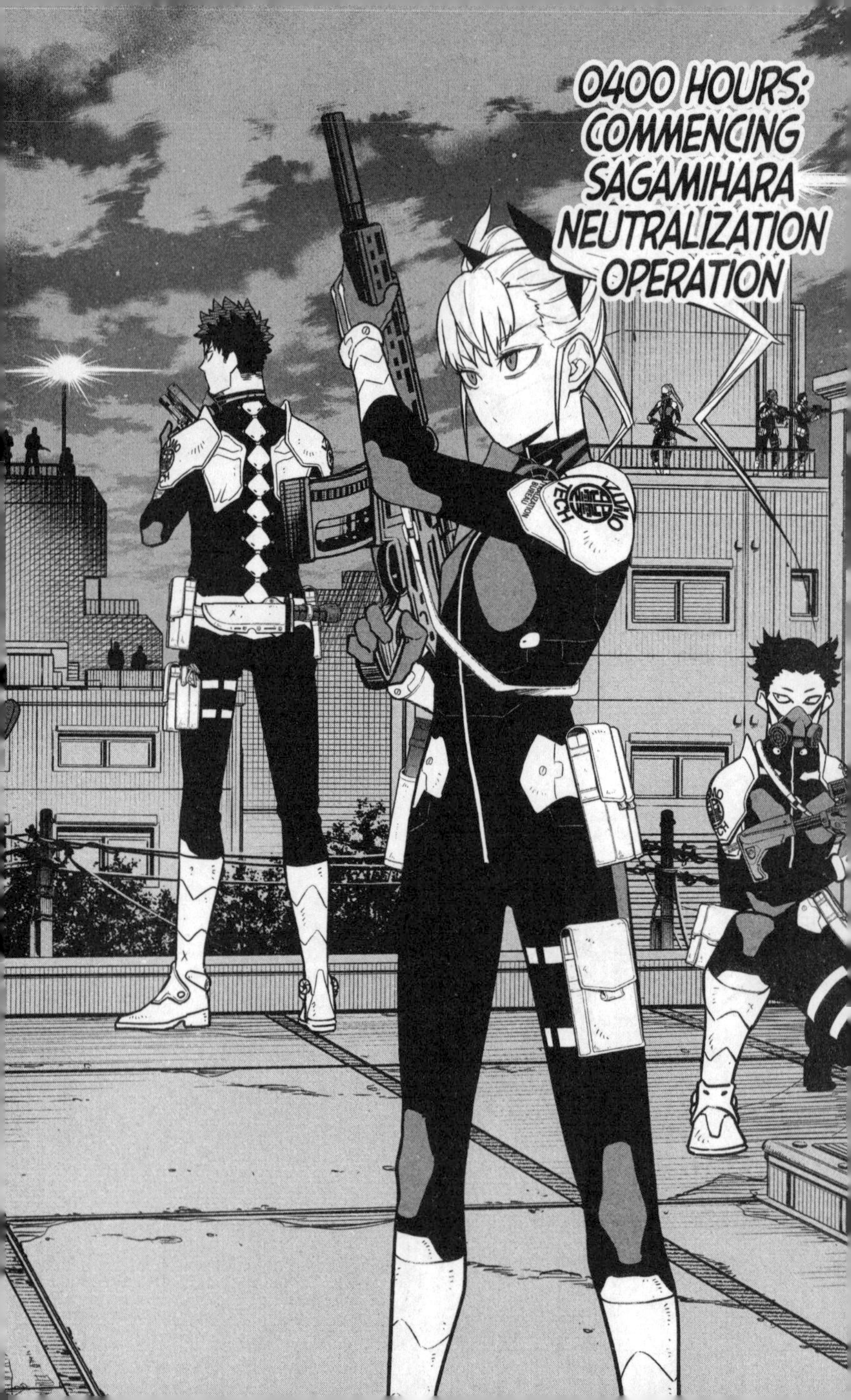
0400 HOURS: COMMENCING SAGAMIHARA NEUTRALIZATION OPERATION

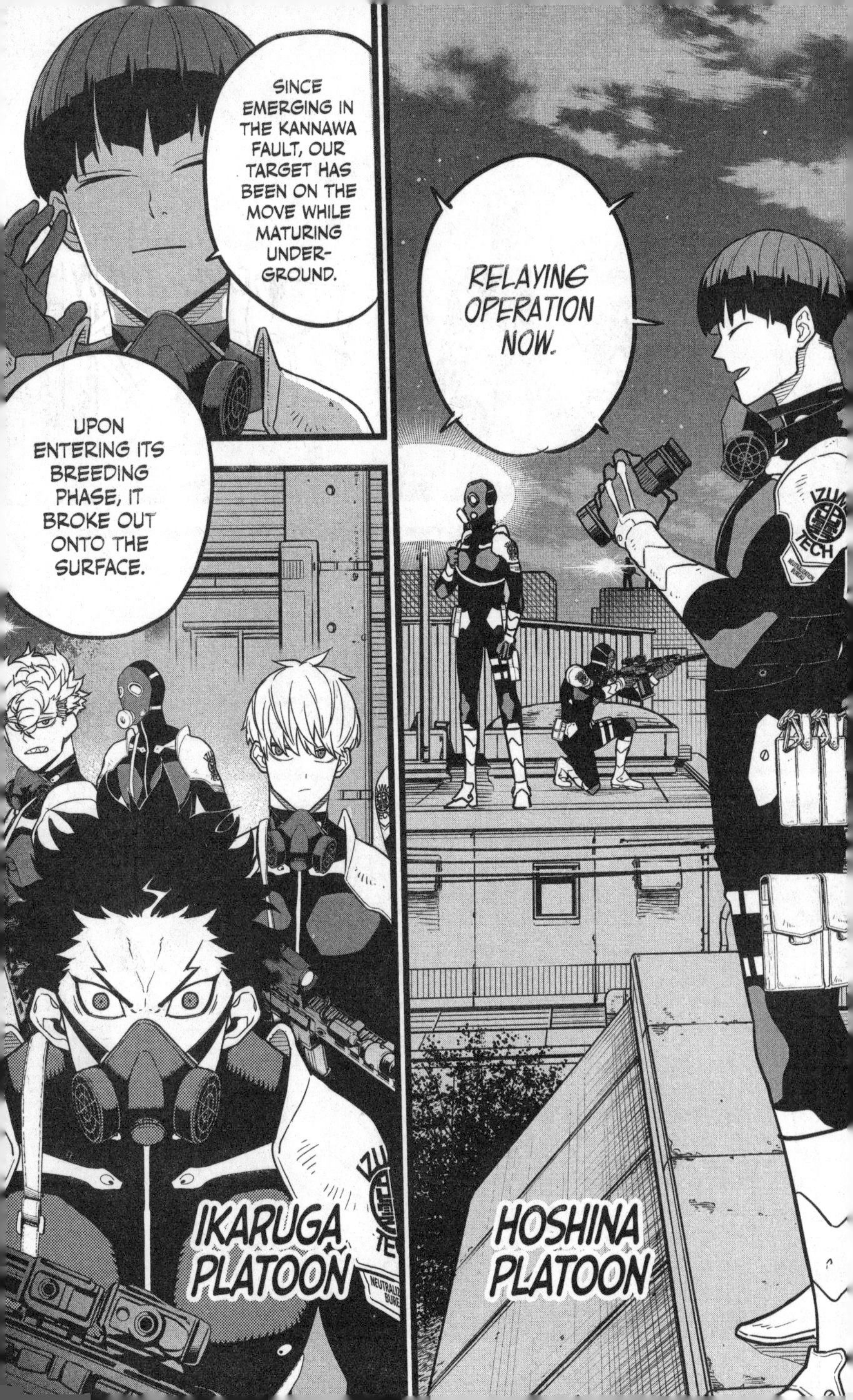
RELAYING OPERATION NOW.
HOSHINA PLATOON
SINCE EMERGING IN THE KANNAWA FAULT, OUR TARGET HAS BEEN ON THE MOVE WHILE MATURING UNDER-GROUND.
UPON ENTERING ITS BREEDING PHASE, IT BROKE OUT ONTO THE SURFACE.
IKARUGA PLATOON

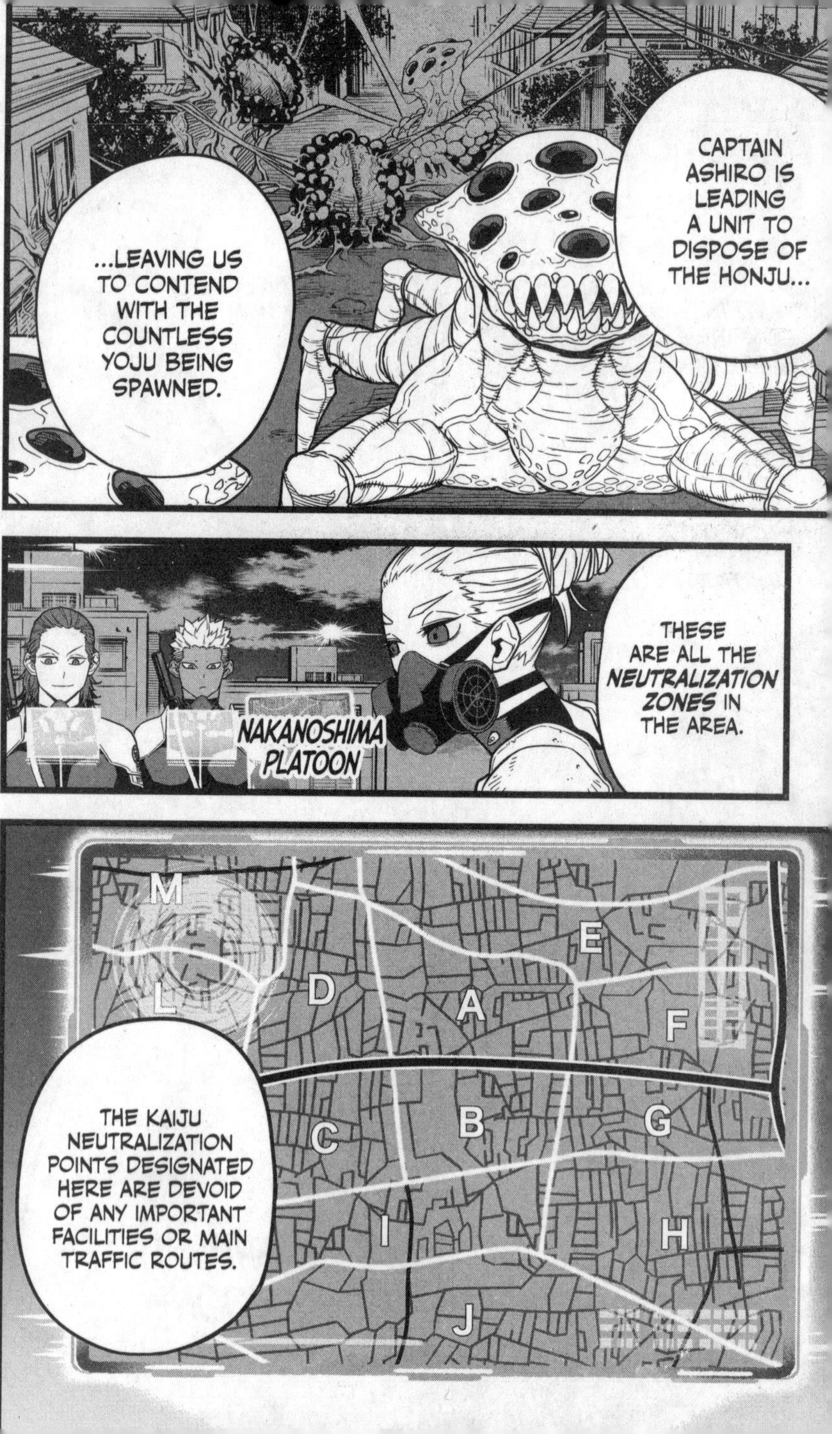
CAPTAIN ASHIRO IS LEADING A UNIT TO DISPOSE OF THE HONJU...
...LEAVING US TO CONTEND WITH THE COUNTLESS YOJU BEING SPAWNED.
THESE ARE ALL THE *NEUTRALIZATION ZONES* IN THE AREA.
NAKANOSHIMA PLATOON
M
E
D
A
L
F
B
C
G
I
H
J
THE KAIJU NEUTRALIZATION POINTS DESIGNATED HERE ARE DEVOID OF ANY IMPORTANT FACILITIES OR MAIN TRAFFIC ROUTES.

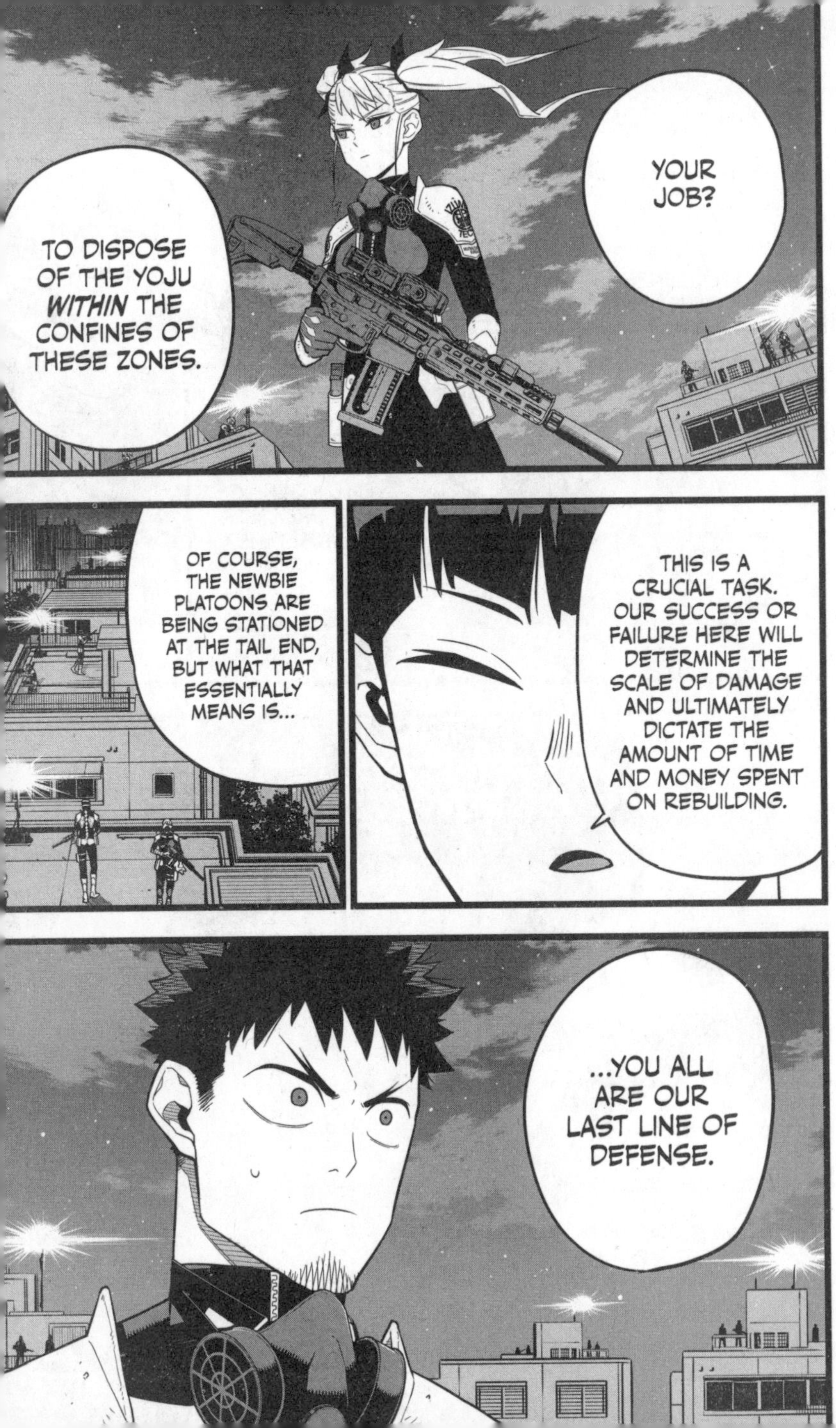
YOUR JOB?
TO DISPOSE OF THE YOJU *WITHIN* THE CONFINES OF THESE ZONES.
THIS IS A CRUCIAL TASK. OUR SUCCESS OR FAILURE HERE WILL DETERMINE THE SCALE OF DAMAGE AND ULTIMATELY DICTATE THE AMOUNT OF TIME AND MONEY SPENT ON REBUILDING.
OF COURSE, THE NEWBIE PLATOONS ARE BEING STATIONED AT THE TAIL END, BUT WHAT THAT ESSENTIALLY MEANS IS...
...YOU ALL ARE OUR LAST LINE OF DEFENSE.

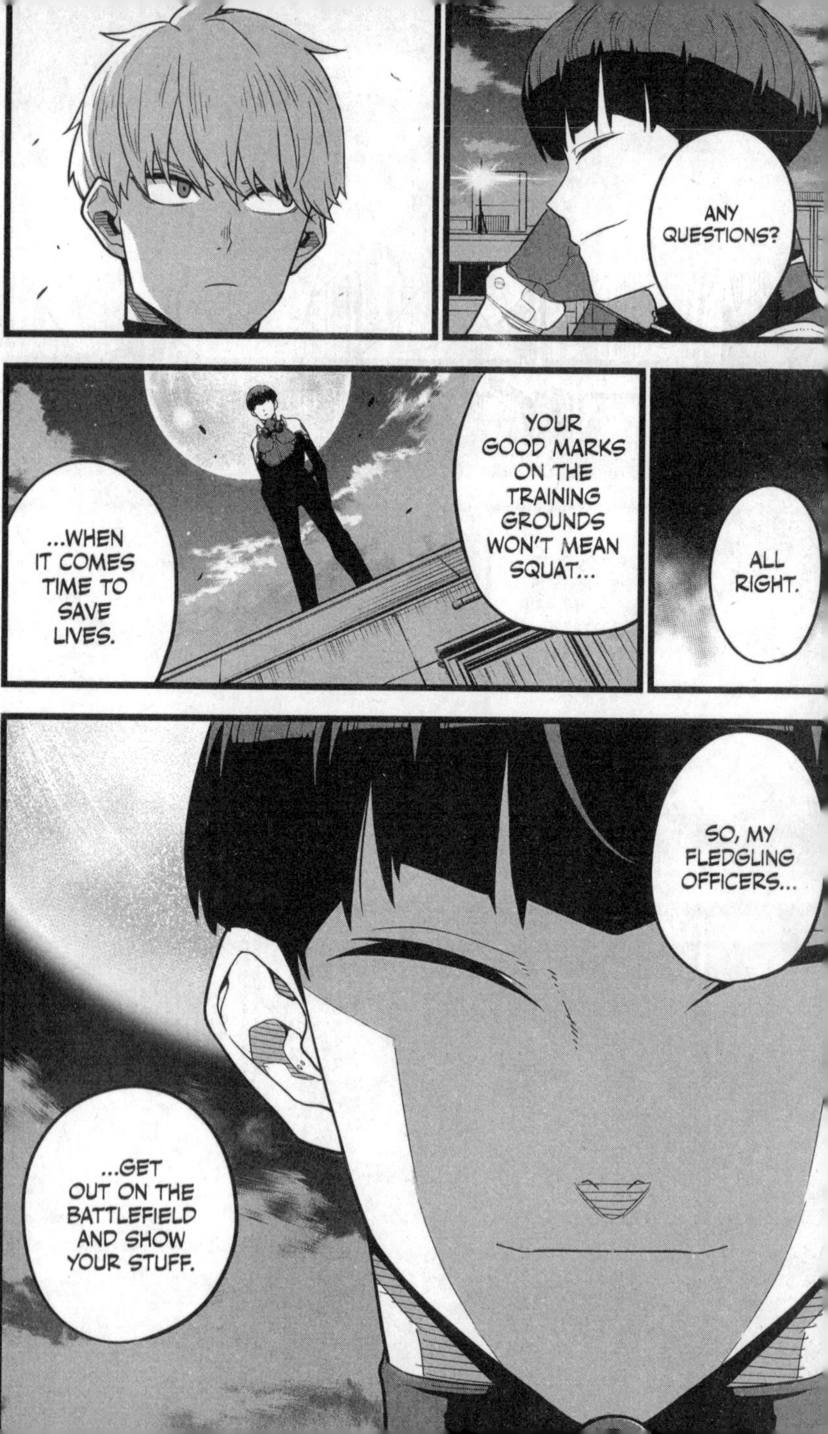
ANY QUESTIONS?
ALL RIGHT.
YOUR GOOD MARKS ON THE TRAINING GROUNDS WON'T MEAN SQUAT...
...WHEN IT COMES TIME TO SAVE LIVES.
SO, MY FLEDGLING OFFICERS...
...GET OUT ON THE BATTLEFIELD AND SHOW YOUR STUFF.

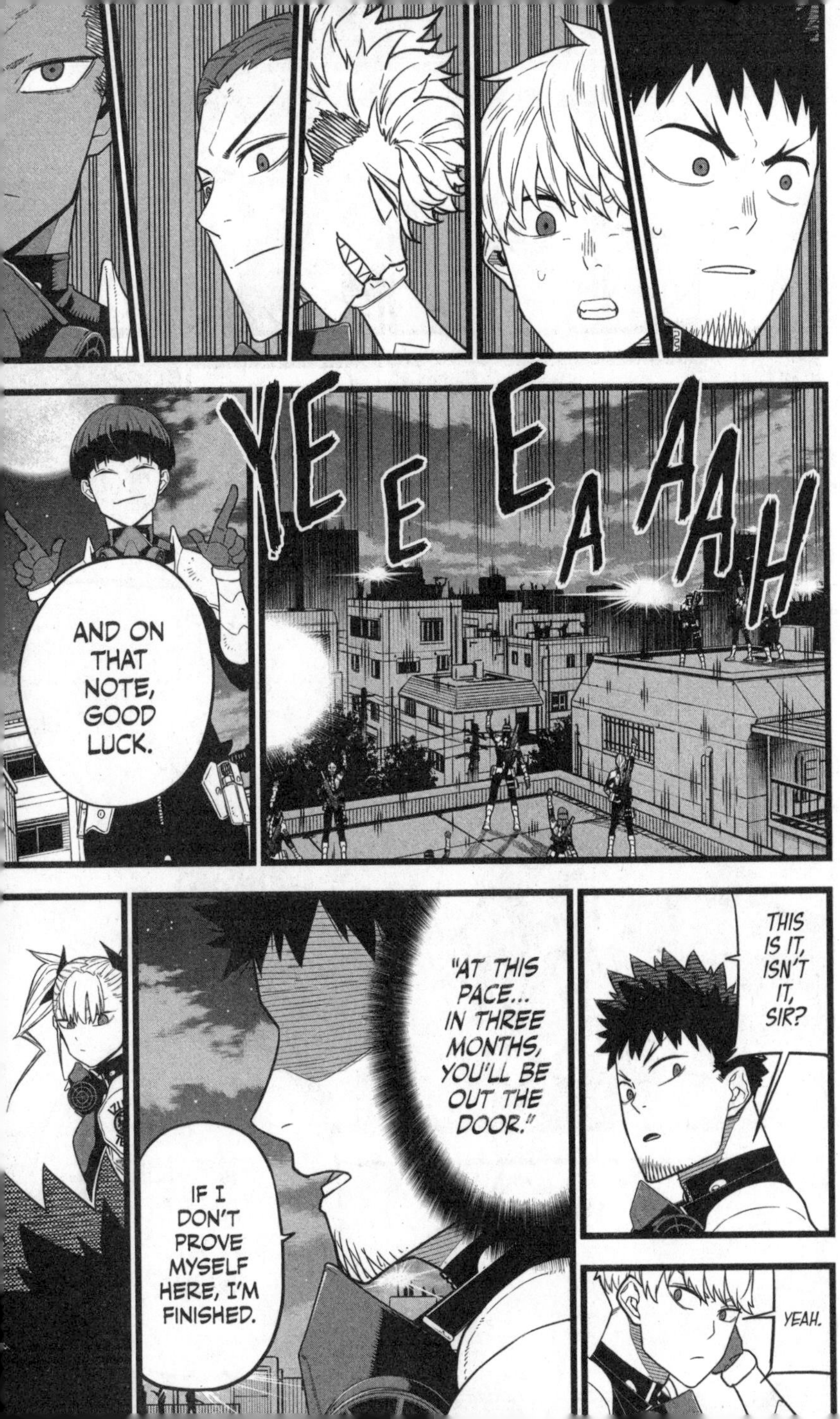
YEEEAAAH
AND ON THAT NOTE, GOOD LUCK.
THIS IS IT, ISN'T IT, SIR?
YEAH.
"AT THIS PACE... IN THREE MONTHS, YOU'LL BE OUT THE DOOR."
IF I DON'T PROVE MYSELF HERE, I'M FINISHED.

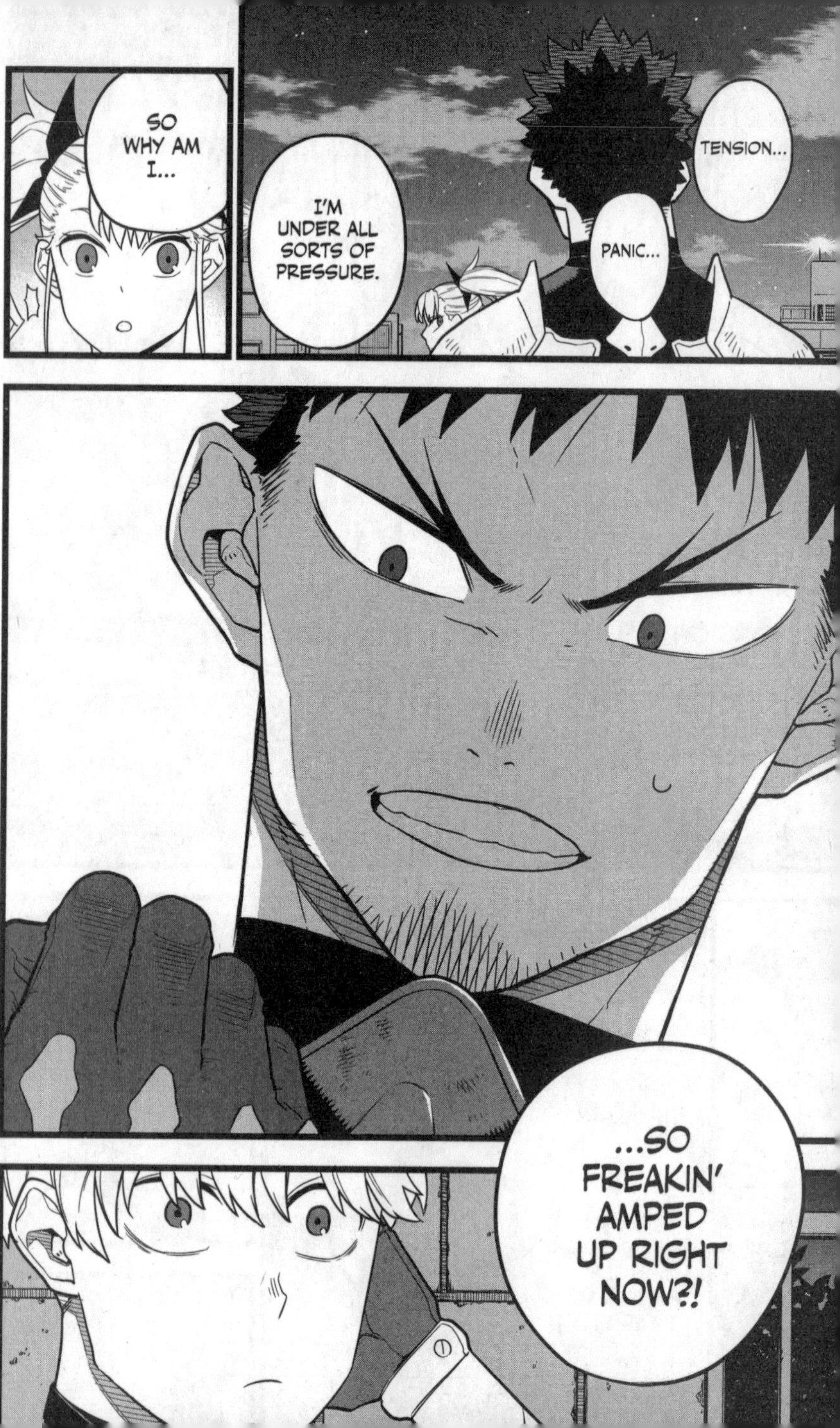
TENSION...
PANIC...
I'M UNDER ALL SORTS OF PRESSURE.
SO WHY AM I...
...SO FREAKIN' AMPED UP RIGHT NOW?!

THIS IS THE JOB YOU'VE ALWAYS WANTED AFTER ALL.

THAT MAKES SENSE.

LET'S MAKE SURE OUR FIRST MISSION IS A SUCCESS!

IZUMO TECH

NEUTRALIZATION BUREAU

YOJU SPOTTED ENTERING ZONE E (ECHO)! ALL OFFICERS IN POSITION, ENGAGE AND NEUTRALIZE!!

THEY'RE HERE...!

LET'S HIT IT, KIKORU!!

GRIp

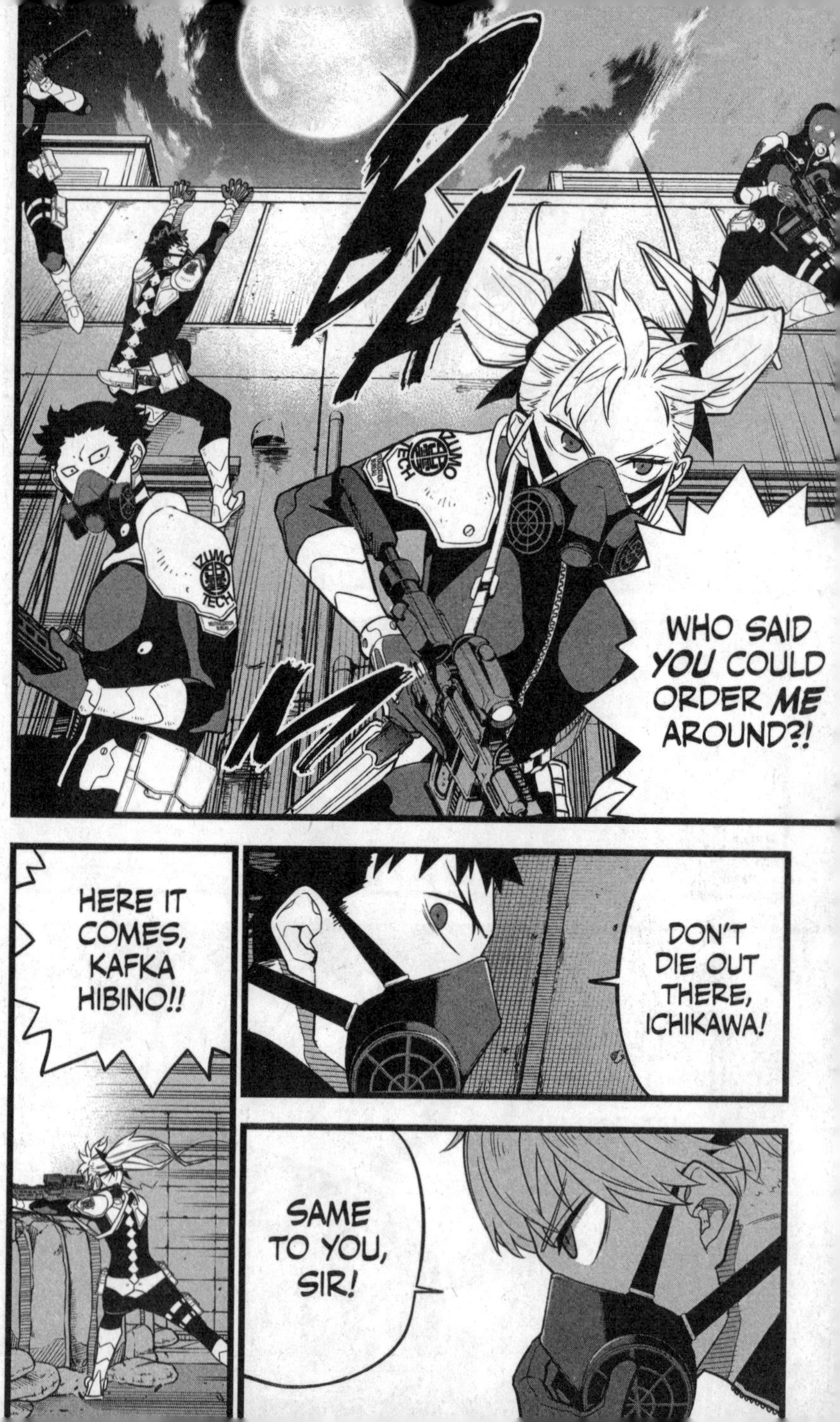
WHO SAID *YOU* COULD ORDER *ME* AROUND?!
DON'T DIE OUT THERE, ICHIKAWA!
HERE IT COMES, KAFKA HIBINO!!
SAME TO YOU, SIR!

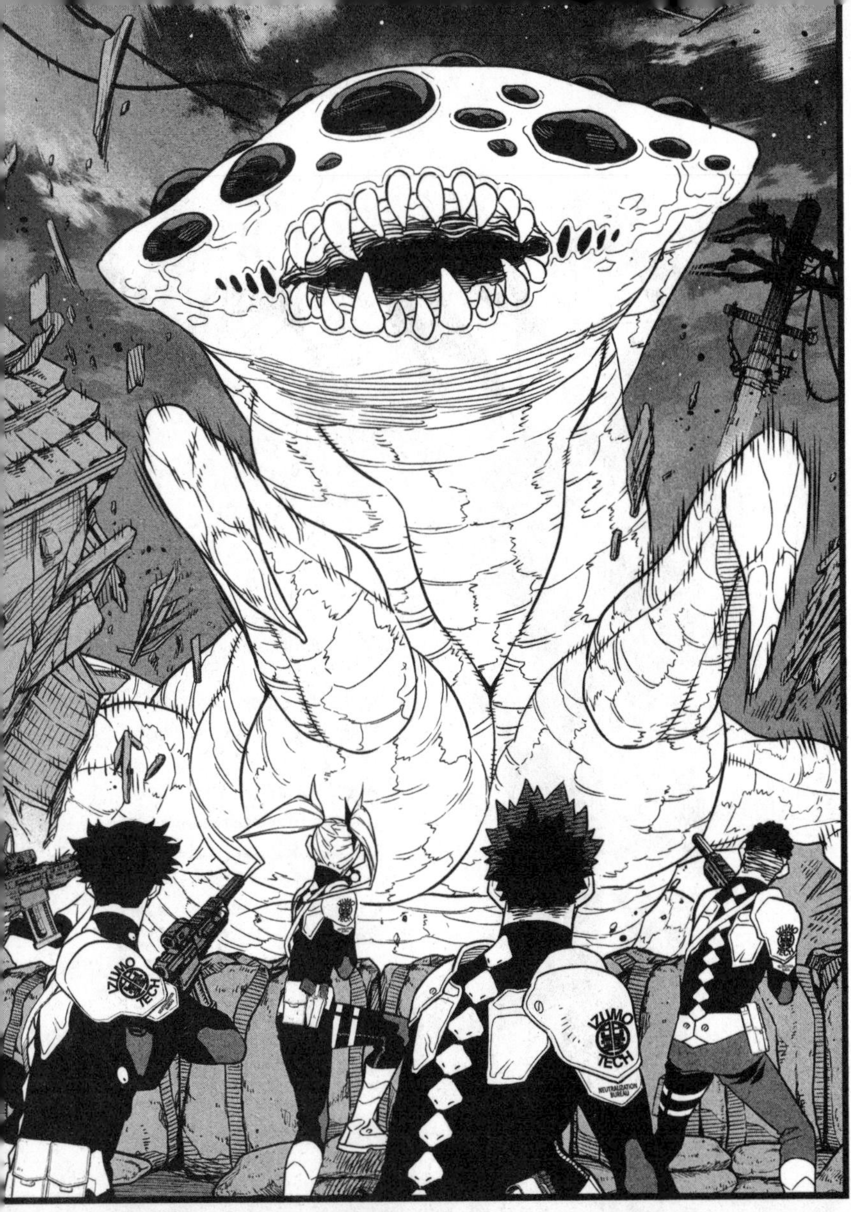
IZUMO TECH
NEUTRALIZATION BUREAU

SOSHIRO HOSHINA

Birthday:
November 21

Height:
171 cm

Likes:
Reading, coffee,
Montblancs, simple folks

Author Comment:
I like that he's different from
the "squinty-eyed character
equals plain" idea. He not only
is the center of a lot of action,
but also acts as a sort of
detective who closes in on the
truth. He's a go-to character
for the author.

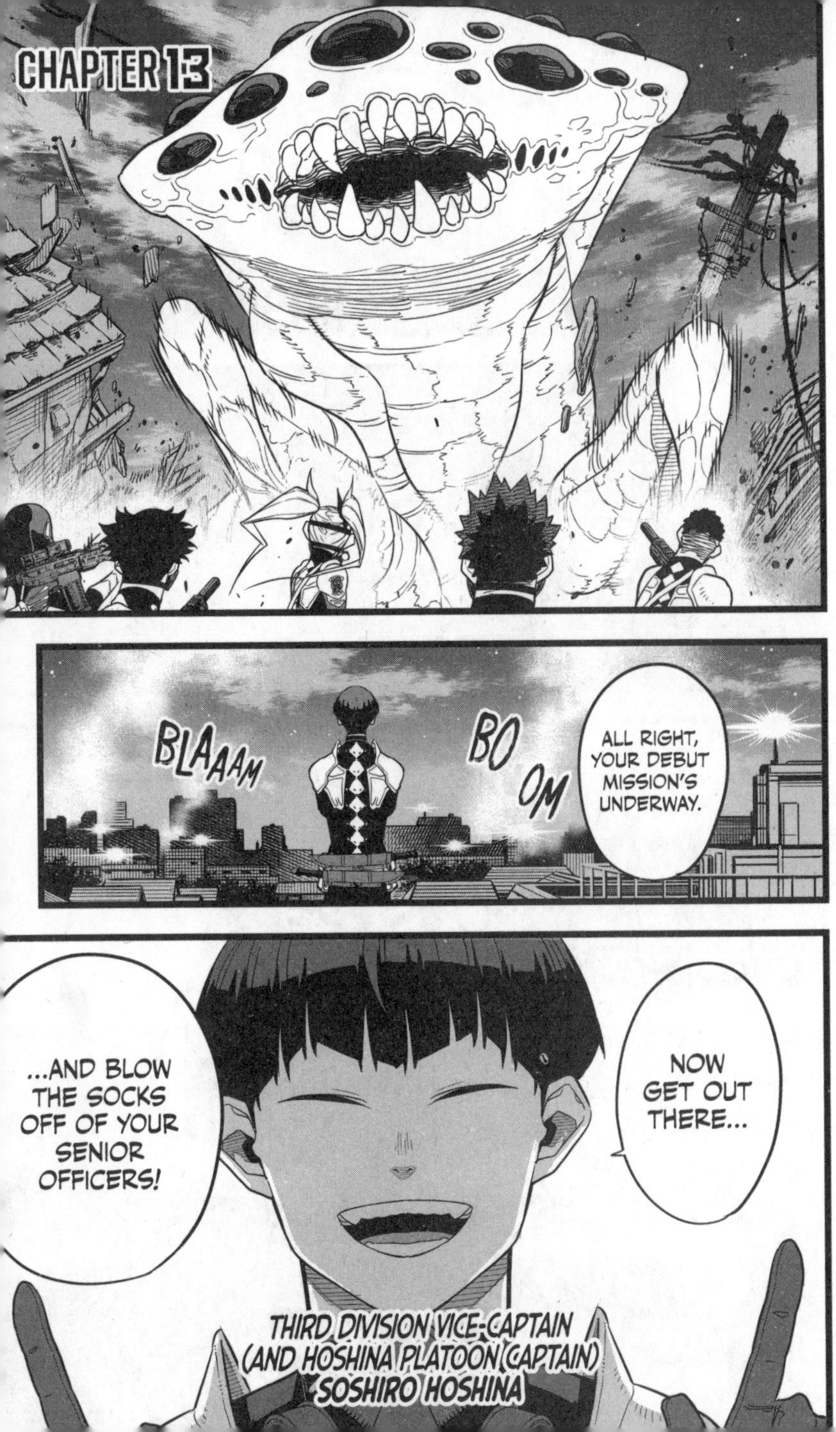
CHAPTER 13
ALL RIGHT, YOUR DEBUT MISSION'S UNDERWAY.
BOOM
BLAAAM
NOW GET OUT THERE...
...AND BLOW THE SOCKS OFF OF YOUR SENIOR OFFICERS!
THIRD DIVISION VICE-CAPTAIN (AND HOSHINA PLATOON CAPTAIN) SOSHIRO HOSHINA

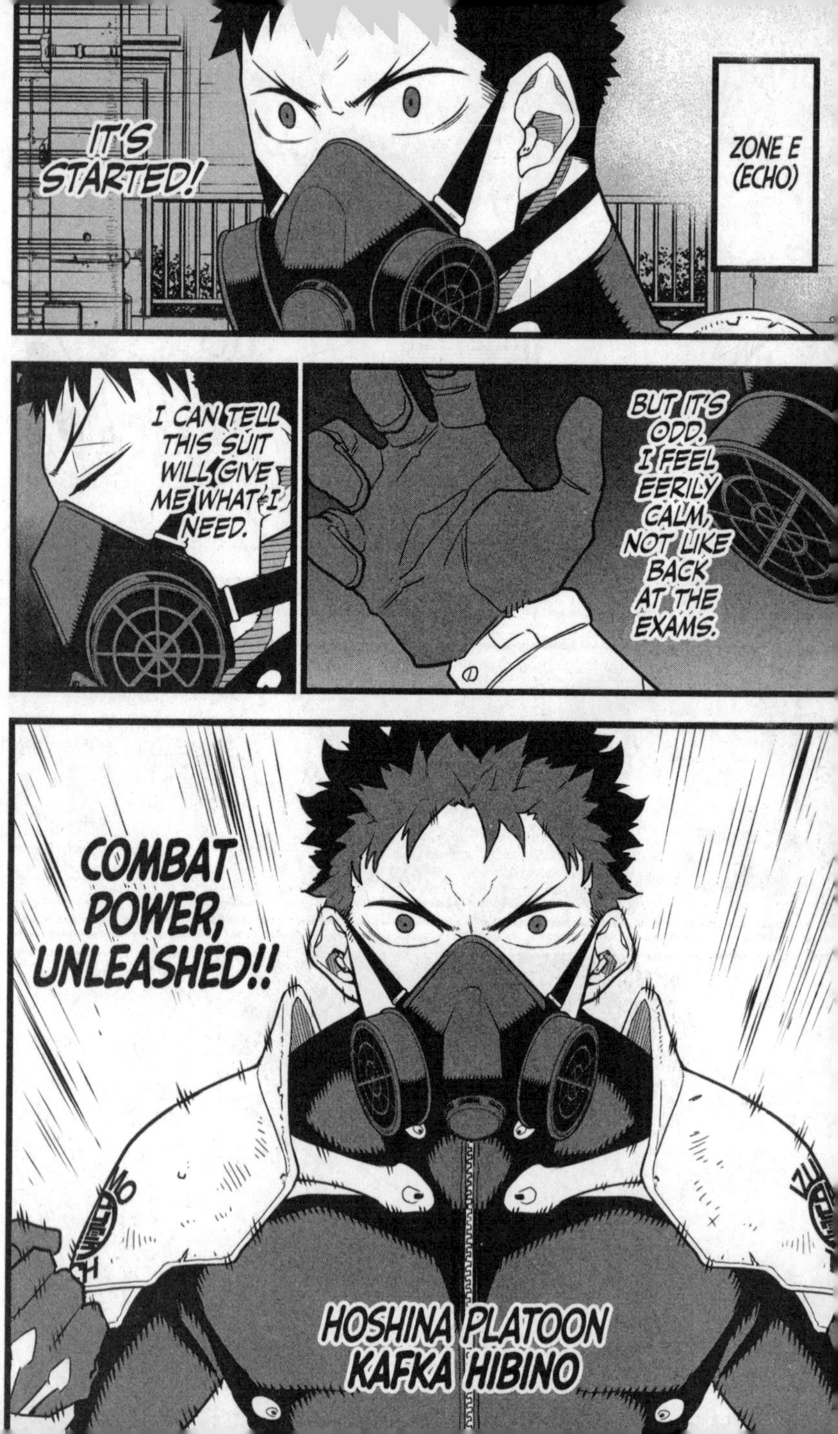
ZONE E (ECHO)
IT'S STARTED!
BUT IT'S ODD. I FEEL EERILY CALM, NOT LIKE BACK AT THE EXAMS.
I CAN TELL THIS SUIT WILL GIVE ME WHAT I NEED.
COMBAT POWER, UNLEASHED!!
HOSHINA PLATOON KAFKA HIBINO

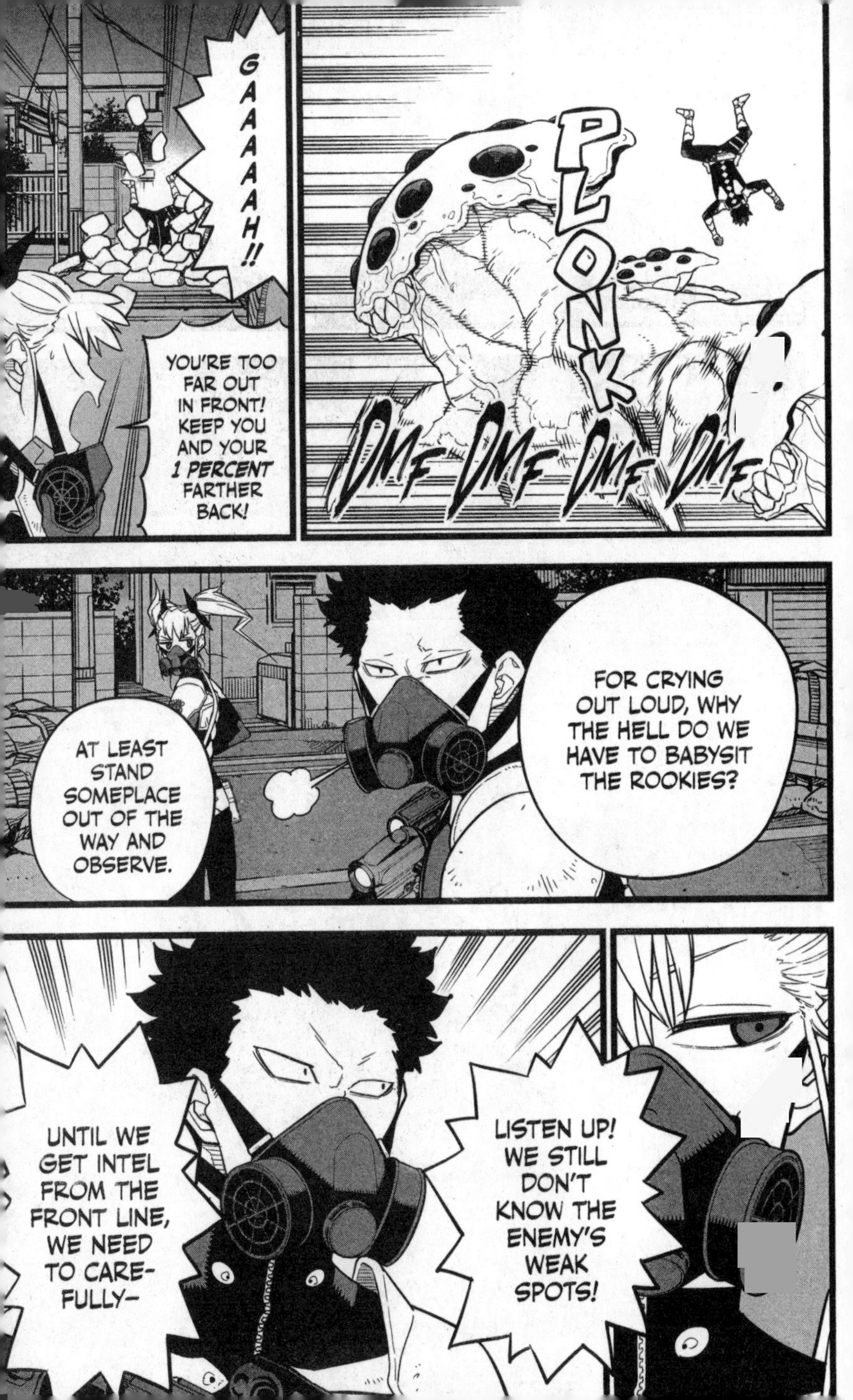
PLONK
DMF DMF DMF DMF
GAAAAAAH!!
YOU'RE TOO FAR OUT IN FRONT! KEEP YOU AND YOUR 1 PERCENT FARTHER BACK!
FOR CRYING OUT LOUD, WHY THE HELL DO WE HAVE TO BABYSIT THE ROOKIES?
AT LEAST STAND SOMEPLACE OUT OF THE WAY AND OBSERVE.
LISTEN UP! WE STILL DON'T KNOW THE ENEMY'S WEAK SPOTS!
UNTIL WE GET INTEL FROM THE FRONT LINE, WE NEED TO CARE-FULLY-

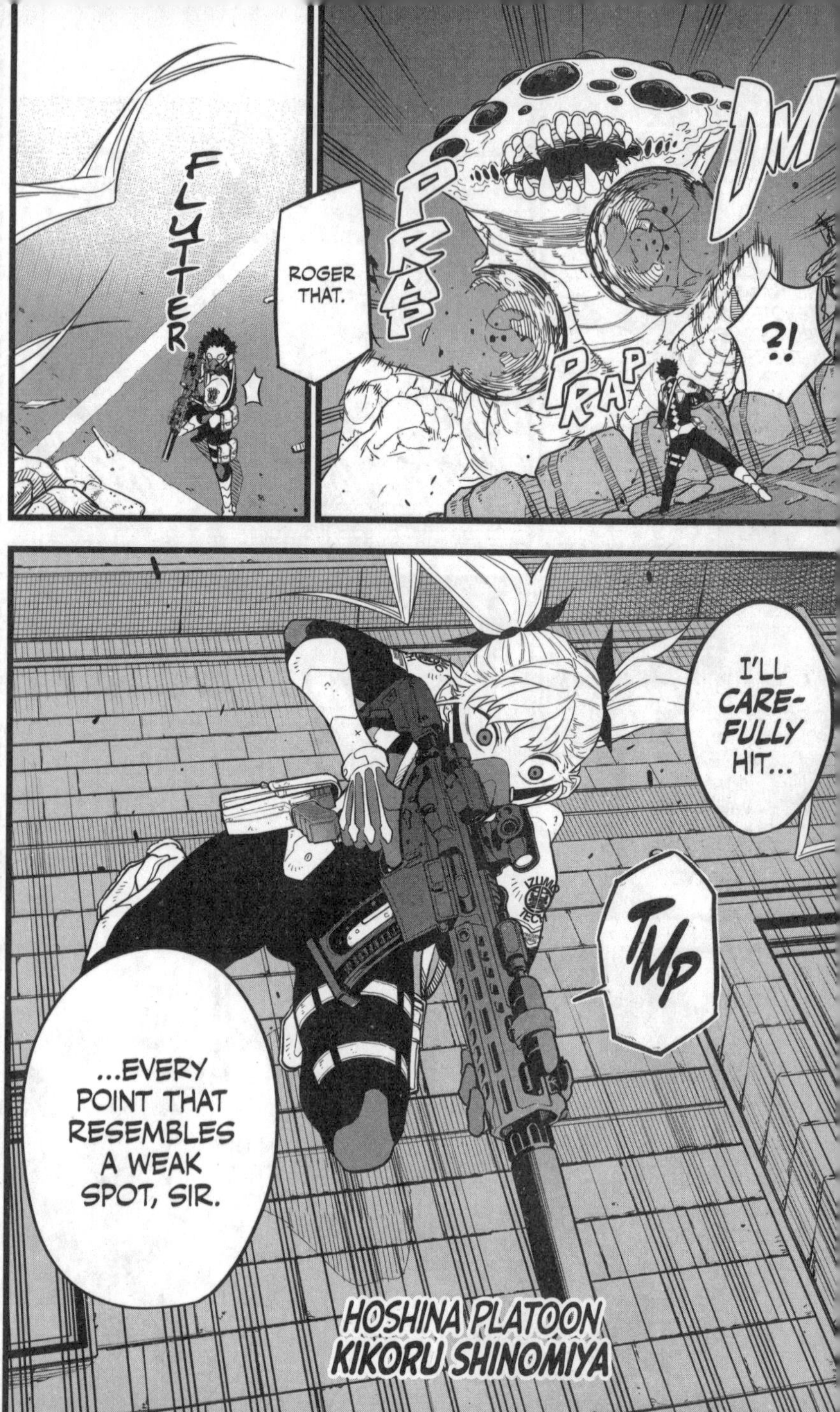
DM
PRAP
?!
PRAP
ROGER THAT.
FLUTTER
I'LL CAREFULLY HIT...
TMP
...EVERY POINT THAT RESEMBLES A WEAK SPOT, SIR.
HOSHINA PLATOON
KIKORU SHINOMIYA

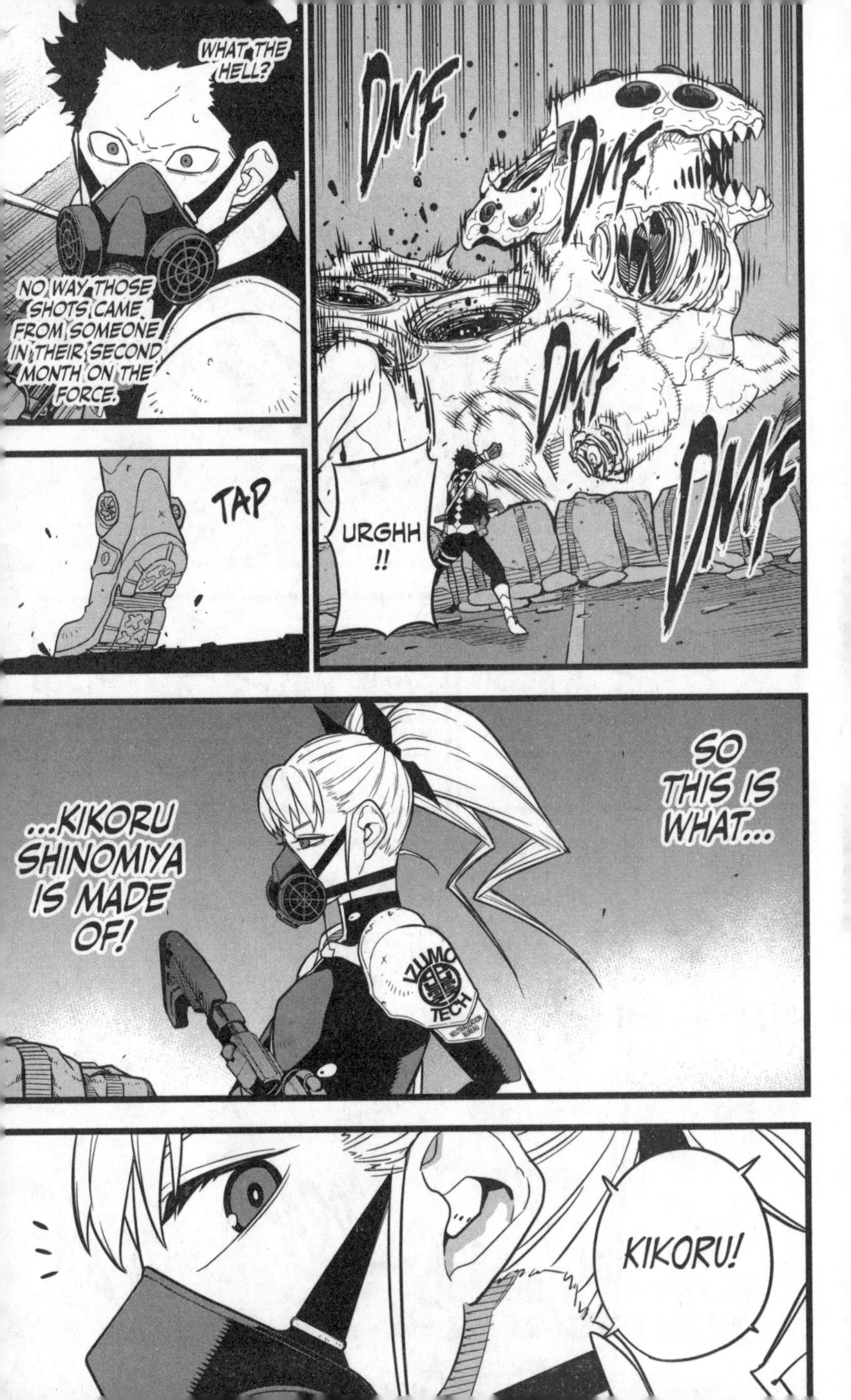
DMF
DMF
DMF
DMF
URGHH !!
WHAT THE HELL?
NO WAY THOSE SHOTS CAME FROM SOMEONE IN THEIR SECOND MONTH ON THE FORCE.
TAP
SO THIS IS WHAT...
...KIKORU SHINOMIYA IS MADE OF!
IZUMO TECH
KIKORU!

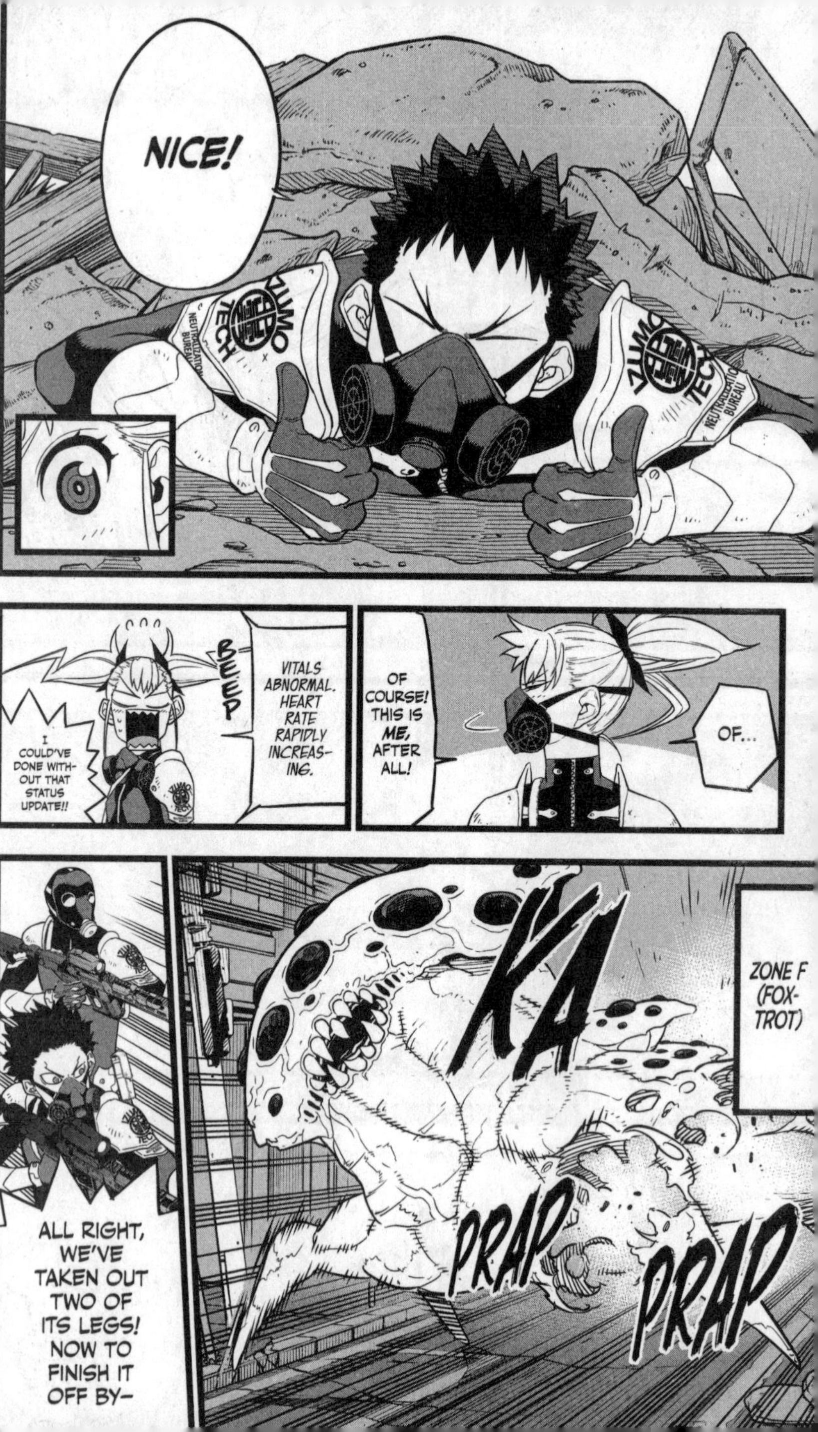
NICE!
OF...
OF COURSE! THIS IS ME, AFTER ALL!
BEEP
VITALS ABNORMAL. HEART RATE RAPIDLY INCREASING.
I COULD'VE DONE WITHOUT THAT STATUS UPDATE!!
ZONE F (FOXTROT)
KA
PRAP
PRAP
ALL RIGHT, WE'VE TAKEN OUT TWO OF ITS LEGS! NOW TO FINISH IT OFF BY—

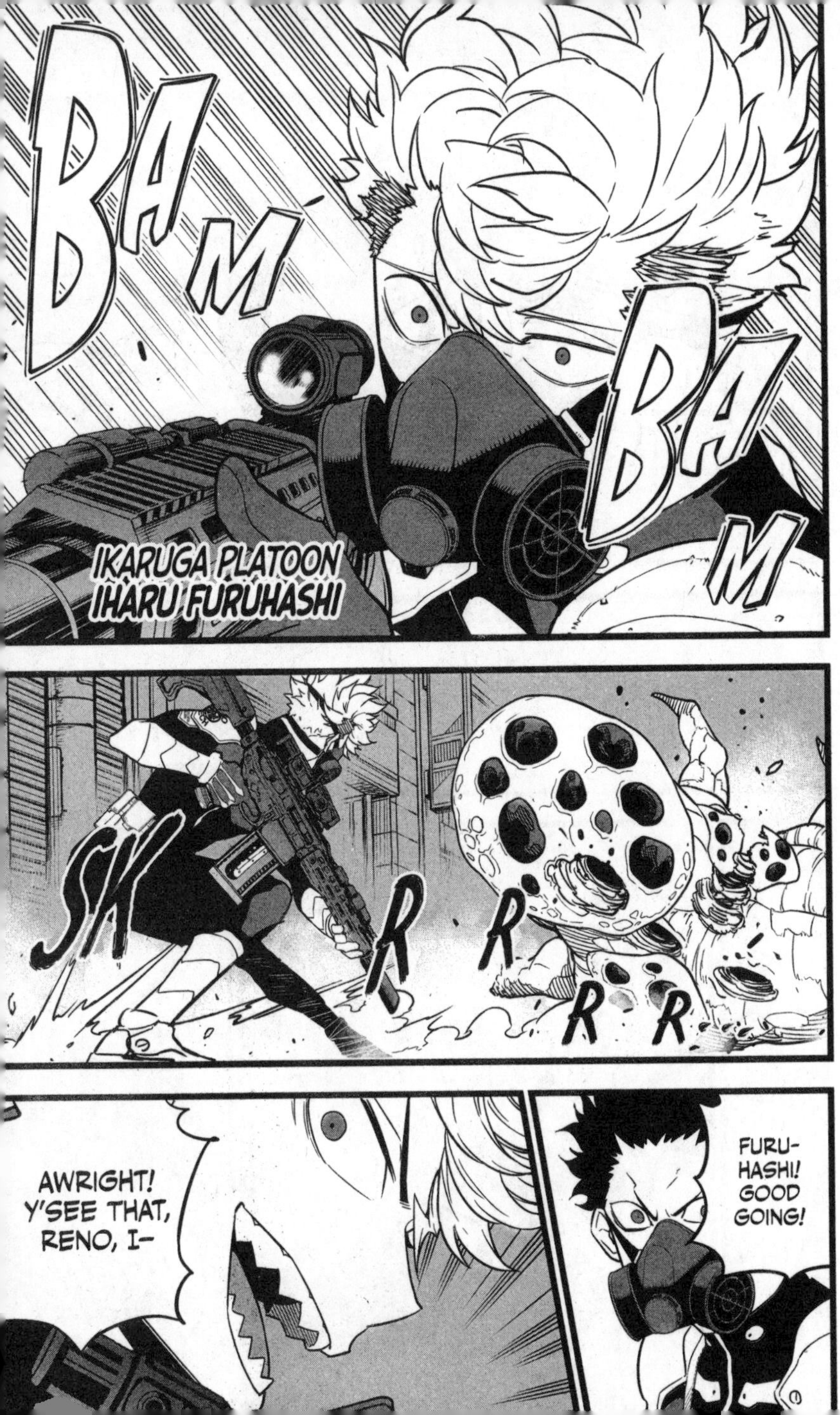
BAM
BAM
IKARUGA PLATOON
IHARU FURUHASHI
SKRRRRR
FURU-HASHI! GOOD GOING!
AWRIGHT! Y'SEE THAT, RENO, I-

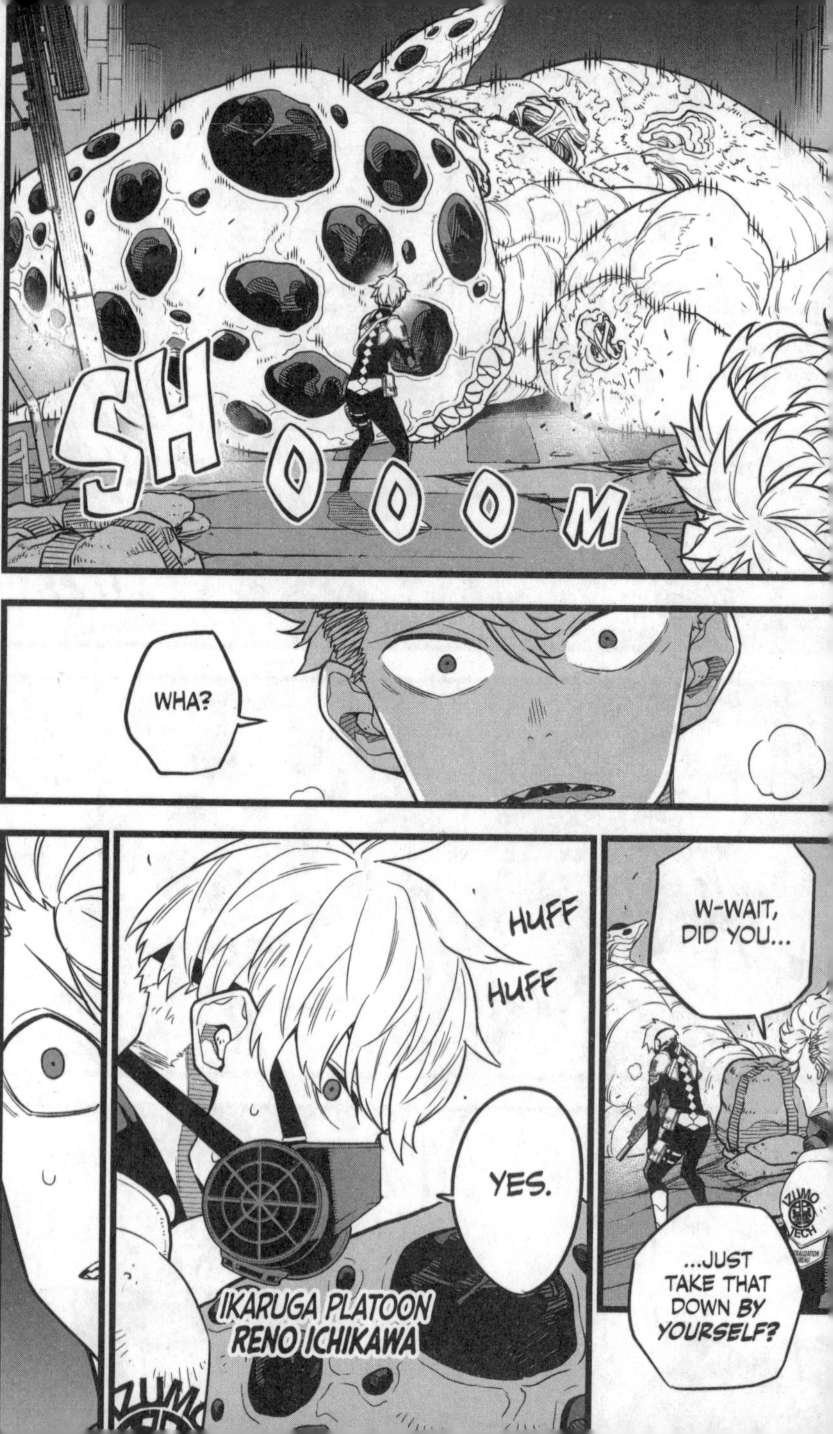
SHOOOOM
WHA?
W-WAIT, DID YOU...
...JUST TAKE THAT DOWN BY YOURSELF?
HUFF
HUFF
YES.
IKARUGA PLATOON RENO ICHIKAWA

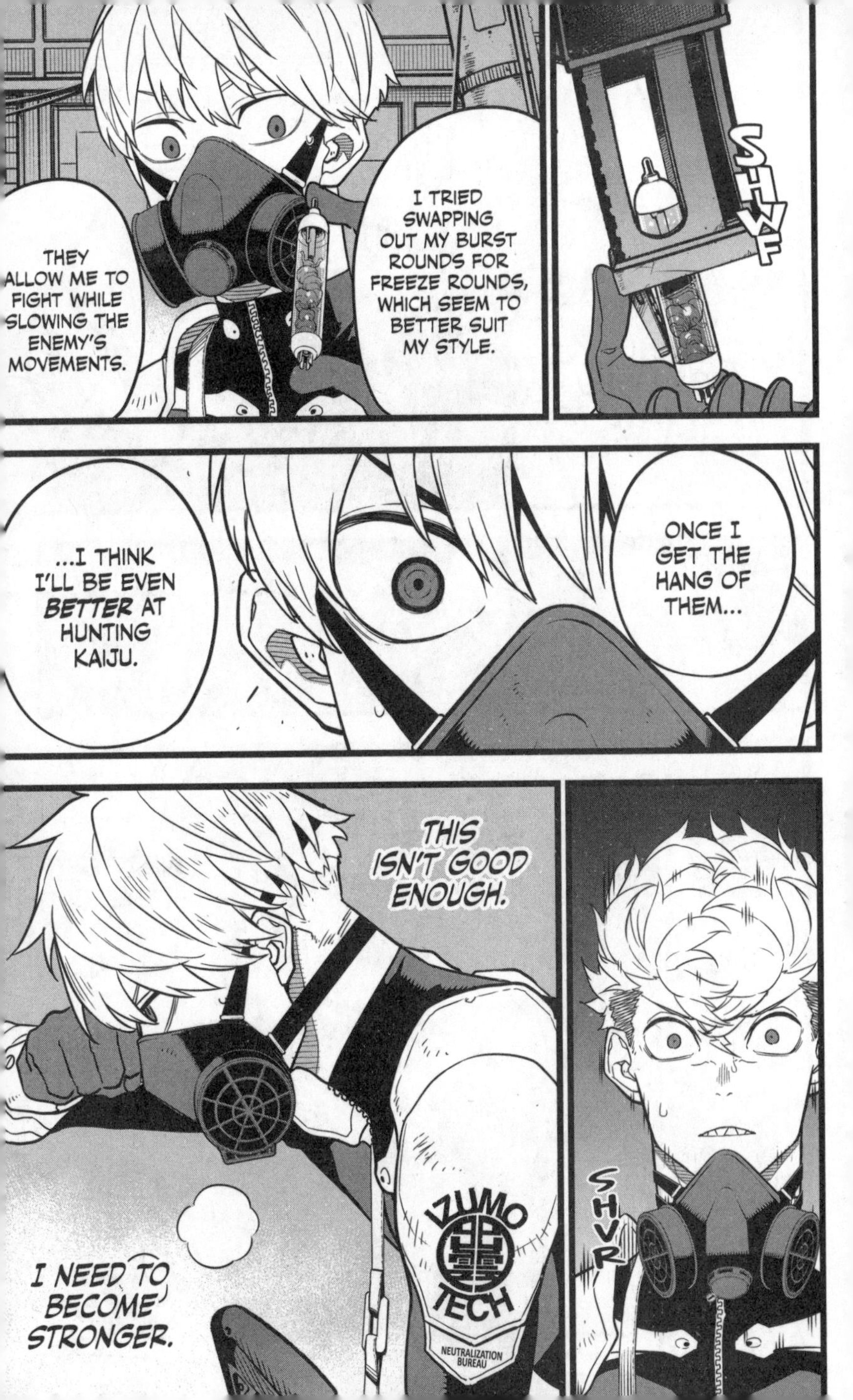
SHWF
I TRIED SWAPPING OUT MY BURST ROUNDS FOR FREEZE ROUNDS, WHICH SEEM TO BETTER SUIT MY STYLE.
THEY ALLOW ME TO FIGHT WHILE SLOWING THE ENEMY'S MOVEMENTS.
ONCE I GET THE HANG OF THEM...
...I THINK I'LL BE EVEN *BETTER* AT HUNTING KAIJU.
SHVR
THIS ISN'T GOOD ENOUGH.
IZUMO TECH
NEUTRALIZATION BUREAU
I NEED TO BECOME STRONGER.

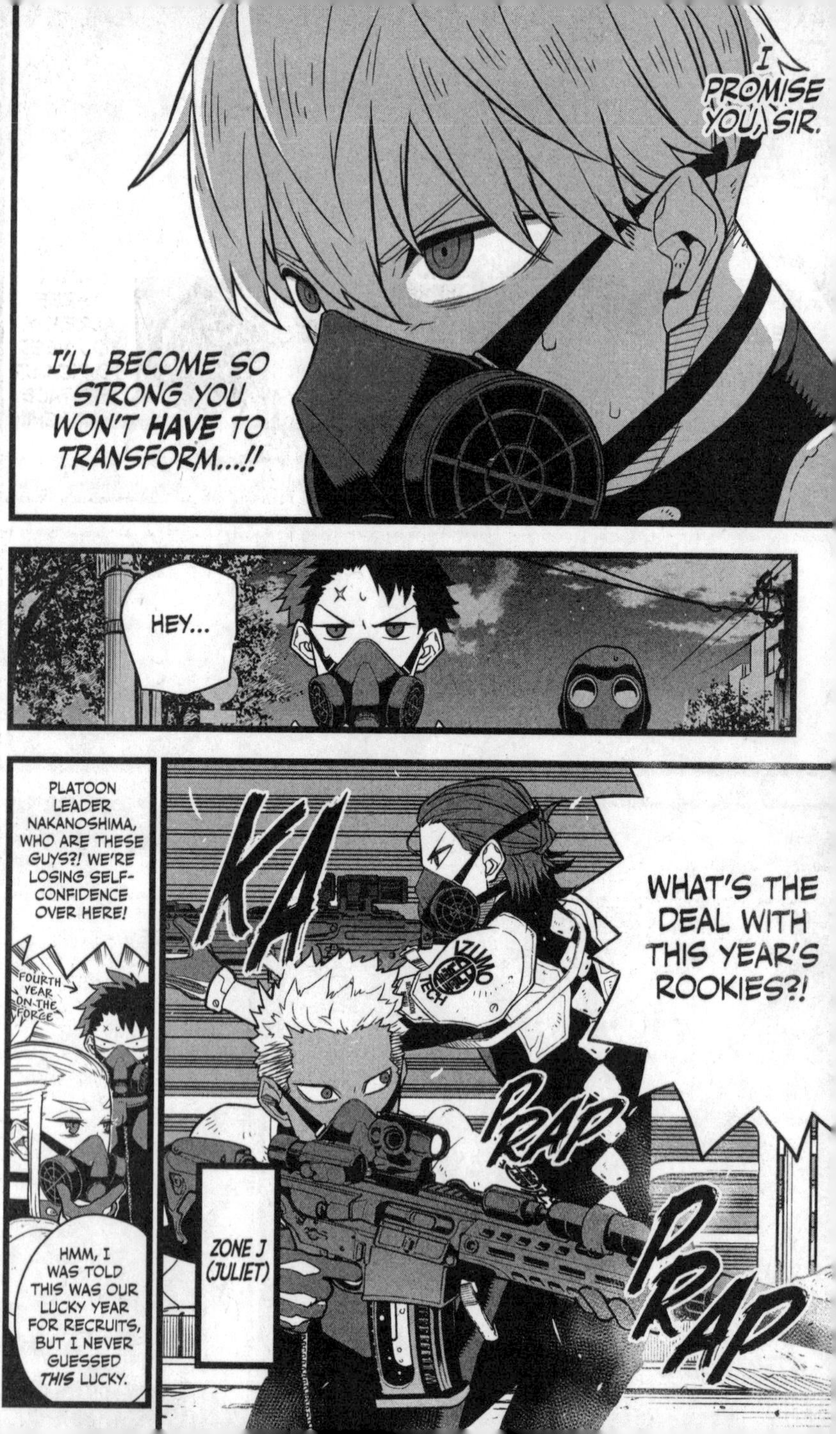
I PROMISE YOU, SIR.
I'LL BECOME SO STRONG YOU WON'T HAVE TO TRANSFORM...!!
HEY...
WHAT'S THE DEAL WITH THIS YEAR'S ROOKIES?!
KA
PLATOON LEADER NAKANOSHIMA, WHO ARE THESE GUYS?! WE'RE LOSING SELF-CONFIDENCE OVER HERE!
FOURTH YEAR ON THE FORCE
IZUMO TECH
PRAP
PRAP
ZONE J (JULIET)
HMM, I WAS TOLD THIS WAS OUR LUCKY YEAR FOR RECRUITS, BUT I NEVER GUESSED THIS LUCKY.

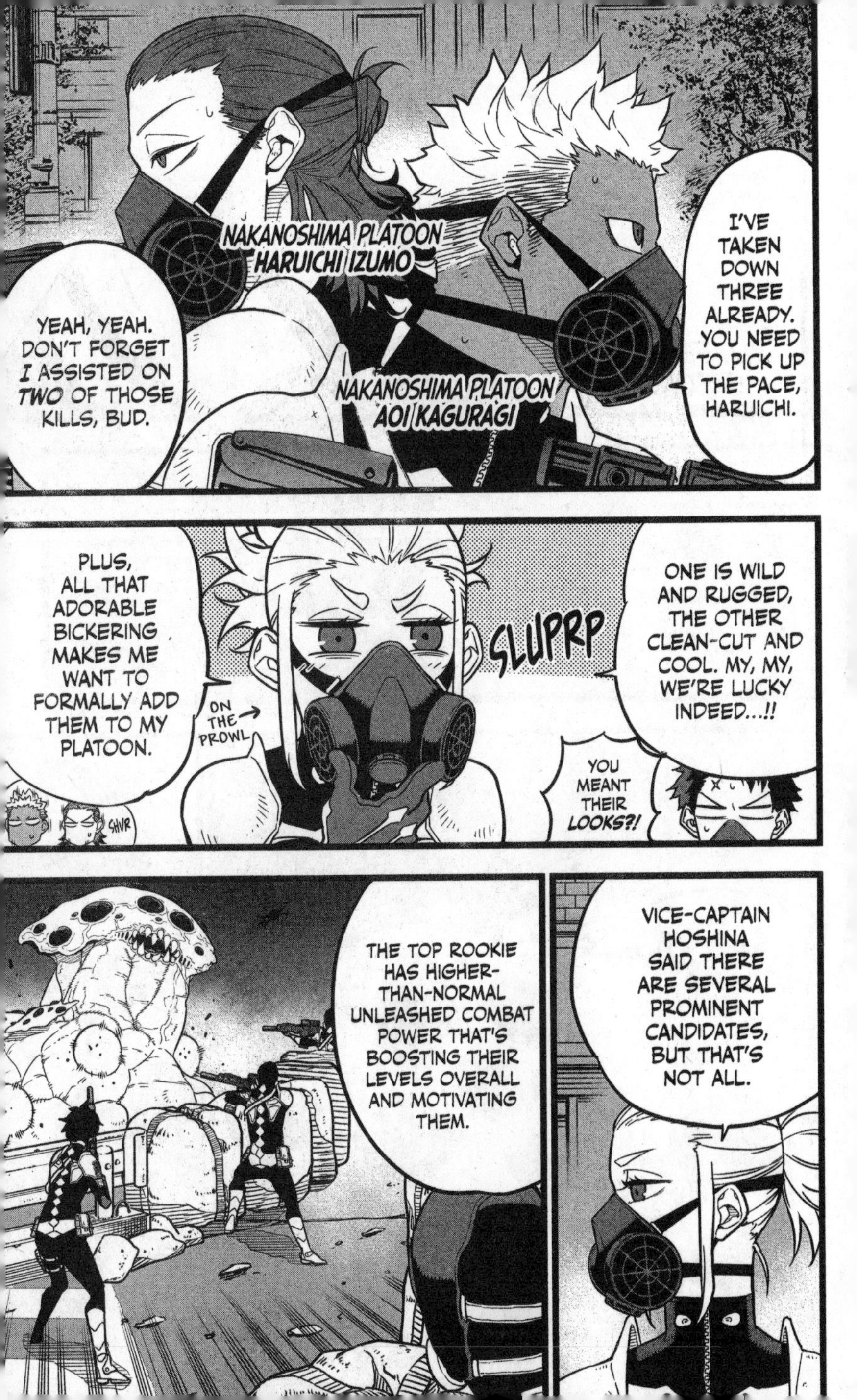
I'VE TAKEN DOWN THREE ALREADY. YOU NEED TO PICK UP THE PACE, HARUICHI.
NAKANOSHIMA PLATOON HARUICHI IZUMO
NAKANOSHIMA PLATOON AOI KAGURAGI
YEAH, YEAH. DON'T FORGET *I* ASSISTED ON *TWO* OF THOSE KILLS, BUD.
ONE IS WILD AND RUGGED, THE OTHER CLEAN-CUT AND COOL. MY, MY, WE'RE LUCKY INDEED...!!
YOU MEANT THEIR *LOOKS?!*
SLUPRP
ON THE PROWL
PLUS, ALL THAT ADORABLE BICKERING MAKES ME WANT TO FORMALLY ADD THEM TO MY PLATOON.
SHVR
VICE-CAPTAIN HOSHINA SAID THERE ARE SEVERAL PROMINENT CANDIDATES, BUT THAT'S NOT ALL.
THE TOP ROOKIE HAS HIGHER-THAN-NORMAL UNLEASHED COMBAT POWER THAT'S BOOSTING THEIR LEVELS OVERALL AND MOTIVATING THEM.

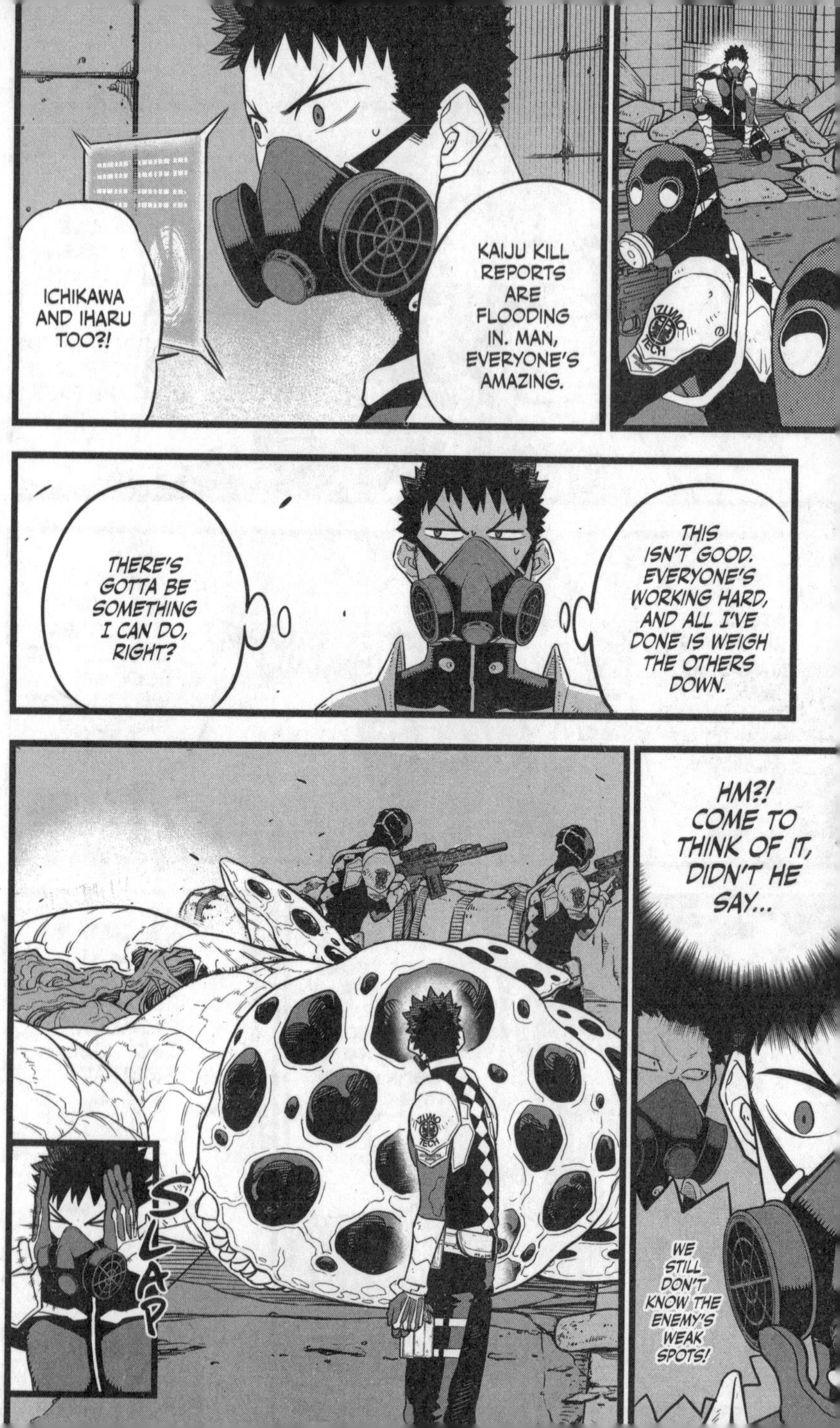
KAIJU KILL REPORTS ARE FLOODING IN. MAN, EVERYONE'S AMAZING.
ICHIKAWA AND IHARU TOO?!
THIS ISN'T GOOD. EVERYONE'S WORKING HARD, AND ALL I'VE DONE IS WEIGH THE OTHERS DOWN.
THERE'S GOTTA BE SOMETHING I CAN DO, RIGHT?
HM?! COME TO THINK OF IT, DIDN'T HE SAY...
WE STILL DON'T KNOW THE ENEMY'S WEAK SPOTS!
SLAP

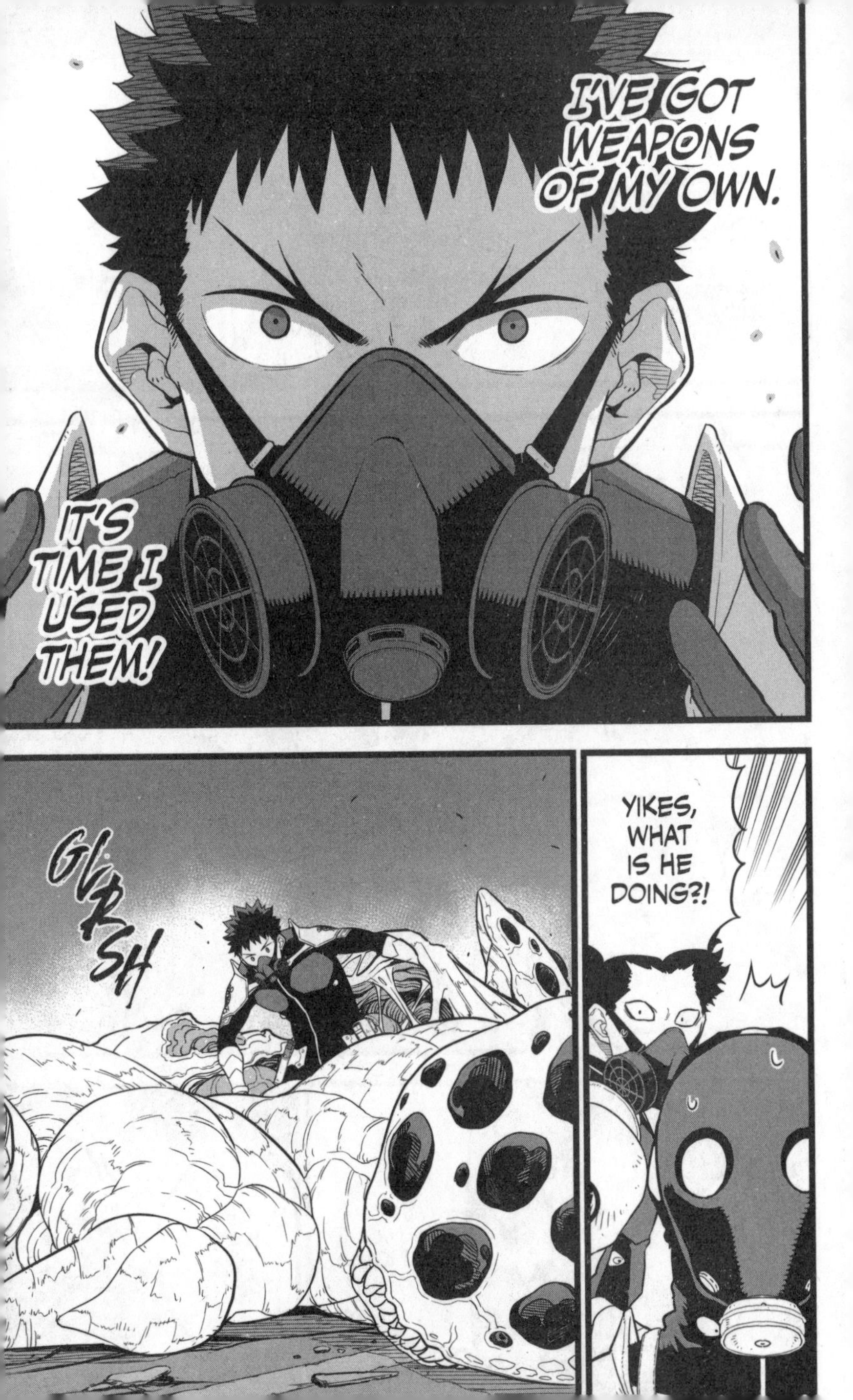
I'VE GOT WEAPONS OF MY OWN.
IT'S TIME I USED THEM!
YIKES, WHAT IS HE DOING?!
GLRSH

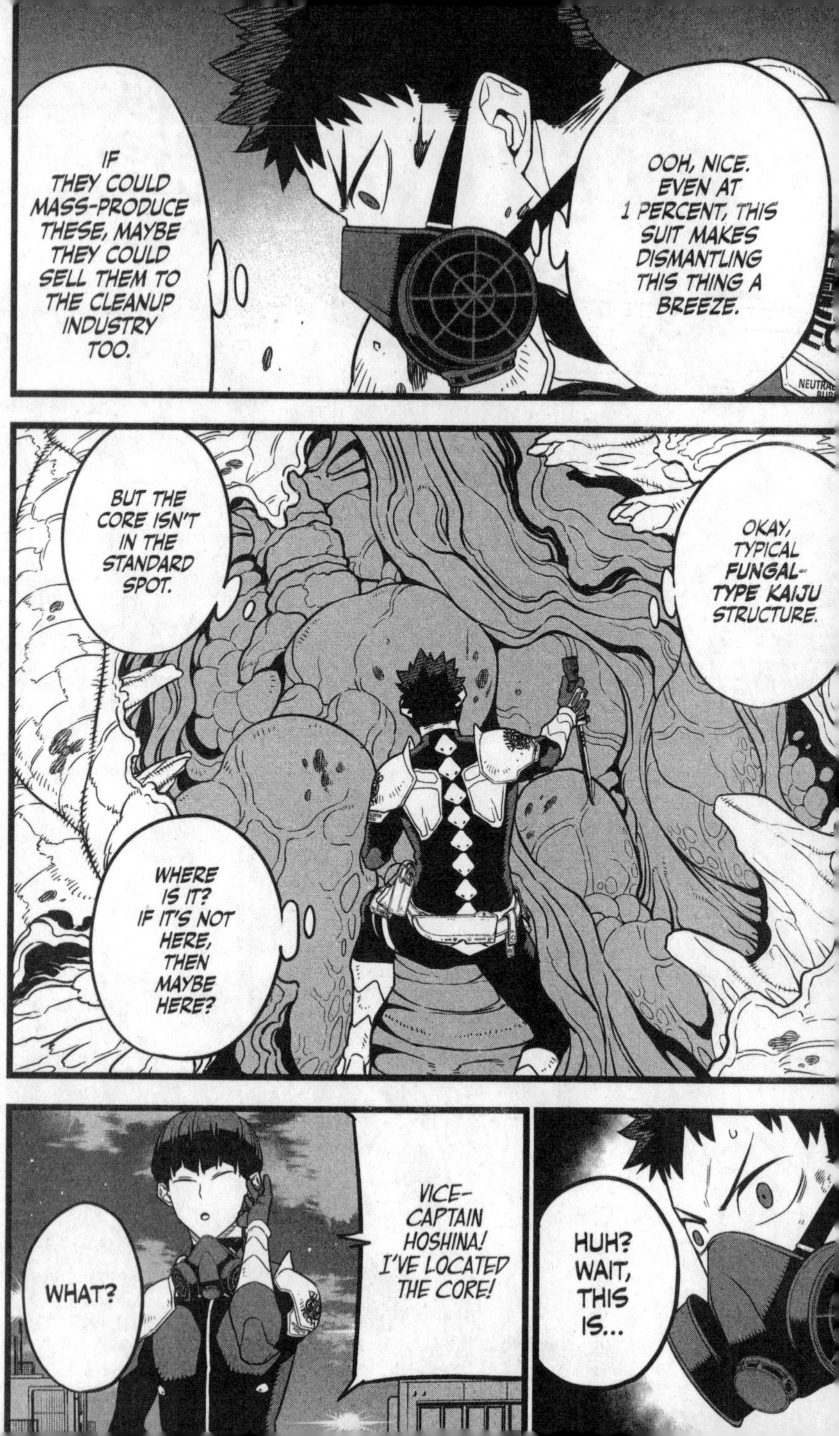
OOH, NICE. EVEN AT 1 PERCENT, THIS SUIT MAKES DISMANTLING THIS THING A BREEZE.
IF THEY COULD MASS-PRODUCE THESE, MAYBE THEY COULD SELL THEM TO THE CLEANUP INDUSTRY TOO.
OKAY, TYPICAL FUNGAL-TYPE KAIJU STRUCTURE.
BUT THE CORE ISN'T IN THE STANDARD SPOT.
WHERE IS IT? IF IT'S NOT HERE, THEN MAYBE HERE?
HUH? WAIT, THIS IS...
VICE-CAPTAIN HOSHINA! I'VE LOCATED THE CORE!
WHAT?

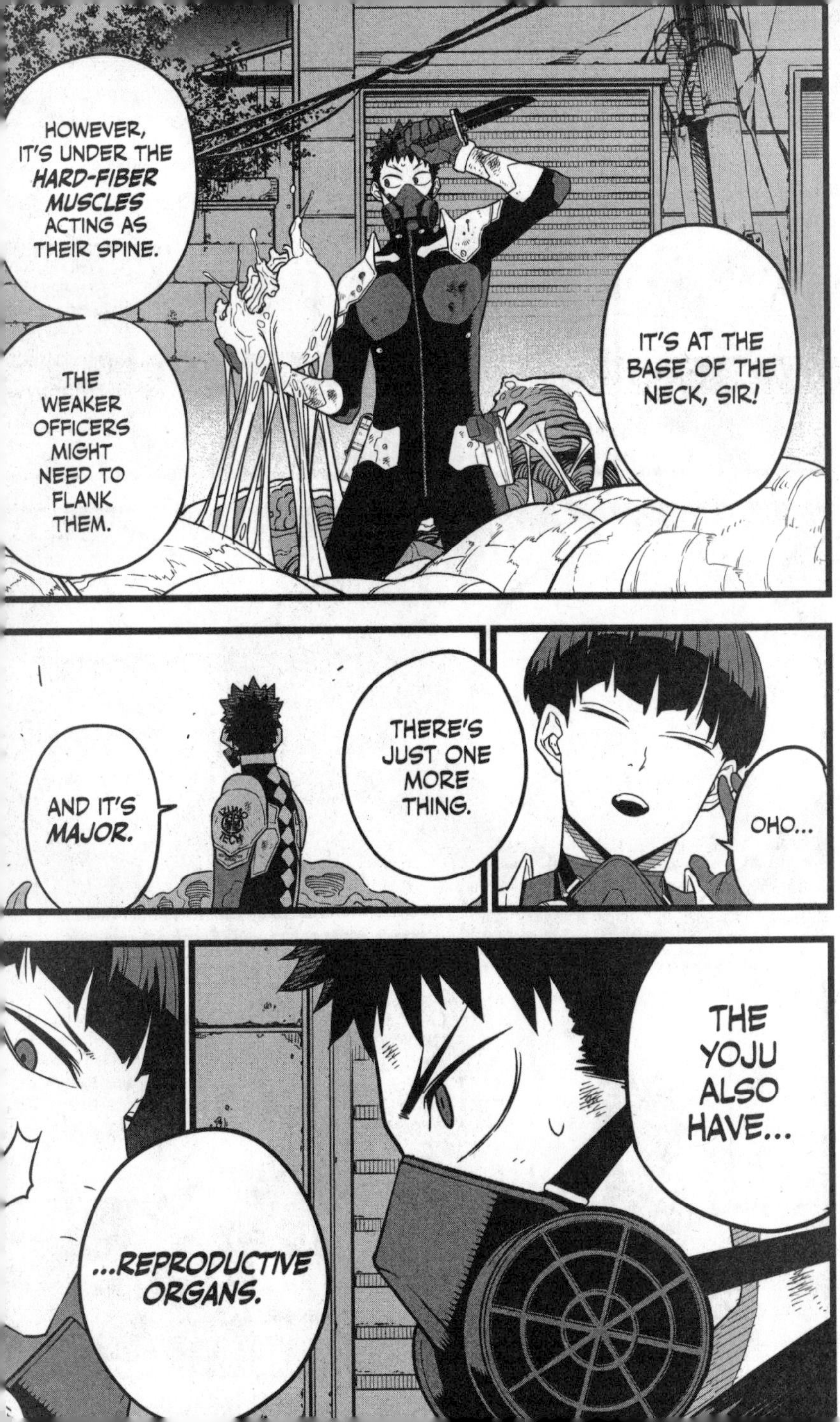
IT'S AT THE BASE OF THE NECK, SIR!
HOWEVER, IT'S UNDER THE HARD-FIBER MUSCLES ACTING AS THEIR SPINE.
THE WEAKER OFFICERS MIGHT NEED TO FLANK THEM.
OHO...
THERE'S JUST ONE MORE THING.
AND IT'S MAJOR.
THE YOJU ALSO HAVE...
...REPRODUCTIVE ORGANS.

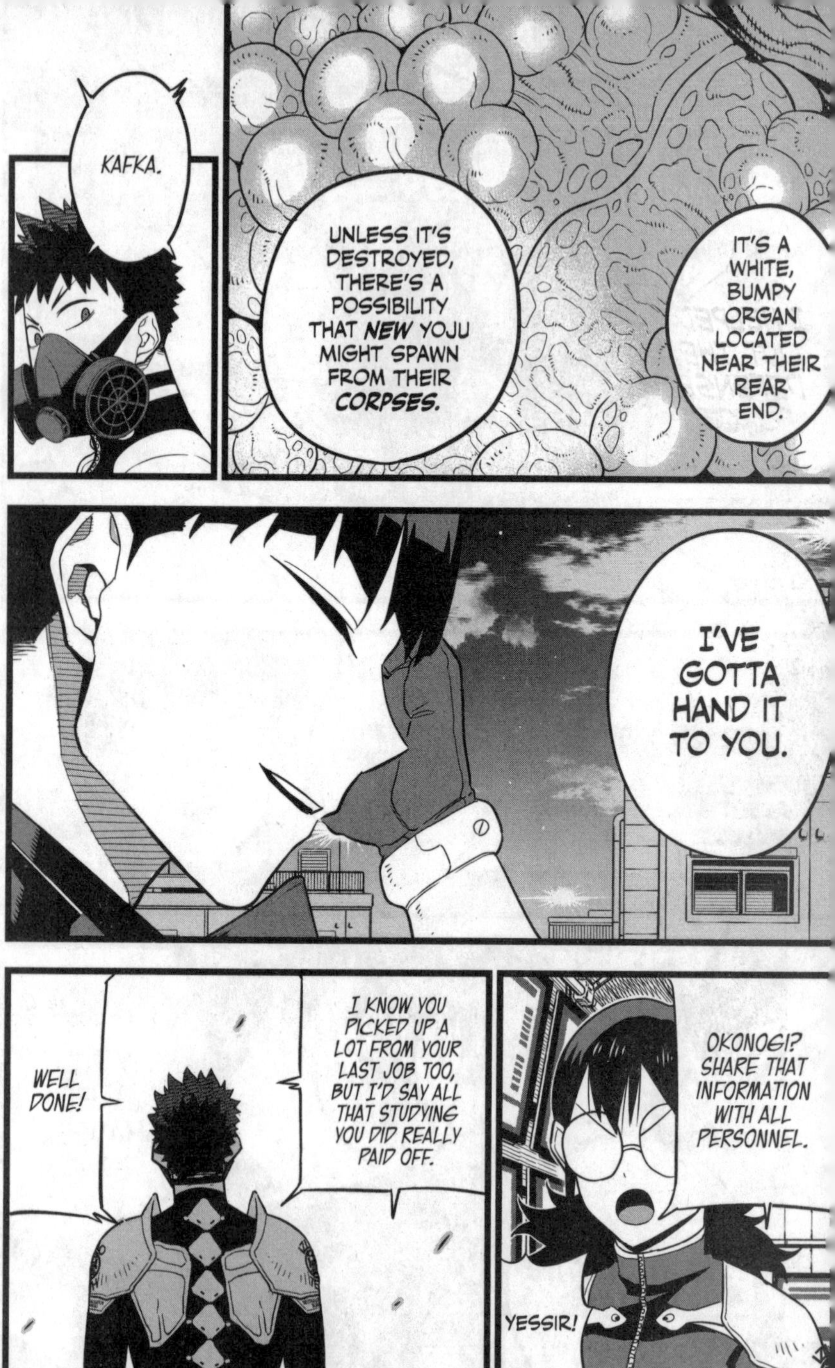
IT'S A WHITE, BUMPY ORGAN LOCATED NEAR THEIR REAR END.
UNLESS IT'S DESTROYED, THERE'S A POSSIBILITY THAT NEW YOJU MIGHT SPAWN FROM THEIR CORPSES.
KAFKA.
I'VE GOTTA HAND IT TO YOU.
OKONOGI? SHARE THAT INFORMATION WITH ALL PERSONNEL.
YESSIR!
I KNOW YOU PICKED UP A LOT FROM YOUR LAST JOB TOO, BUT I'D SAY ALL THAT STUDYING YOU DID REALLY PAID OFF.
WELL DONE!

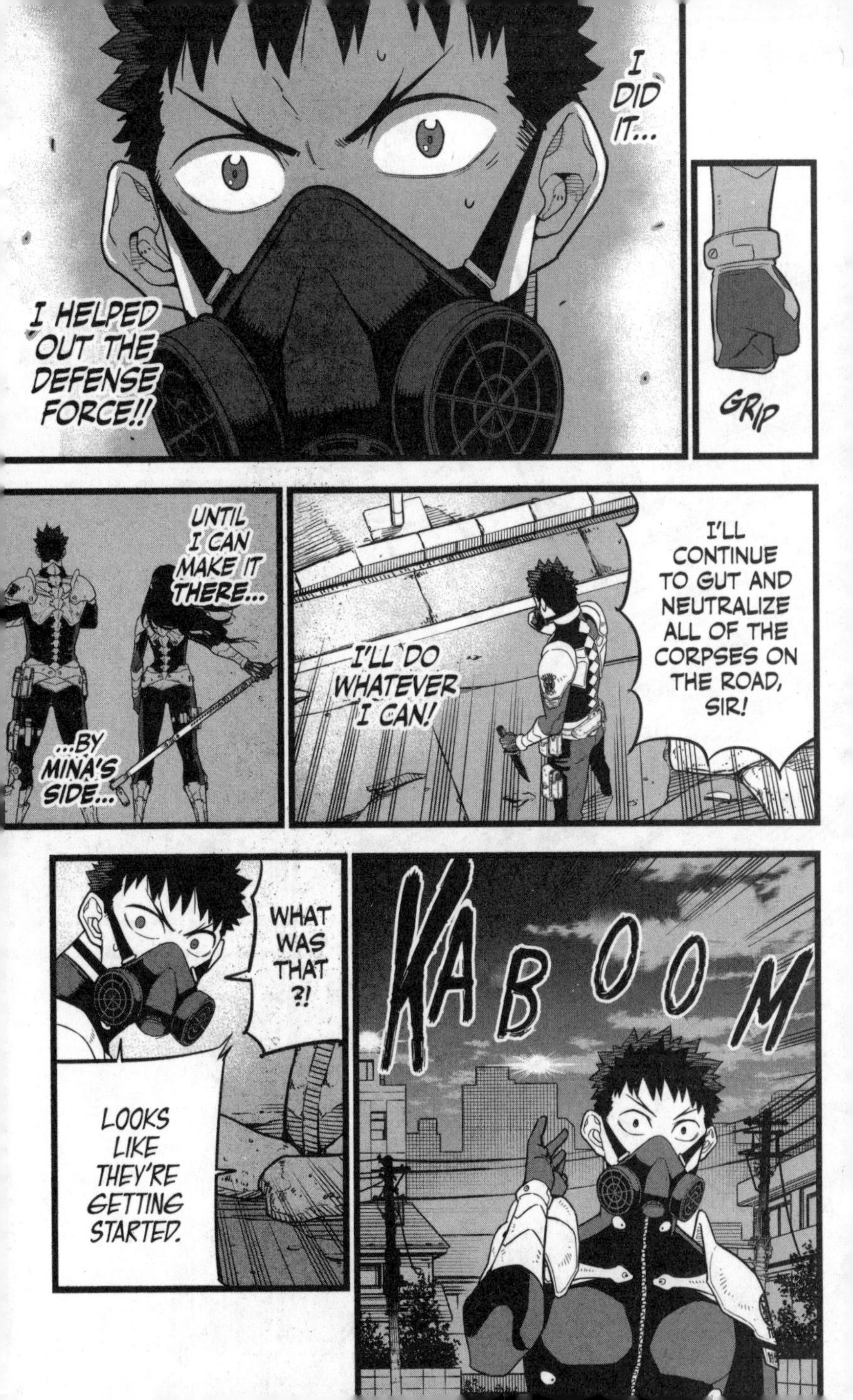
GRIP
I DID IT...
I HELPED OUT THE DEFENSE FORCE!!
I'LL CONTINUE TO GUT AND NEUTRALIZE ALL OF THE CORPSES ON THE ROAD, SIR!
I'LL DO WHATEVER I CAN!
UNTIL I CAN MAKE IT THERE...
...BY MINA'S SIDE...
KABOOM
WHAT WAS THAT?!
LOOKS LIKE THEY'RE GETTING STARTED.

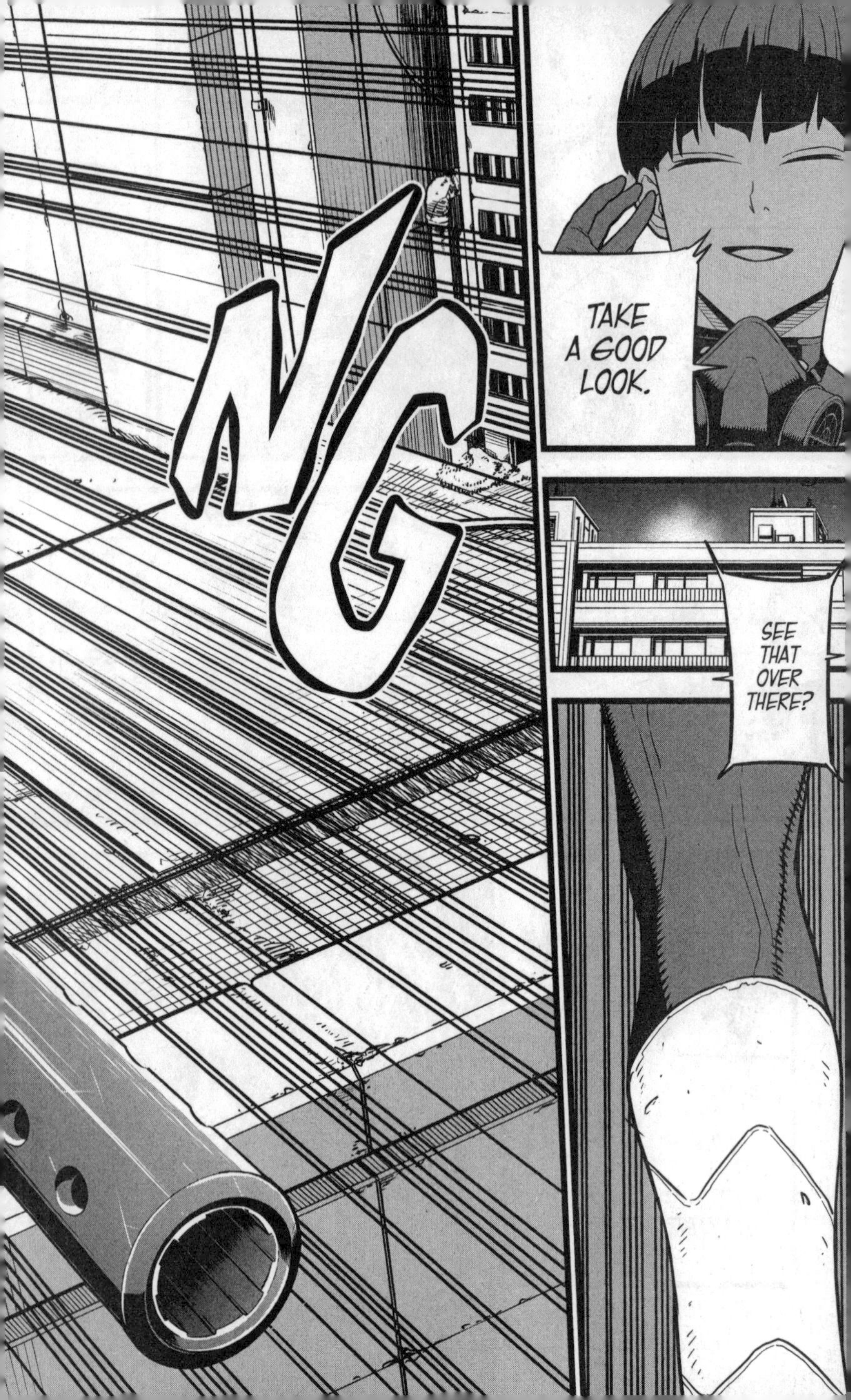
TAKE A GOOD LOOK.
SEE THAT OVER THERE?
NG

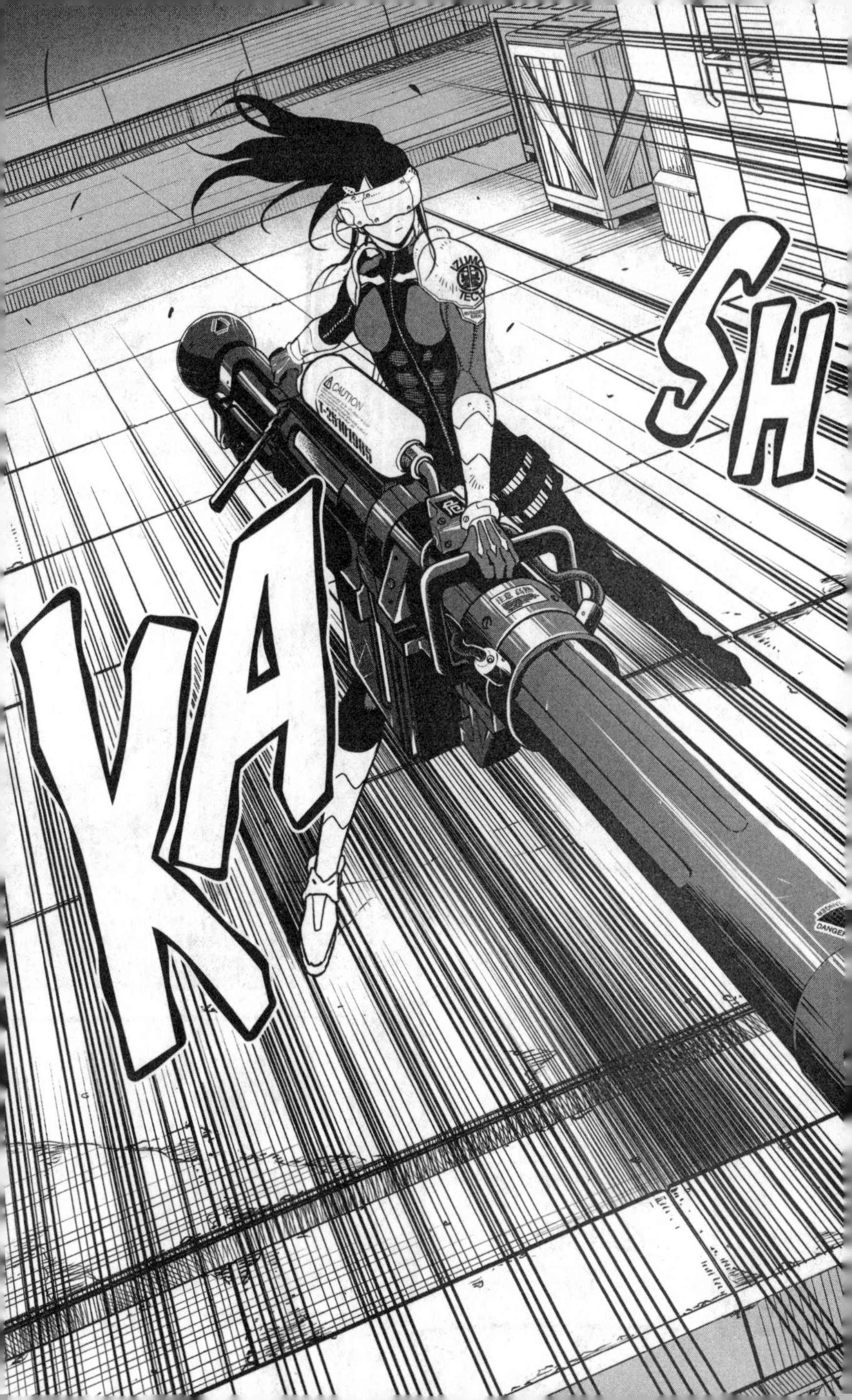
KA
SH
CAUTION
T-25101905
DANGER

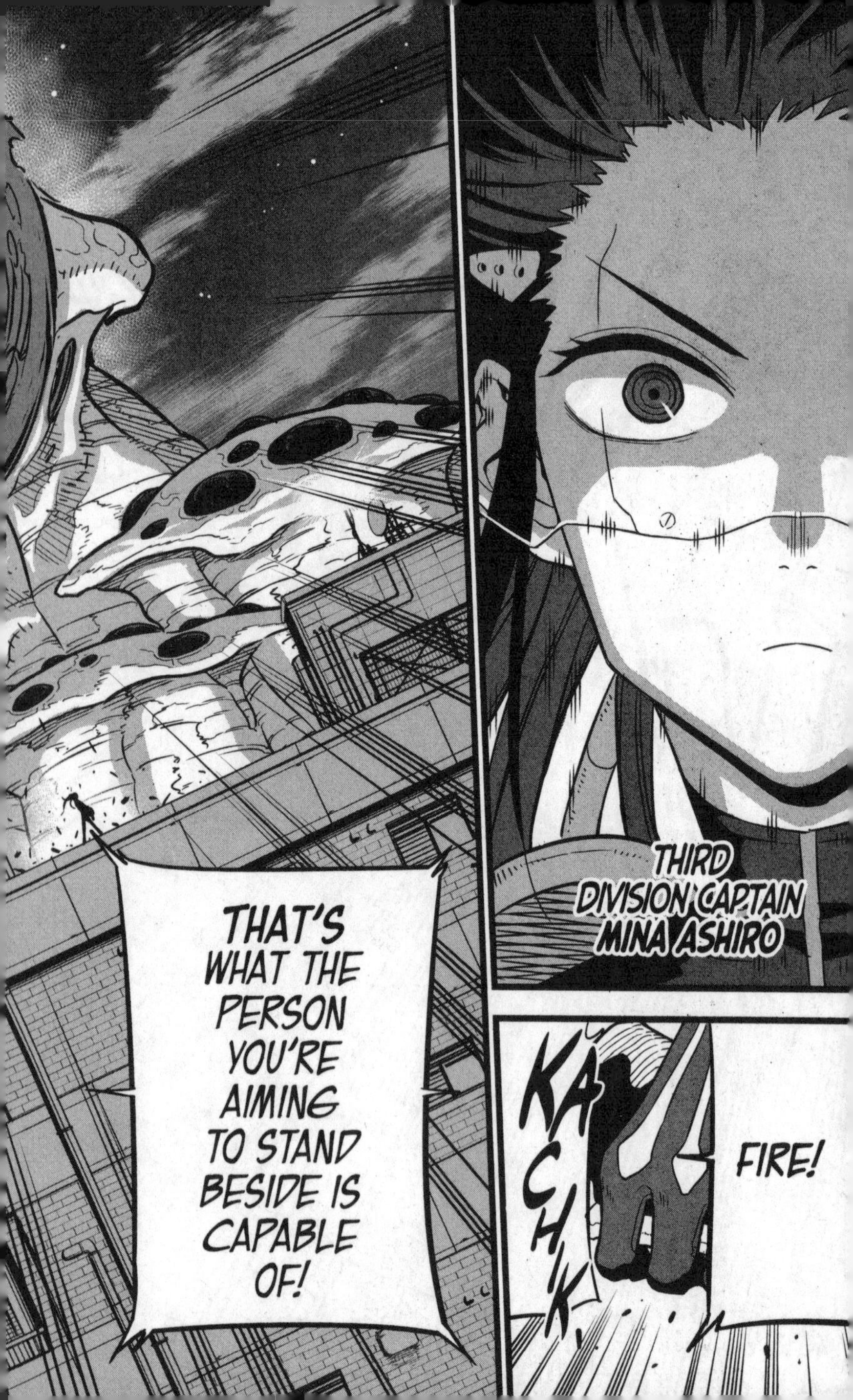
THIRD DIVISION CAPTAIN MINA ASHIRO
KACHIK
FIRE!
THAT'S WHAT THE PERSON YOU'RE AIMING TO STAND BESIDE IS CAPABLE OF!

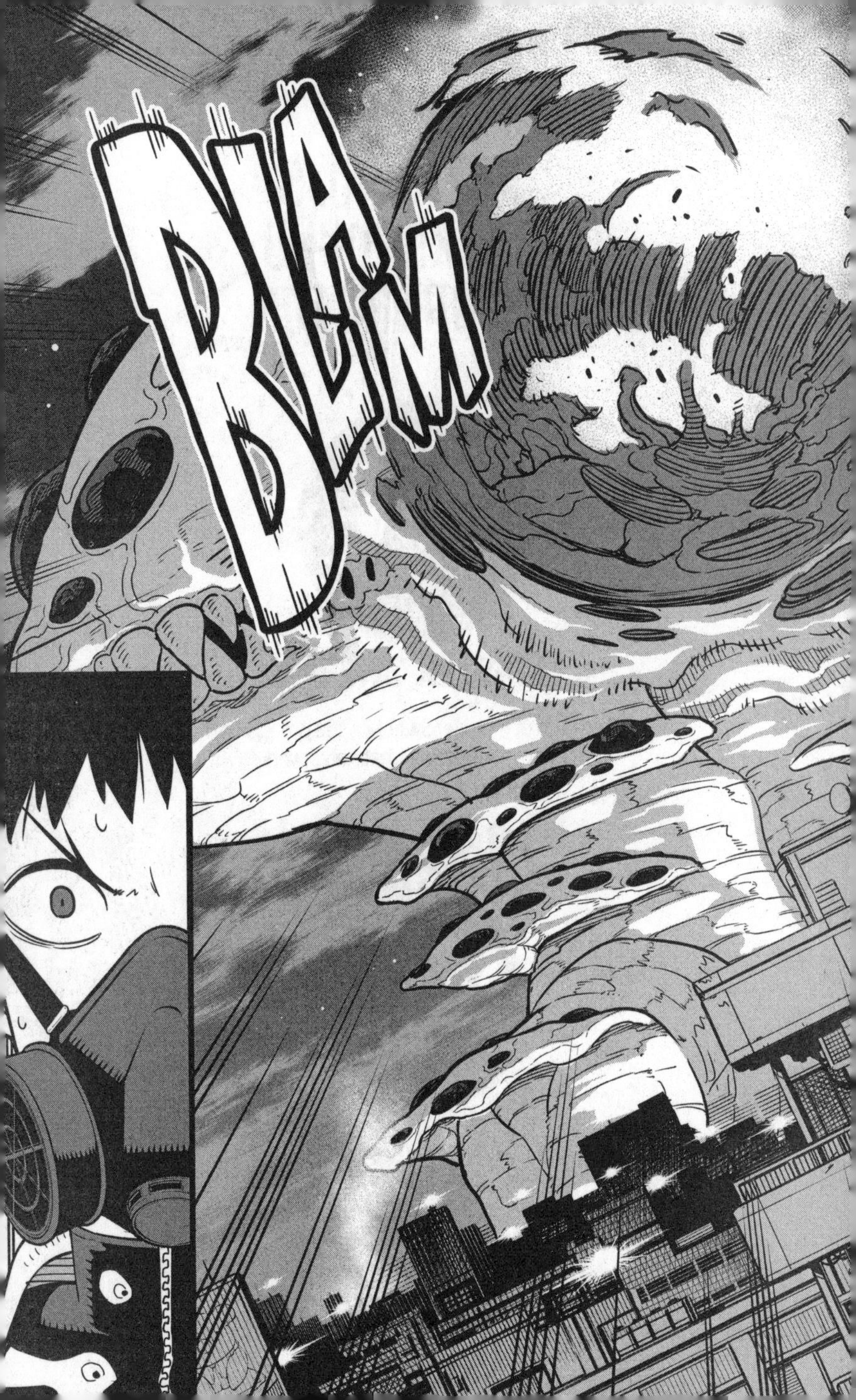
BLEM

KAIJU NO. 8
BACKGROUND
INFORMATION

MONSTER SWEEPER

The logo of Monster Sweeper, the professional kaiju cleaning company that Kafka worked for.

The logo of Izumo Tech, manufacturers of anti-kaiju weaponry. This is featured on the shoulder part of the suits.

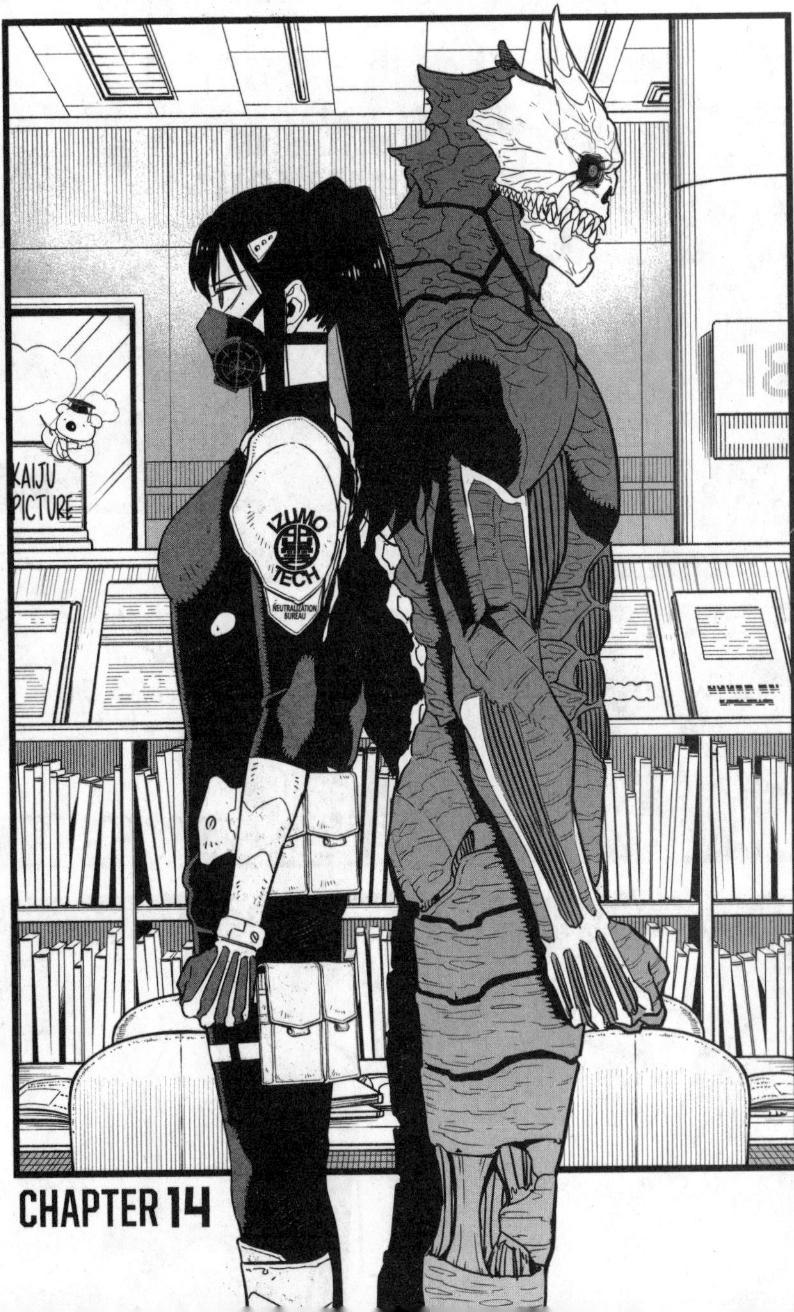
KAIJU
PICTURE
IZUMO
TECH
NEUTRALIZATION
BUREAU
18

CHAPTER 14

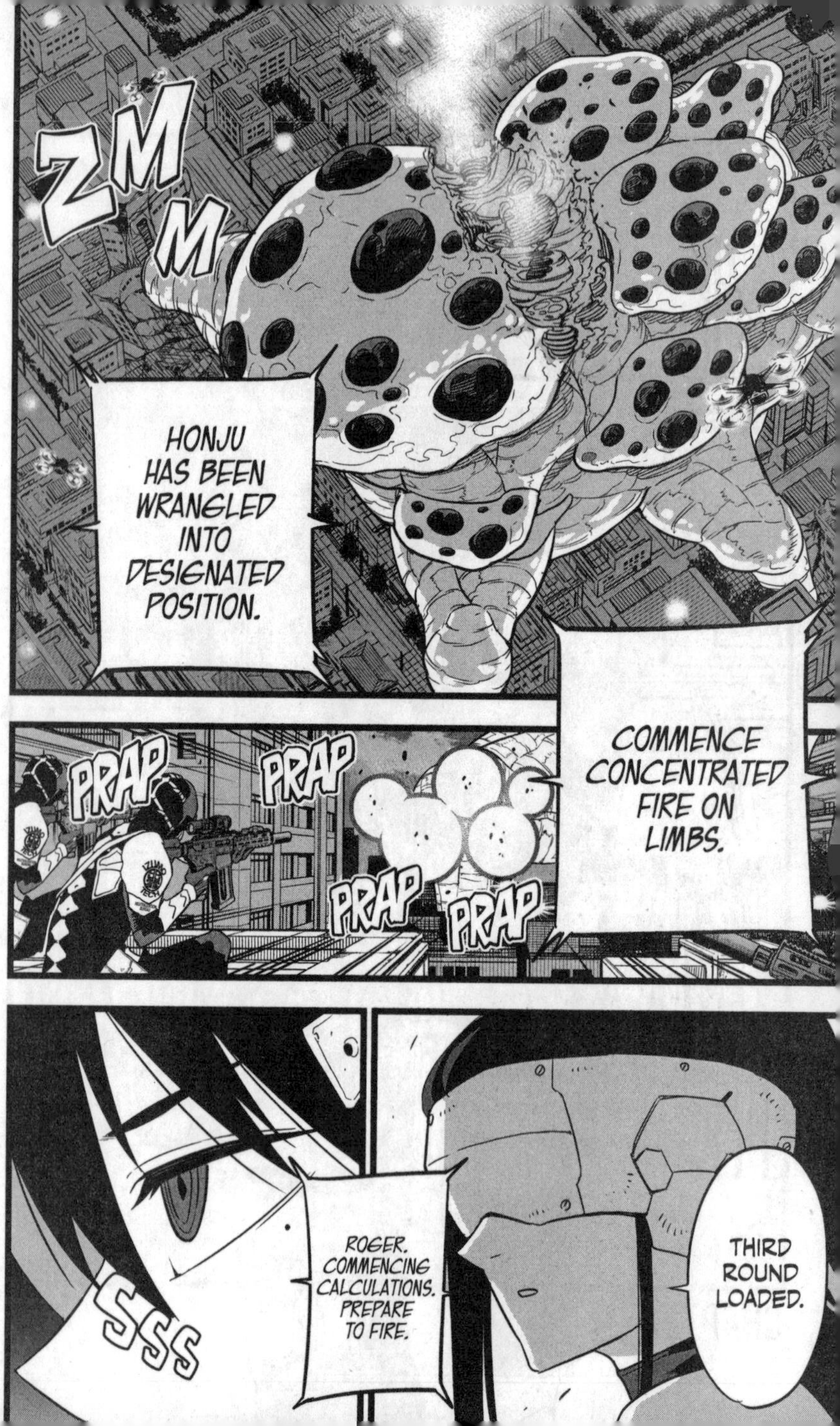
ZMMM
HONJU HAS BEEN WRANGLED INTO DESIGNATED POSITION.
COMMENCE CONCENTRATED FIRE ON LIMBS.
PRAP
PRAP
PRAP
PRAP
THIRD ROUND LOADED.
ROGER. COMMENCING CALCULATIONS. PREPARE TO FIRE.
SSS

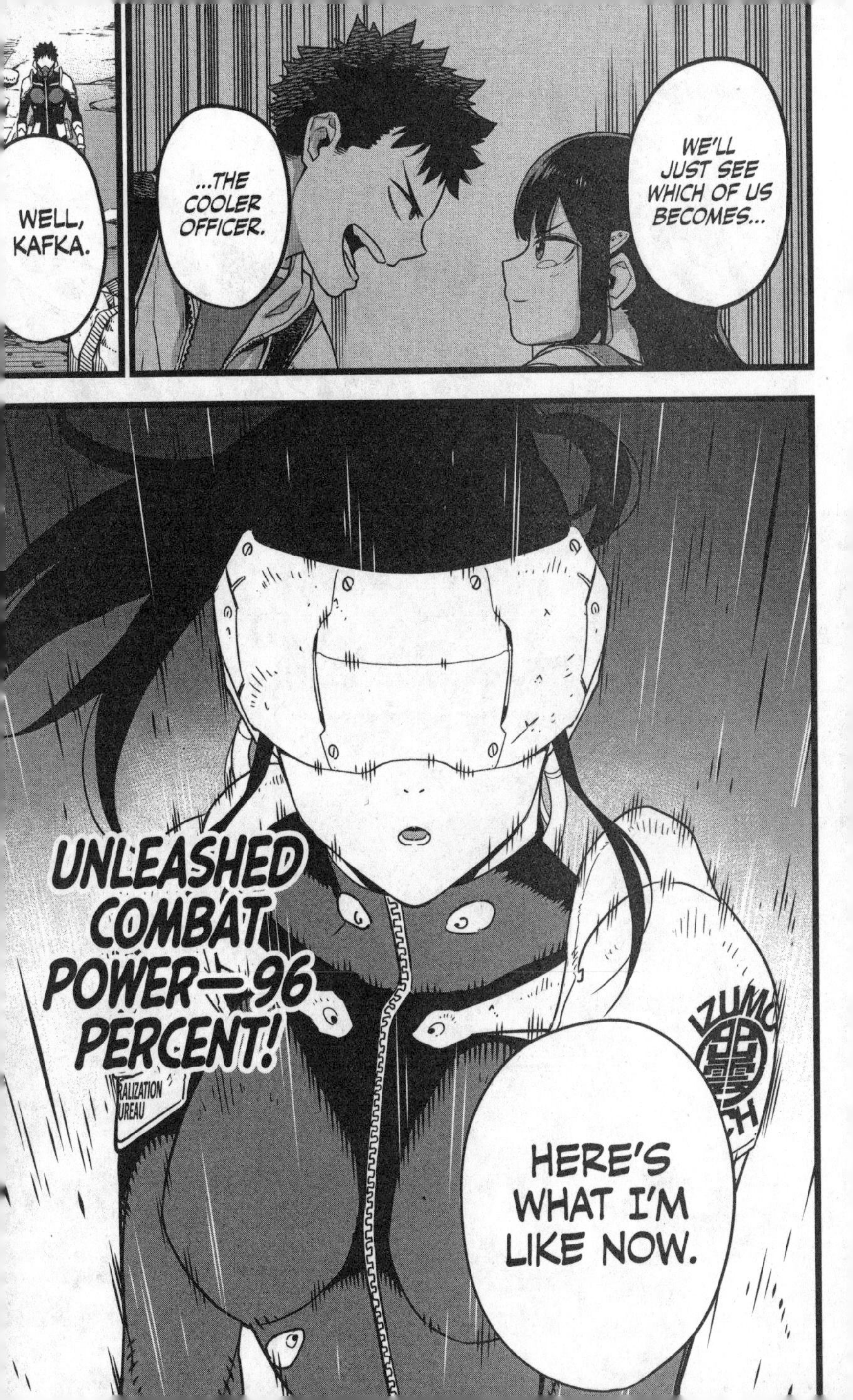
WE'LL JUST SEE WHICH OF US BECOMES...
...THE COOLER OFFICER.
WELL, KAFKA.
UNLEASHED COMBAT POWER—96 PERCENT!
IZUMO
HERE'S WHAT I'M LIKE NOW.

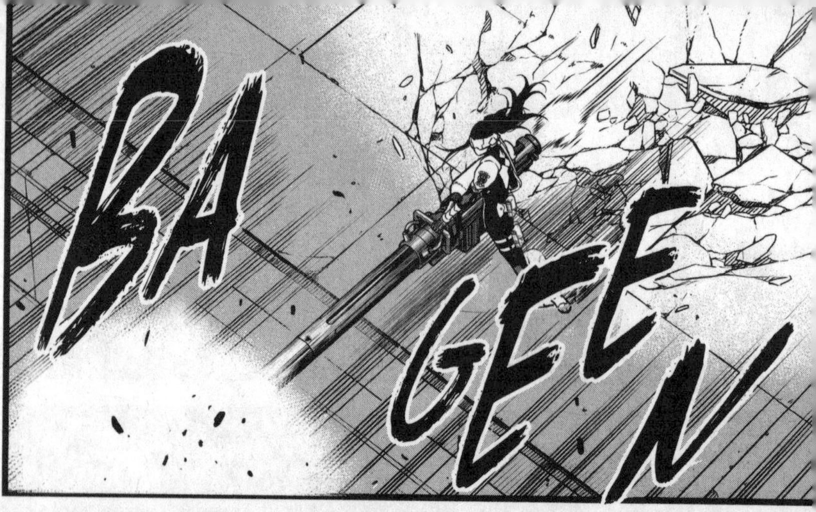
BAGEEN
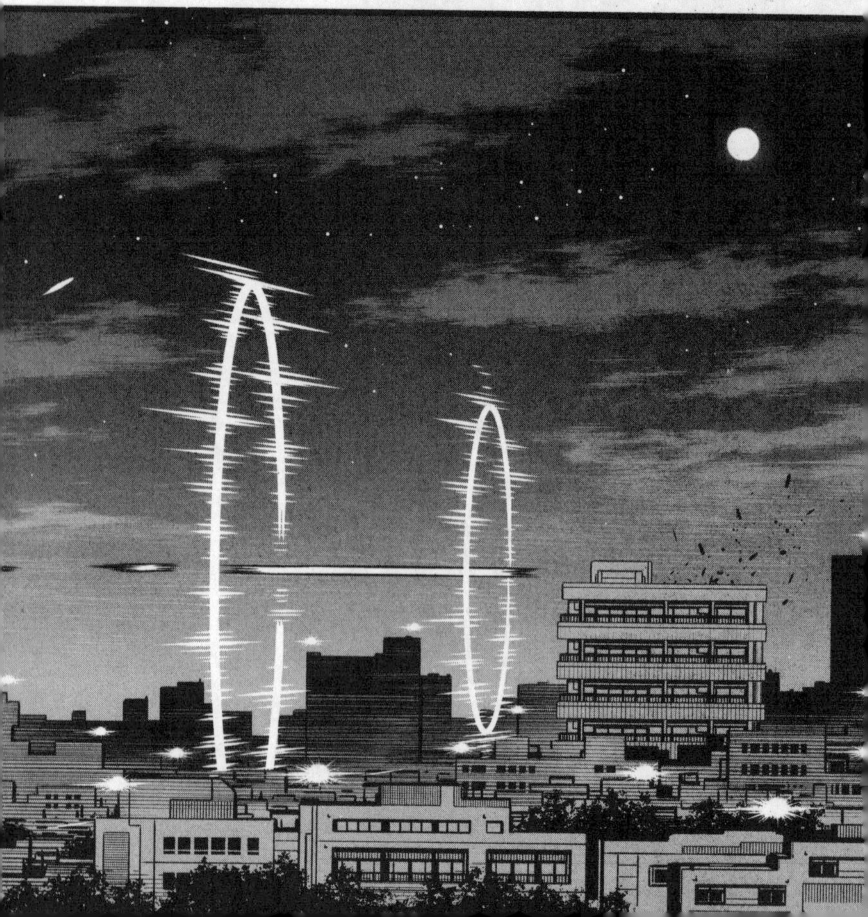

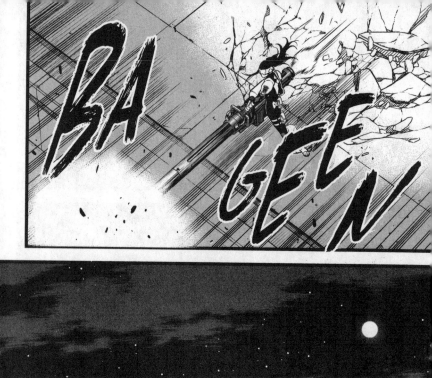

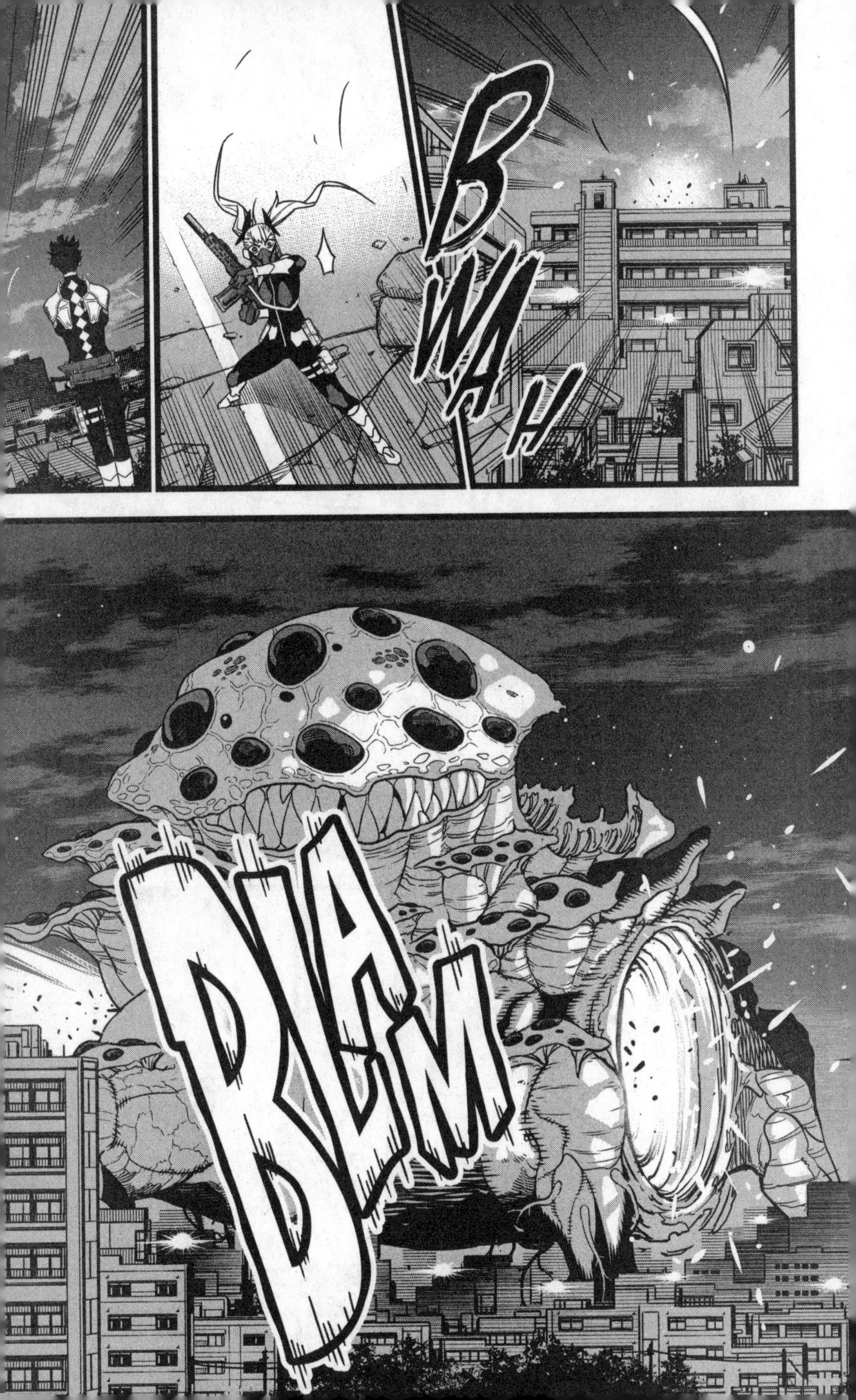
BWAHH
BLAM

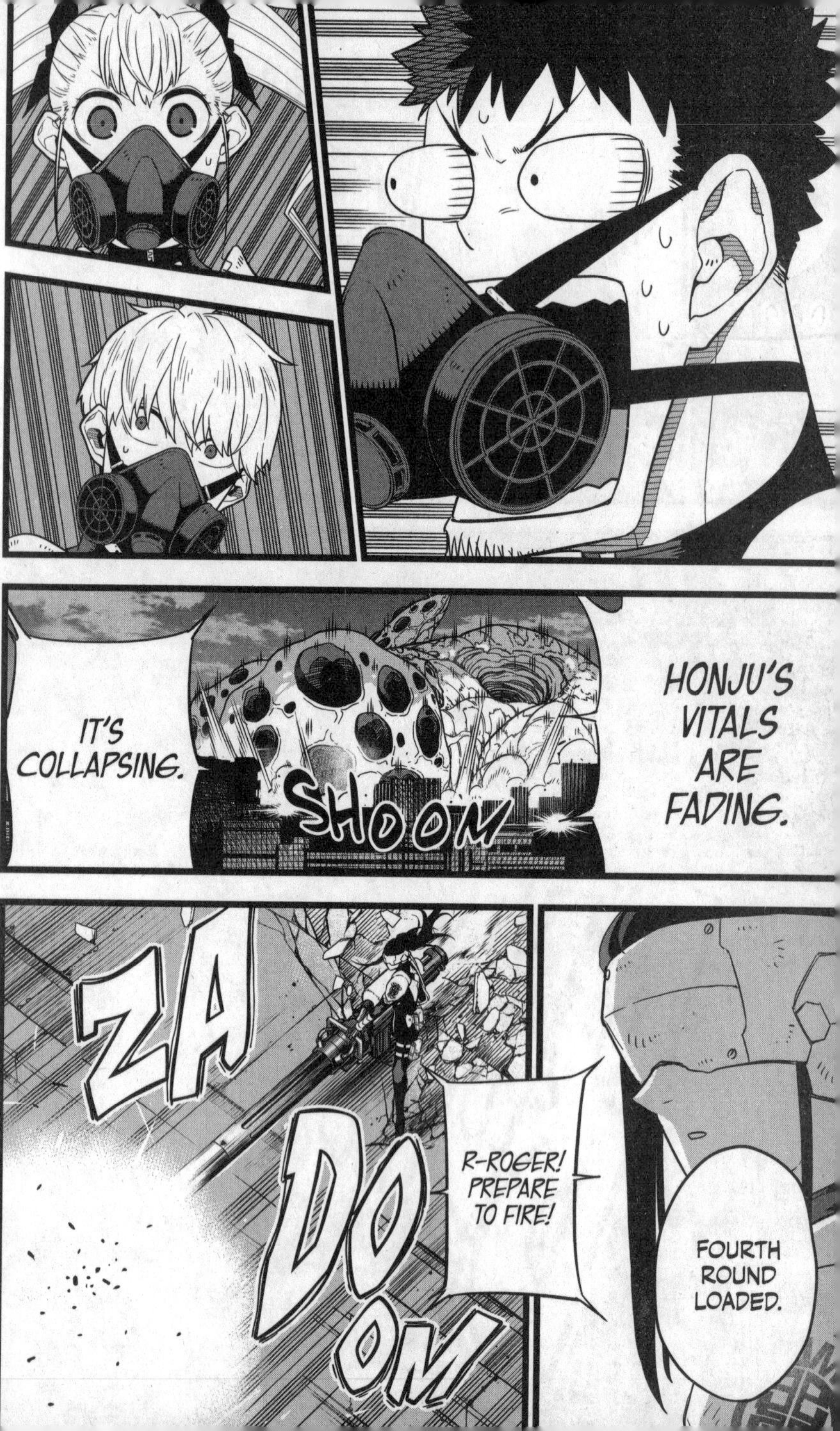
HONJU'S VITALS ARE FADING.
IT'S COLLAPSING.
SHOOM
FOURTH ROUND LOADED.
R-ROGER! PREPARE TO FIRE!
ZA
DOOM

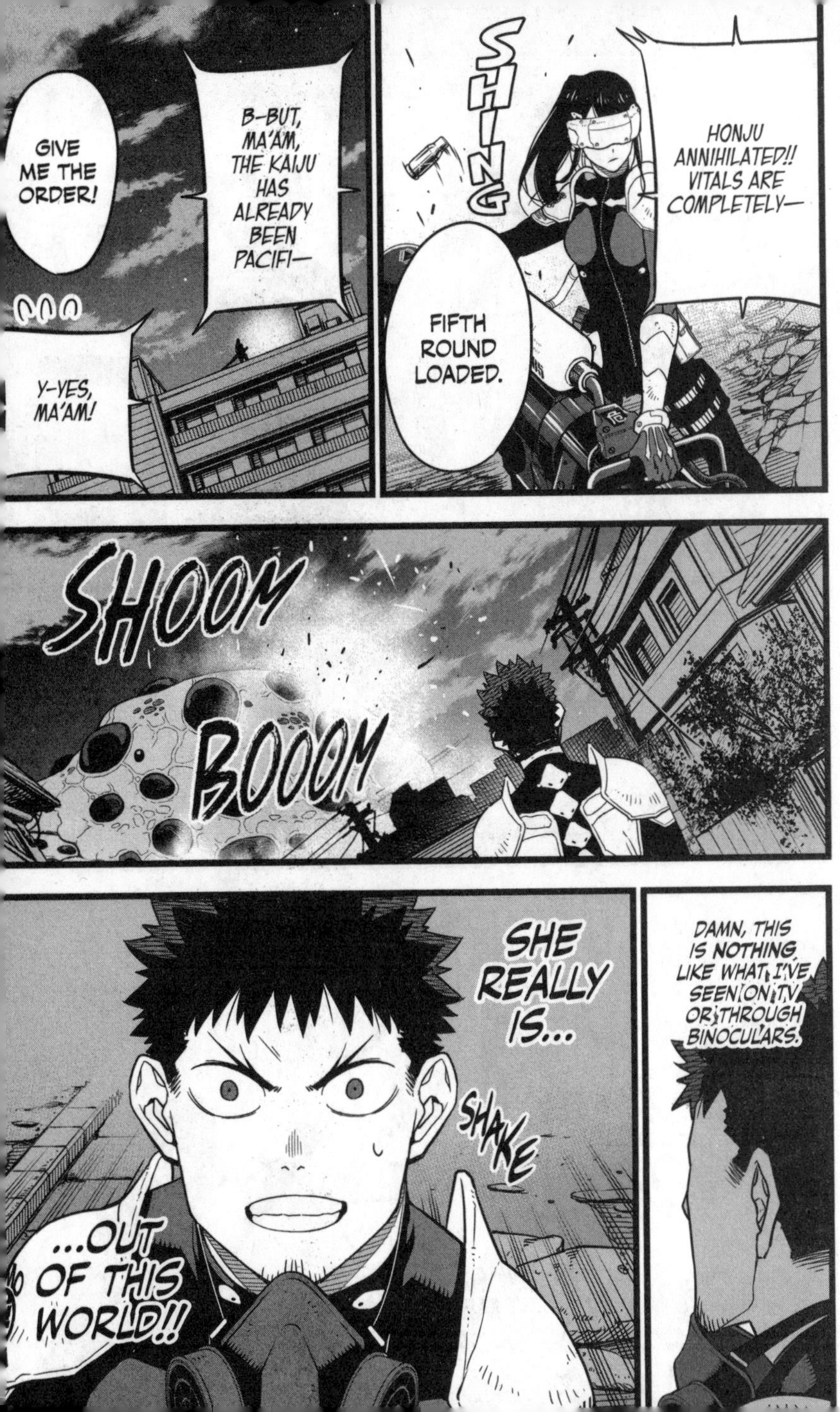
HONJU ANNIHILATED!! VITALS ARE COMPLETELY—
SHING
FIFTH ROUND LOADED.
B-BUT, MA'AM, THE KAIJU HAS ALREADY BEEN PACIFI—
GIVE ME THE ORDER!
Y-YES, MA'AM!
SHOOM
BOOOM
DAMN, THIS IS NOTHING LIKE WHAT I'VE SEEN ON TV OR THROUGH BINOCULARS.
SHE REALLY IS...
SHAKE
...OUT OF THIS WORLD!!

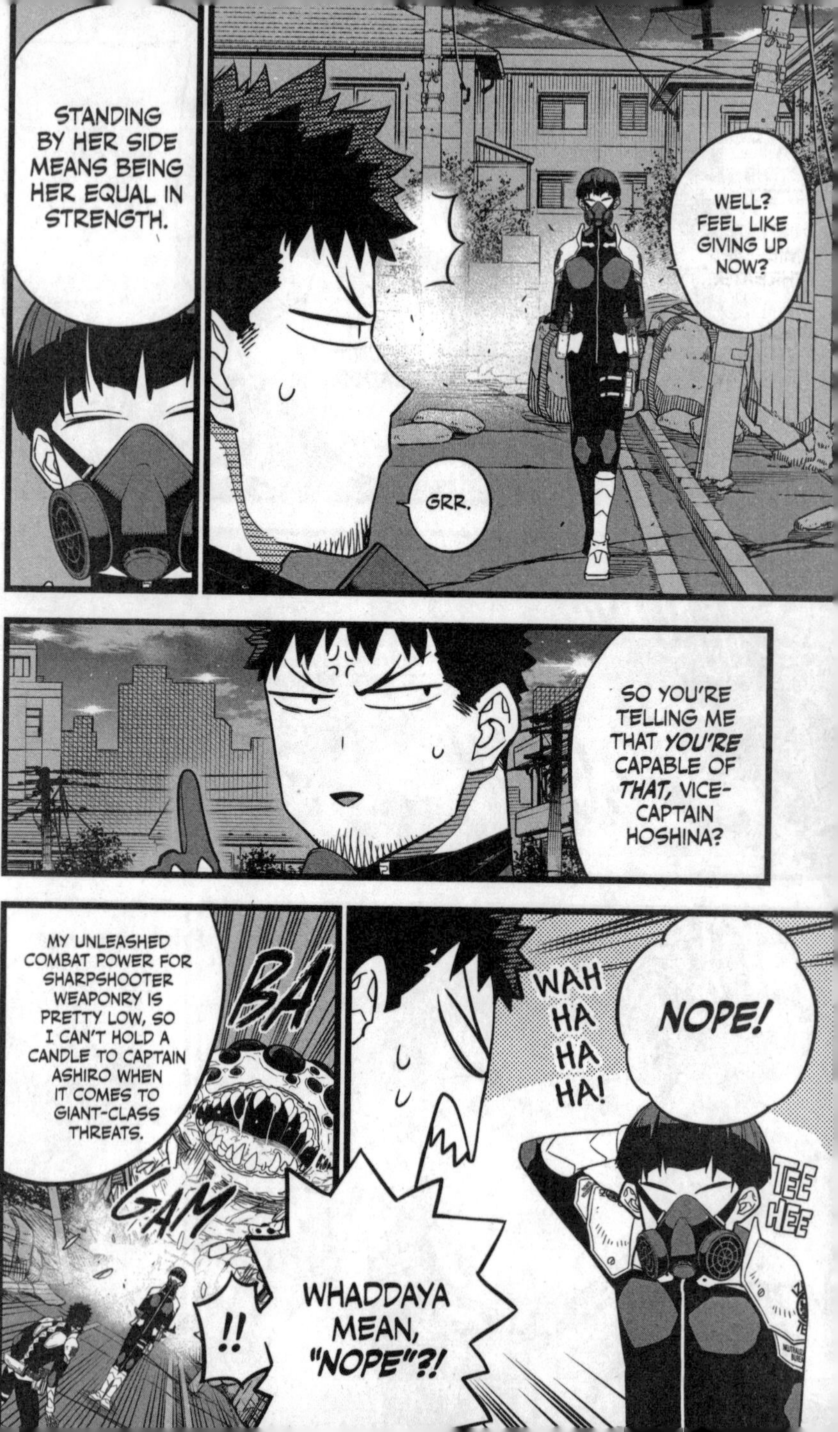
WELL? FEEL LIKE GIVING UP NOW?
GRR.
STANDING BY HER SIDE MEANS BEING HER EQUAL IN STRENGTH.
SO YOU'RE TELLING ME THAT *YOU'RE* CAPABLE OF *THAT,* VICE-CAPTAIN HOSHINA?
NOPE!
WAH HA HA HA!
TEE HEE
WHADDAYA MEAN, "*NOPE*"?!
MY UNLEASHED COMBAT POWER FOR SHARPSHOOTER WEAPONRY IS PRETTY LOW, SO I CAN'T HOLD A CANDLE TO CAPTAIN ASHIRO WHEN IT COMES TO GIANT-CLASS THREATS.
BA
GAM
!!

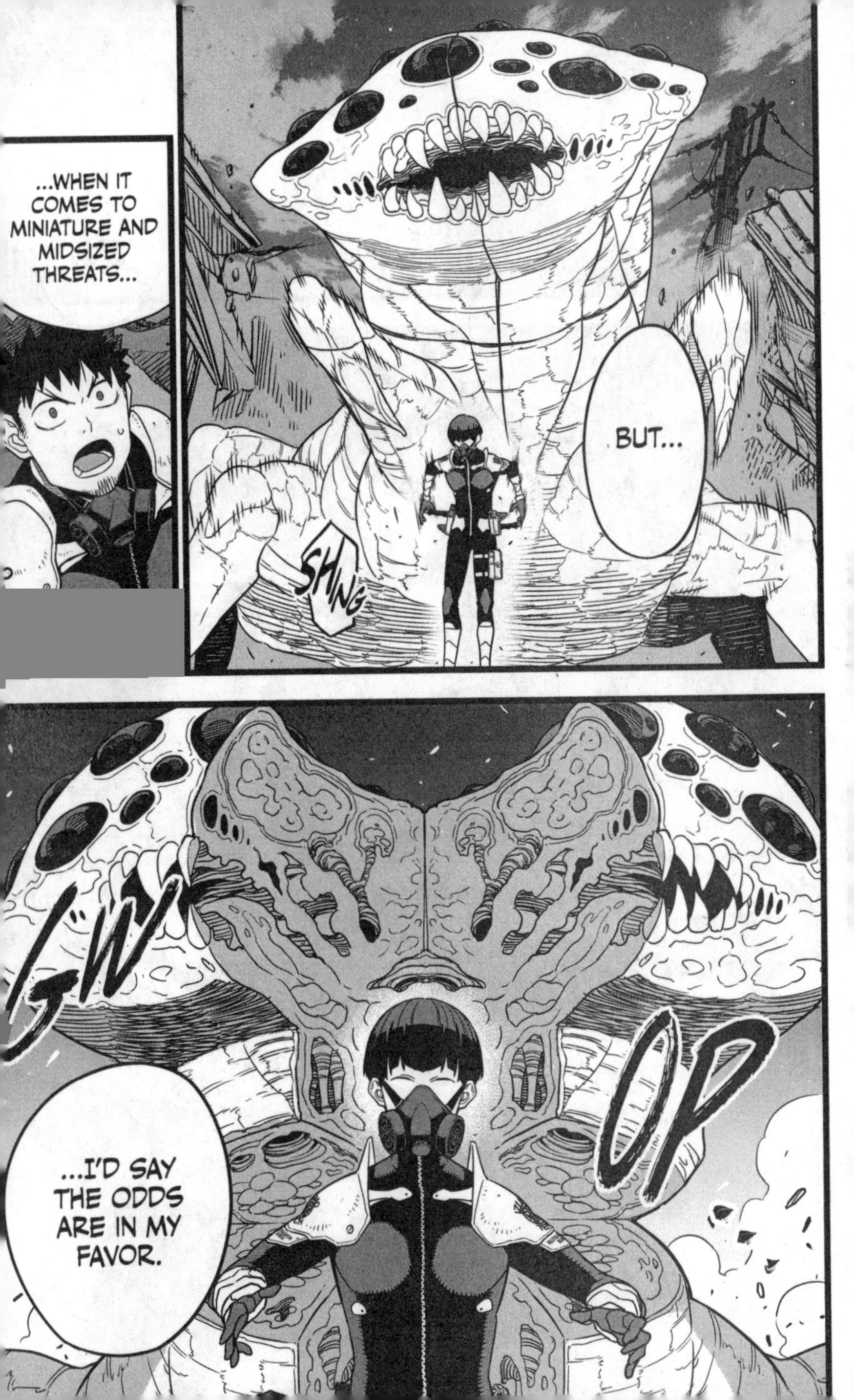
BUT...
SHING
...WHEN IT COMES TO MINIATURE AND MIDSIZED THREATS...
GWOP
...I'D SAY THE ODDS ARE IN MY FAVOR.

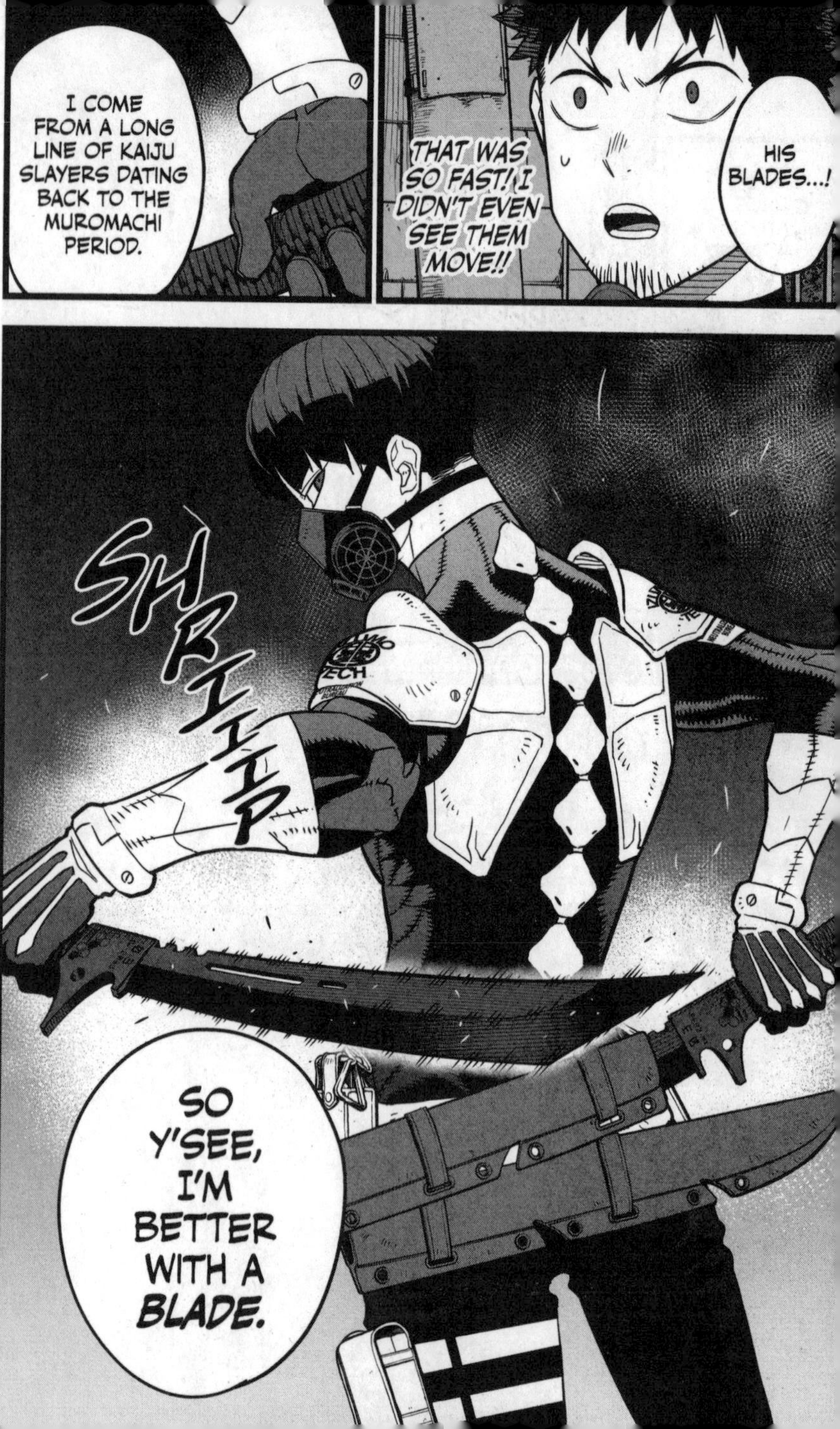
HIS BLADES...!
THAT WAS SO FAST! I DIDN'T EVEN SEE THEM MOVE!!
I COME FROM A LONG LINE OF KAIJU SLAYERS DATING BACK TO THE MUROMACHI PERIOD.
SHRIIIIP
SO Y'SEE, I'M BETTER WITH A BLADE.

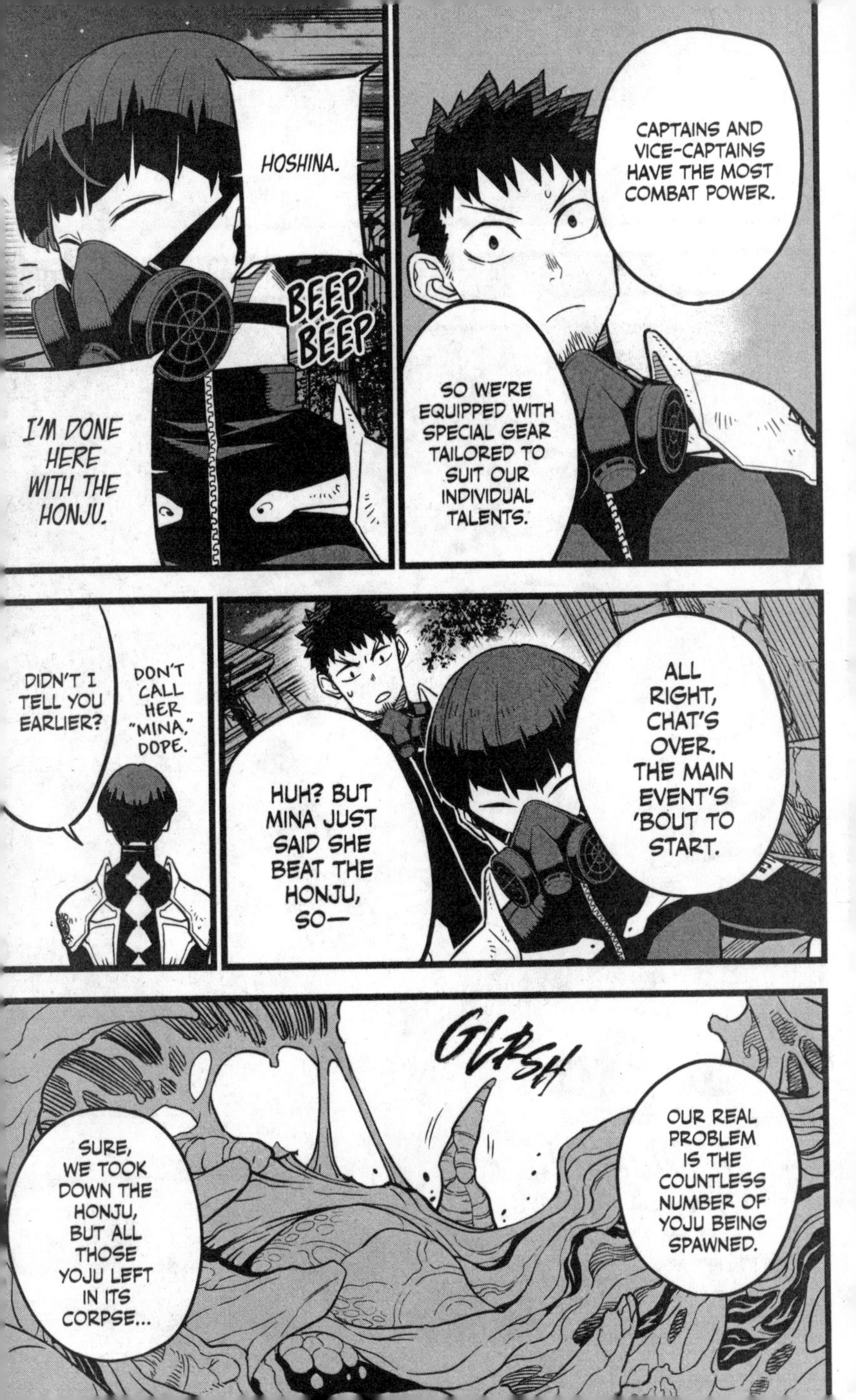
CAPTAINS AND VICE-CAPTAINS HAVE THE MOST COMBAT POWER.
SO WE'RE EQUIPPED WITH SPECIAL GEAR TAILORED TO SUIT OUR INDIVIDUAL TALENTS.
HOSHINA.
BEEP BEEP
I'M DONE HERE WITH THE HONJU.
ALL RIGHT, CHAT'S OVER. THE MAIN EVENT'S 'BOUT TO START.
HUH? BUT MINA JUST SAID SHE BEAT THE HONJU, SO—
DON'T CALL HER "MINA," DOPE.
DIDN'T I TELL YOU EARLIER?
GLRSH
OUR REAL PROBLEM IS THE COUNTLESS NUMBER OF YOJU BEING SPAWNED.
SURE, WE TOOK DOWN THE HONJU, BUT ALL THOSE YOJU LEFT IN ITS CORPSE...

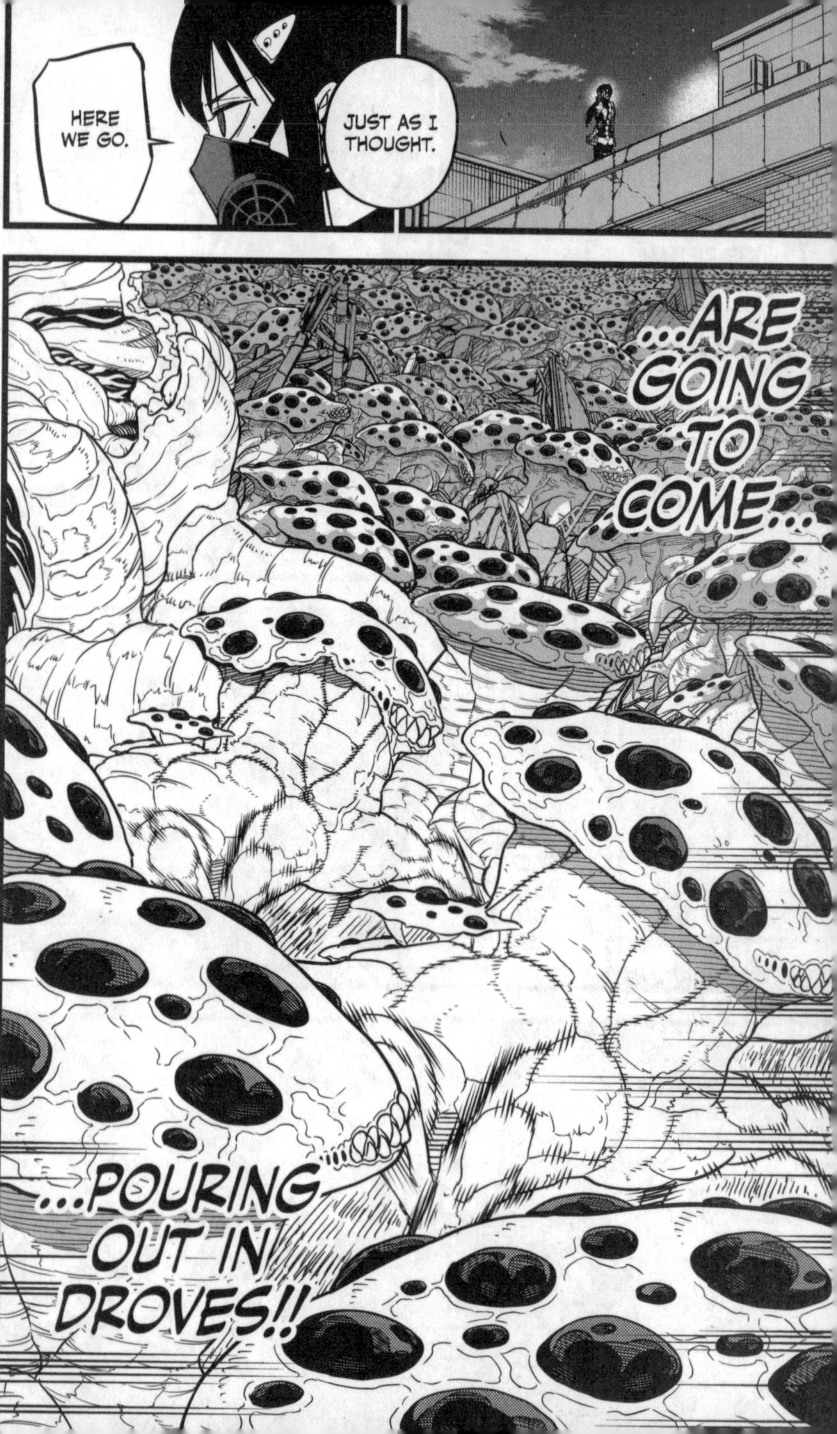
JUST AS I THOUGHT.
HERE WE GO.
...ARE GOING TO COME...
...POURING OUT IN DROVES!!

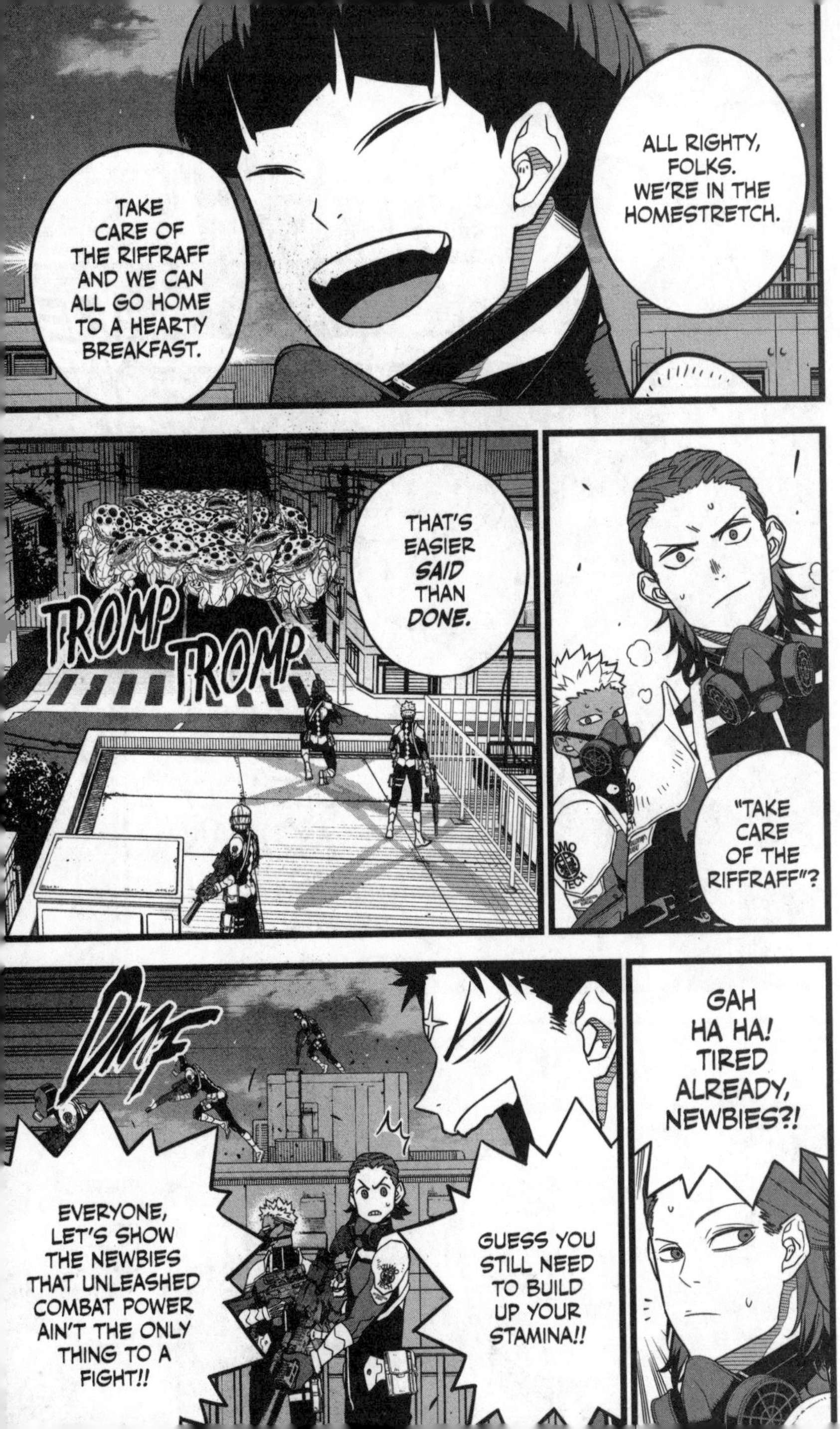
ALL RIGHTY, FOLKS. WE'RE IN THE HOMESTRETCH.
TAKE CARE OF THE RIFFRAFF AND WE CAN ALL GO HOME TO A HEARTY BREAKFAST.
"TAKE CARE OF THE RIFFRAFF"?
THAT'S EASIER SAID THAN DONE.
TROMP TROMP
GAH HA HA! TIRED ALREADY, NEWBIES?!
DMF
GUESS YOU STILL NEED TO BUILD UP YOUR STAMINA!!
EVERYONE, LET'S SHOW THE NEWBIES THAT UNLEASHED COMBAT POWER AIN'T THE ONLY THING TO A FIGHT!!

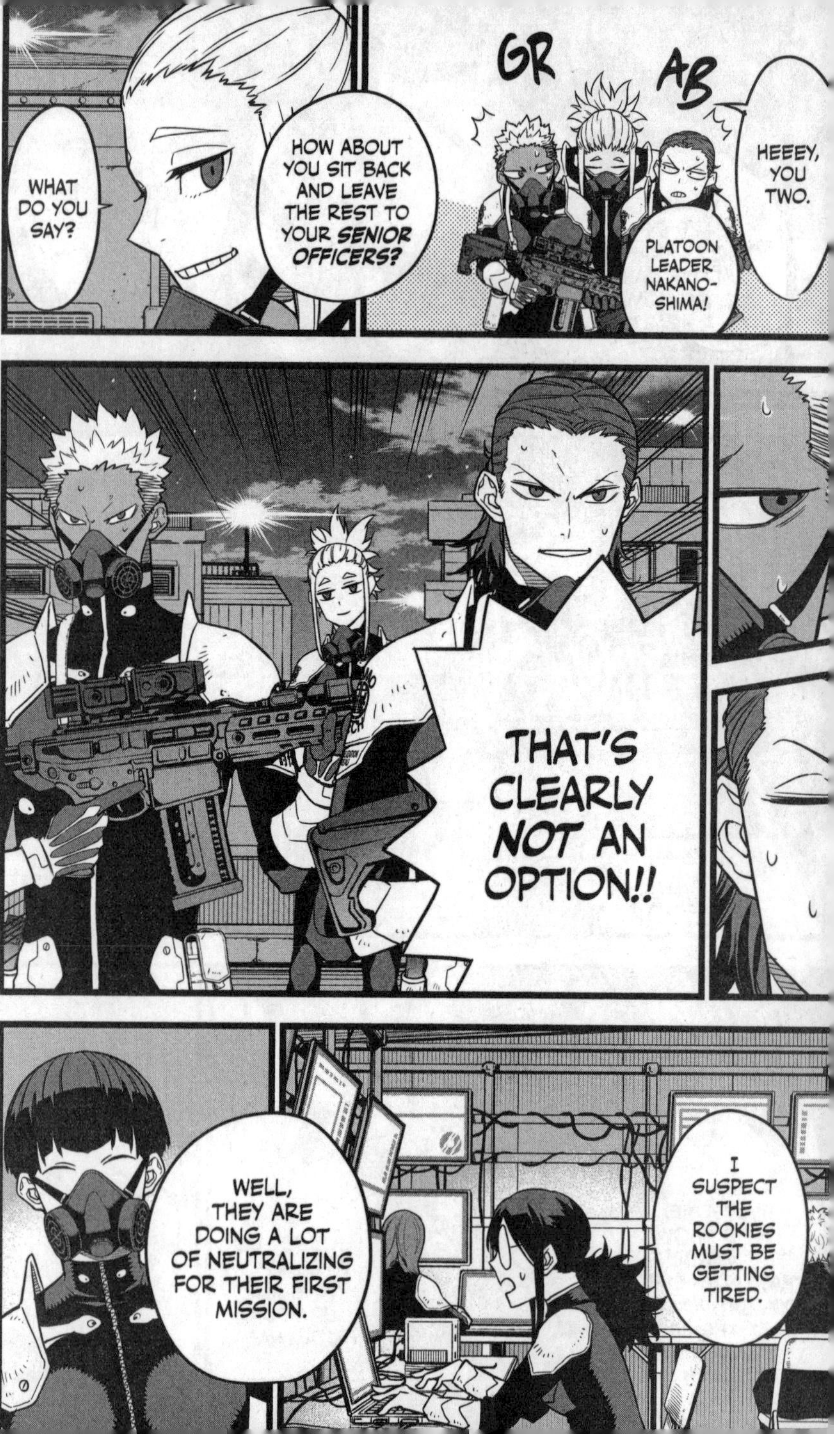
GR AB
HEEEY, YOU TWO.
PLATOON LEADER NAKANO-SHIMA!
HOW ABOUT YOU SIT BACK AND LEAVE THE REST TO YOUR *SENIOR OFFICERS?*
WHAT DO YOU SAY?
THAT'S CLEARLY *NOT* AN OPTION!!
I SUSPECT THE ROOKIES MUST BE GETTING TIRED.
WELL, THEY ARE DOING A LOT OF NEUTRALIZING FOR THEIR FIRST MISSION.

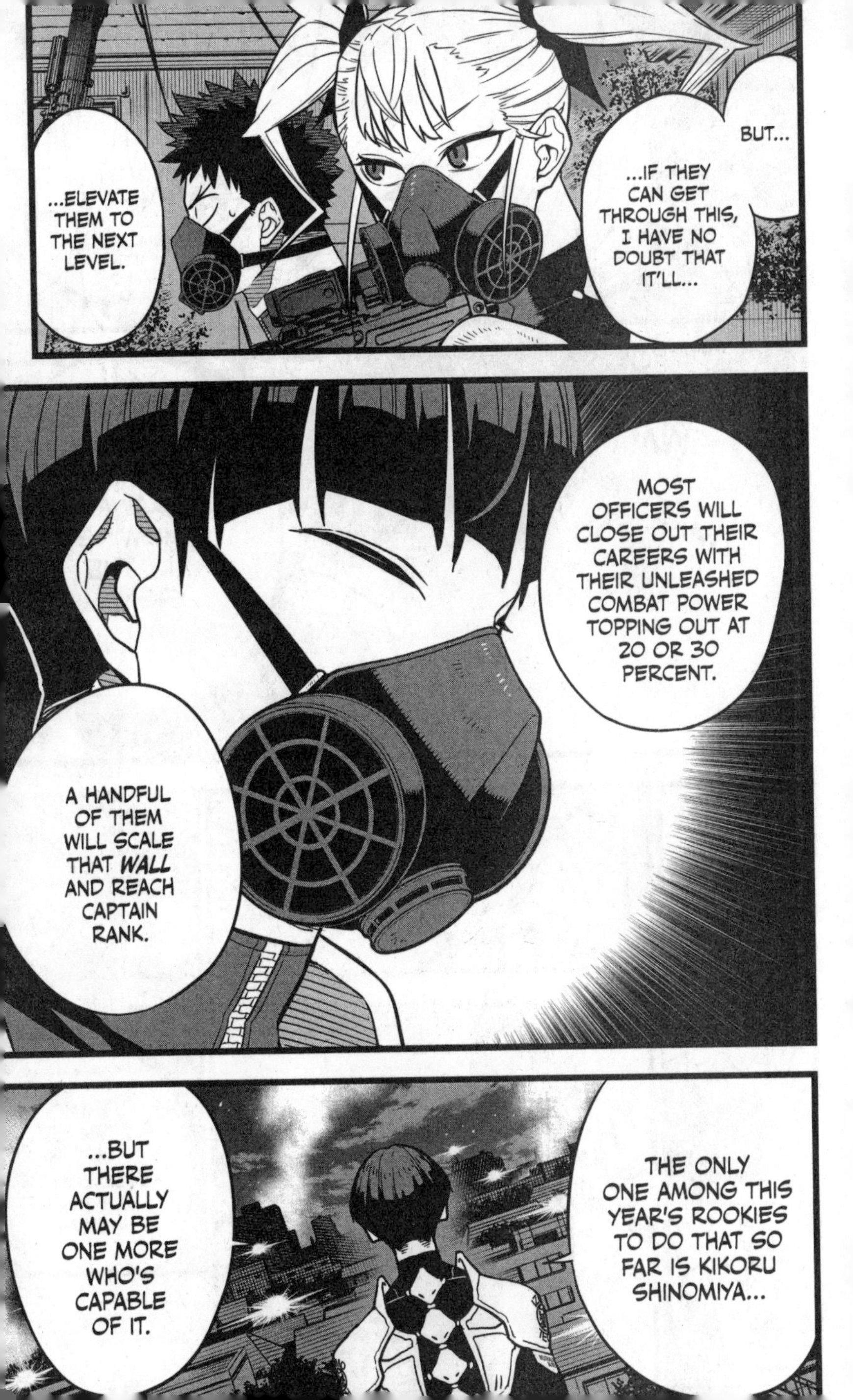
BUT...
...IF THEY CAN GET THROUGH THIS, I HAVE NO DOUBT THAT IT'LL...
...ELEVATE THEM TO THE NEXT LEVEL.
MOST OFFICERS WILL CLOSE OUT THEIR CAREERS WITH THEIR UNLEASHED COMBAT POWER TOPPING OUT AT 20 OR 30 PERCENT.
A HANDFUL OF THEM WILL SCALE THAT *WALL* AND REACH CAPTAIN RANK.
THE ONLY ONE AMONG THIS YEAR'S ROOKIES TO DO THAT SO FAR IS KIKORU SHINOMIYA...
...BUT THERE ACTUALLY MAY BE ONE MORE WHO'S CAPABLE OF IT.

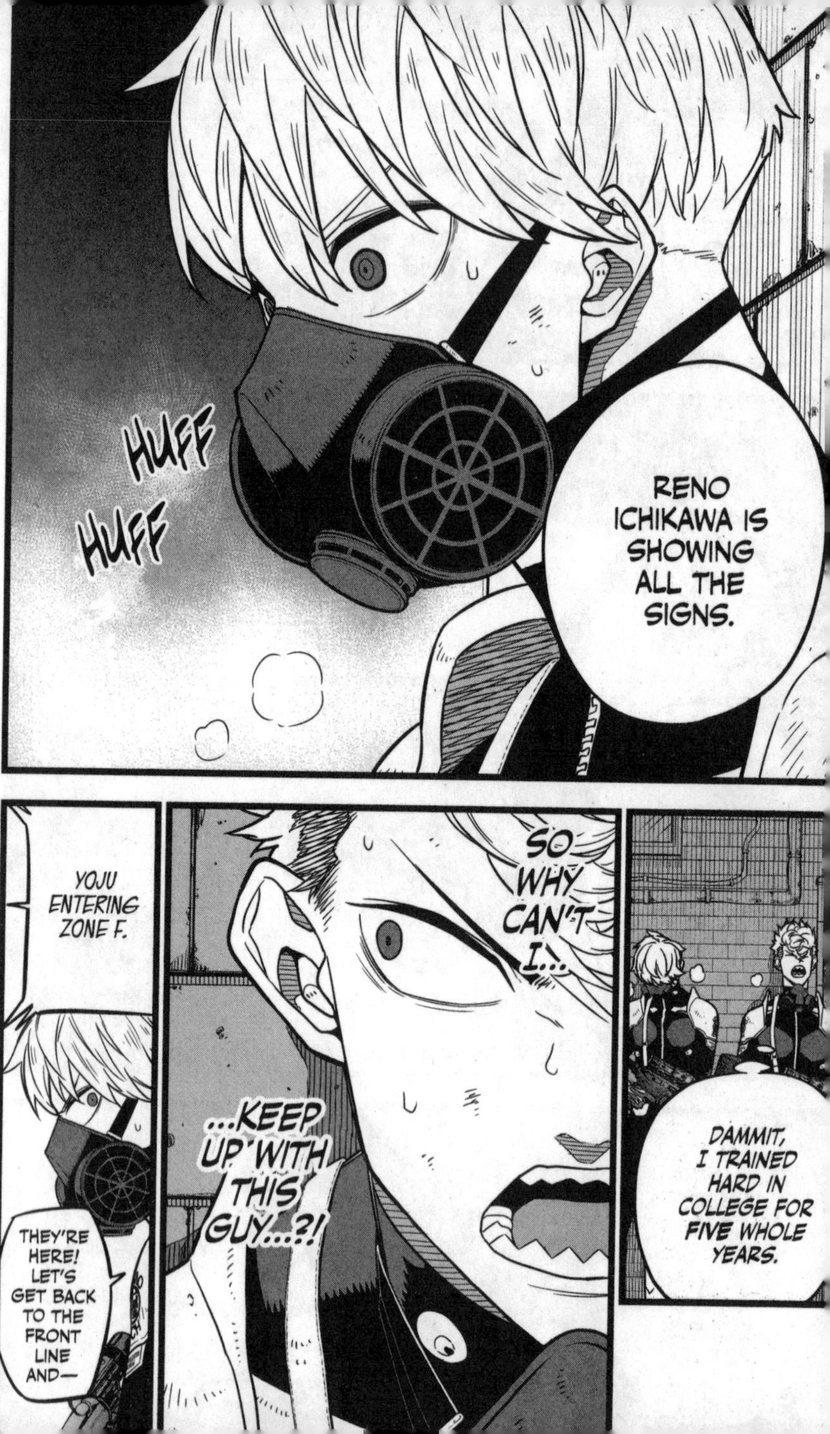
RENO ICHIKAWA IS SHOWING ALL THE SIGNS.
HUFF
HUFF
DAMMIT, I TRAINED HARD IN COLLEGE FOR FIVE WHOLE YEARS.
SO WHY CAN'T I...
...KEEP UP WITH THIS GUY...?!
YOJU ENTERING ZONE F.
THEY'RE HERE! LET'S GET BACK TO THE FRONT LINE AND—

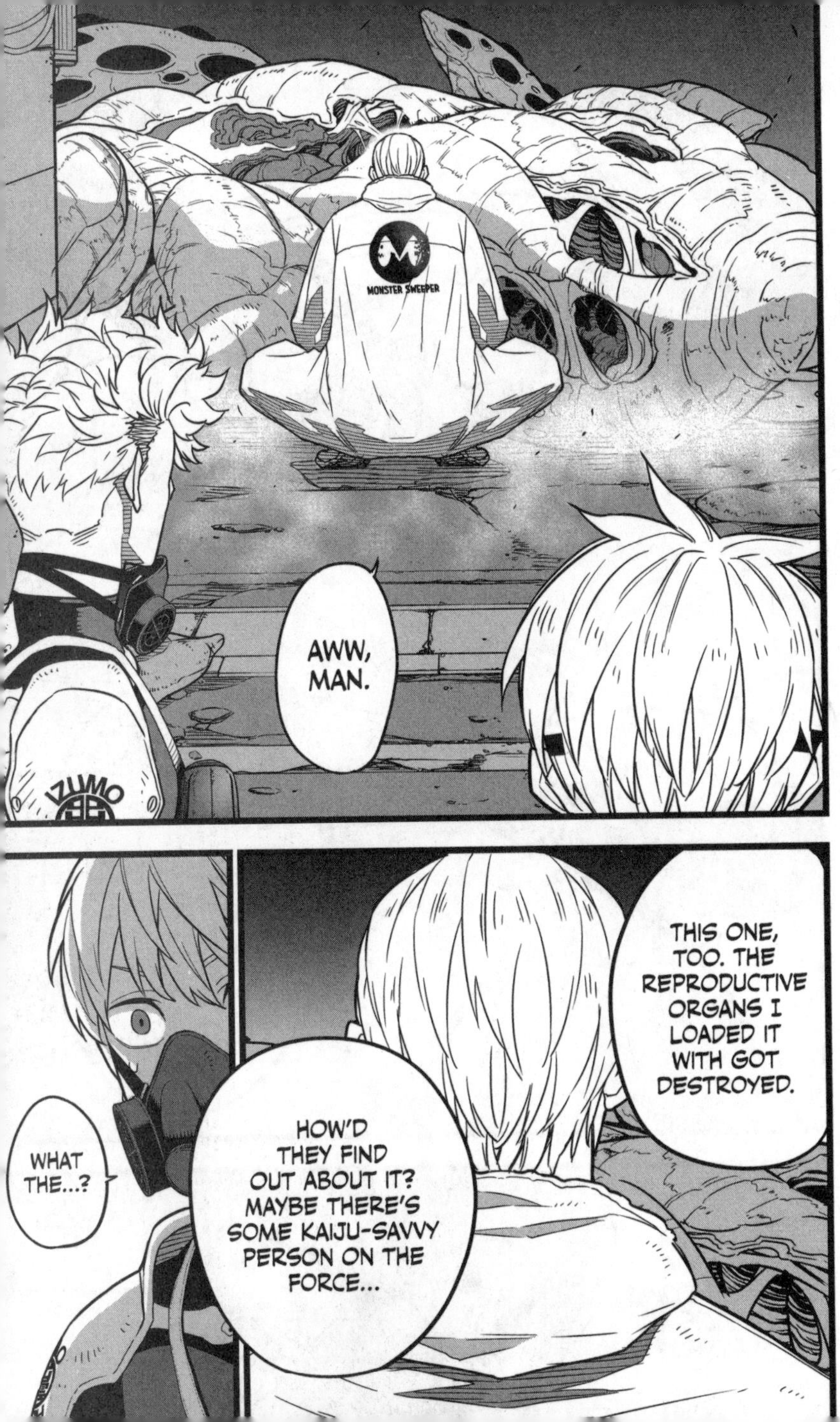
MONSTER SWEEPER
IZUMO
AWW, MAN.
THIS ONE, TOO. THE REPRODUCTIVE ORGANS I LOADED IT WITH GOT DESTROYED.
HOW'D THEY FIND OUT ABOUT IT? MAYBE THERE'S SOME KAIJU-SAVVY PERSON ON THE FORCE...
WHAT THE...?

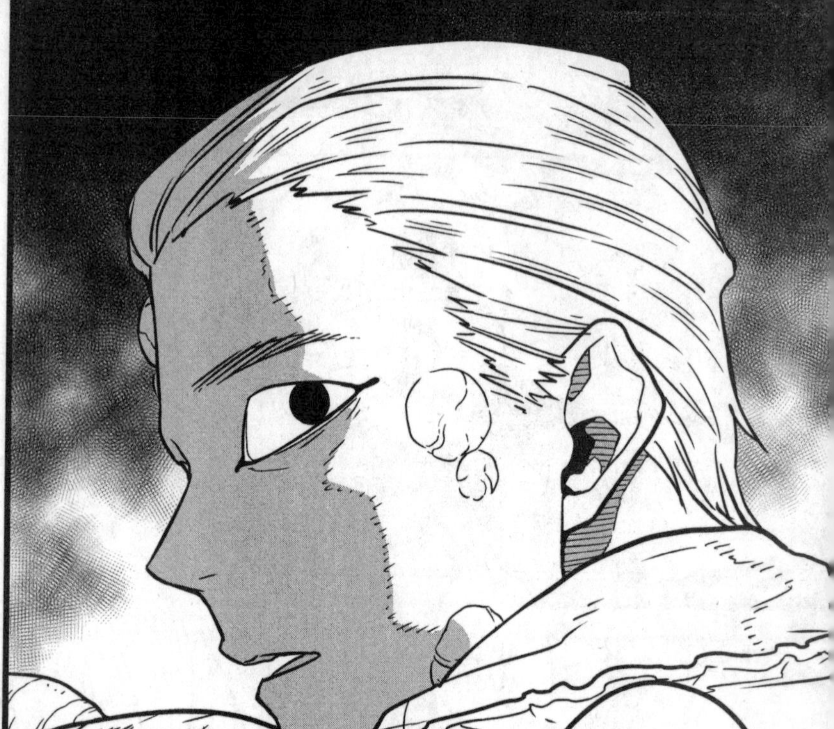
WOULD YOU HAPPEN TO KNOW?
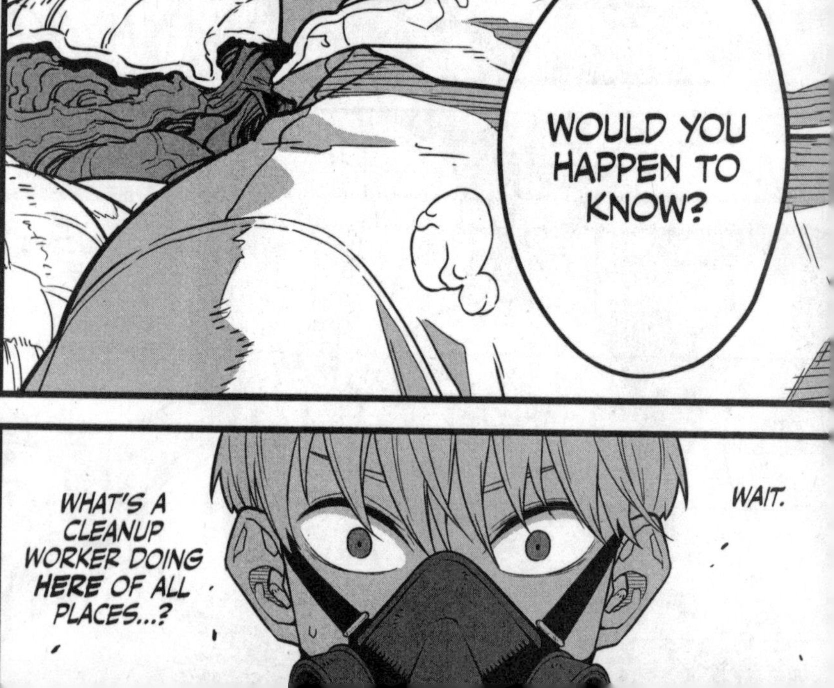
WAIT.
WHAT'S A CLEANUP WORKER DOING HERE OF ALL PLACES...?

CHAPTER 15

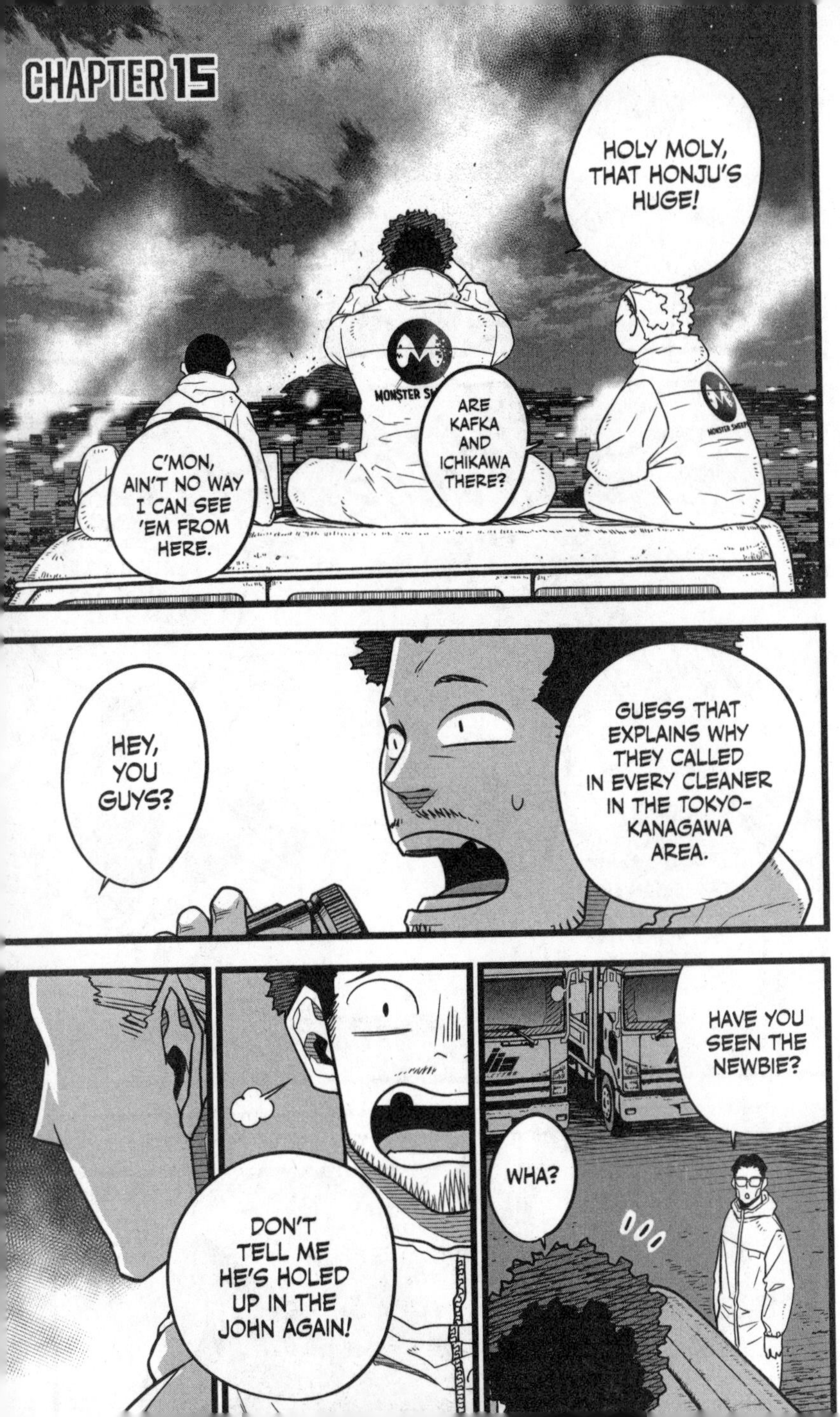
HOLY MOLY, THAT HONJU'S HUGE!
ARE KAFKA AND ICHIKAWA THERE?
C'MON, AIN'T NO WAY I CAN SEE 'EM FROM HERE.
GUESS THAT EXPLAINS WHY THEY CALLED IN EVERY CLEANER IN THE TOKYO-KANAGAWA AREA.
HEY, YOU GUYS?
HAVE YOU SEEN THE NEWBIE?
WHA?
DON'T TELL ME HE'S HOLED UP IN THE JOHN AGAIN!

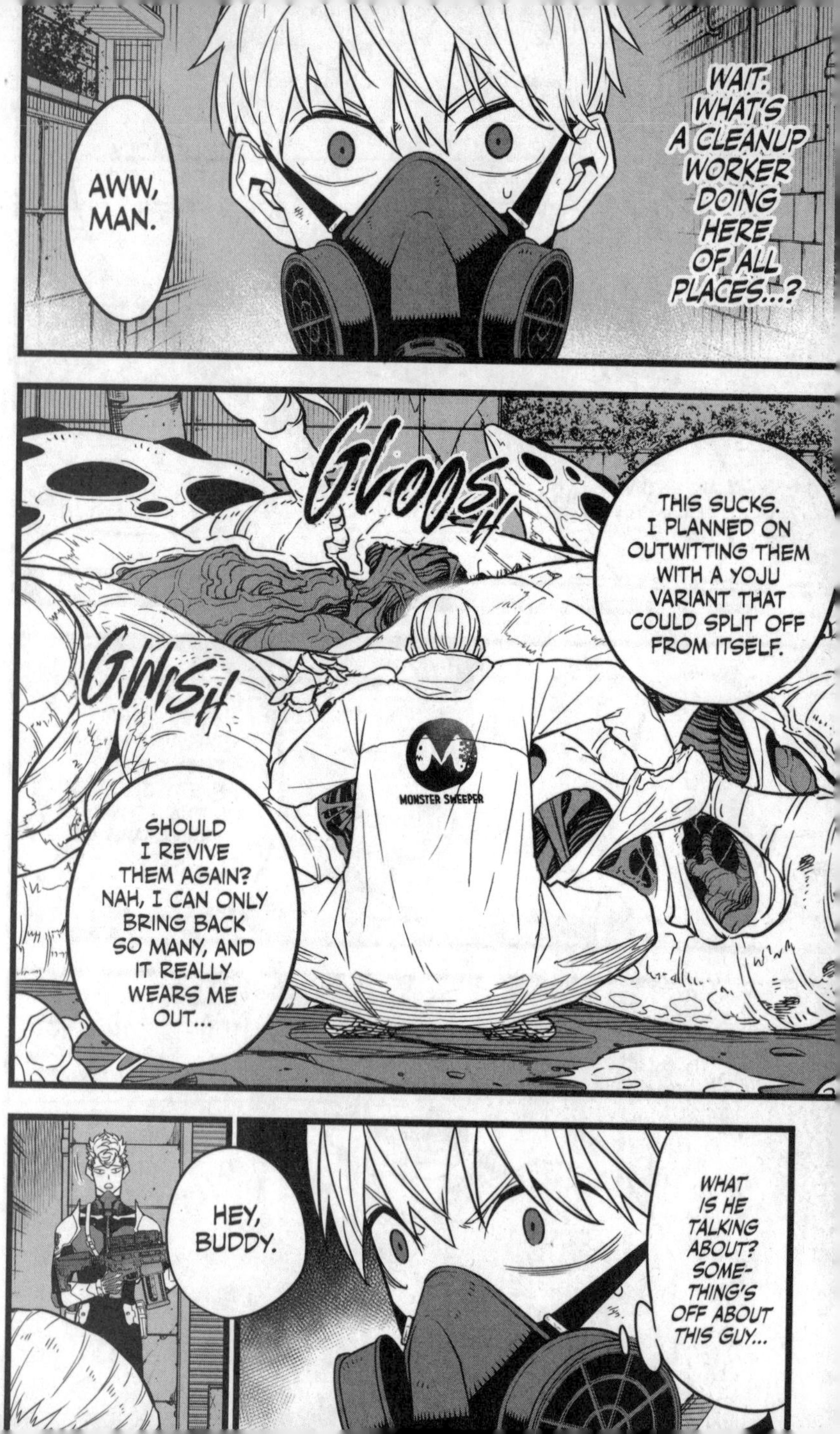
WAIT. WHAT'S A CLEANUP WORKER DOING HERE OF ALL PLACES...?
AWW, MAN.
THIS SUCKS. I PLANNED ON OUTWITTING THEM WITH A YOJU VARIANT THAT COULD SPLIT OFF FROM ITSELF.
GLOOSH
GWISH
MONSTER SWEEPER
SHOULD I REVIVE THEM AGAIN? NAH, I CAN ONLY BRING BACK SO MANY, AND IT REALLY WEARS ME OUT...
WHAT IS HE TALKING ABOUT? SOME-THING'S OFF ABOUT THIS GUY...
HEY, BUDDY.

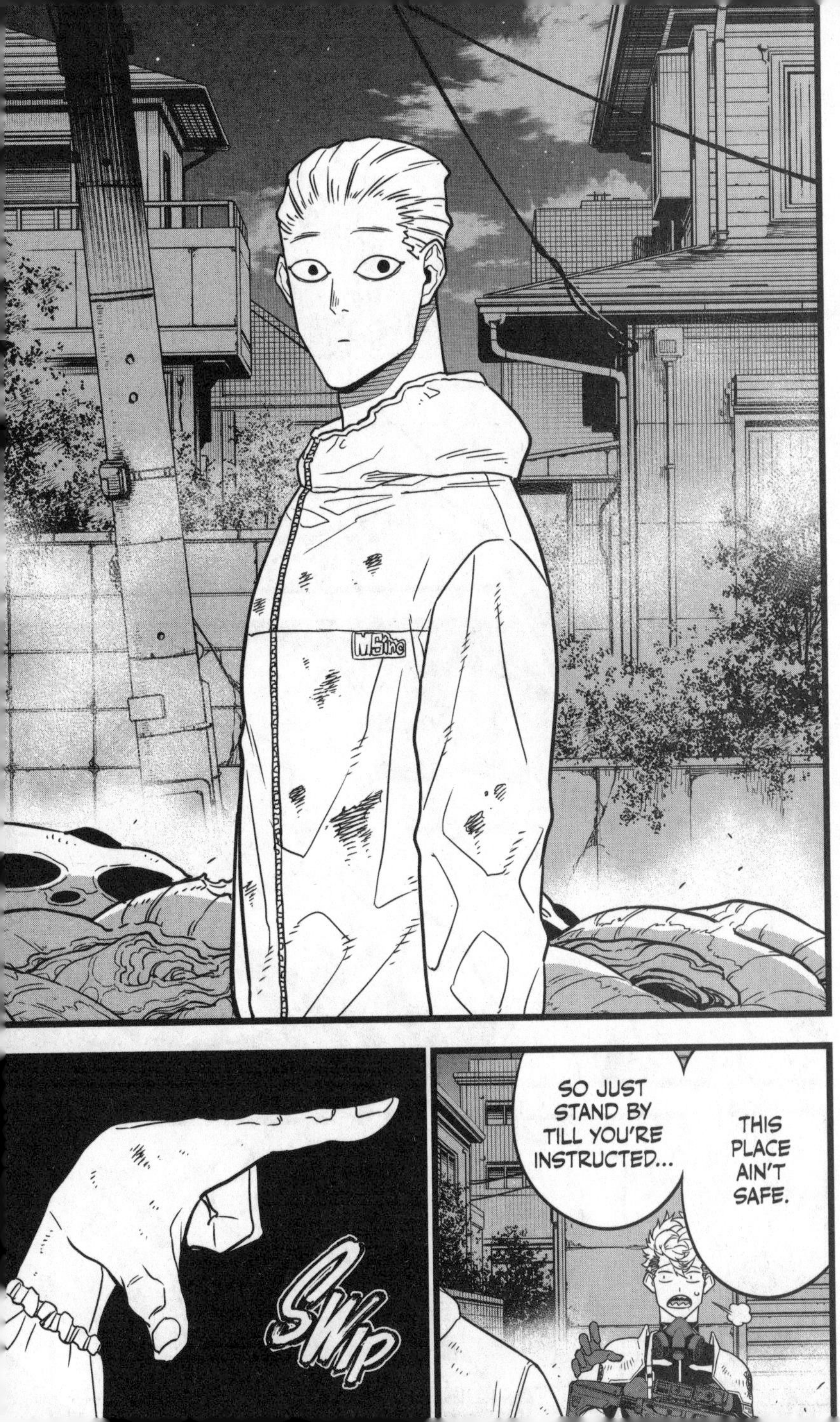
THIS PLACE AIN'T SAFE.
SO JUST STAND BY TILL YOU'RE INSTRUCTED...
SWIP

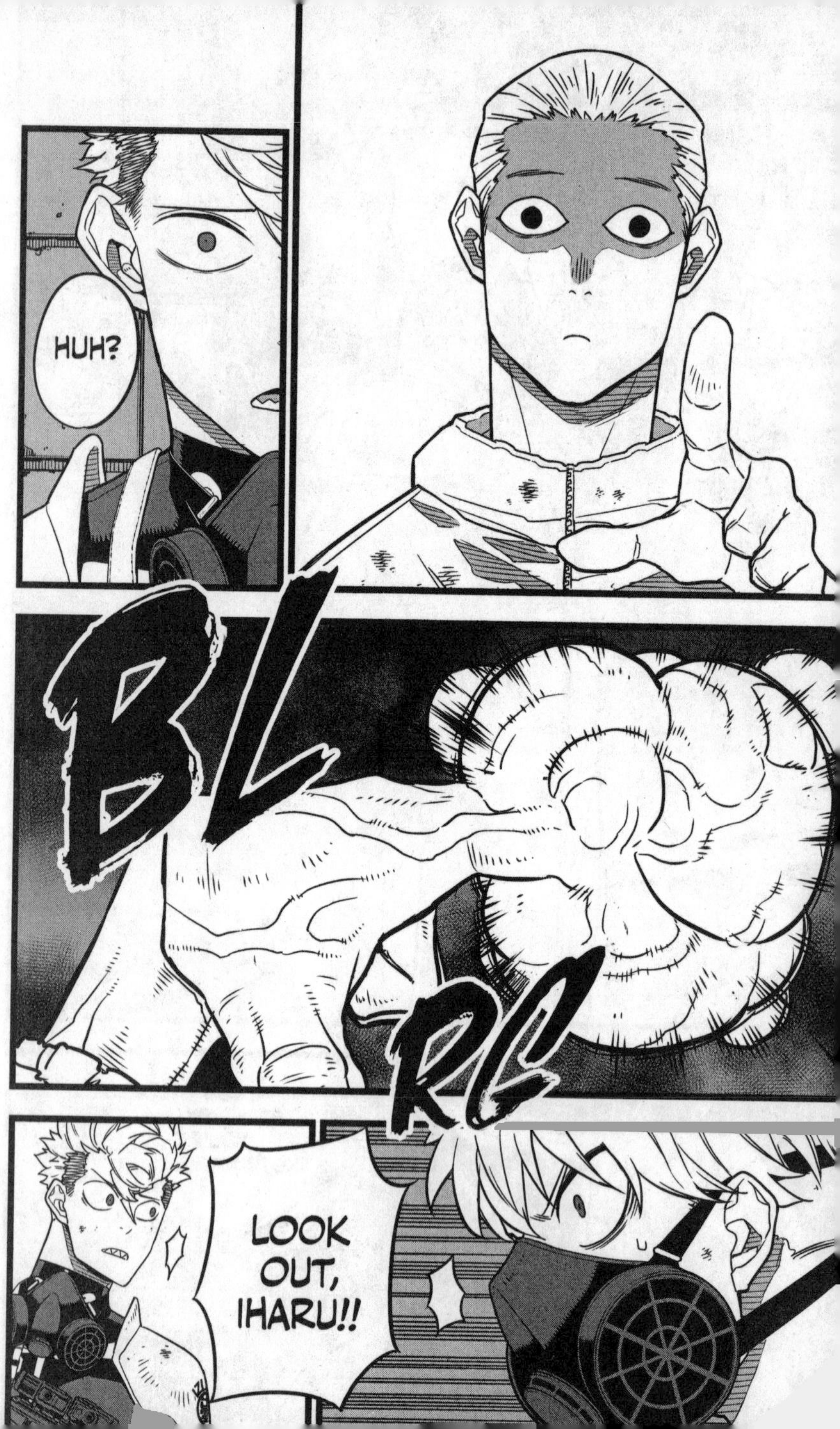
HUH?
BLRC
LOOK OUT, IHARU!!

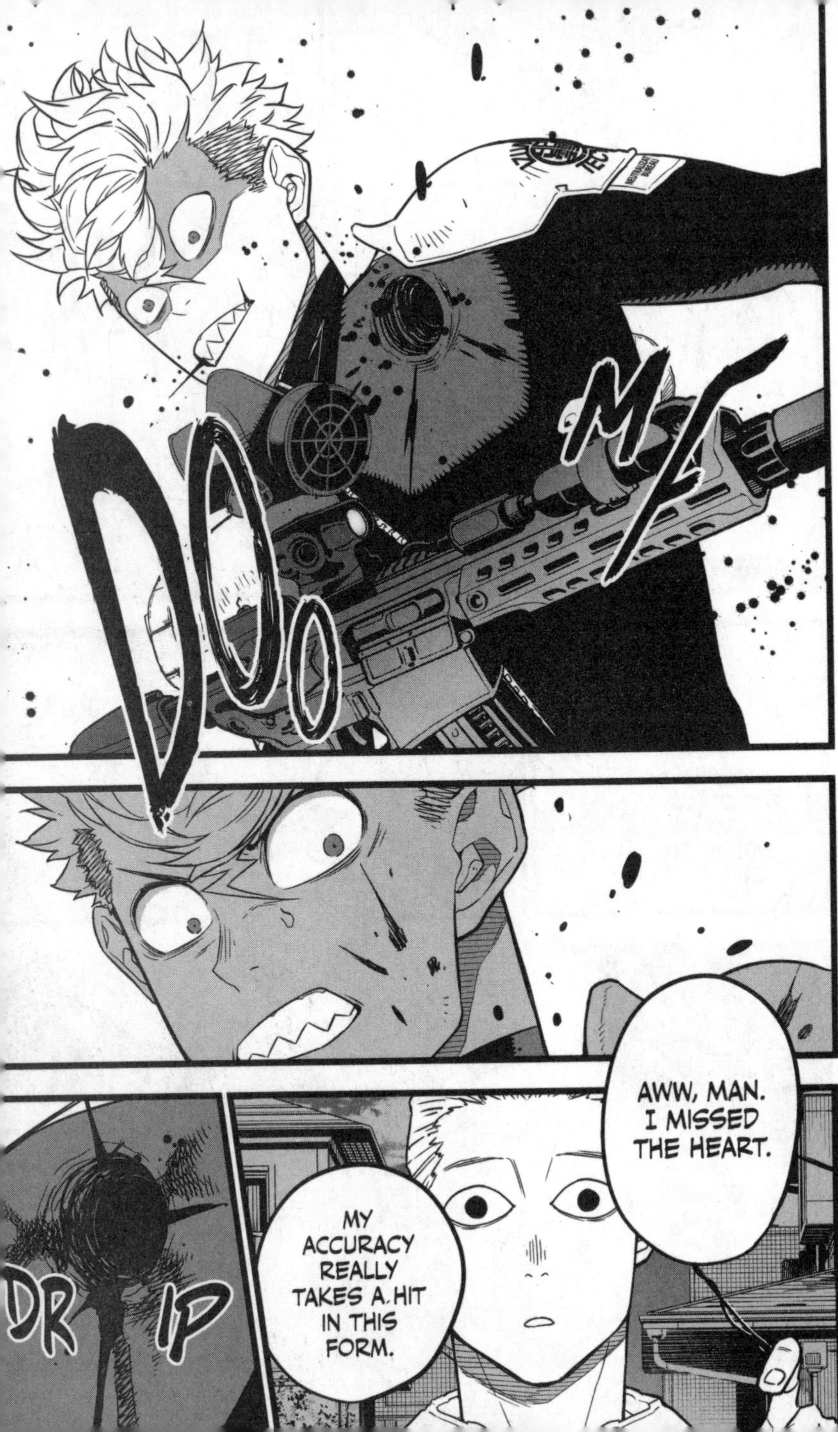
DOOO
AWW, MAN. I MISSED THE HEART.
MY ACCURACY REALLY TAKES A HIT IN THIS FORM.
DRIP

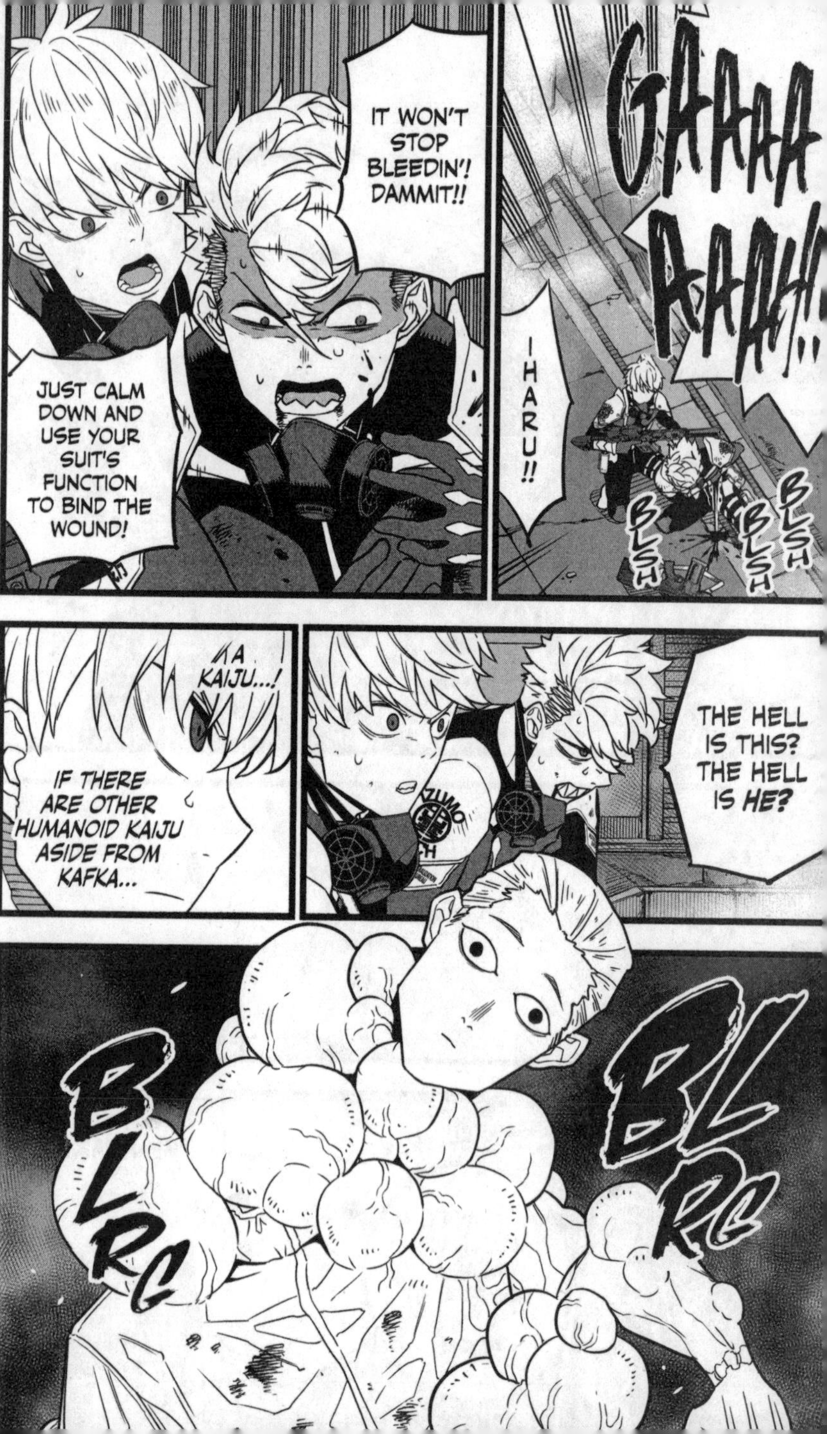
GAAAA AAAH!!
IHARU!!
BLSH
BLSH
BLSH
IT WON'T STOP BLEEDIN'! DAMMIT!!
JUST CALM DOWN AND USE YOUR SUIT'S FUNCTION TO BIND THE WOUND!
THE HELL IS THIS? THE HELL IS HE?
A KAIJU...!
IF THERE ARE OTHER HUMANOID KAIJU ASIDE FROM KAFKA...
BLRG
BLRG

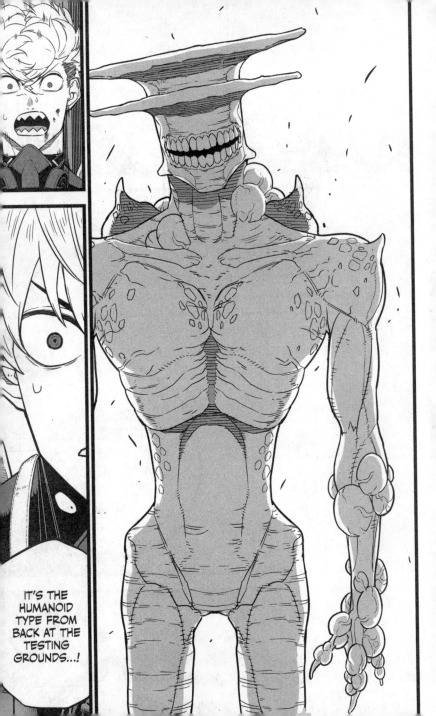

IT'S THE HUMANOID TYPE FROM BACK AT THE TESTING GROUNDS...!

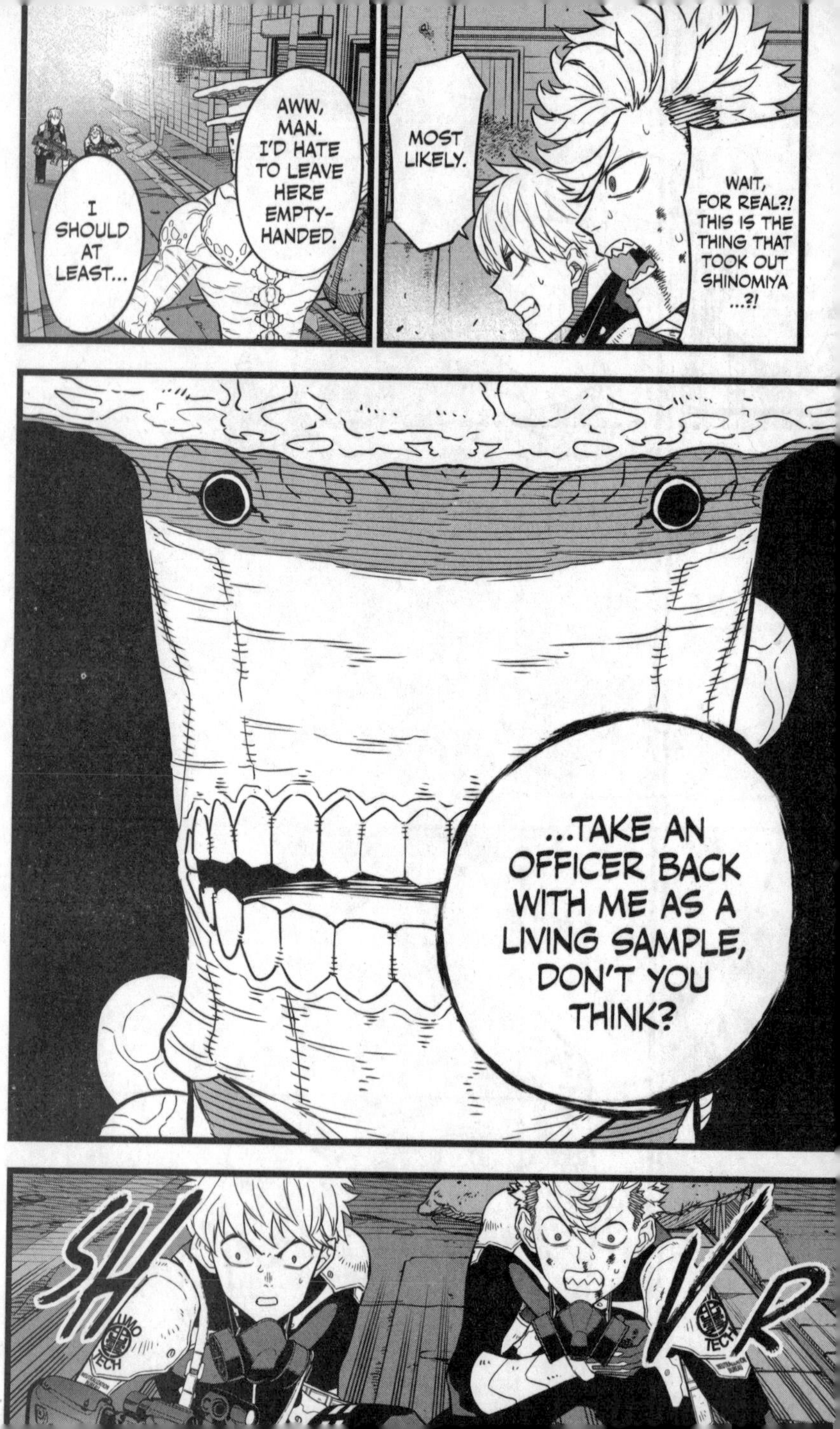
WAIT, FOR REAL?! THIS IS THE THING THAT TOOK OUT SHINOMIYA ...?!
MOST LIKELY.
AWW, MAN. I'D HATE TO LEAVE HERE EMPTY-HANDED.
I SHOULD AT LEAST...
...TAKE AN OFFICER BACK WITH ME AS A LIVING SAMPLE, DON'T YOU THINK?

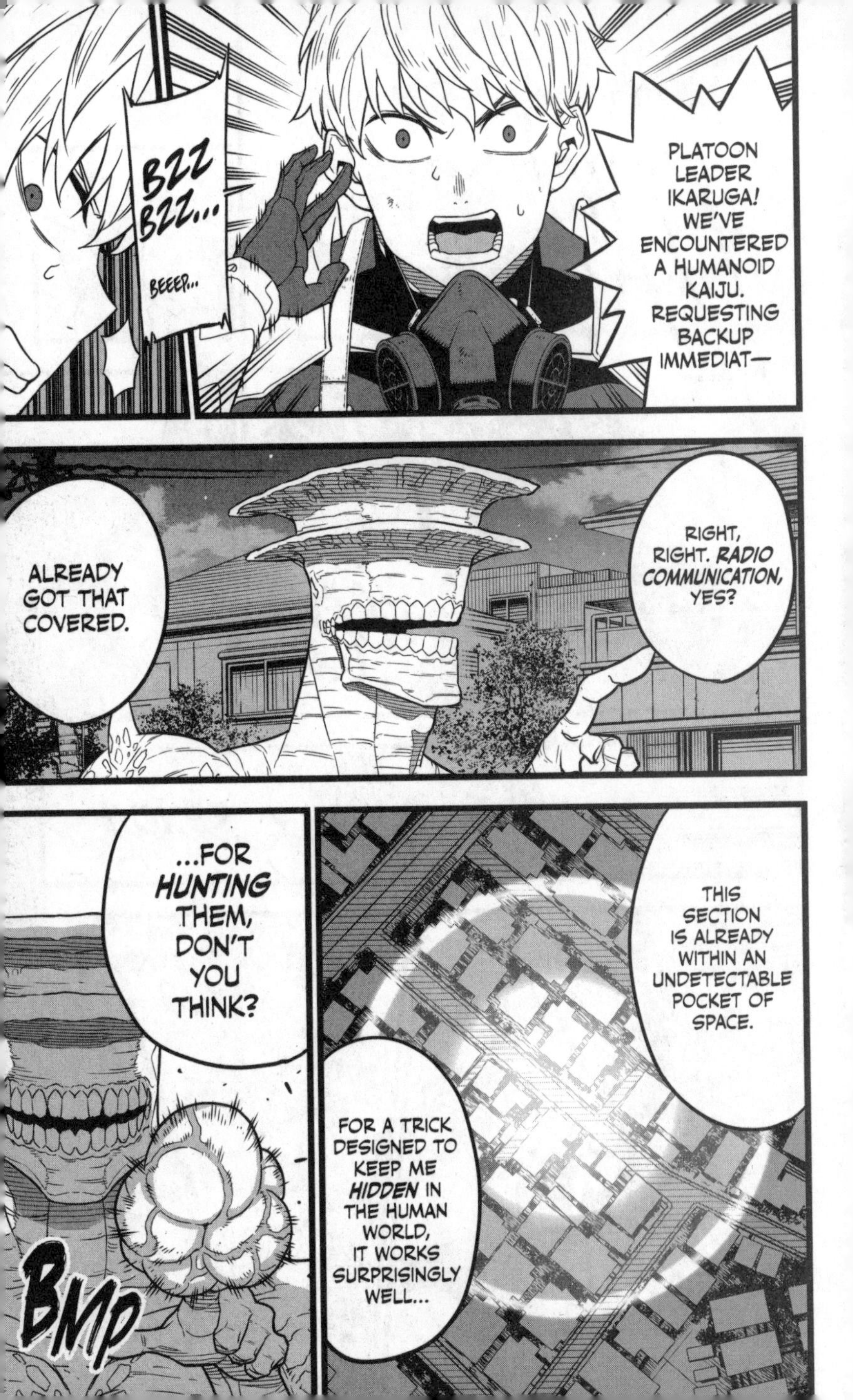
PLATOON LEADER IKARUGA! WE'VE ENCOUNTERED A HUMANOID KAIJU. REQUESTING BACKUP IMMEDIAT—
BZZ BZZ...
BEEEP...
RIGHT, RIGHT. RADIO COMMUNICATION, YES?
ALREADY GOT THAT COVERED.
THIS SECTION IS ALREADY WITHIN AN UNDETECTABLE POCKET OF SPACE.
FOR A TRICK DESIGNED TO KEEP ME HIDDEN IN THE HUMAN WORLD, IT WORKS SURPRISINGLY WELL...
...FOR HUNTING THEM, DON'T YOU THINK?
BMP

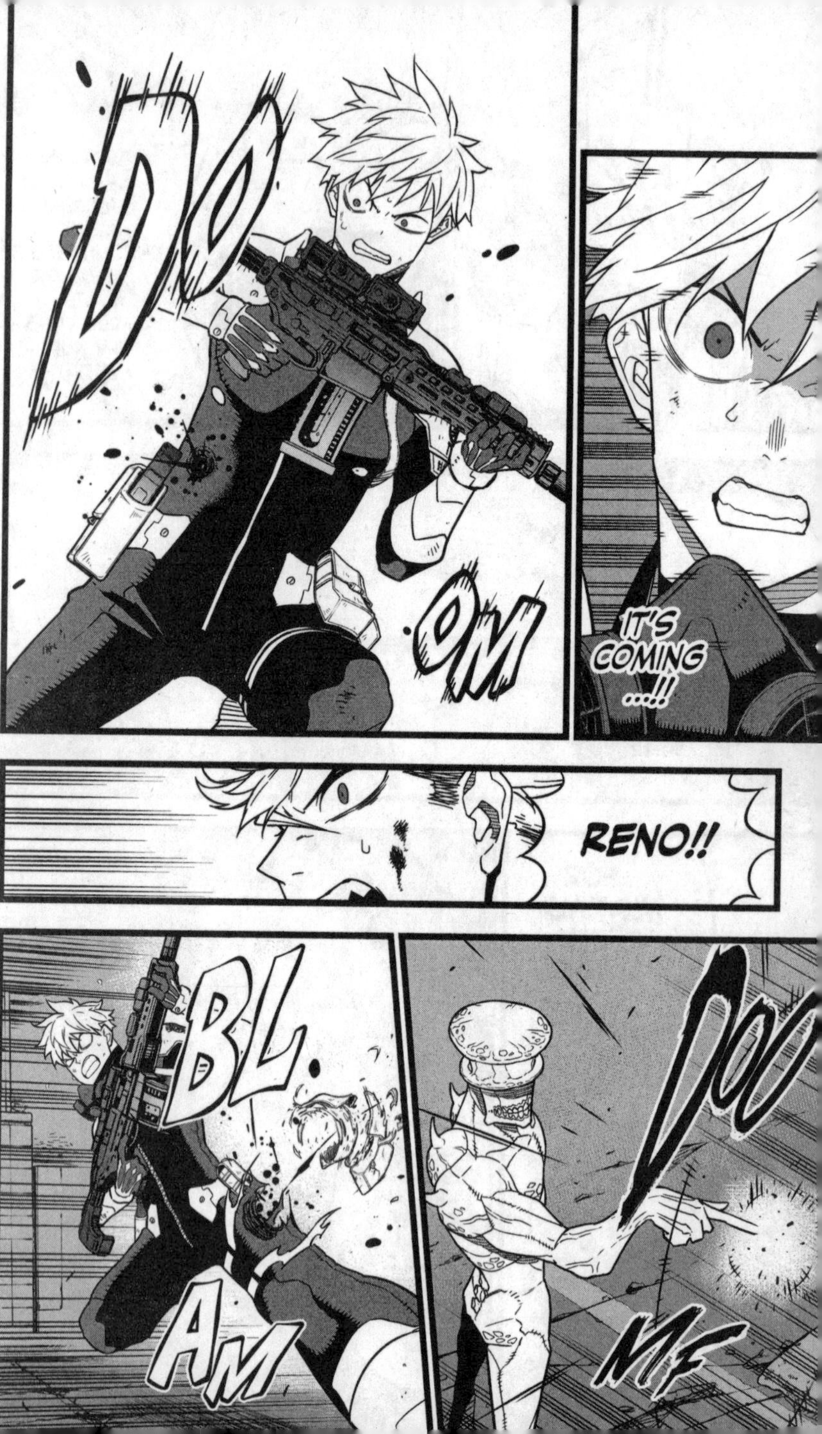
IT'S COMING ...!!
DO OM
RENO!!
DOO MF
BL AM

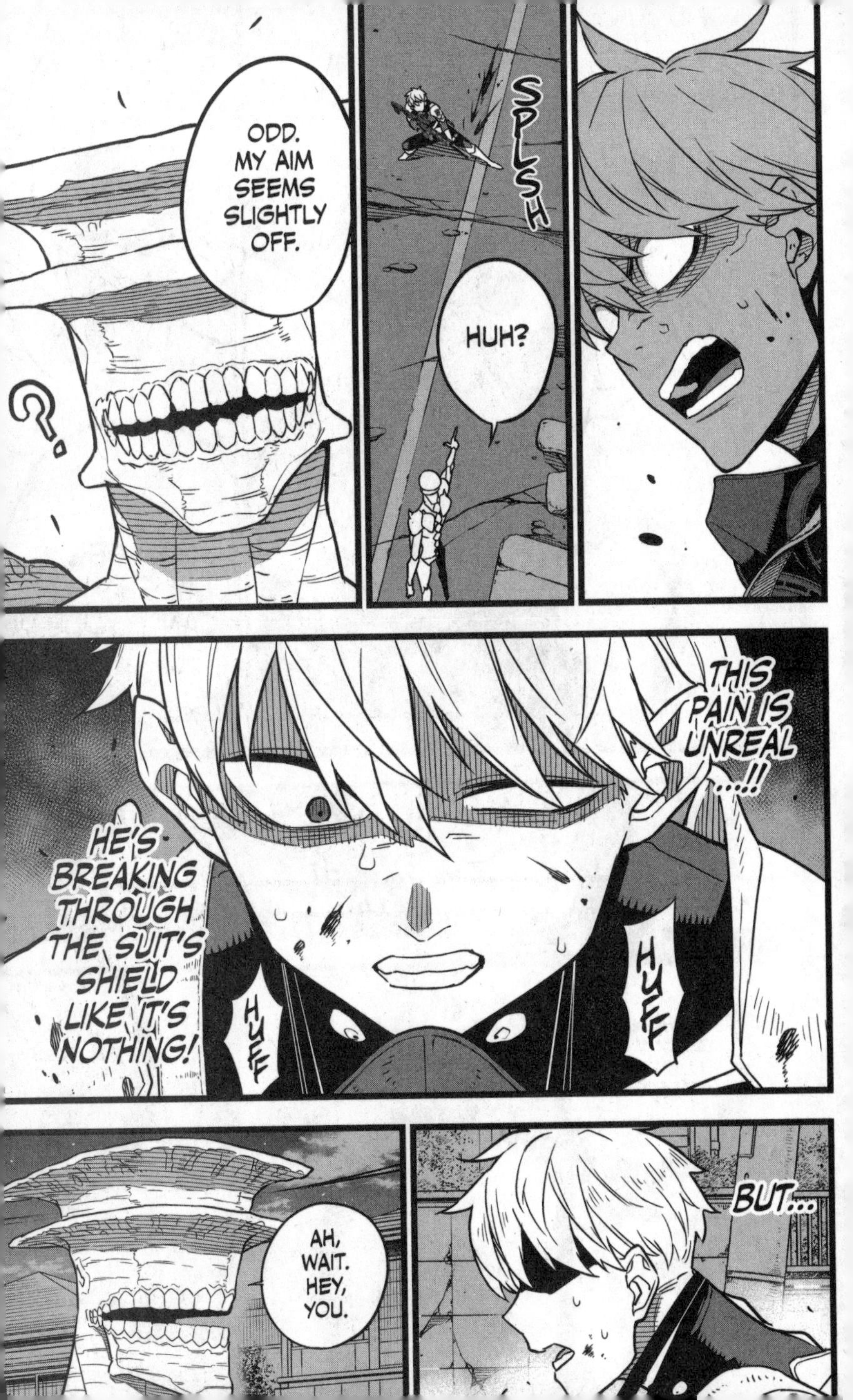
SPLSH
HUH?
ODD. MY AIM SEEMS SLIGHTLY OFF.
?
THIS PAIN IS UNREAL...!!
HUFF
HE'S BREAKING THROUGH THE SUIT'S SHIELD LIKE IT'S NOTHING!
HUFF
BUT...
AH, WAIT. HEY, YOU.

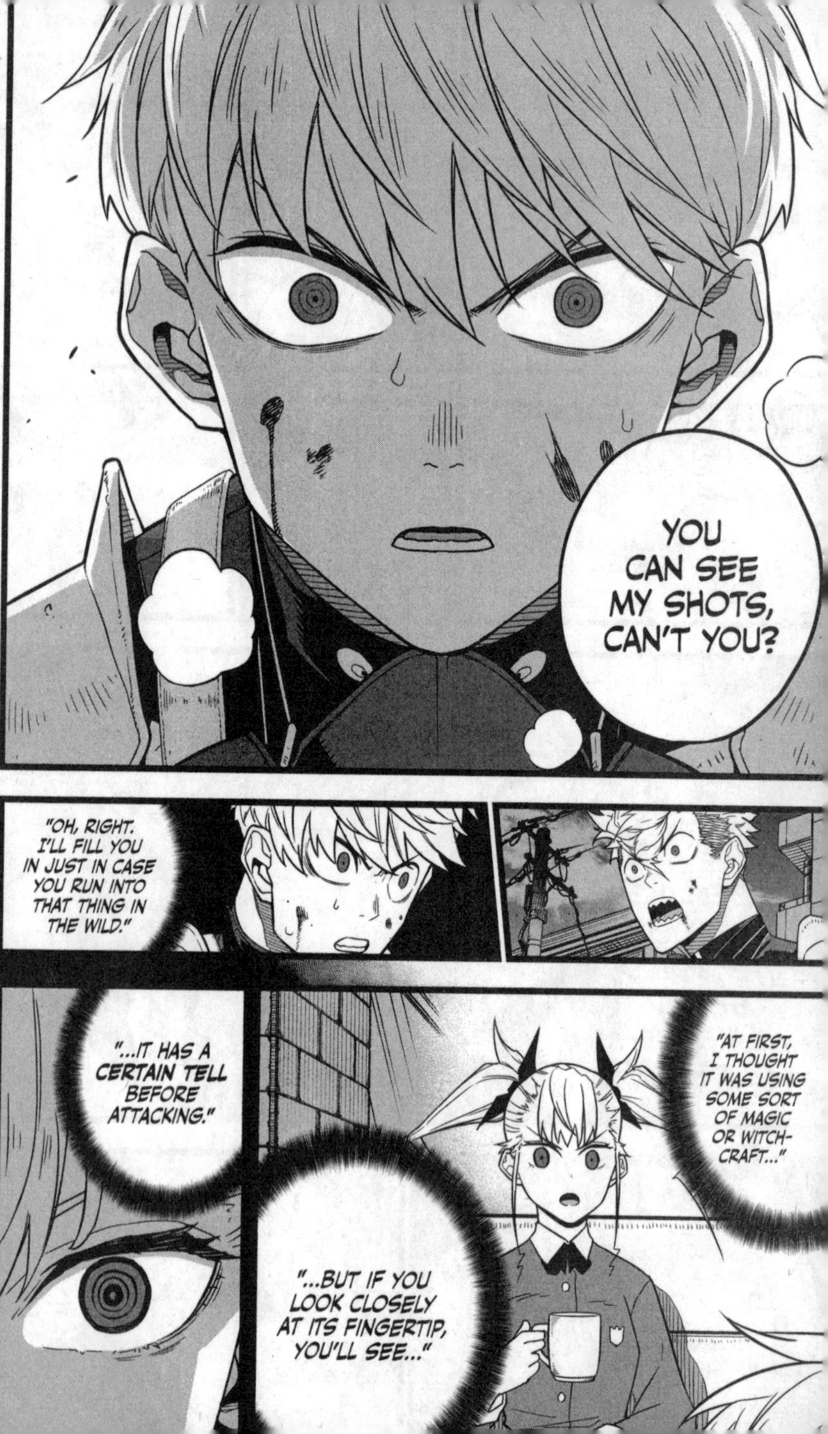
YOU CAN SEE MY SHOTS, CAN'T YOU?
"OH, RIGHT. I'LL FILL YOU IN JUST IN CASE YOU RUN INTO THAT THING IN THE WILD."
"AT FIRST, I THOUGHT IT WAS USING SOME SORT OF MAGIC OR WITCH-CRAFT..."
"...IT HAS A CERTAIN TELL BEFORE ATTACKING."
"...BUT IF YOU LOOK CLOSELY AT ITS FINGERTIP, YOU'LL SEE..."

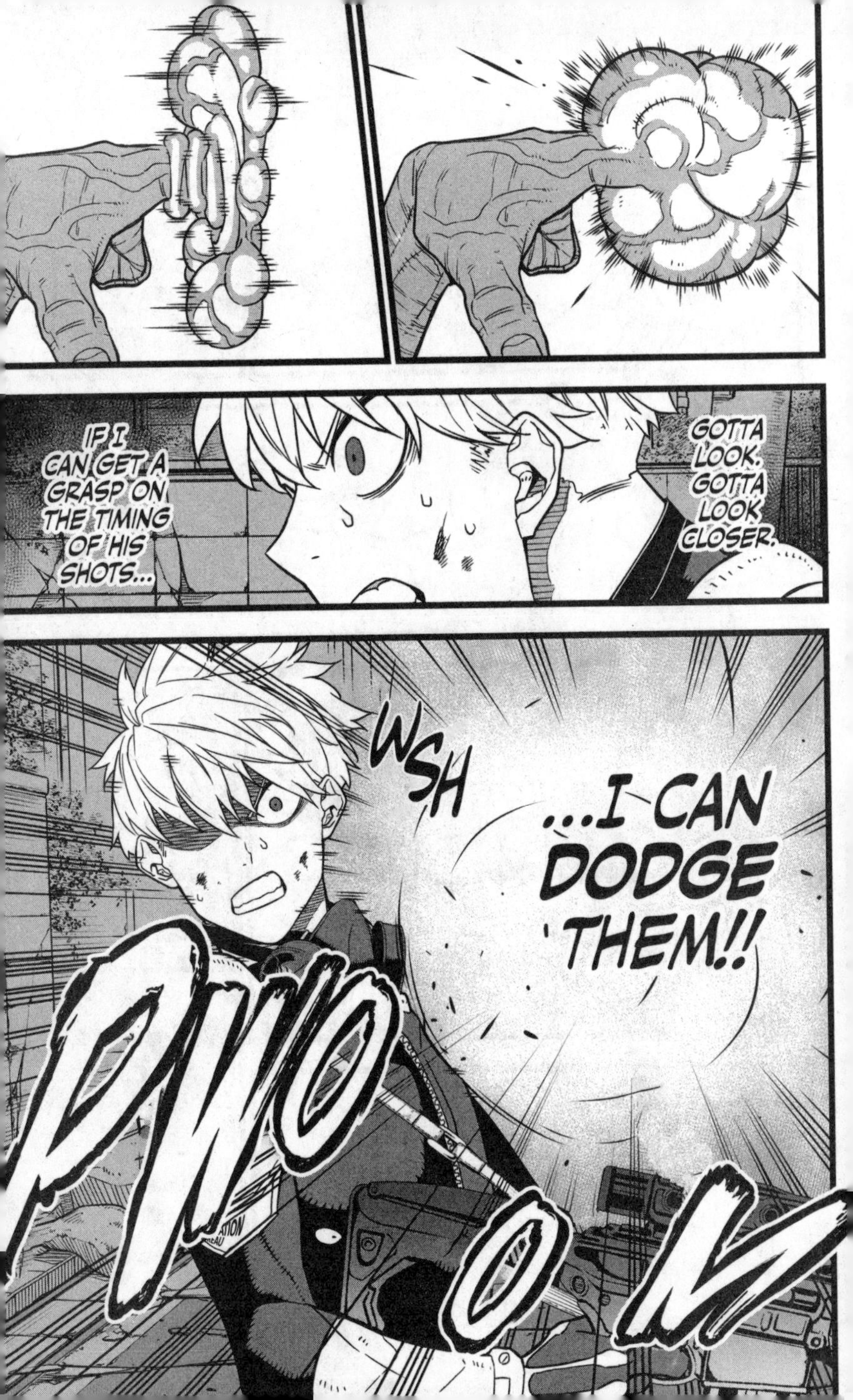
GOTTA LOOK. GOTTA LOOK CLOSER.
IF I CAN GET A GRASP ON THE TIMING OF HIS SHOTS...
WSH
...I CAN DODGE THEM!!
PWOOM

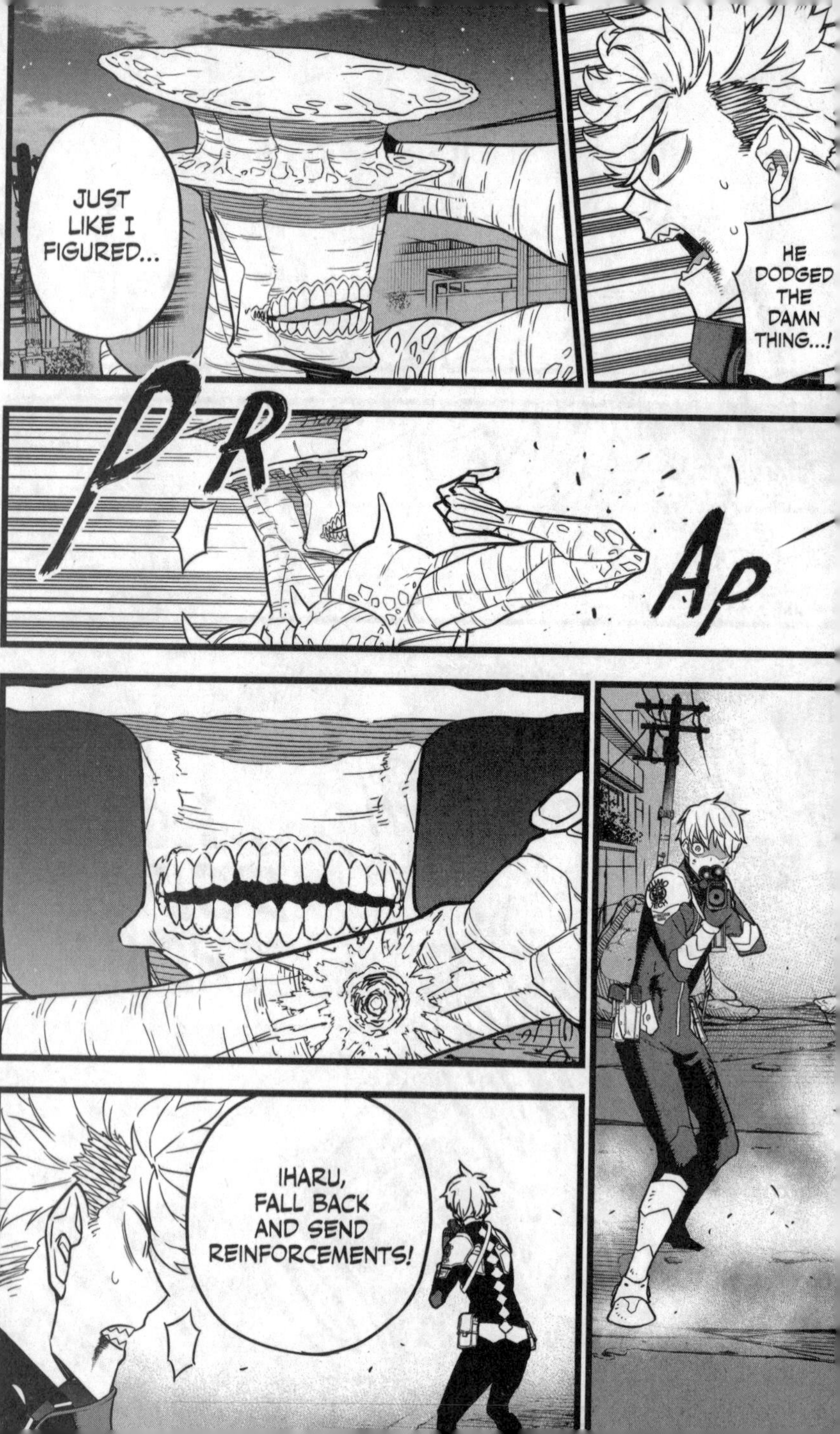
HE DODGED THE DAMN THING...!
JUST LIKE I FIGURED...
PRAP
IHARU, FALL BACK AND SEND REINFORCEMENTS!

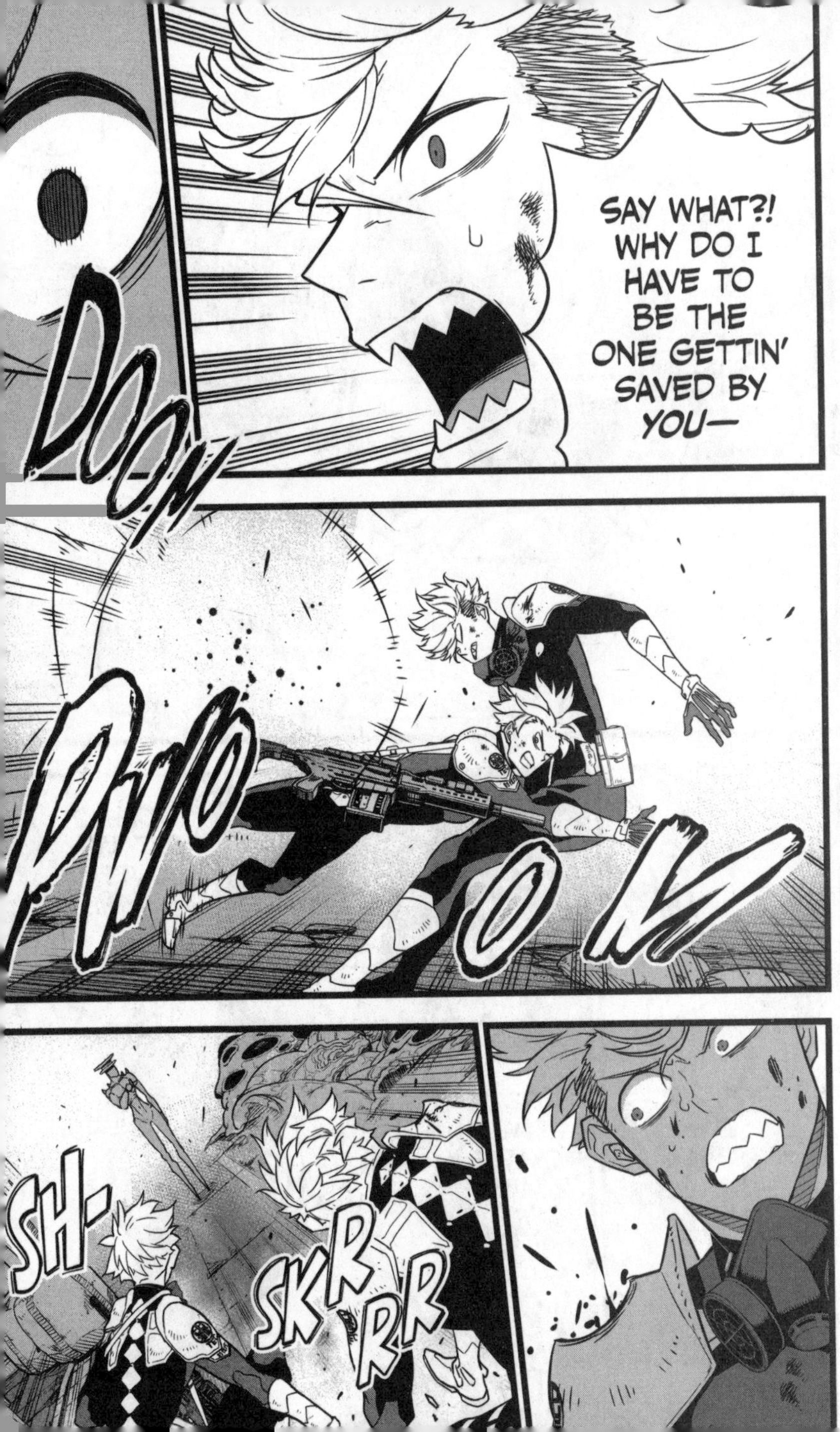
SAY WHAT?! WHY DO I HAVE TO BE THE ONE GETTIN' SAVED BY YOU—
DOOM
PWOOOM
SH-
SKRRRR

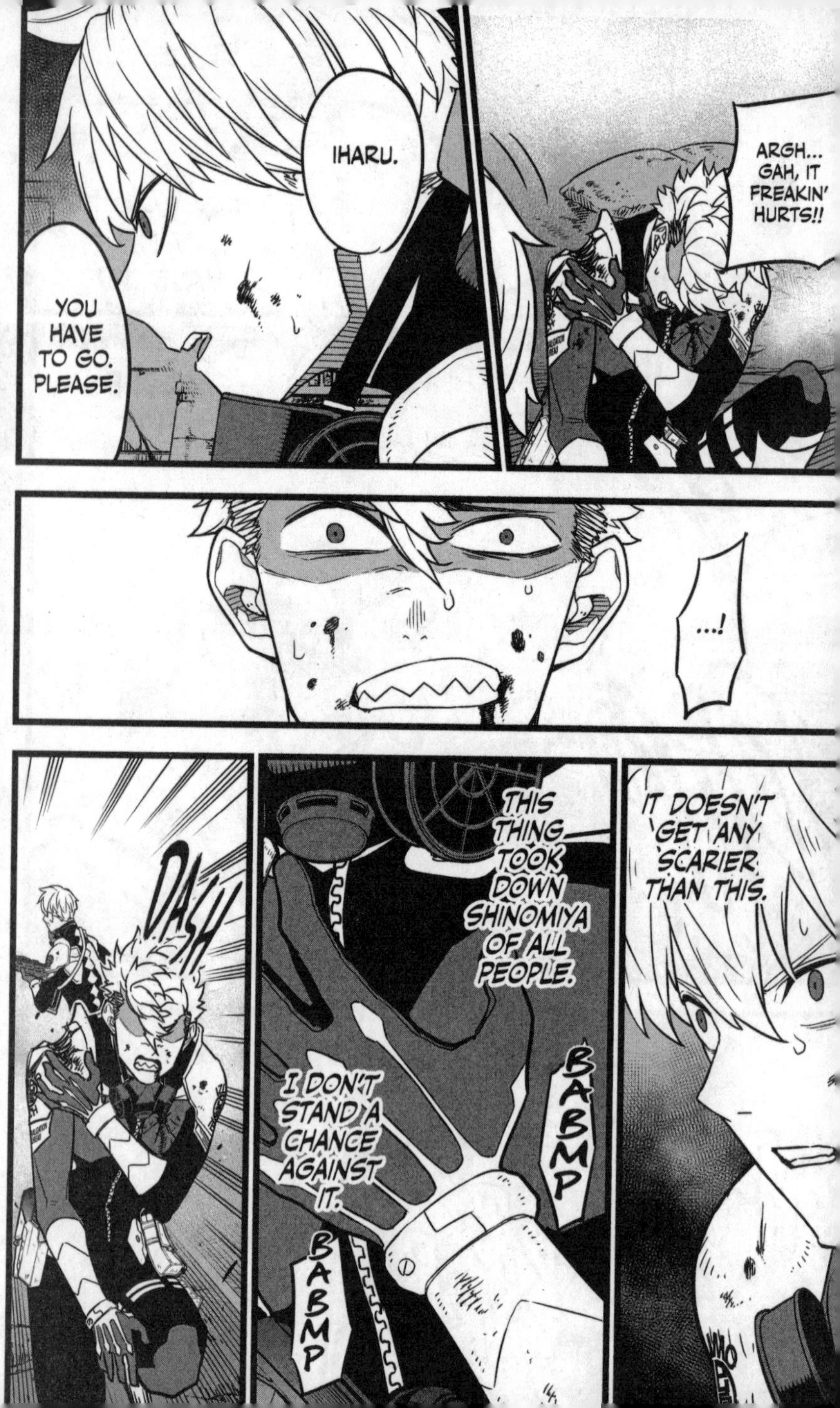
ARGH... GAH, IT FREAKIN' HURTS!!
IHARU.
YOU HAVE TO GO. PLEASE.
...!
IT DOESN'T GET ANY SCARIER THAN THIS.
THIS THING TOOK DOWN SHINOMIYA OF ALL PEOPLE.
BABMP
I DON'T STAND A CHANCE AGAINST IT.
BABMP
DASH

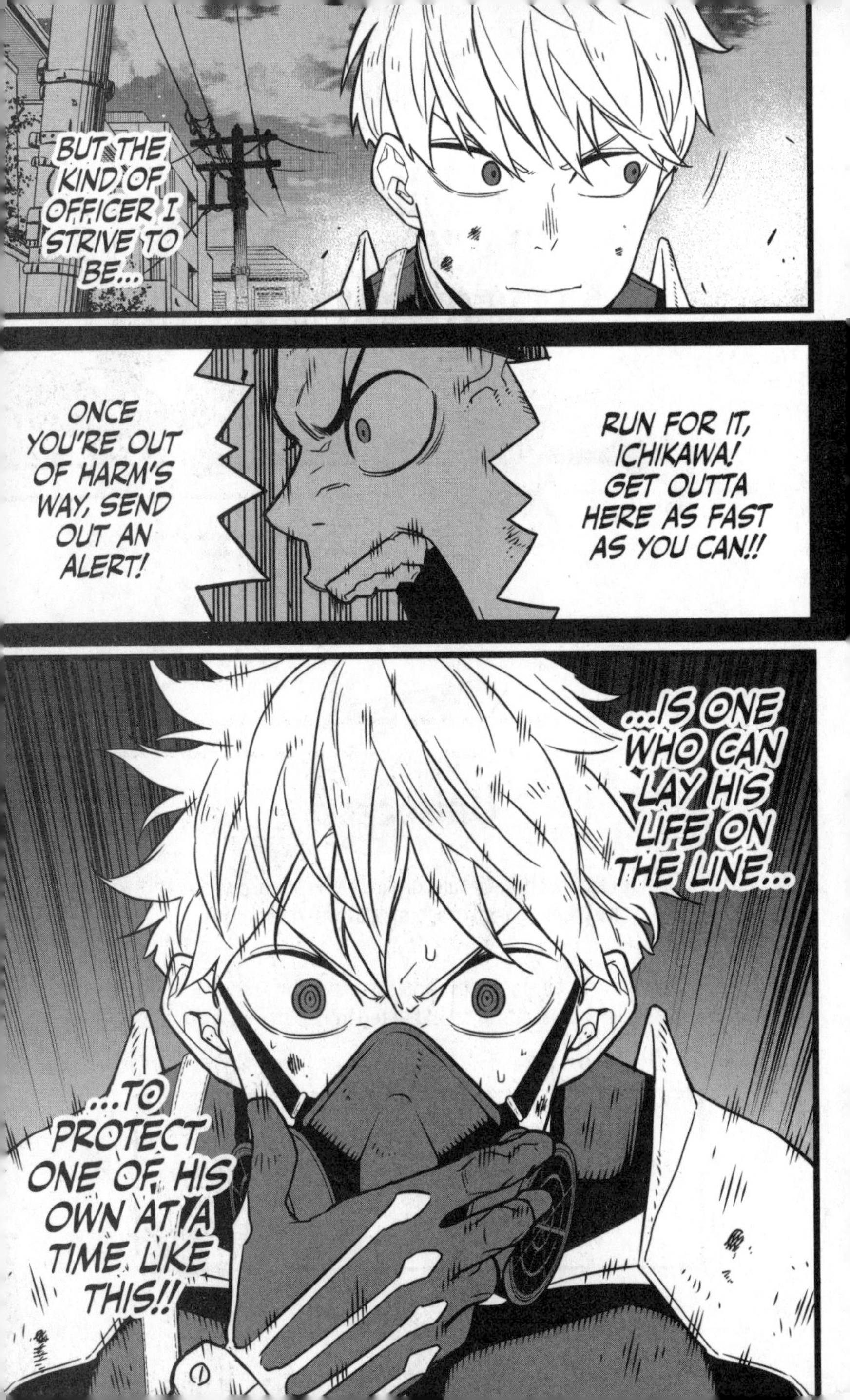
BUT THE KIND OF OFFICER I STRIVE TO BE...
RUN FOR IT, ICHIKAWA! GET OUTTA HERE AS FAST AS YOU CAN!!
ONCE YOU'RE OUT OF HARM'S WAY, SEND OUT AN ALERT!
...IS ONE WHO CAN LAY HIS LIFE ON THE LINE...
...TO PROTECT ONE OF HIS OWN AT A TIME LIKE THIS!!

KAIJU NO. 8
BACKGROUND
INFORMATION

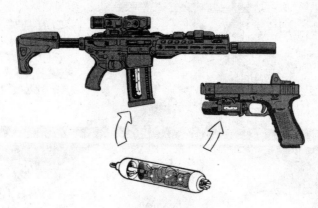

Unisocket

A socket that houses kaiju organs with special attributes (i.e., "uniorgans") or secretions from said organs.

Swapping out the socket's contents allows the ammunition to gain special attributes extracted from different kaiju.

---Examples---

Burst Rounds	**Freeze Rounds**
Collected from a honju that emerged on August 4, 1970	Collected from a honju that emerged on February 19, 1988

THIS THING TOOK DOWN SHINOMIYA.

PANT PANT

CHAPTER 16

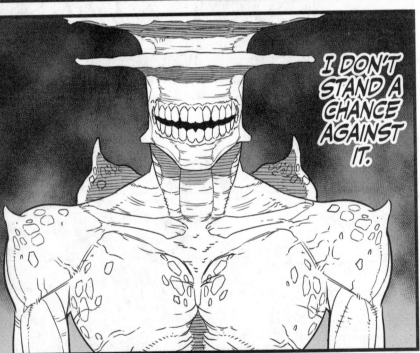

I DON'T STAND A CHANCE AGAINST IT.

YAAAA-AAAH!!

BUT I CAN AT LEAST BUY IHARU SOME TIME TO ESCAPE!!

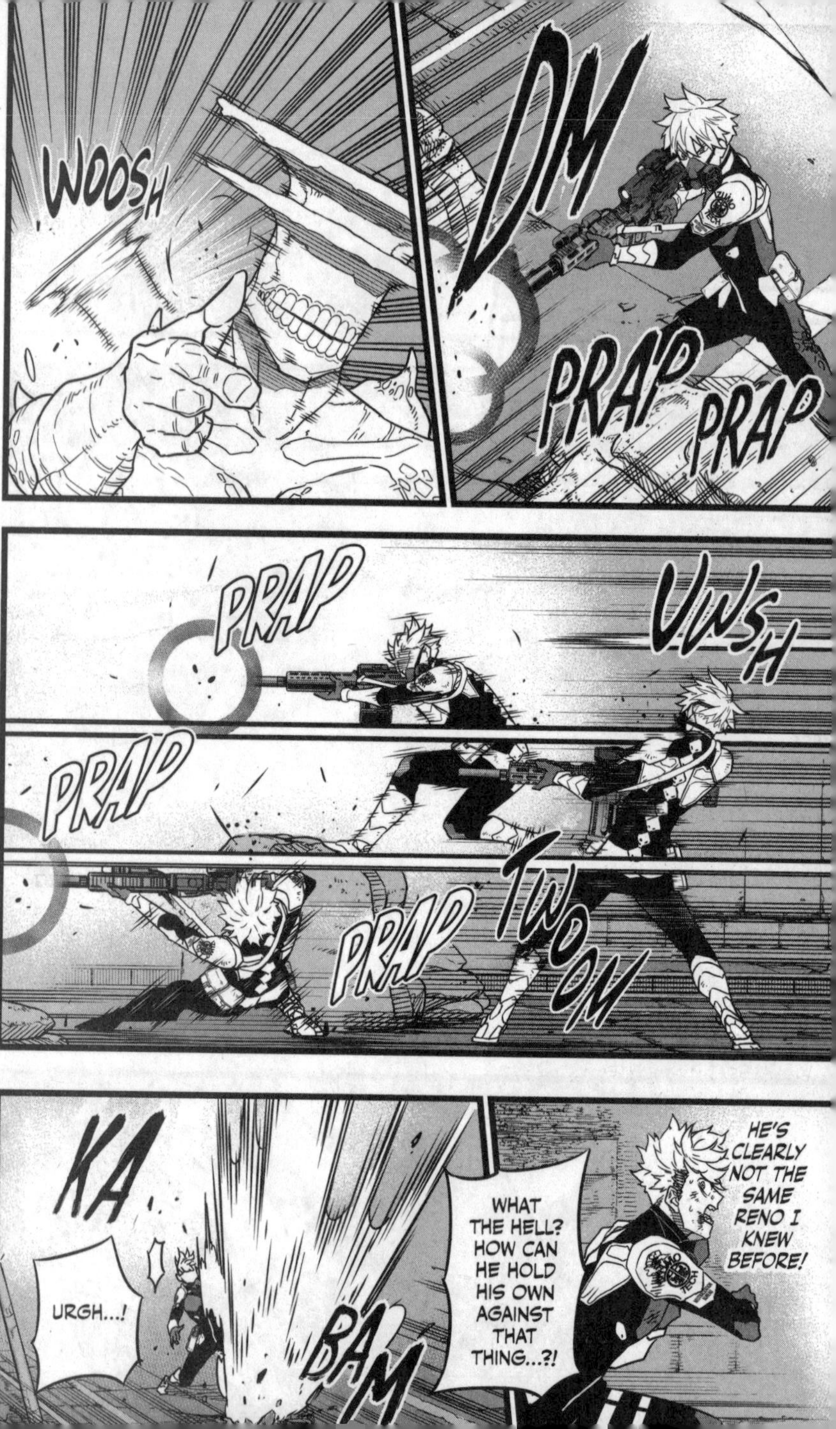
DM
PRAP
PRAP
WOOSH
VWSH
PRAP
PRAP
TWOOM
PRAP
HE'S CLEARLY NOT THE SAME RENO I KNEW BEFORE!
WHAT THE HELL? HOW CAN HE HOLD HIS OWN AGAINST THAT THING...?!
KA
BAM
URGH...!

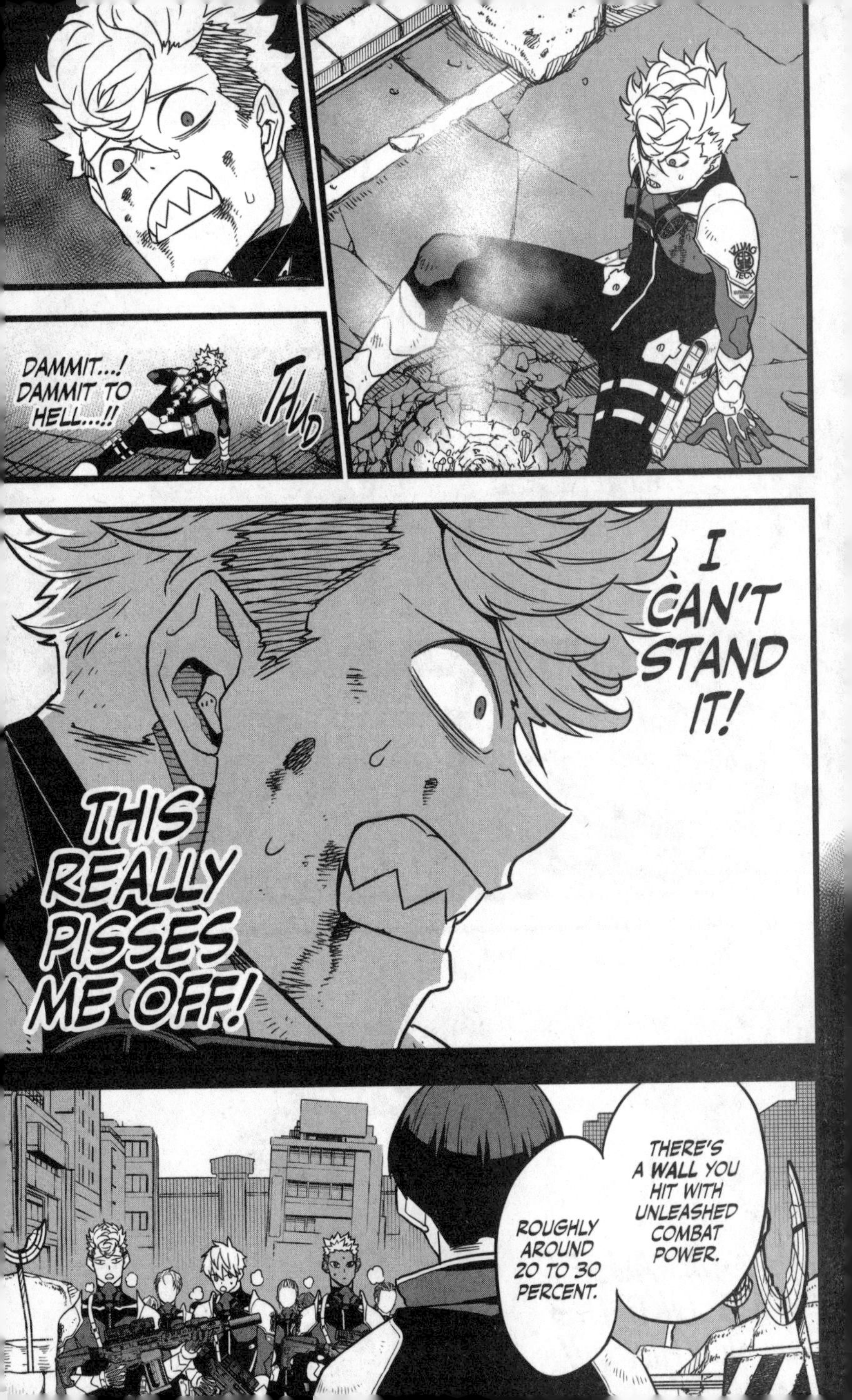
DAMMIT...! DAMMIT TO HELL...!!
THUD
I CAN'T STAND IT!
THIS REALLY PISSES ME OFF!
THERE'S A WALL YOU HIT WITH UNLEASHED COMBAT POWER.
ROUGHLY AROUND 20 TO 30 PERCENT.

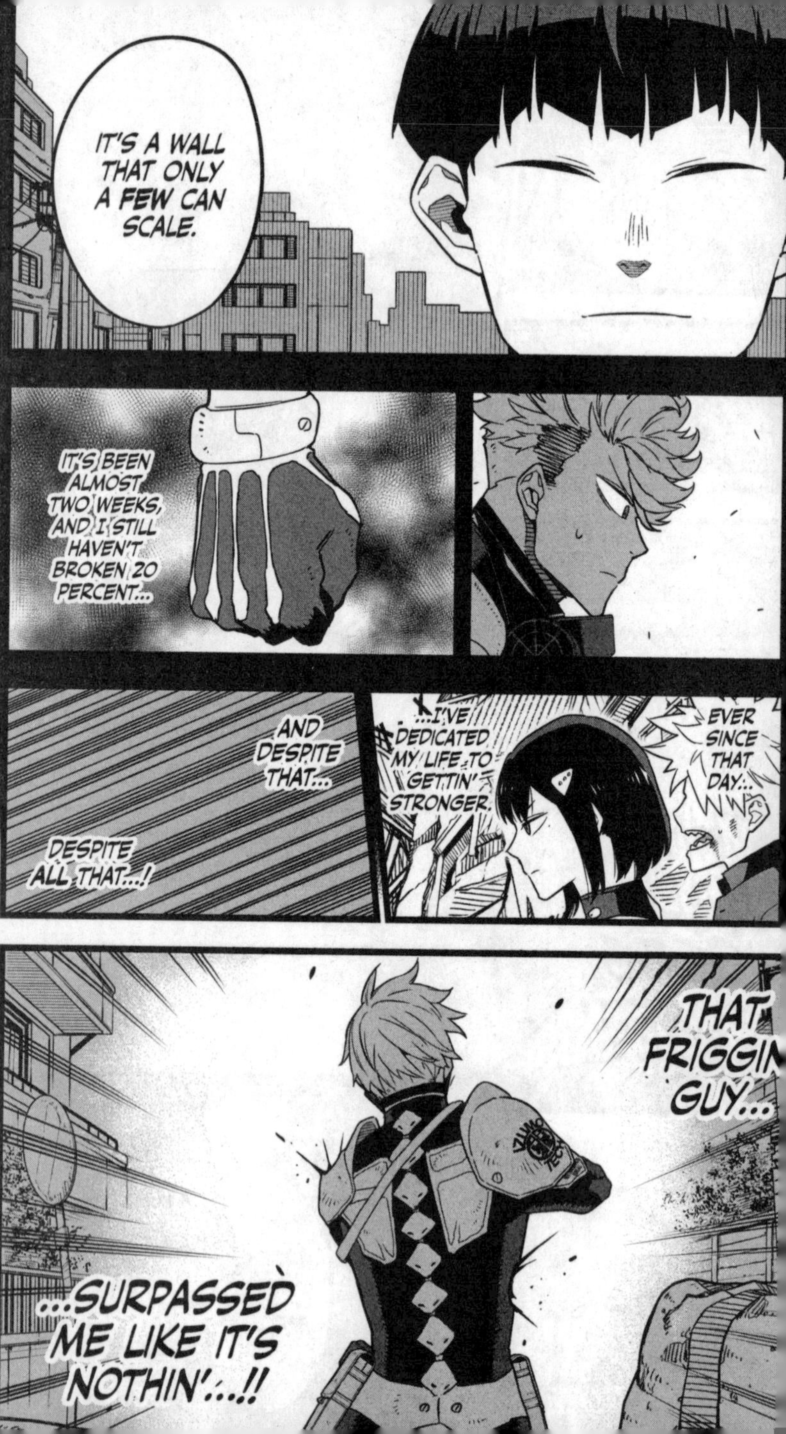
IT'S A WALL THAT ONLY A FEW CAN SCALE.
IT'S BEEN ALMOST TWO WEEKS, AND I STILL HAVEN'T BROKEN 20 PERCENT...
EVER SINCE THAT DAY...
...I'VE DEDICATED MY LIFE TO GETTIN' STRONGER.
AND DESPITE THAT...
DESPITE ALL THAT...!
THAT FRIGGIN GUY...
...SURPASSED ME LIKE IT'S NOTHIN'...!!

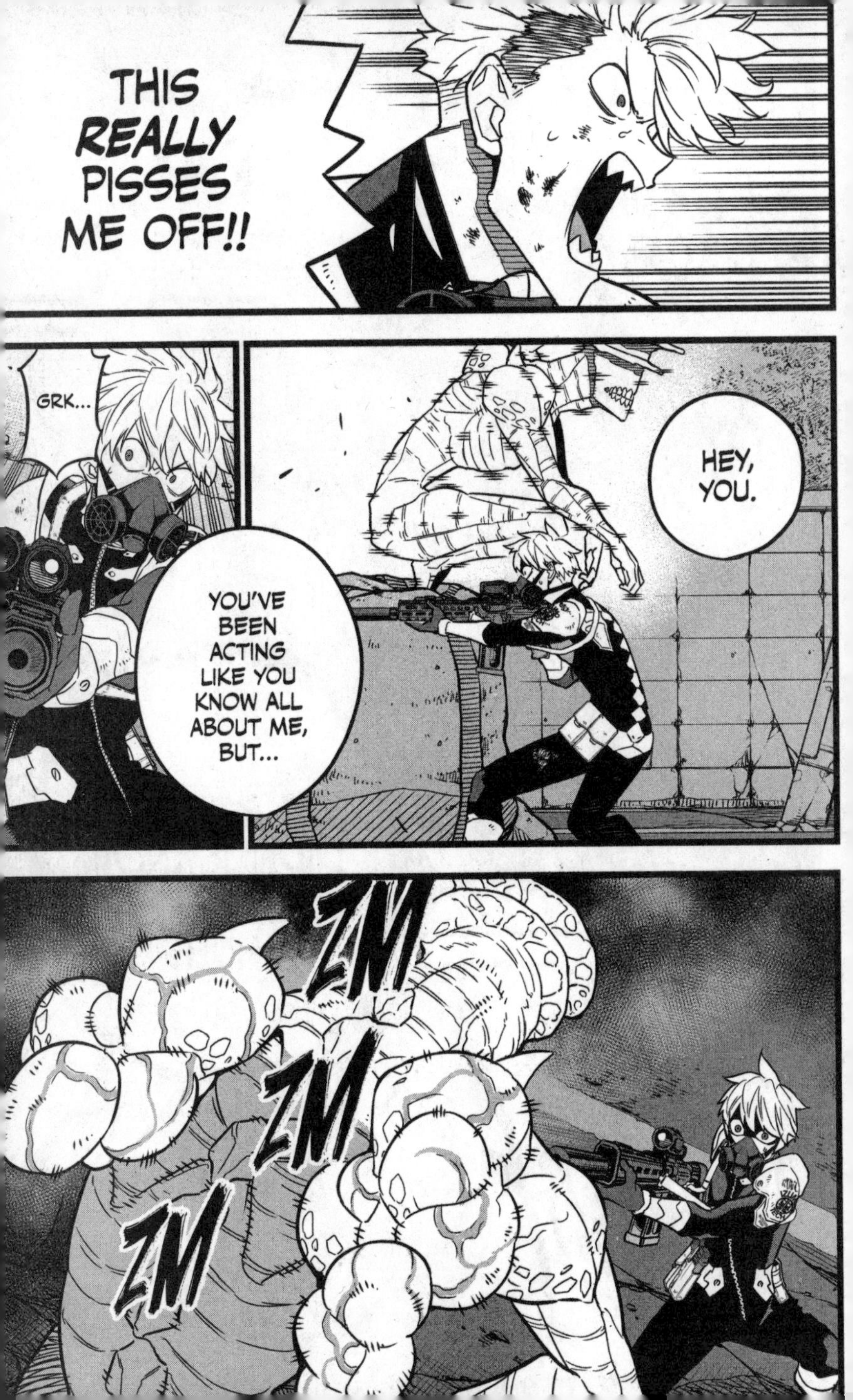
THIS REALLY PISSES ME OFF!!
HEY, YOU.
YOU'VE BEEN ACTING LIKE YOU KNOW ALL ABOUT ME, BUT...
GRK...
ZM
ZM
ZM

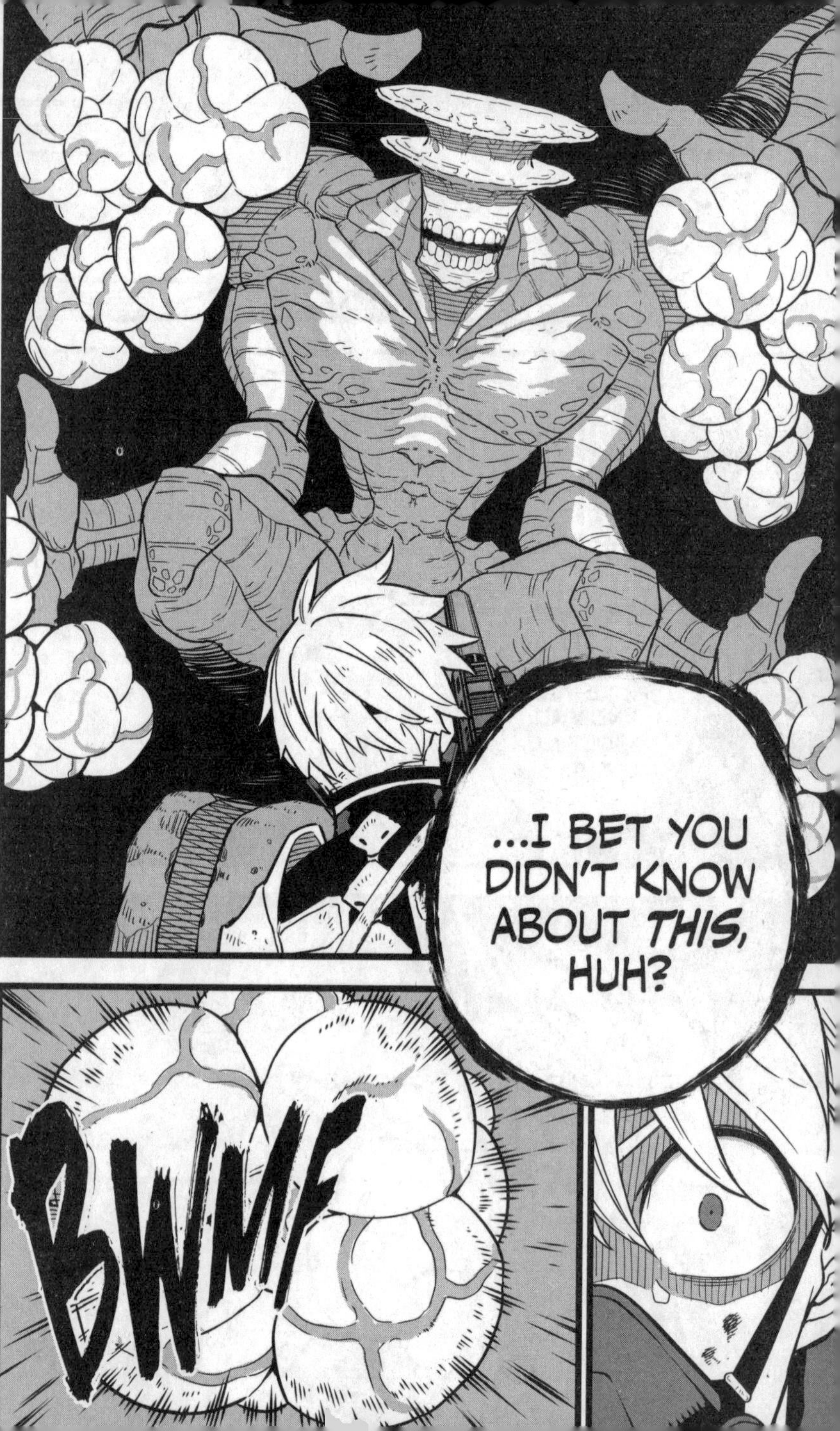
...I BET YOU DIDN'T KNOW ABOUT *THIS*, HUH?
BWMF

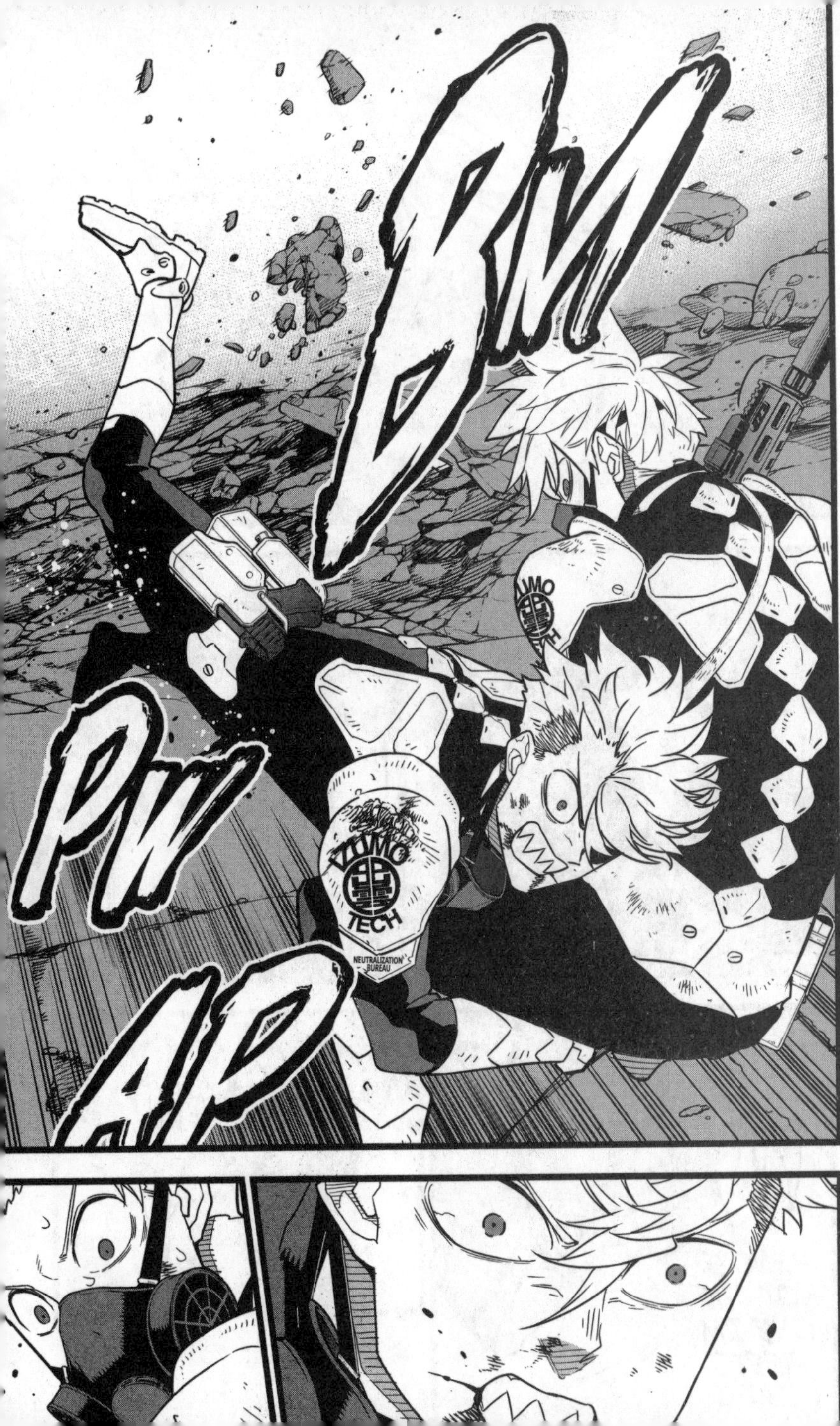
IZUMO TECH
NEUTRALIZATION BUREAU

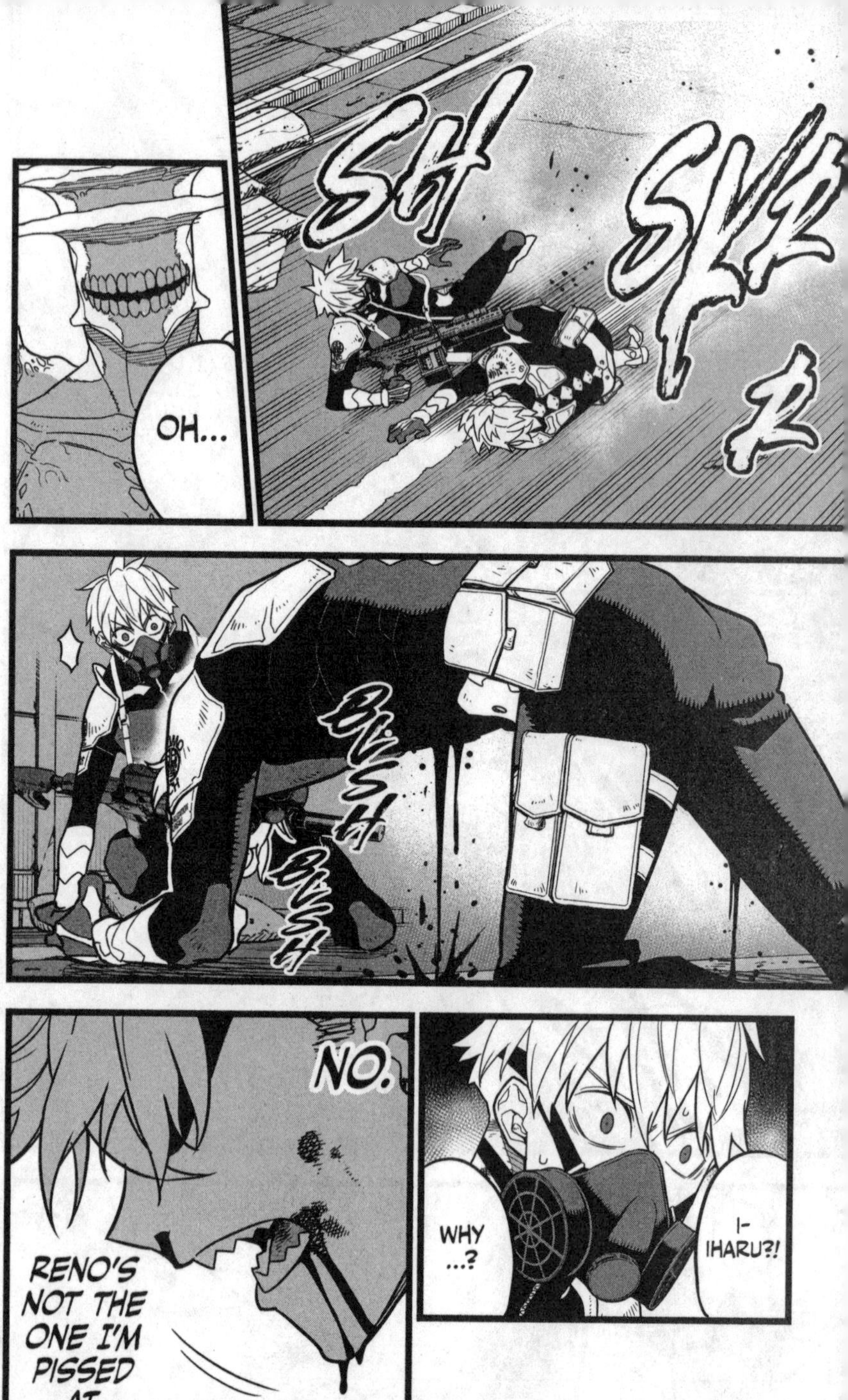
OH...
GUSH GUSH
I- IHARU?!
WHY ...?
NO.
RENO'S NOT THE ONE I'M PISSED AT.

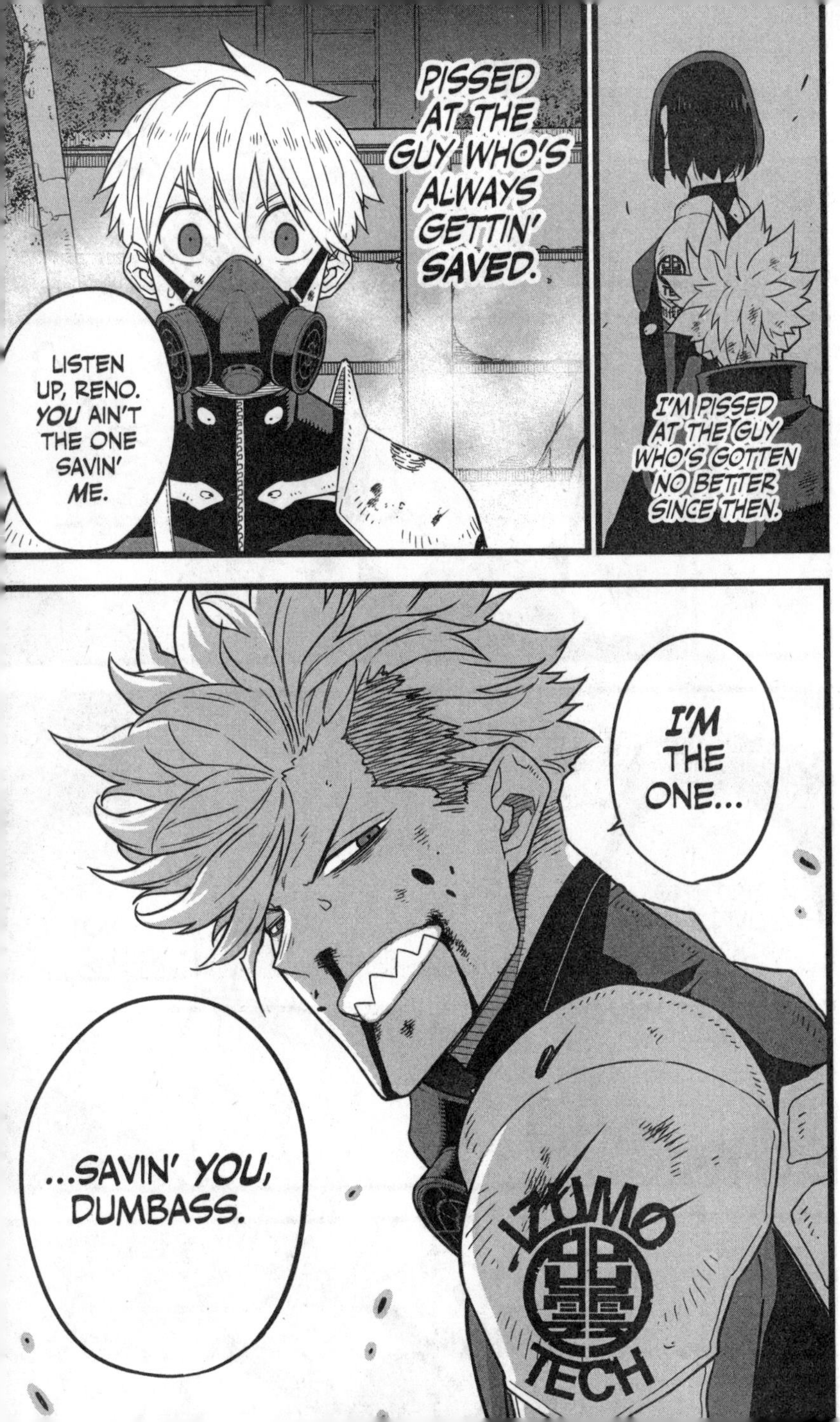
I'M PISSED AT THE GUY WHO'S GOTTEN NO BETTER SINCE THEN.
PISSED AT THE GUY WHO'S ALWAYS GETTIN' SAVED.
LISTEN UP, RENO. YOU AIN'T THE ONE SAVIN' ME.
I'M THE ONE...
...SAVIN' YOU, DUMBASS.
IZUMO TECH

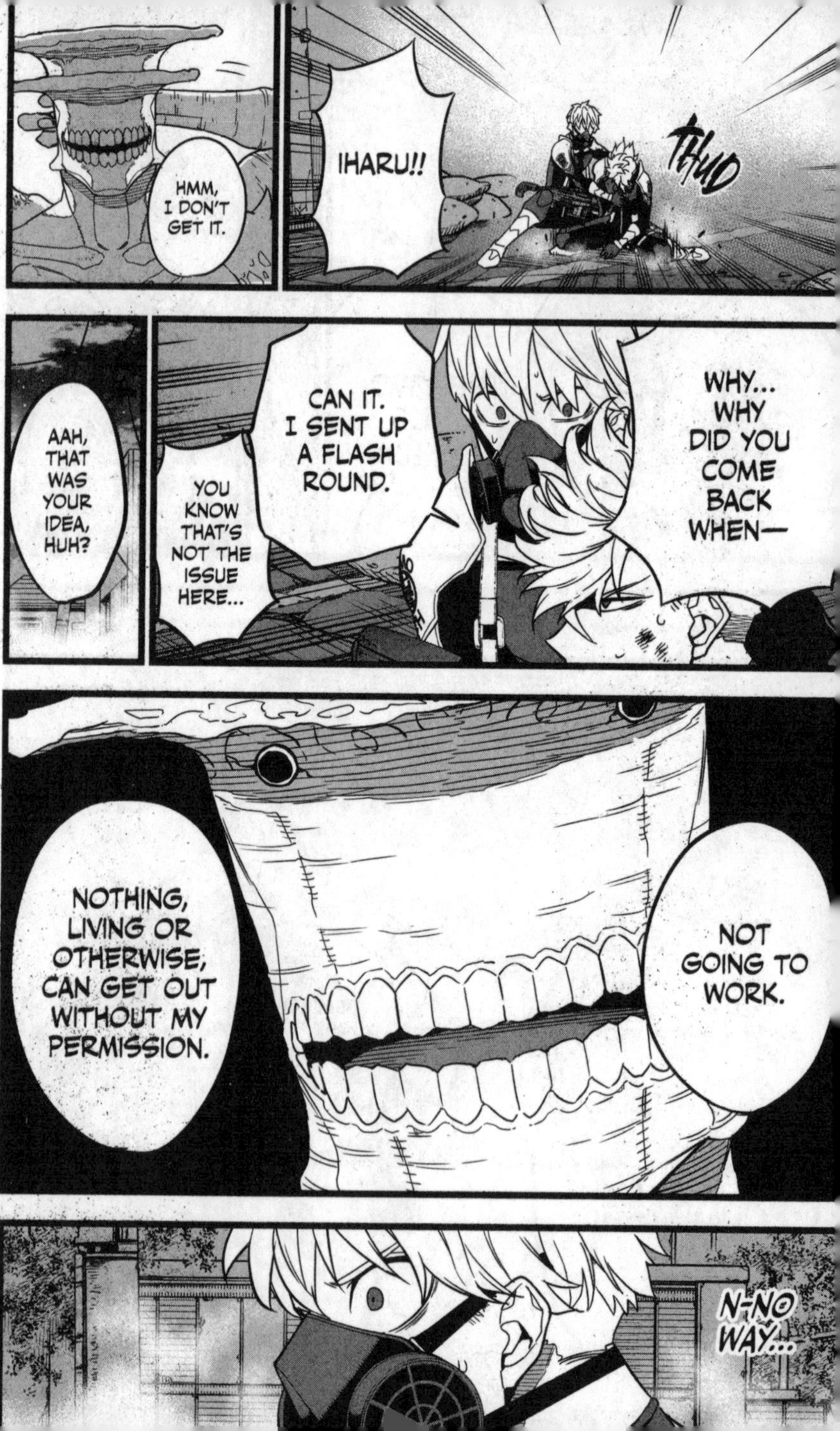
THUD
IHARU!!
HMM, I DON'T GET IT.
WHY... WHY DID YOU COME BACK WHEN—
CAN IT. I SENT UP A FLASH ROUND.
YOU KNOW THAT'S NOT THE ISSUE HERE...
AAH, THAT WAS YOUR IDEA, HUH?
NOT GOING TO WORK.
NOTHING, LIVING OR OTHERWISE, CAN GET OUT WITHOUT MY PERMISSION.
N-NO WAY...

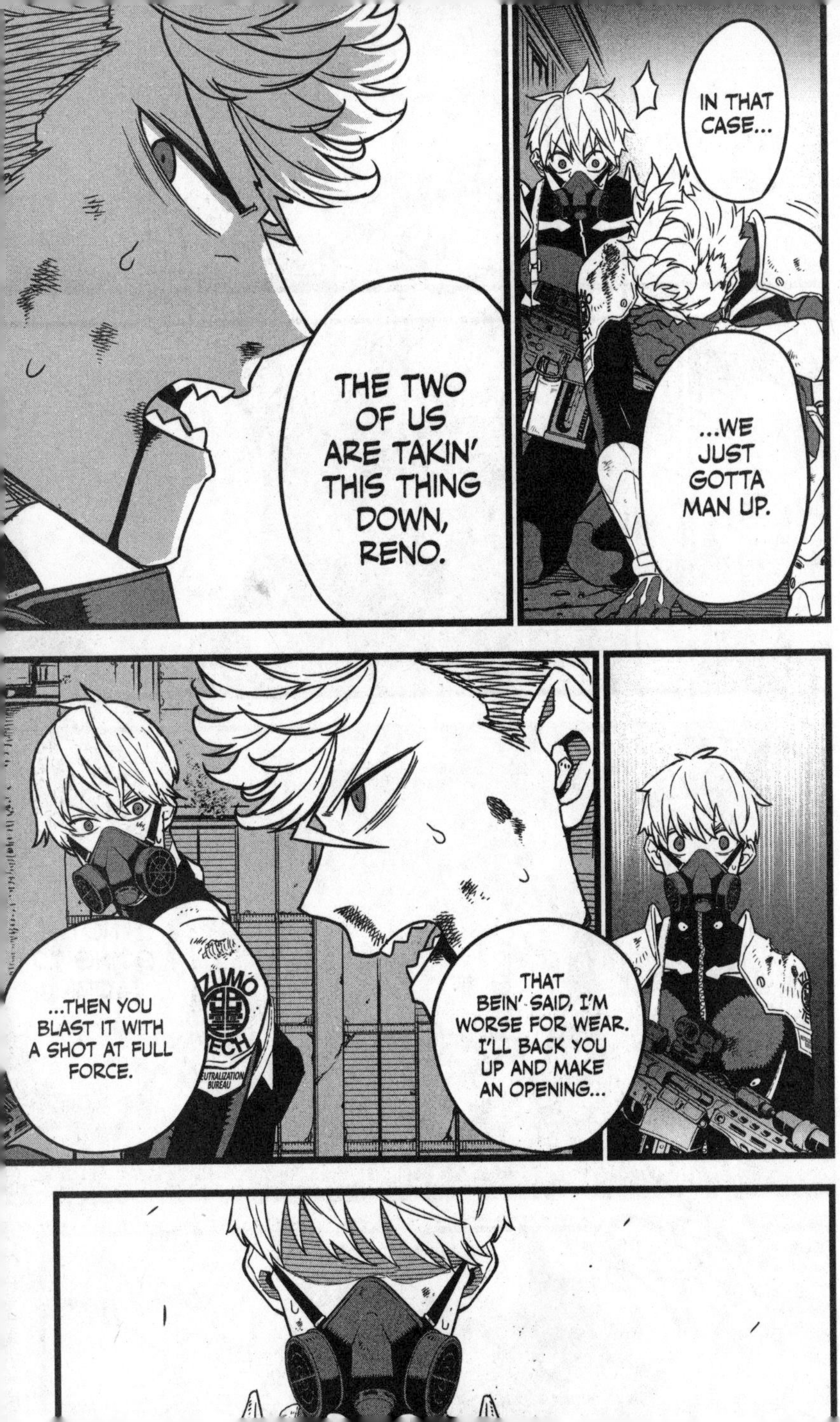
IN THAT CASE...
...WE JUST GOTTA MAN UP.
THE TWO OF US ARE TAKIN' THIS THING DOWN, RENO.
THAT BEIN' SAID, I'M WORSE FOR WEAR. I'LL BACK YOU UP AND MAKE AN OPENING...
...THEN YOU BLAST IT WITH A SHOT AT FULL FORCE.
IZUMO TECH
NEUTRALIZATION BUREAU

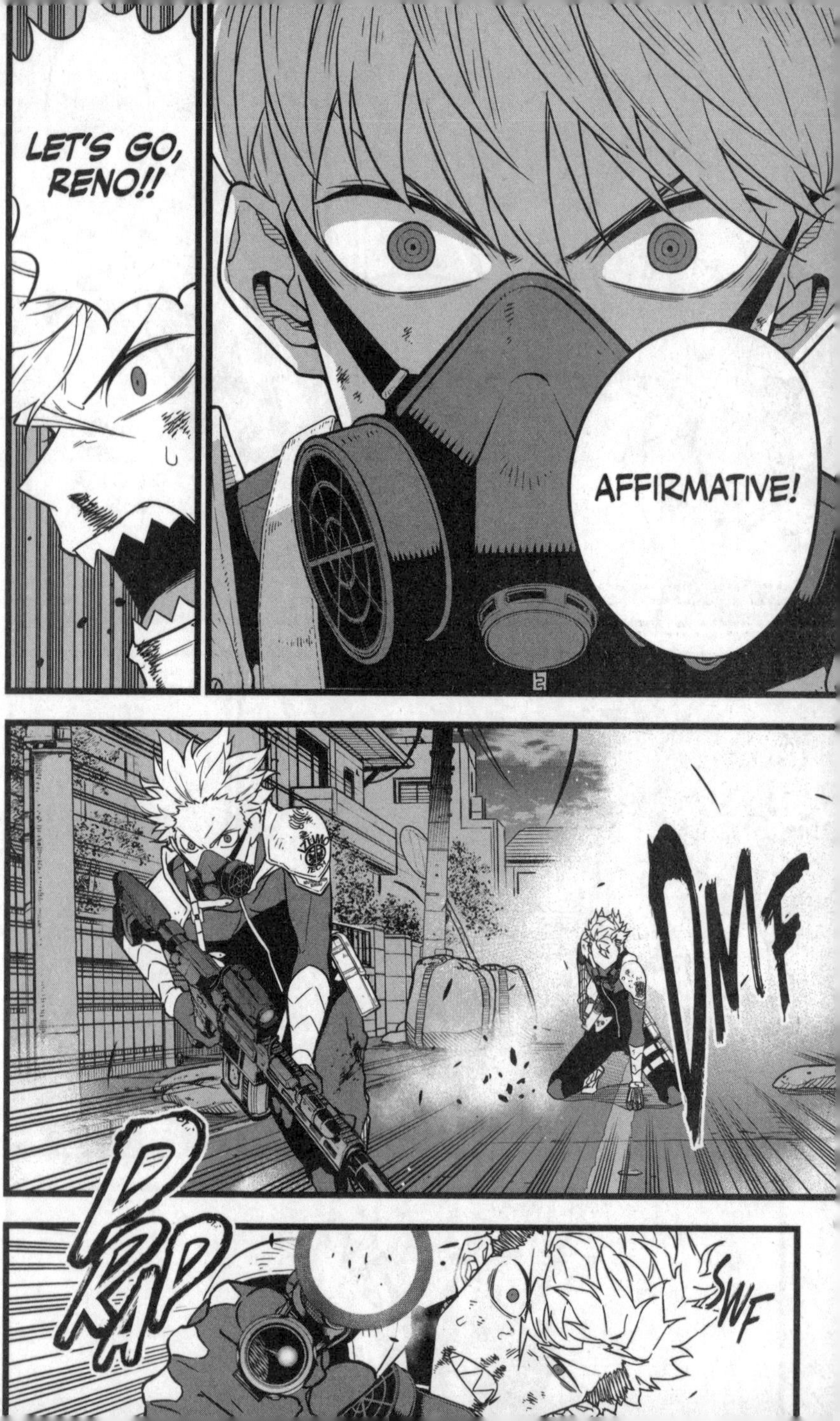
AFFIRMATIVE!
LET'S GO, RENO!!
DMF
SWF
PRAP

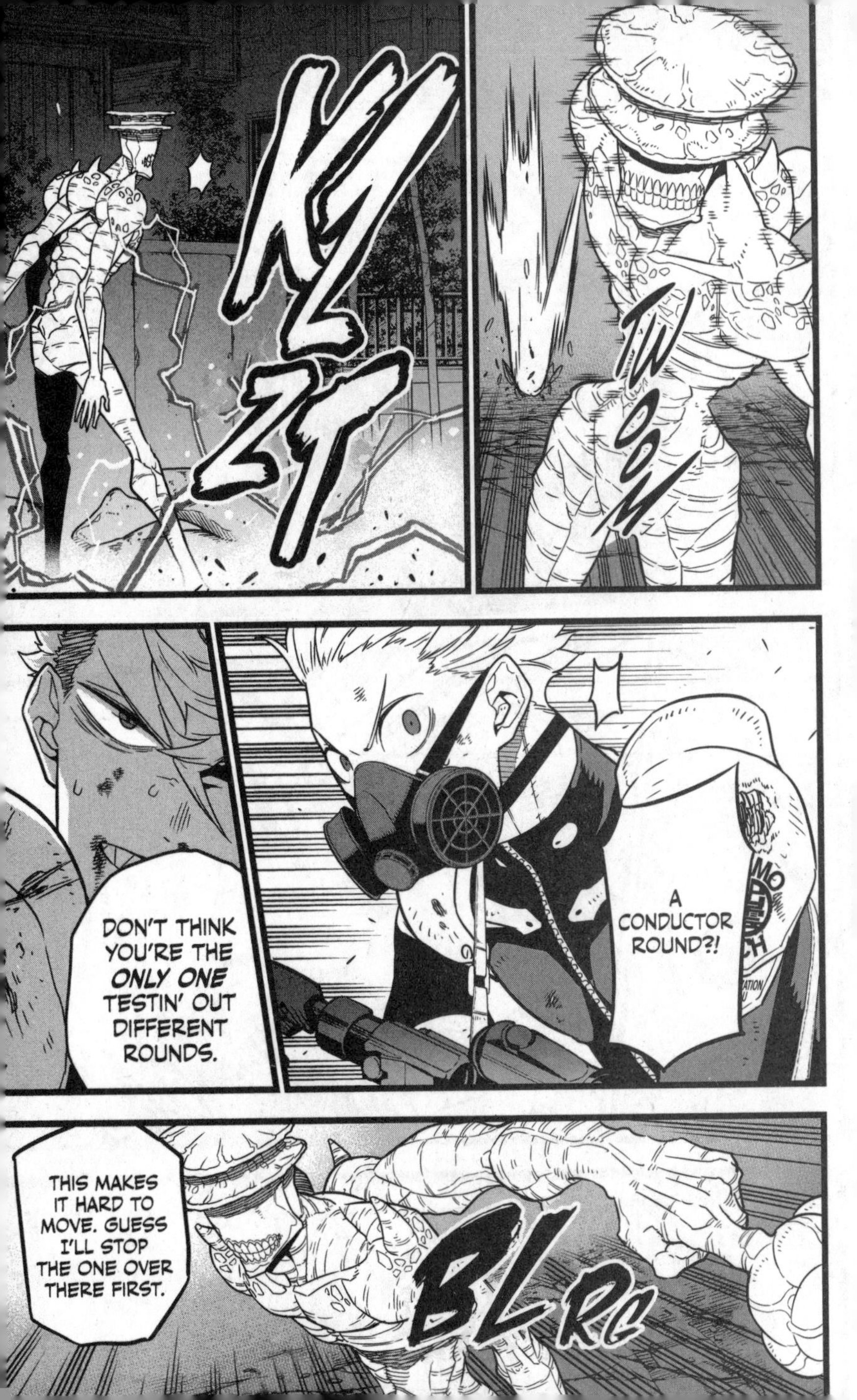
TWOOM
KZZZT
A CONDUCTOR ROUND?!
DON'T THINK YOU'RE THE *ONLY ONE* TESTIN' OUT DIFFERENT ROUNDS.
THIS MAKES IT HARD TO MOVE. GUESS I'LL STOP THE ONE OVER THERE FIRST.
BLRG

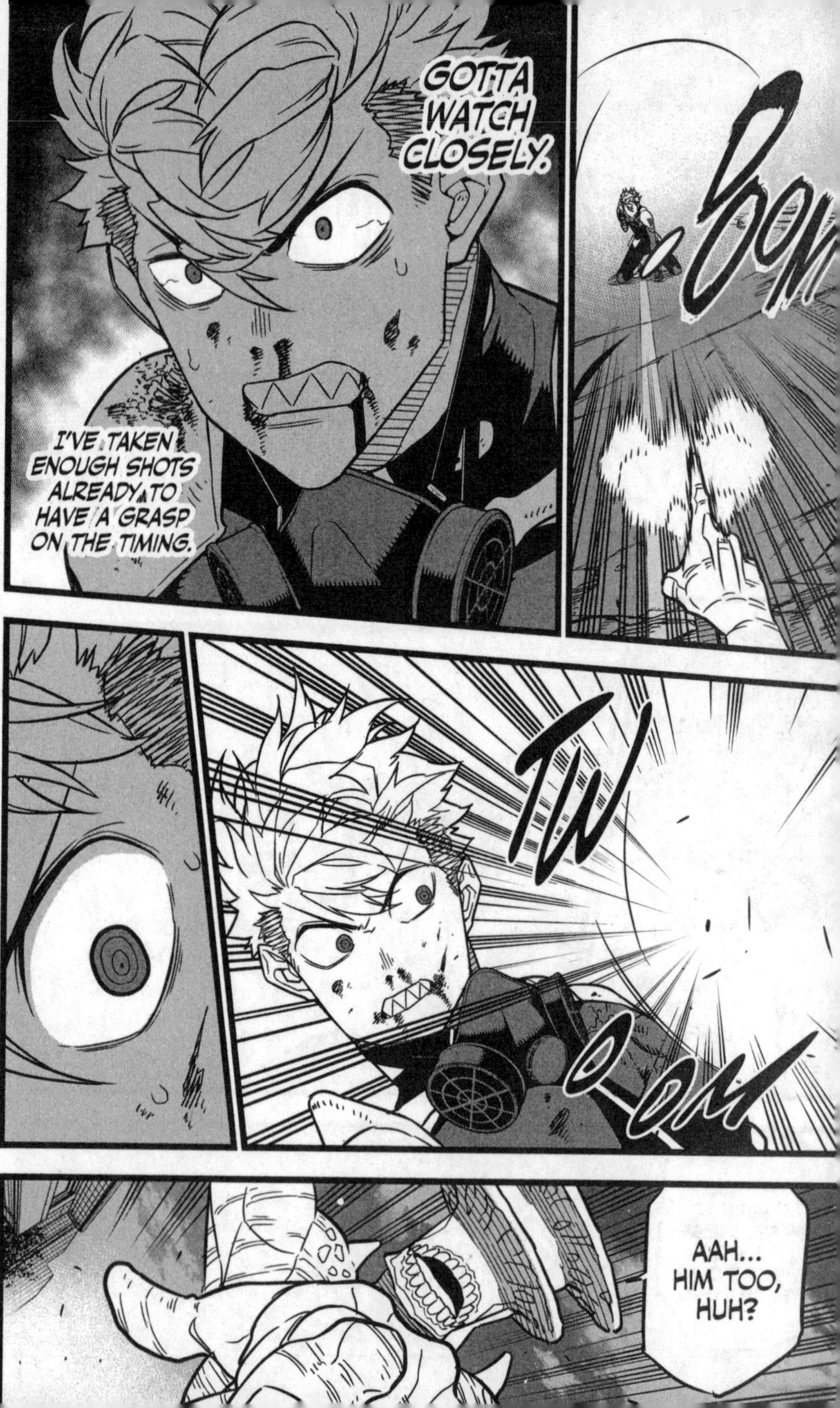
SOM
GOTTA WATCH CLOSELY.
I'VE TAKEN ENOUGH SHOTS ALREADY TO HAVE A GRASP ON THE TIMING.
TW
OOM
AAH... HIM TOO, HUH?

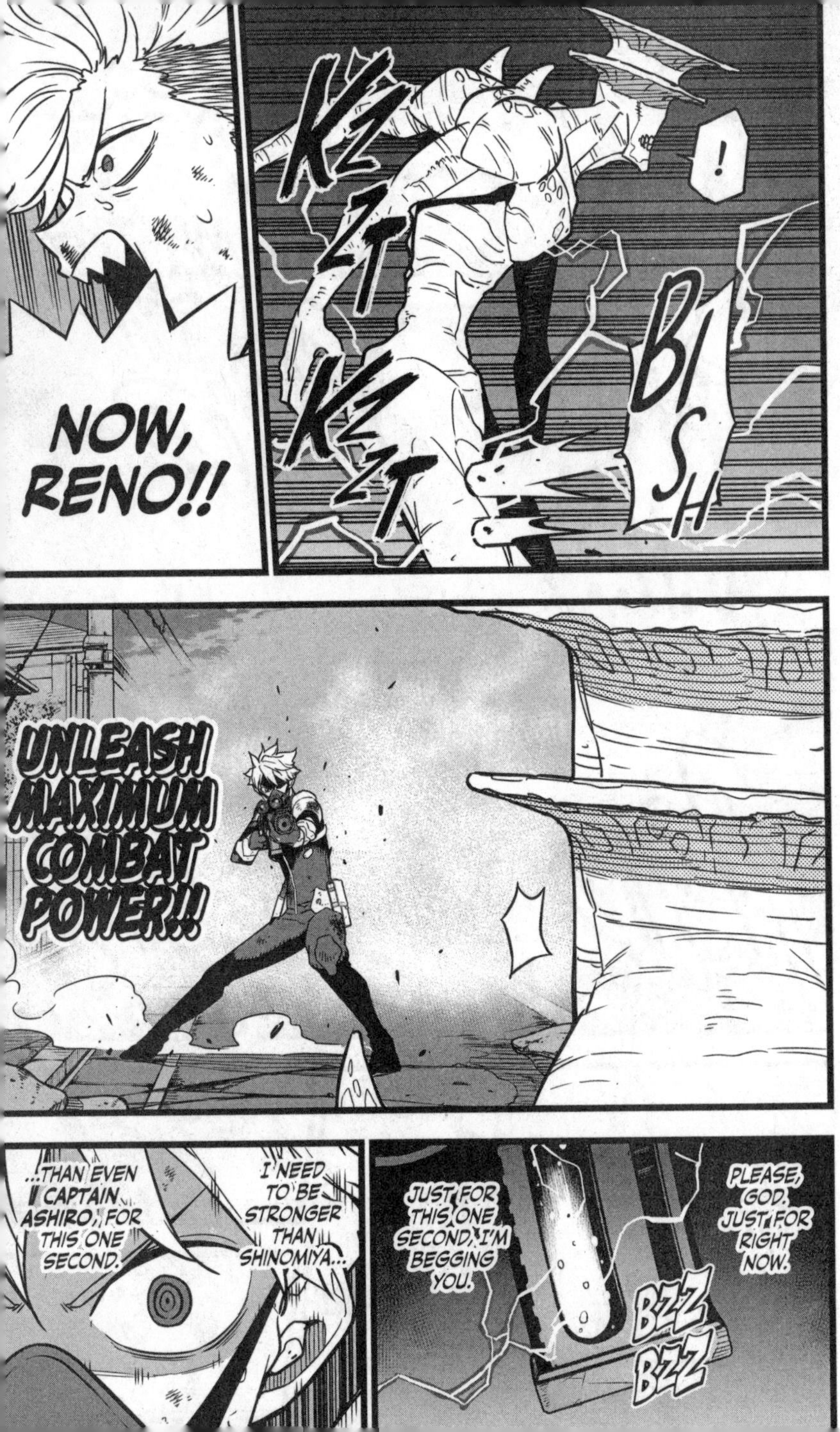
!
KZZT
KZZT
BISH
NOW, RENO!!
UNLEASH MAXIMUM COMBAT POWER!!
PLEASE, GOD. JUST FOR RIGHT NOW.
JUST FOR THIS ONE SECOND, I'M BEGGING YOU.
BZZ
BZZ
I NEED TO BE STRONGER THAN SHINOMIYA...
...THAN EVEN CAPTAIN ASHIRO, FOR THIS ONE SECOND.

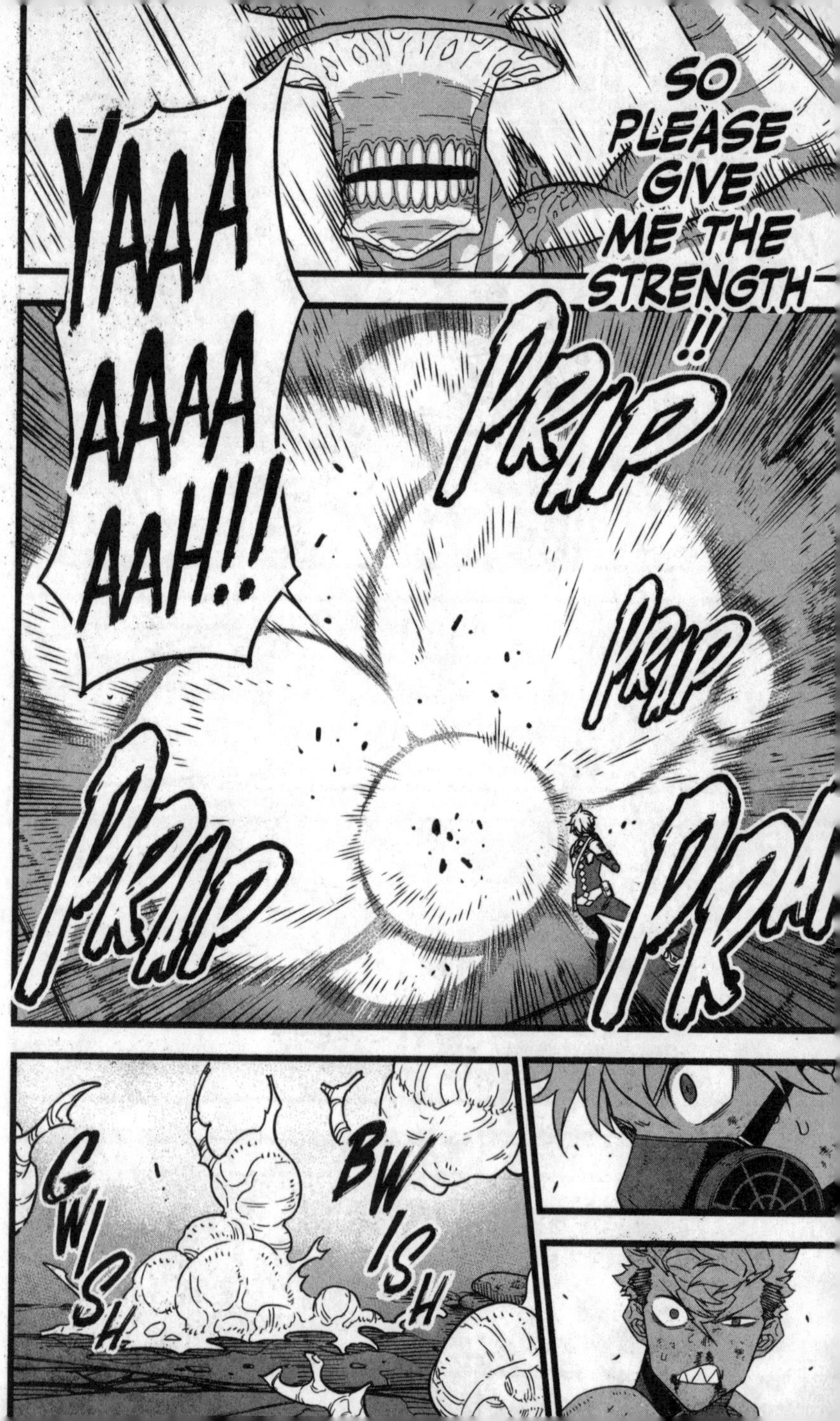
SO PLEASE GIVE ME THE STRENGTH—!!
YAAAAAAAAAH!!
PRAP
PRAP
PRAP
PRAP
BWISH
GWISH

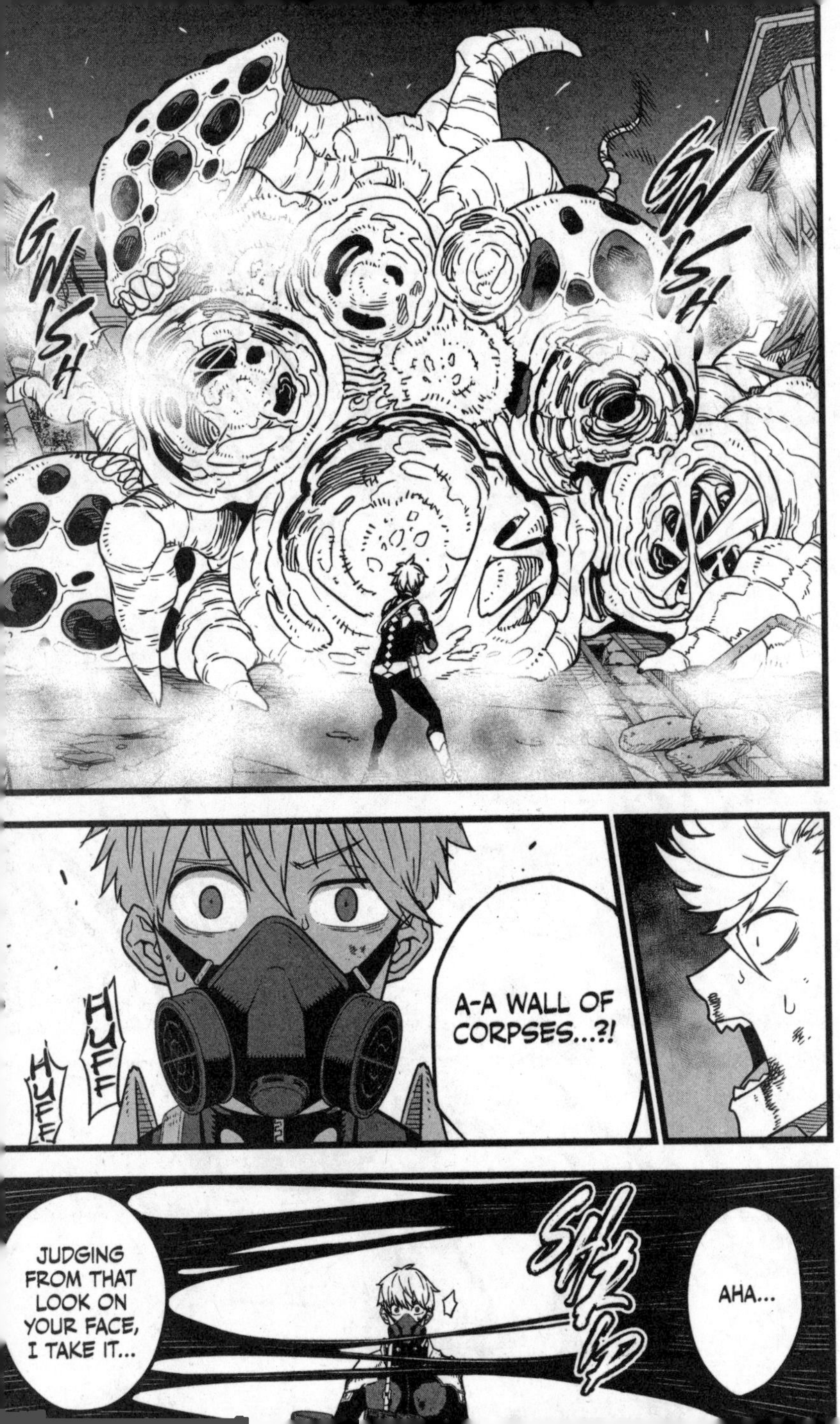
GWISH
GWISH
A-A WALL OF CORPSES...?!
HUFF
HUFF
AHA...
JUDGING FROM THAT LOOK ON YOUR FACE, I TAKE IT...

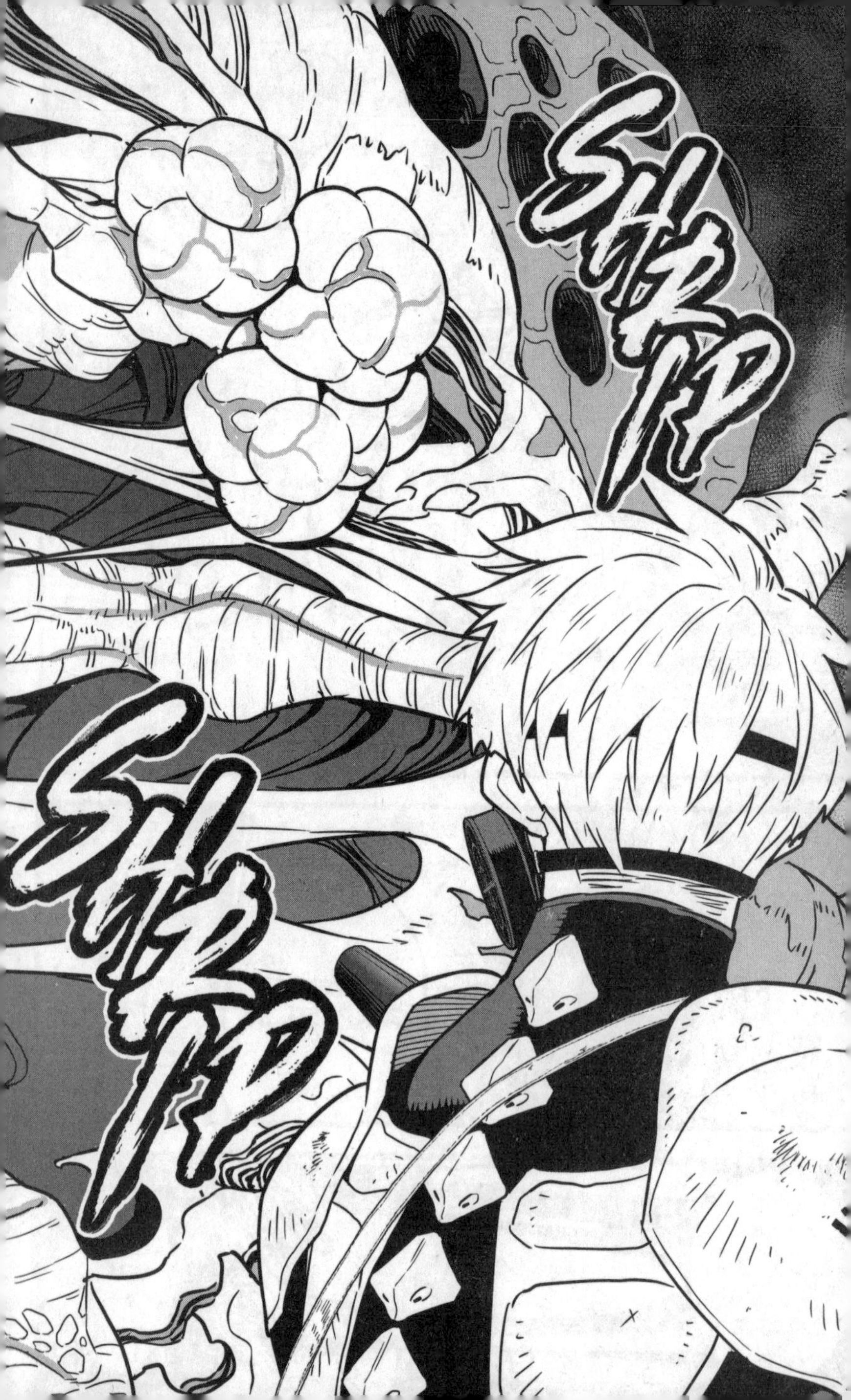
SHRP
SHRP

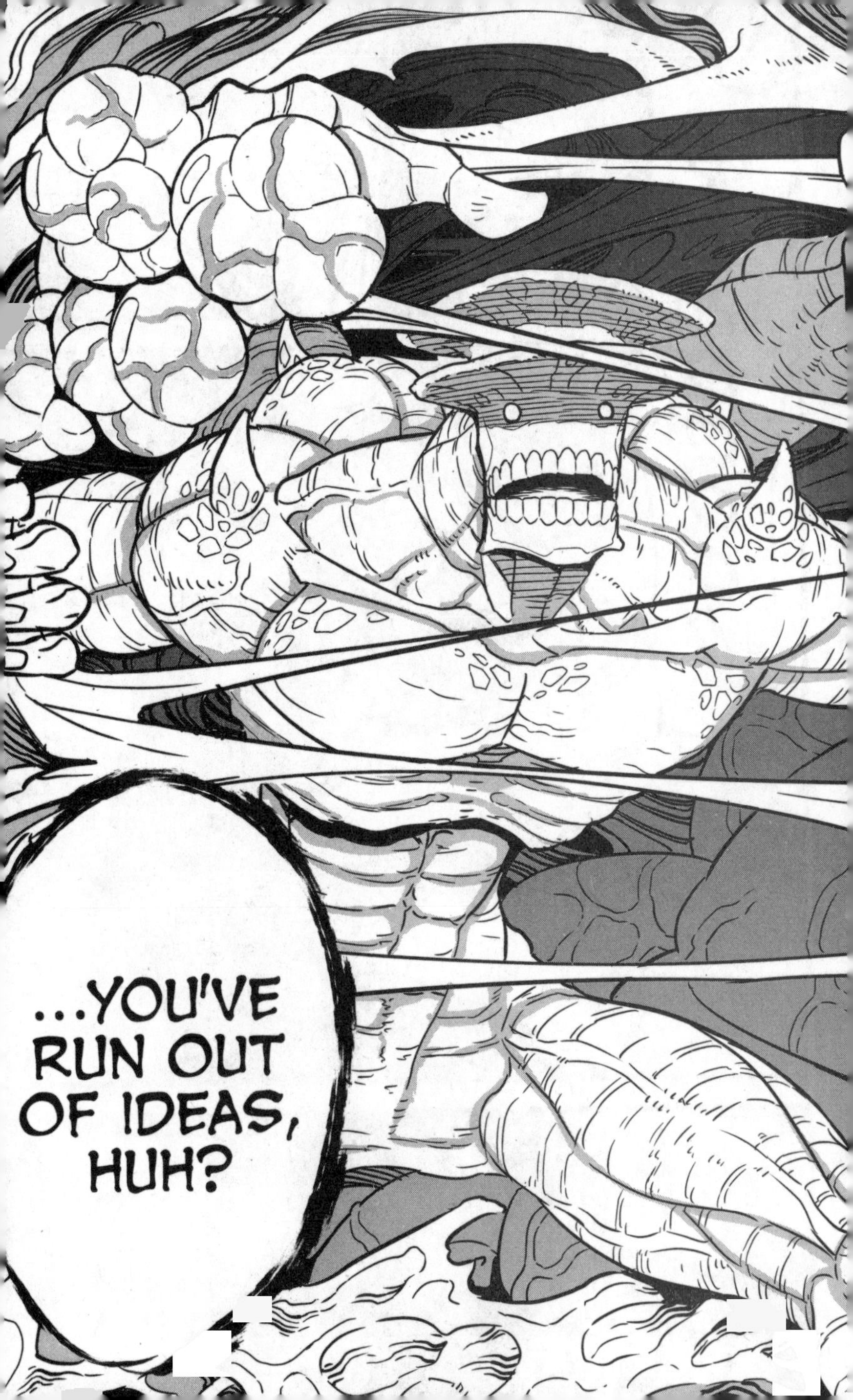
...YOU'VE RUN OUT OF IDEAS, HUH?

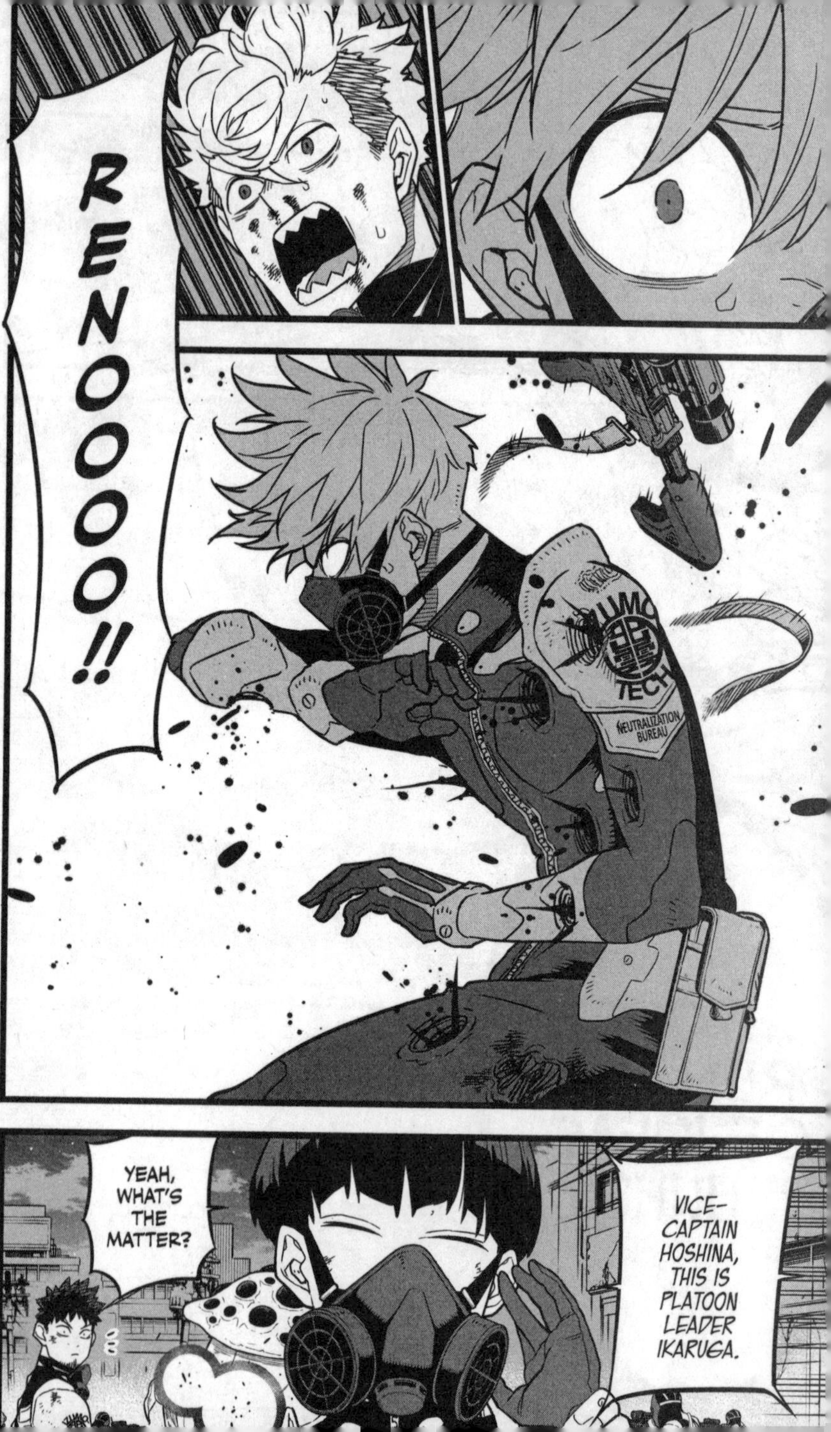
RENOOOO!!
VICE-CAPTAIN HOSHINA, THIS IS PLATOON LEADER IKARUGA.
YEAH, WHAT'S THE MATTER?

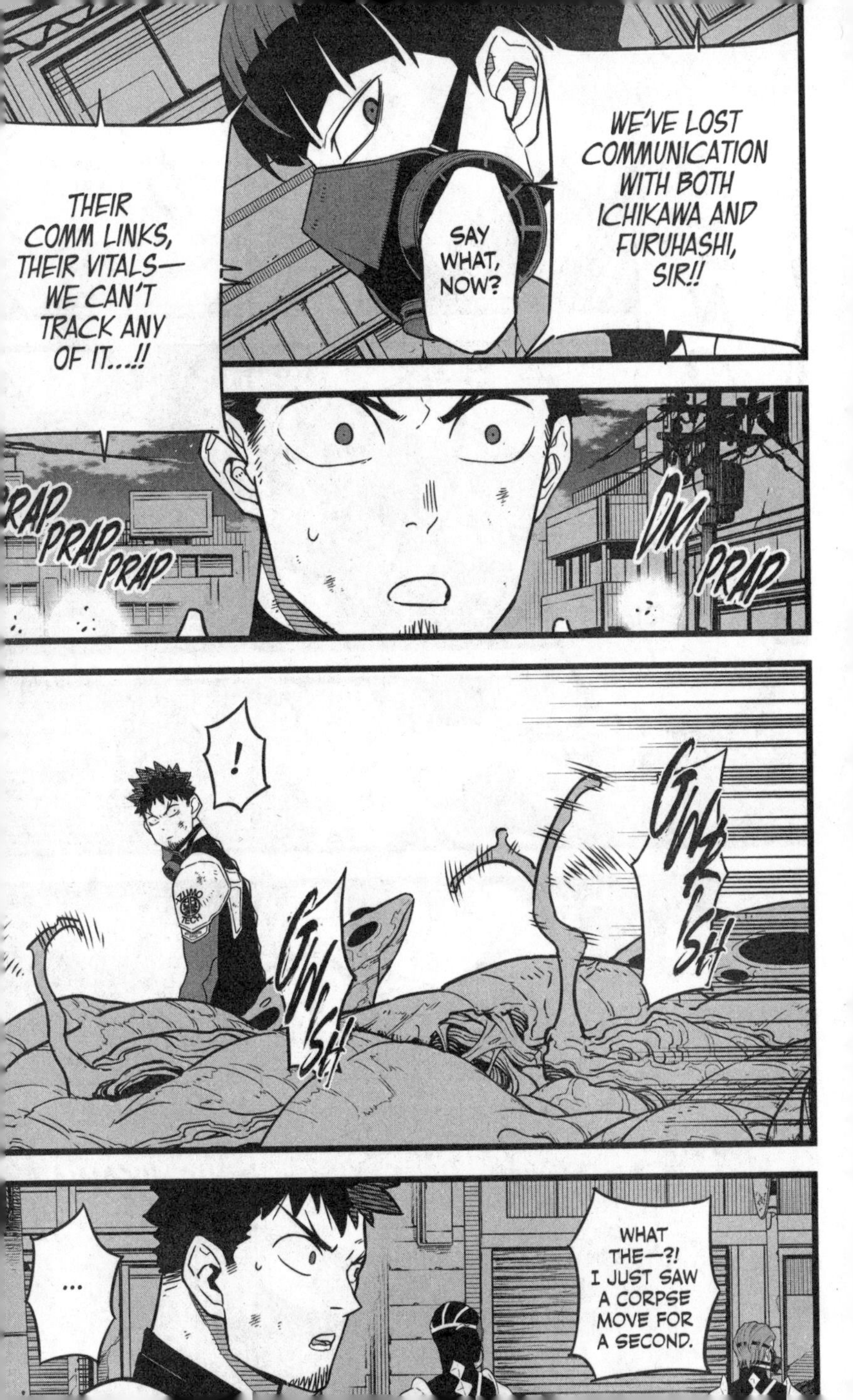
WE'VE LOST COMMUNICATION WITH BOTH ICHIKAWA AND FURUHASHI, SIR!!
SAY WHAT, NOW?
THEIR COMM LINKS, THEIR VITALS— WE CAN'T TRACK ANY OF IT...!!
DM
PRAP
PRAP PRAP PRAP
GWISH
GWISH
!
WHAT THE—?! I JUST SAW A CORPSE MOVE FOR A SECOND.
...

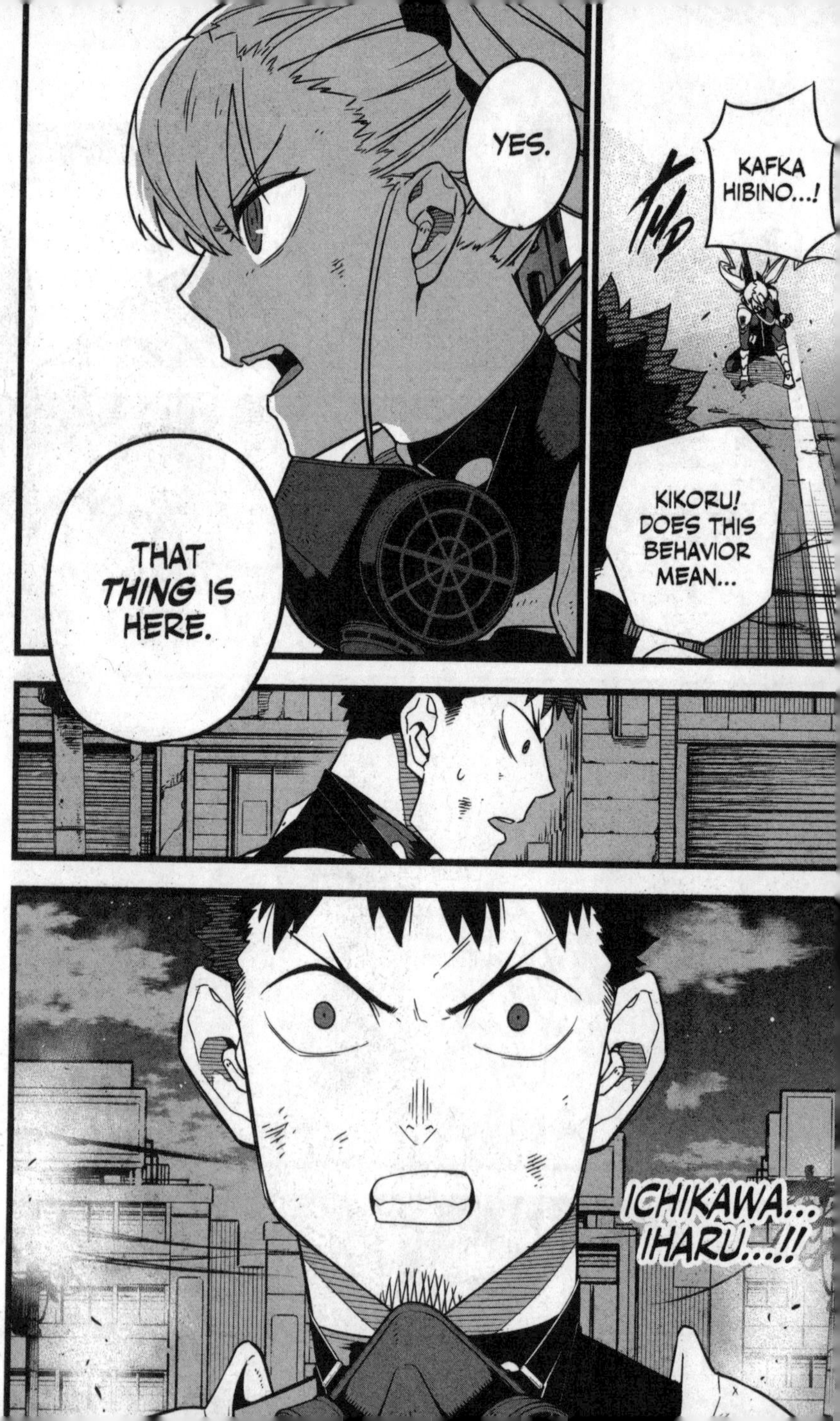
KAFKA HIBINO...!
KIKORU! DOES THIS BEHAVIOR MEAN...
YES.
THAT *THING* IS HERE.
ICHIKAWA... IHARU...!!

CHAPTER 17

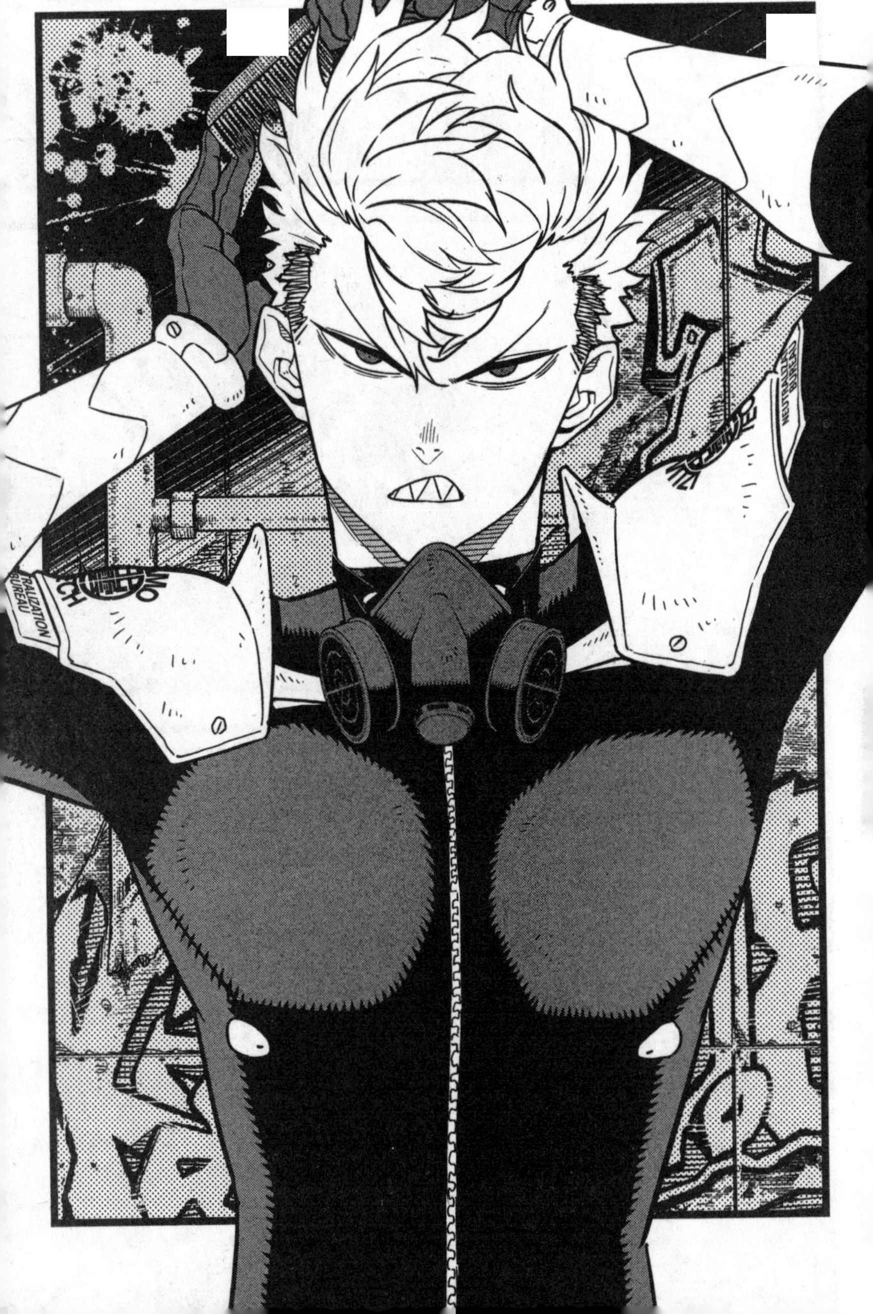

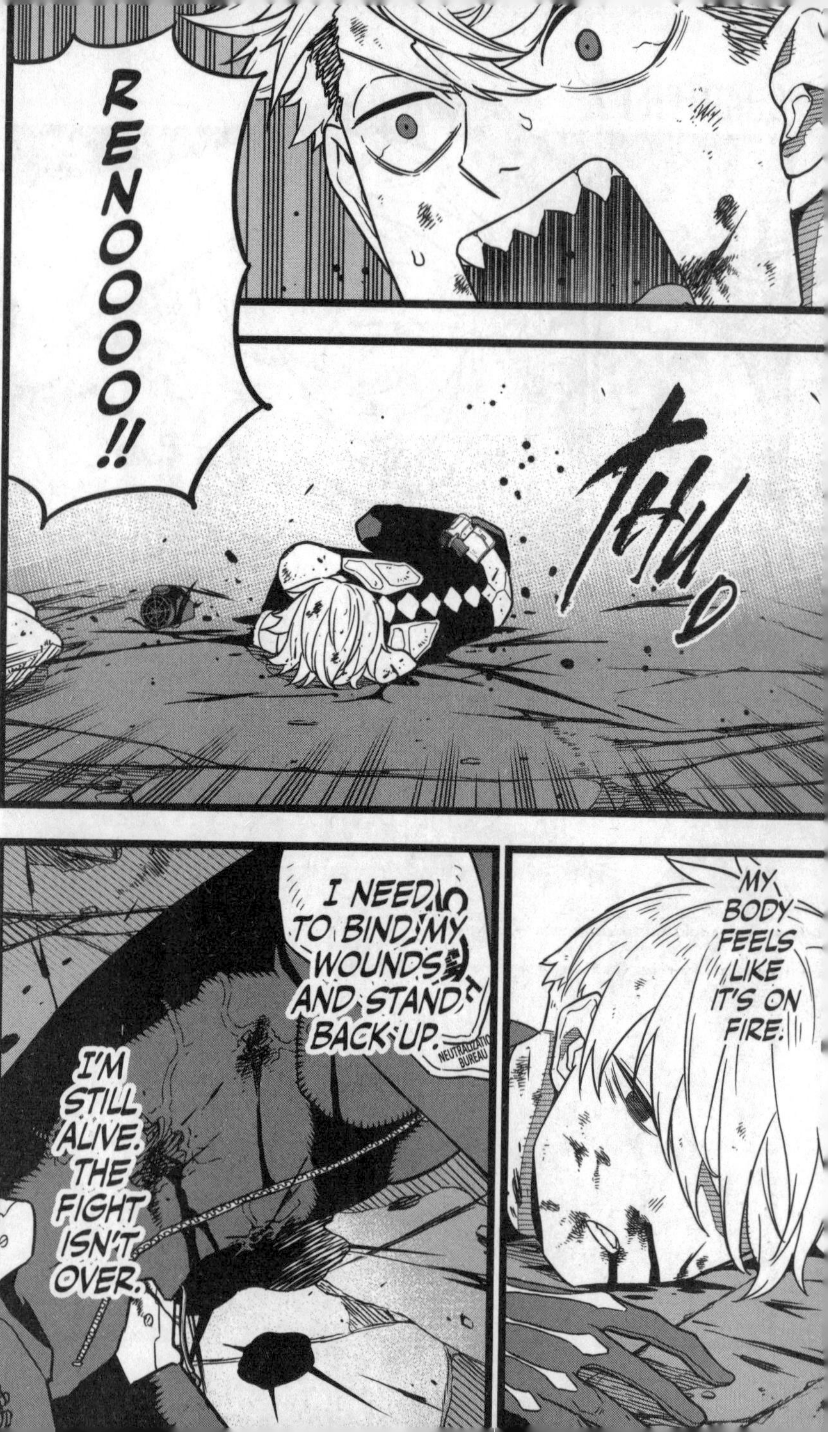
RENOOOOO!!
THUD
MY BODY FEELS LIKE IT'S ON FIRE.
I NEED TO BIND MY WOUNDS AND STAND BACK UP.
I'M STILL ALIVE. THE FIGHT ISN'T OVER.

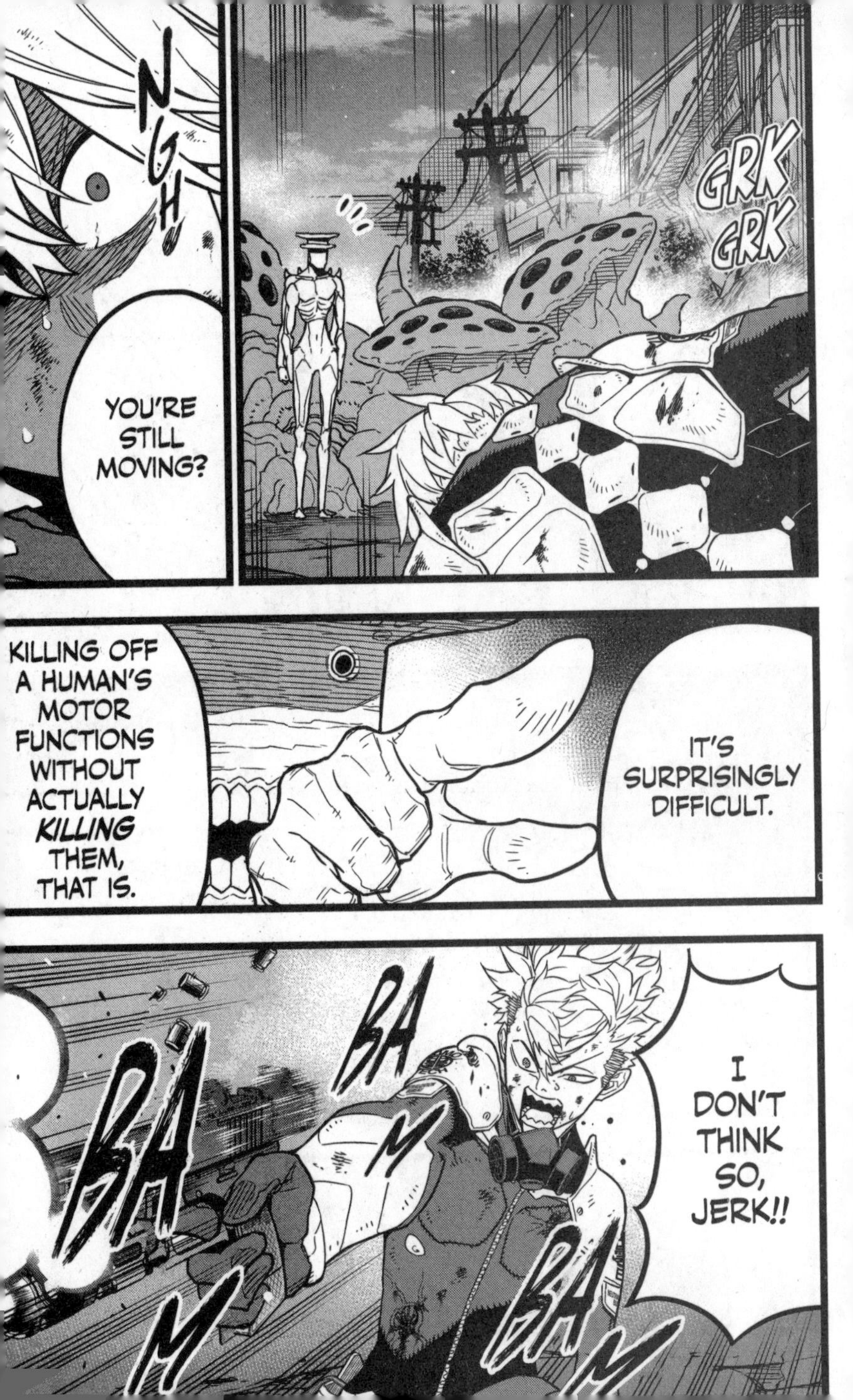
GRK GRK
NGH!
YOU'RE STILL MOVING?
IT'S SURPRISINGLY DIFFICULT.
KILLING OFF A HUMAN'S MOTOR FUNCTIONS WITHOUT ACTUALLY *KILLING* THEM, THAT IS.
I DON'T THINK SO, JERK!!
BAM
BAM
BAM

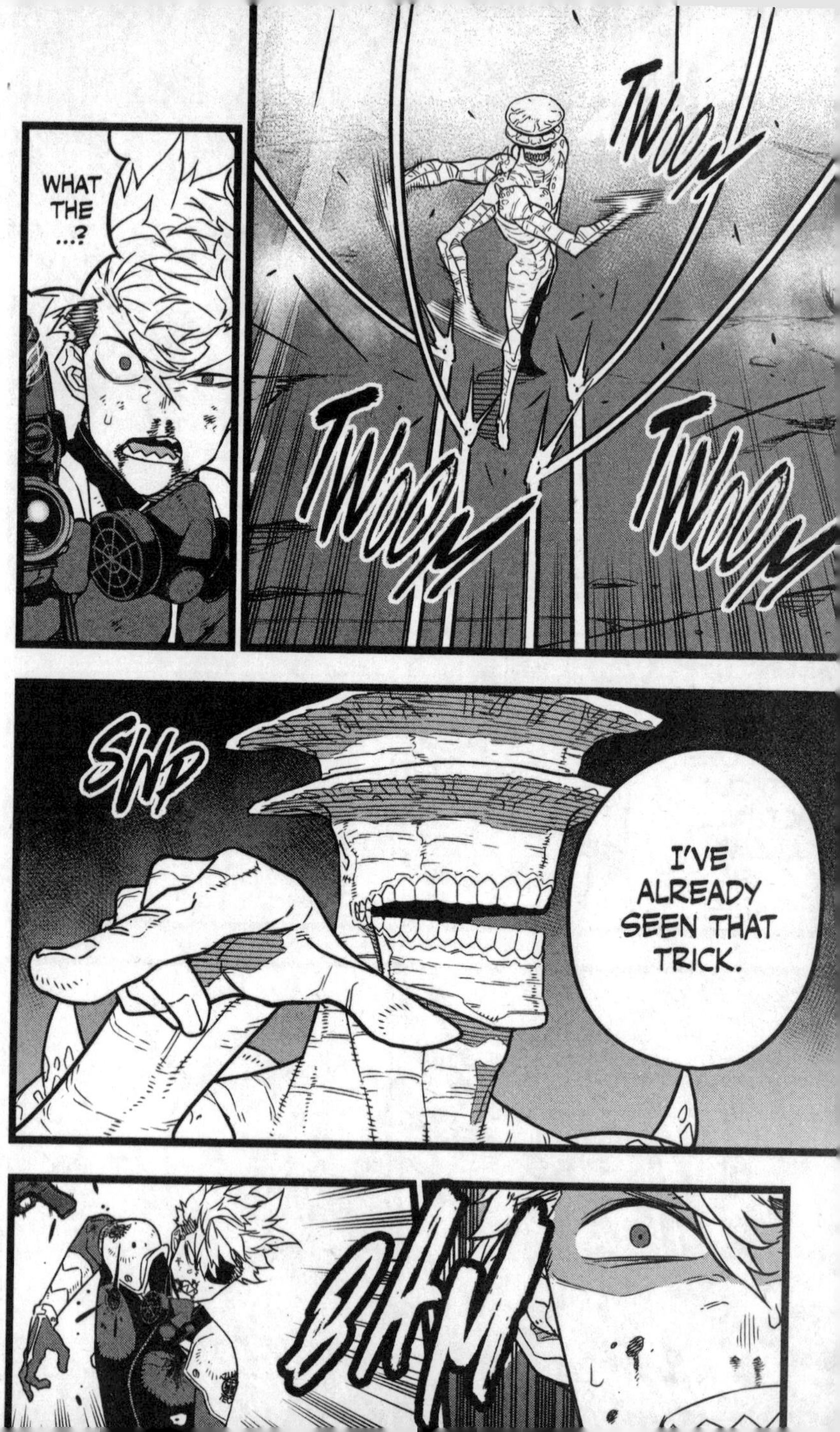
TWOOM
TWOOM
TWOOM
WHAT THE ...?
SWP
I'VE ALREADY SEEN THAT TRICK.

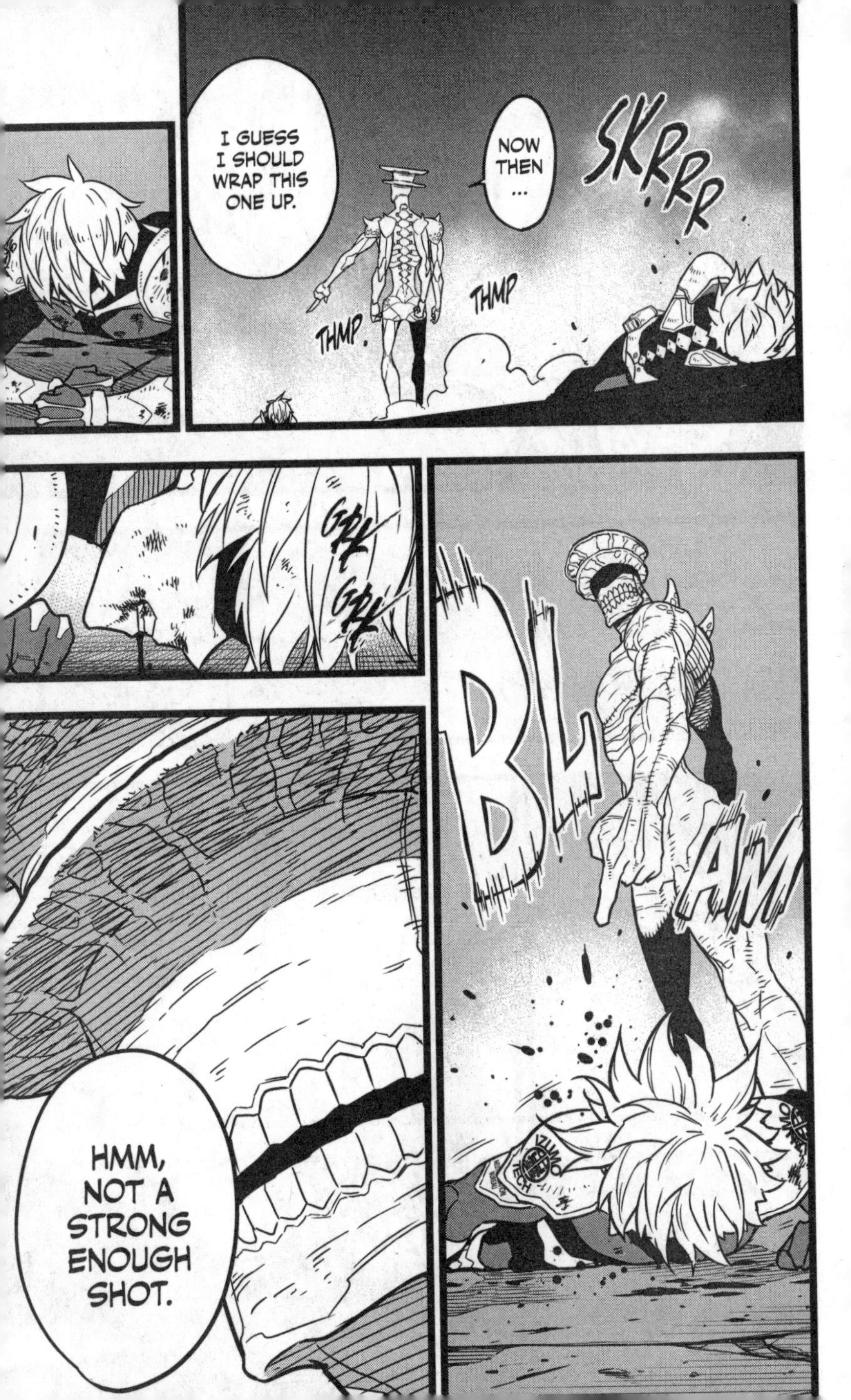
SKRRR
NOW THEN ...
I GUESS I SHOULD WRAP THIS ONE UP.
THMP
THMP
BLAM
GRK GRK
HMM, NOT A STRONG ENOUGH SHOT.

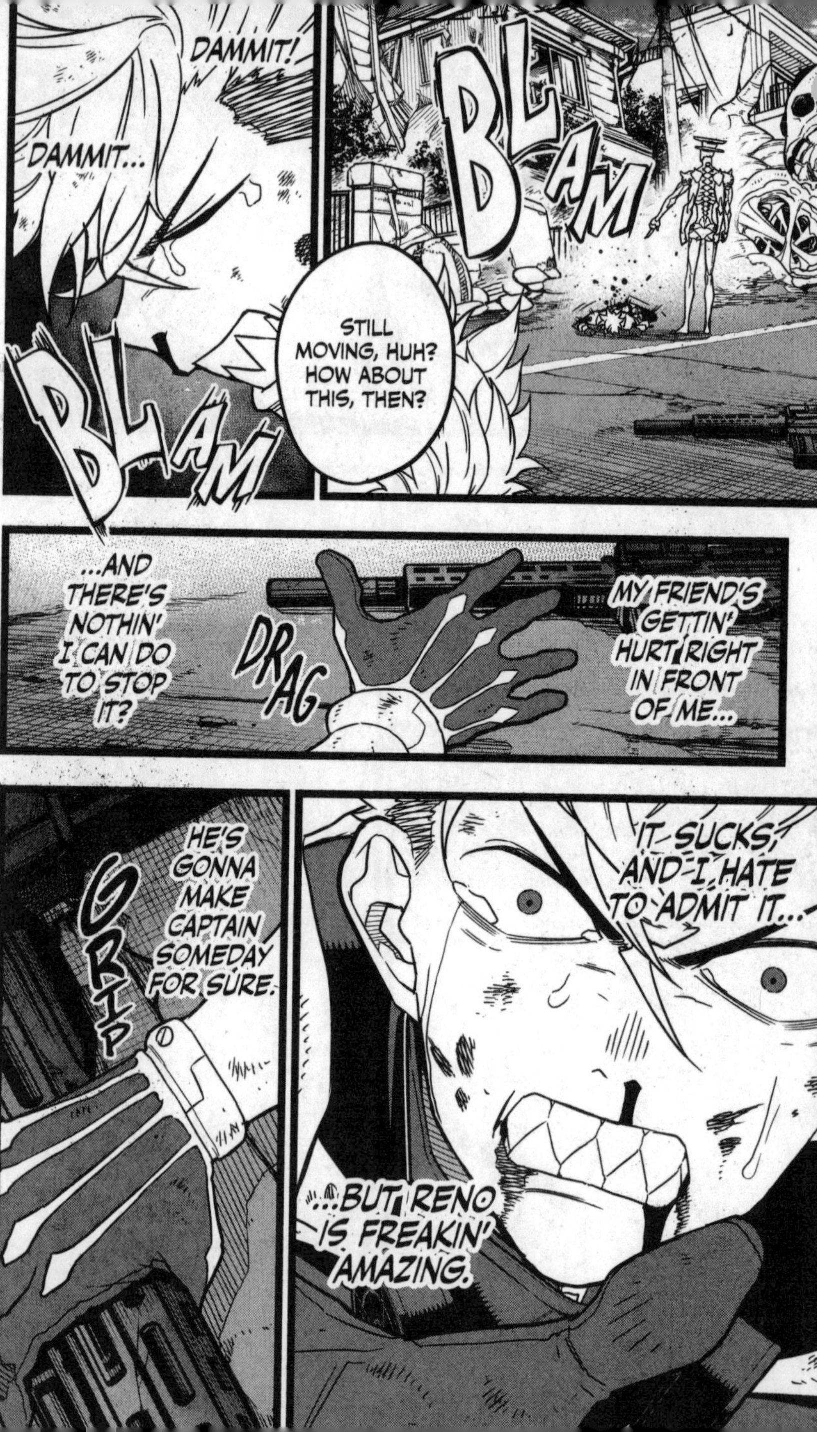
BLAM
STILL MOVING, HUH? HOW ABOUT THIS, THEN?
DAMMIT!
DAMMIT...
BLAM
MY FRIEND'S GETTIN' HURT RIGHT IN FRONT OF ME...
DRAG
...AND THERE'S NOTHIN' I CAN DO TO STOP IT?
IT SUCKS, AND I HATE TO ADMIT IT...
...BUT RENO IS FREAKIN' AMAZING.
HE'S GONNA MAKE CAPTAIN SOMEDAY FOR SURE.
GRIP

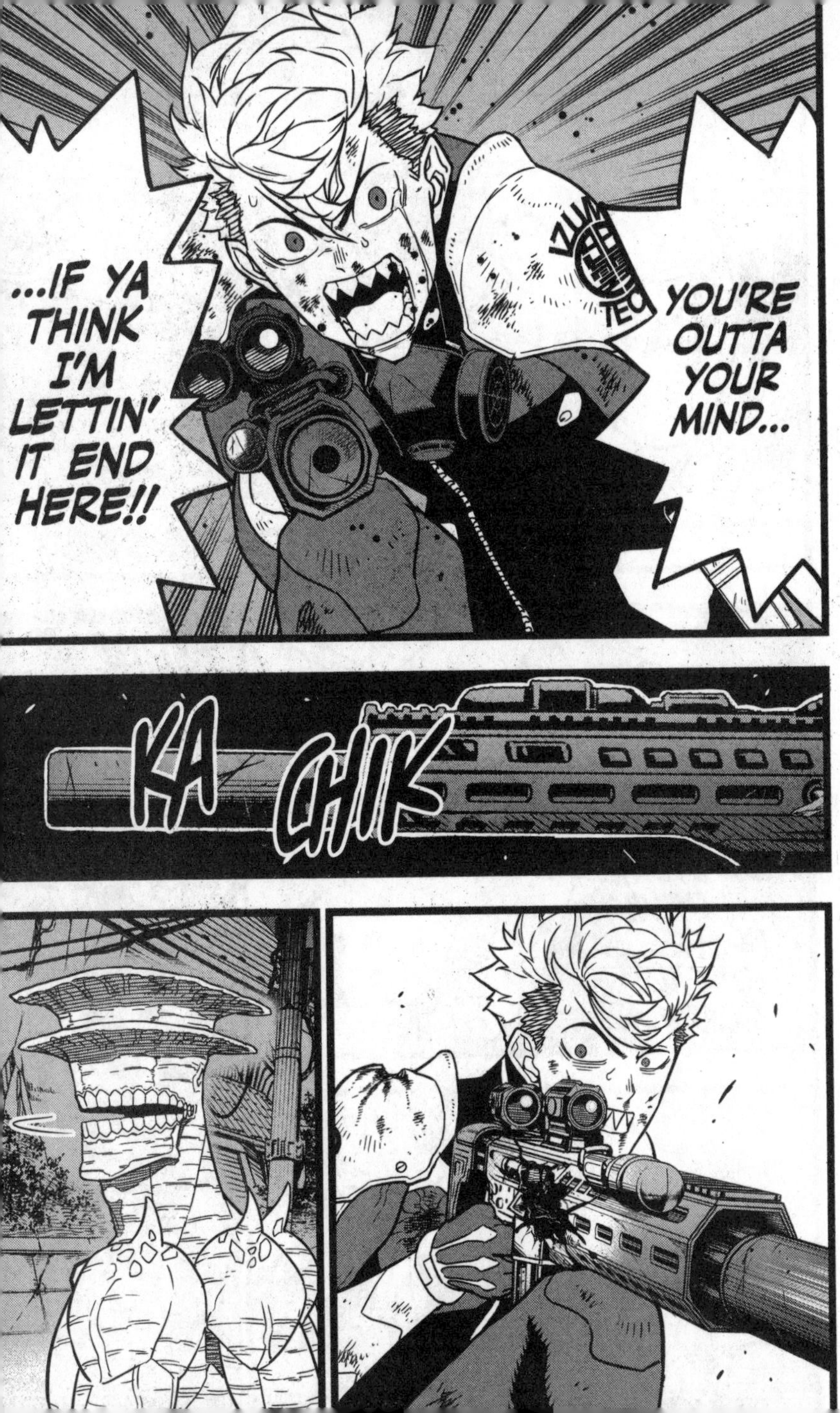
YOU'RE OUTTA YOUR MIND...
...IF YA THINK I'M LETTIN' IT END HERE!!
KA CHIK

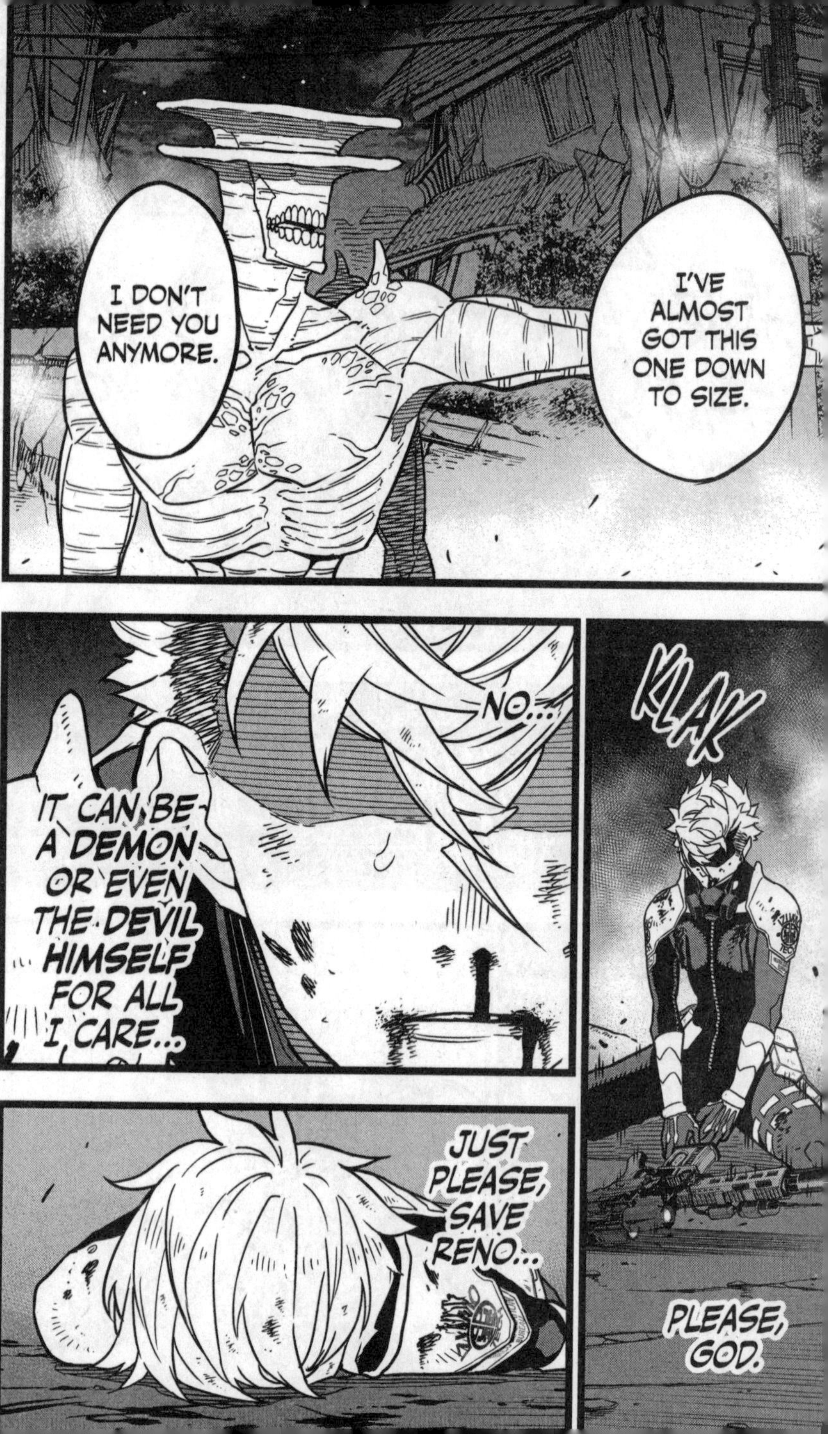
I'VE ALMOST GOT THIS ONE DOWN TO SIZE.
I DON'T NEED YOU ANYMORE.
KLAK
PLEASE, GOD.
NO...
IT CAN BE A DEMON OR EVEN THE DEVIL HIMSELF FOR ALL I CARE...
JUST PLEASE, SAVE RENO...

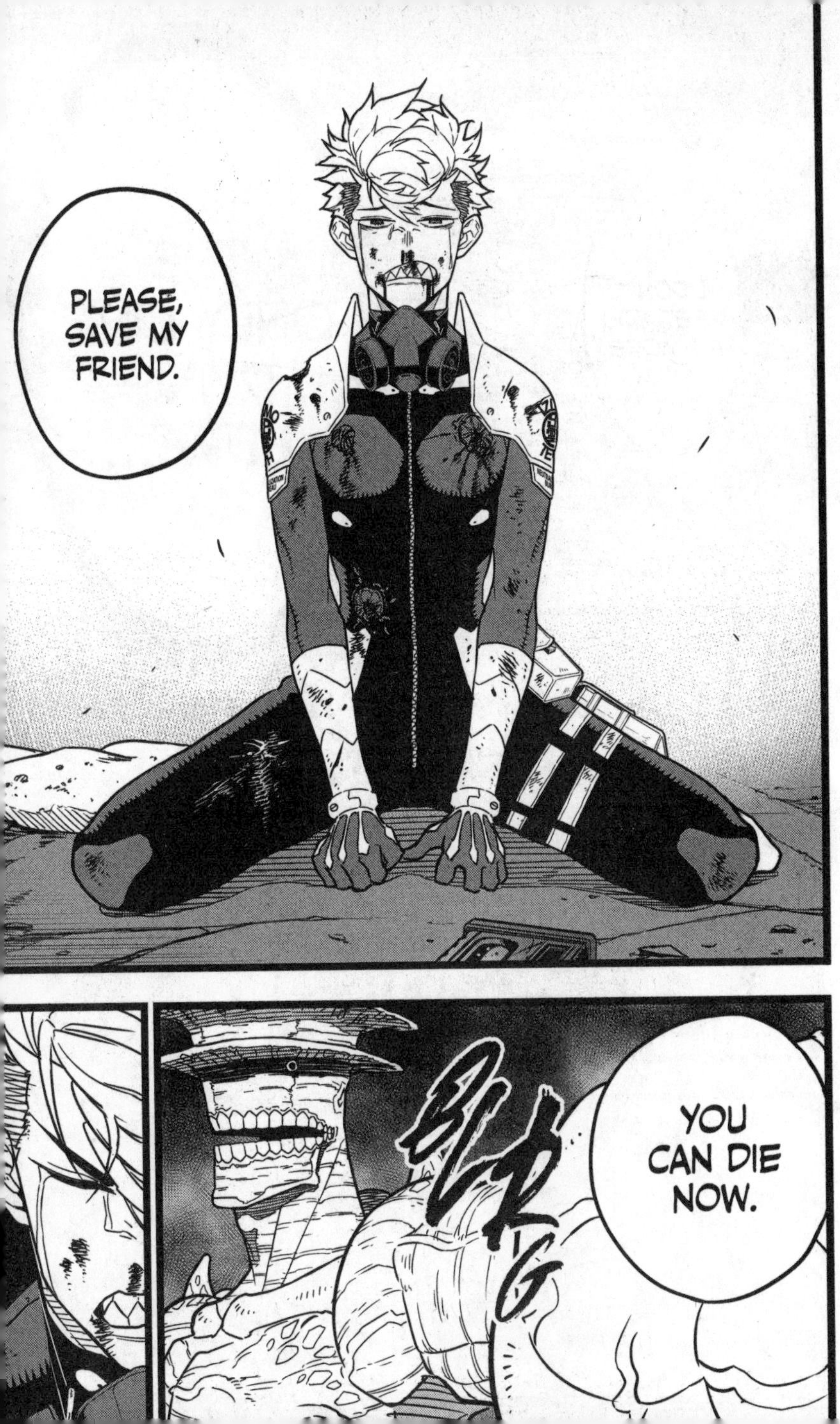
PLEASE, SAVE MY FRIEND.
YOU CAN DIE NOW.

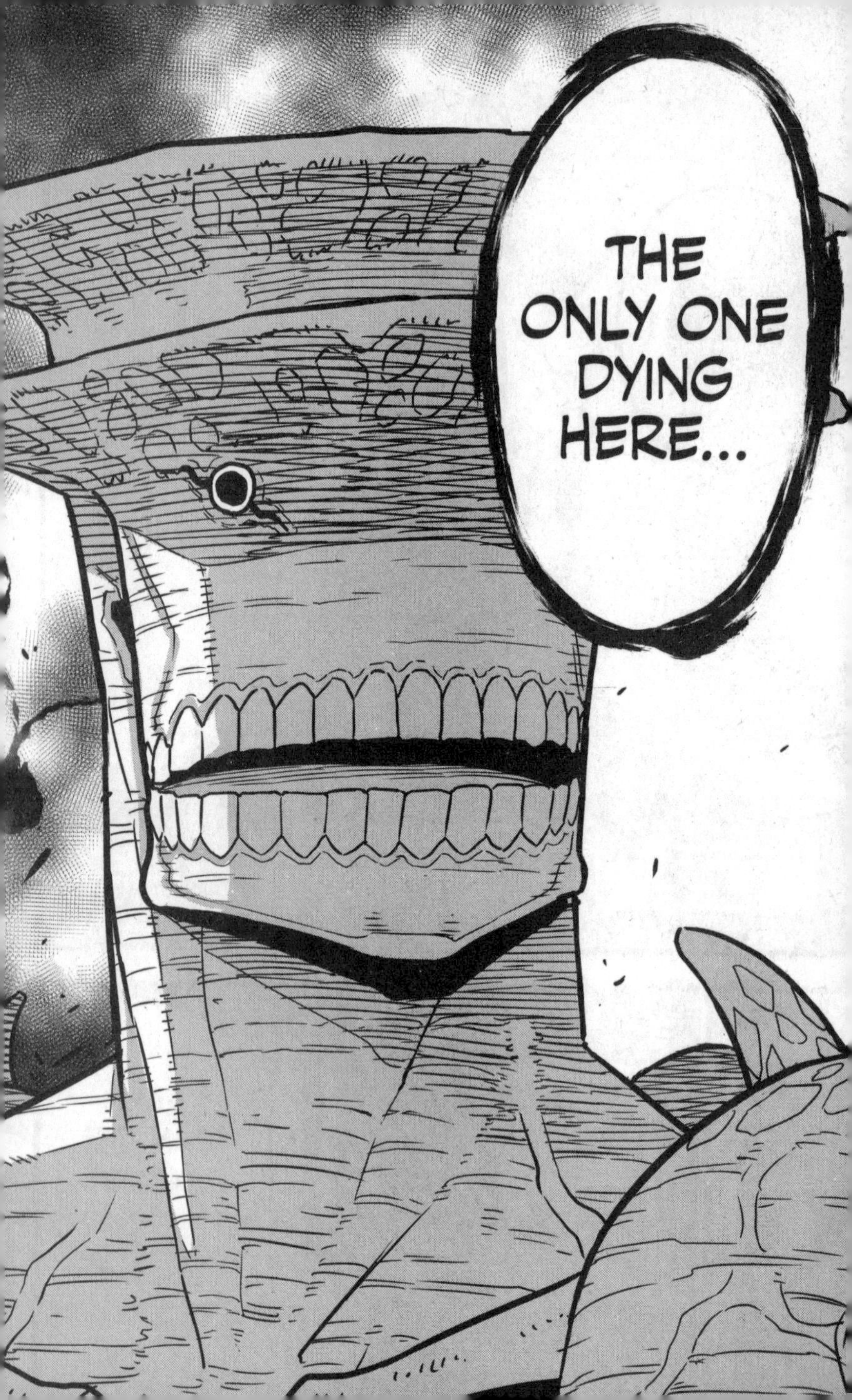
THE ONLY ONE DYING HERE...

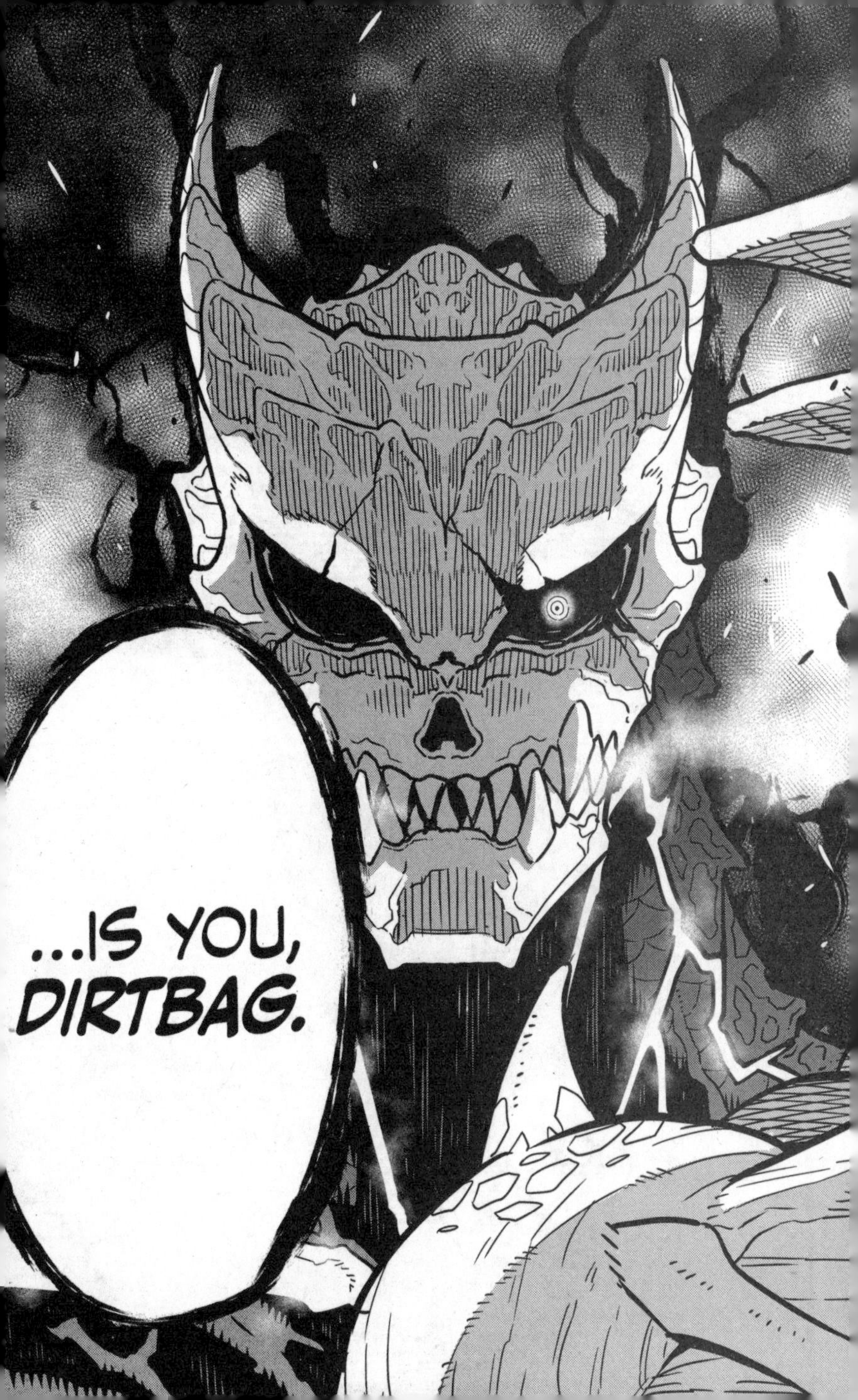
...IS YOU, DIRTBAG.

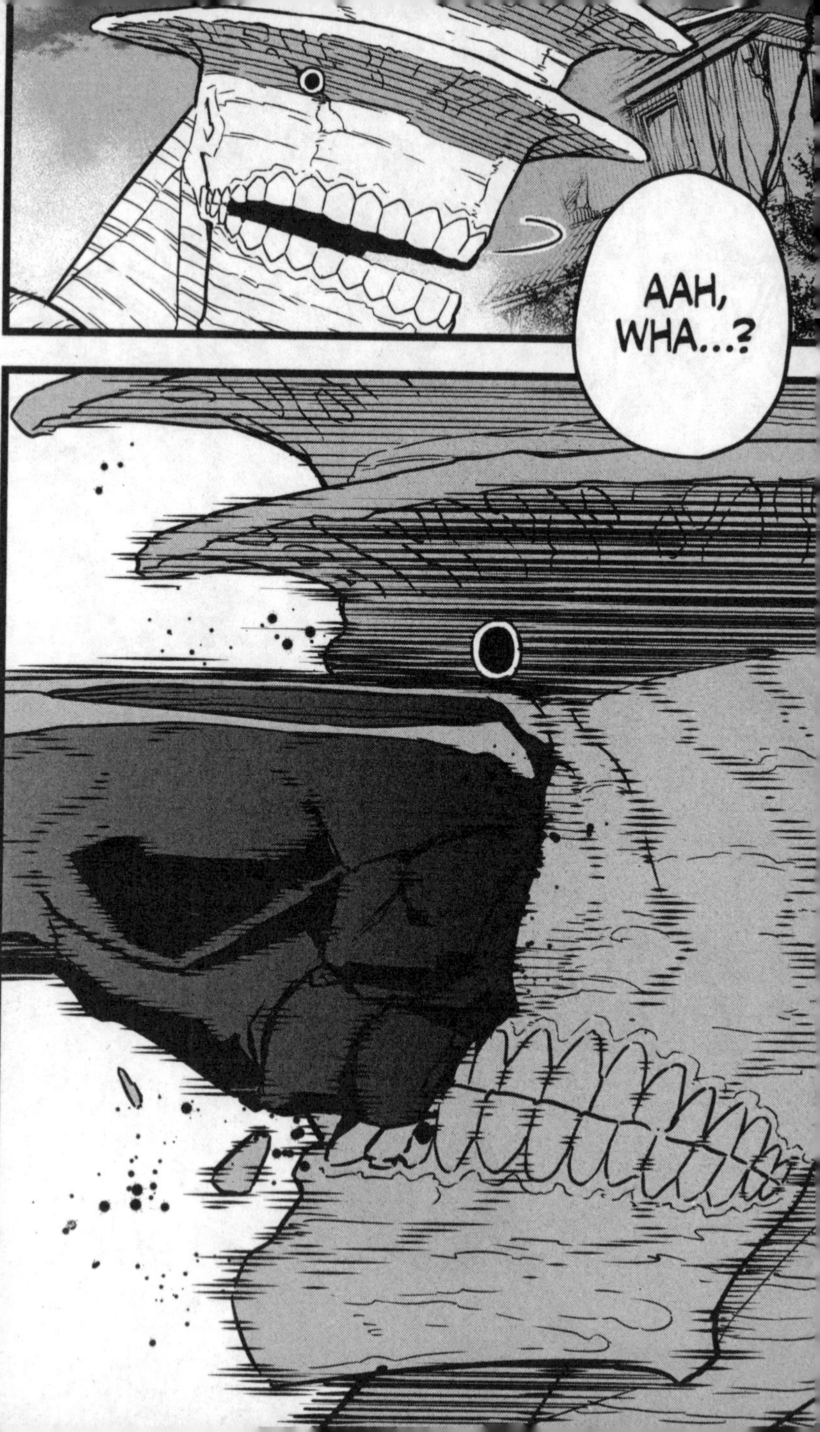
AAH, WHA...?

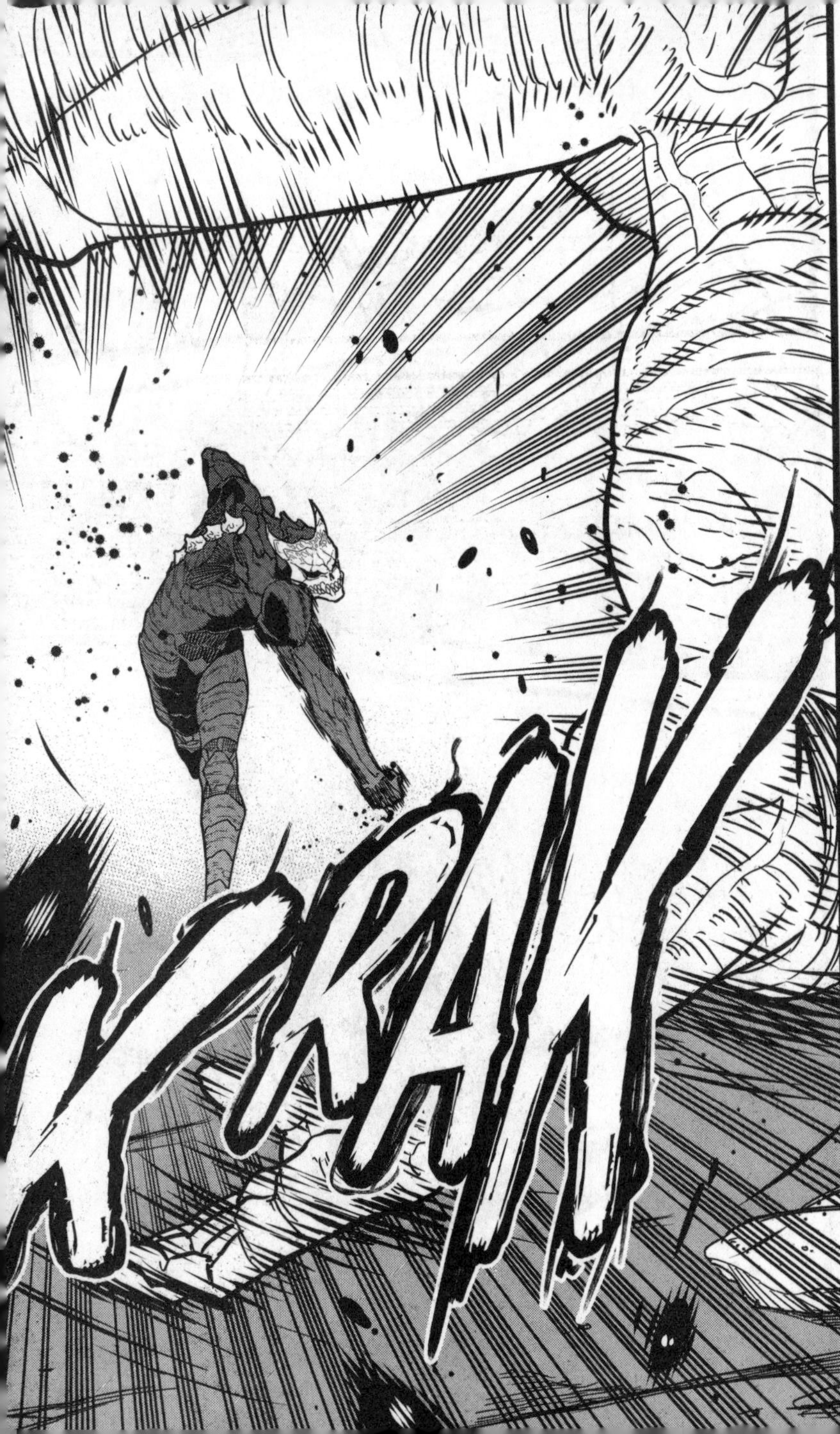

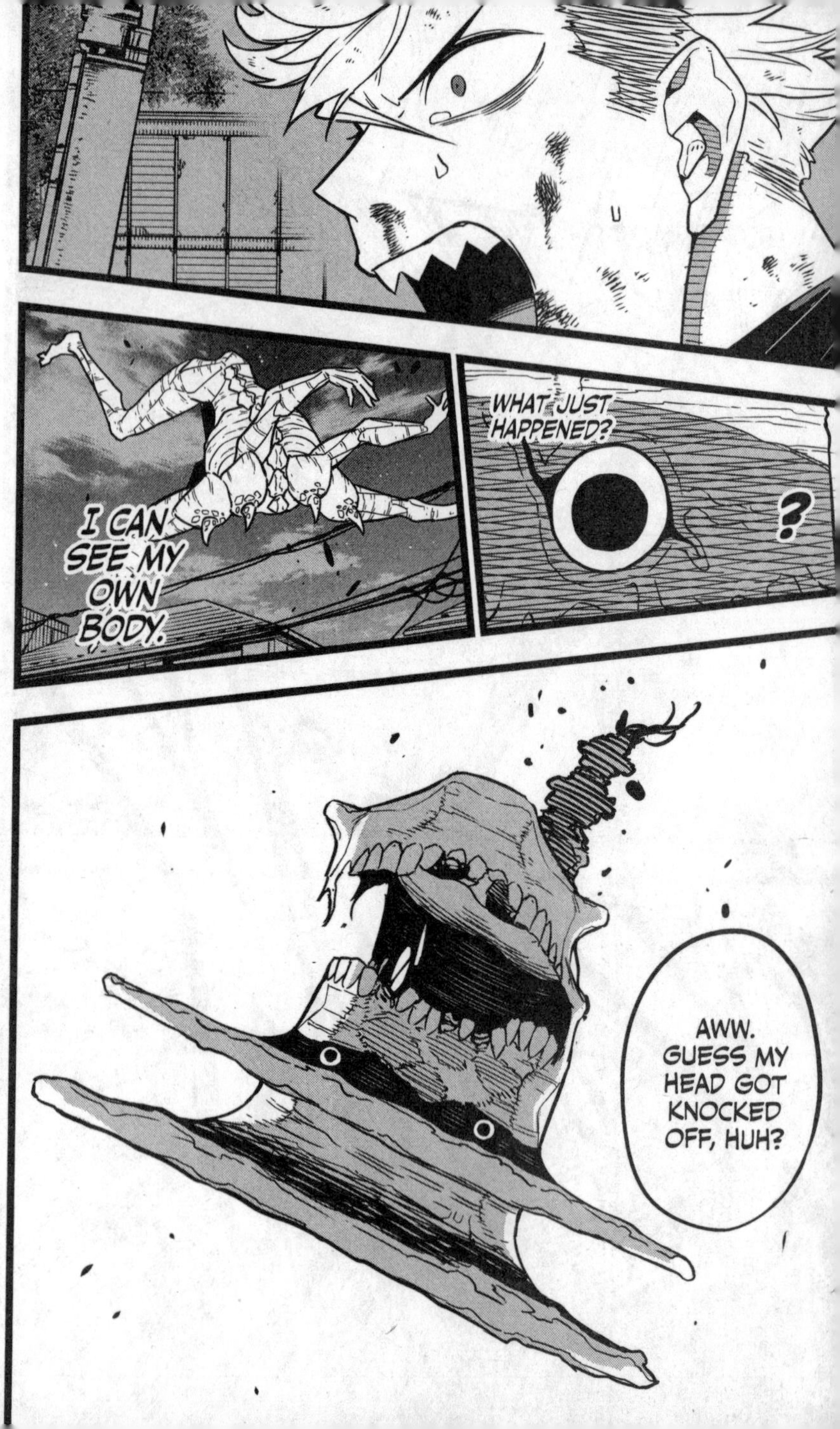
WHAT JUST HAPPENED?
?
I CAN SEE MY OWN BODY.
AWW. GUESS MY HEAD GOT KNOCKED OFF, HUH?

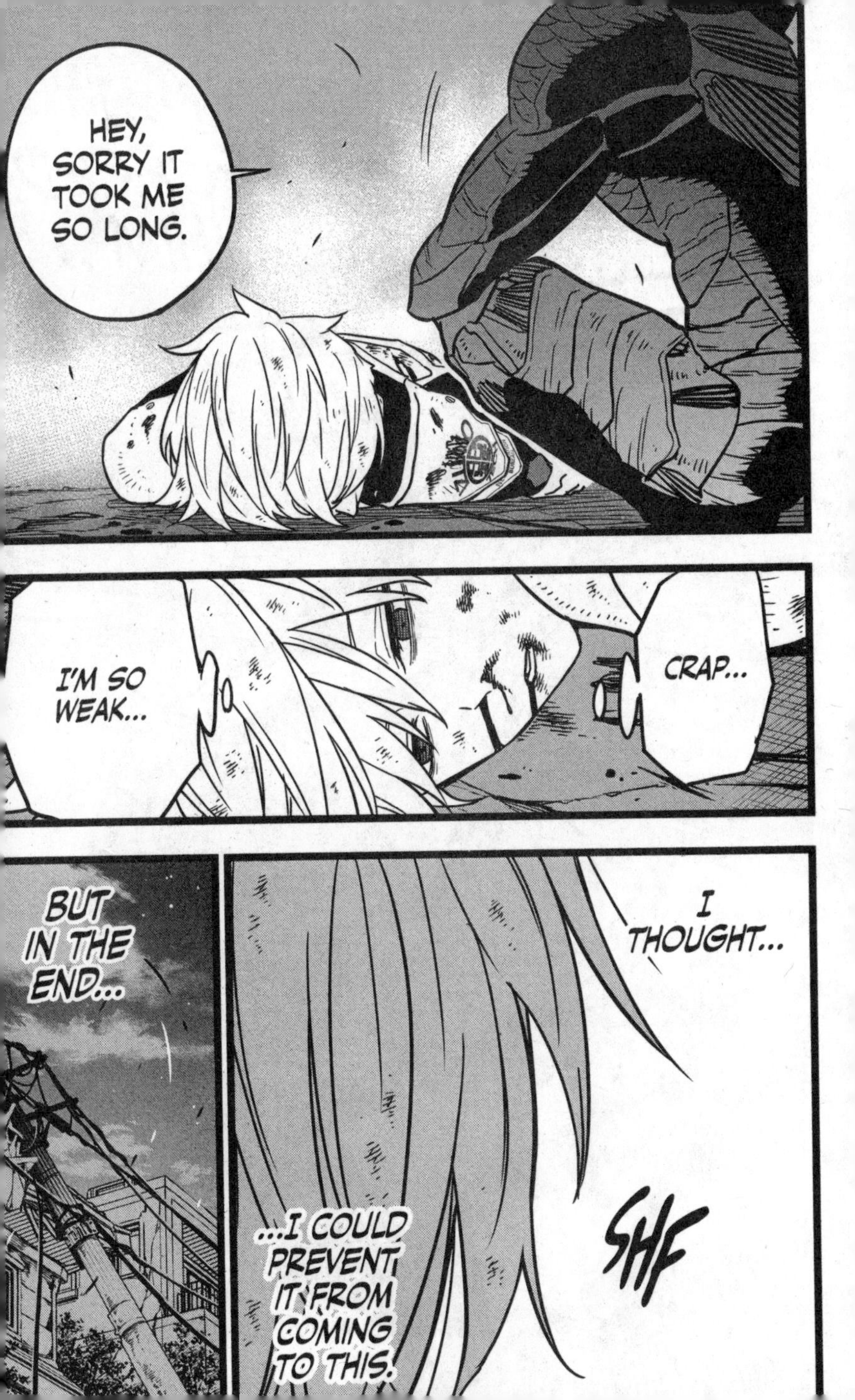
HEY, SORRY IT TOOK ME SO LONG.
CRAP...
I'M SO WEAK...
I THOUGHT...
SHF
...I COULD PREVENT IT FROM COMING TO THIS.
BUT IN THE END...

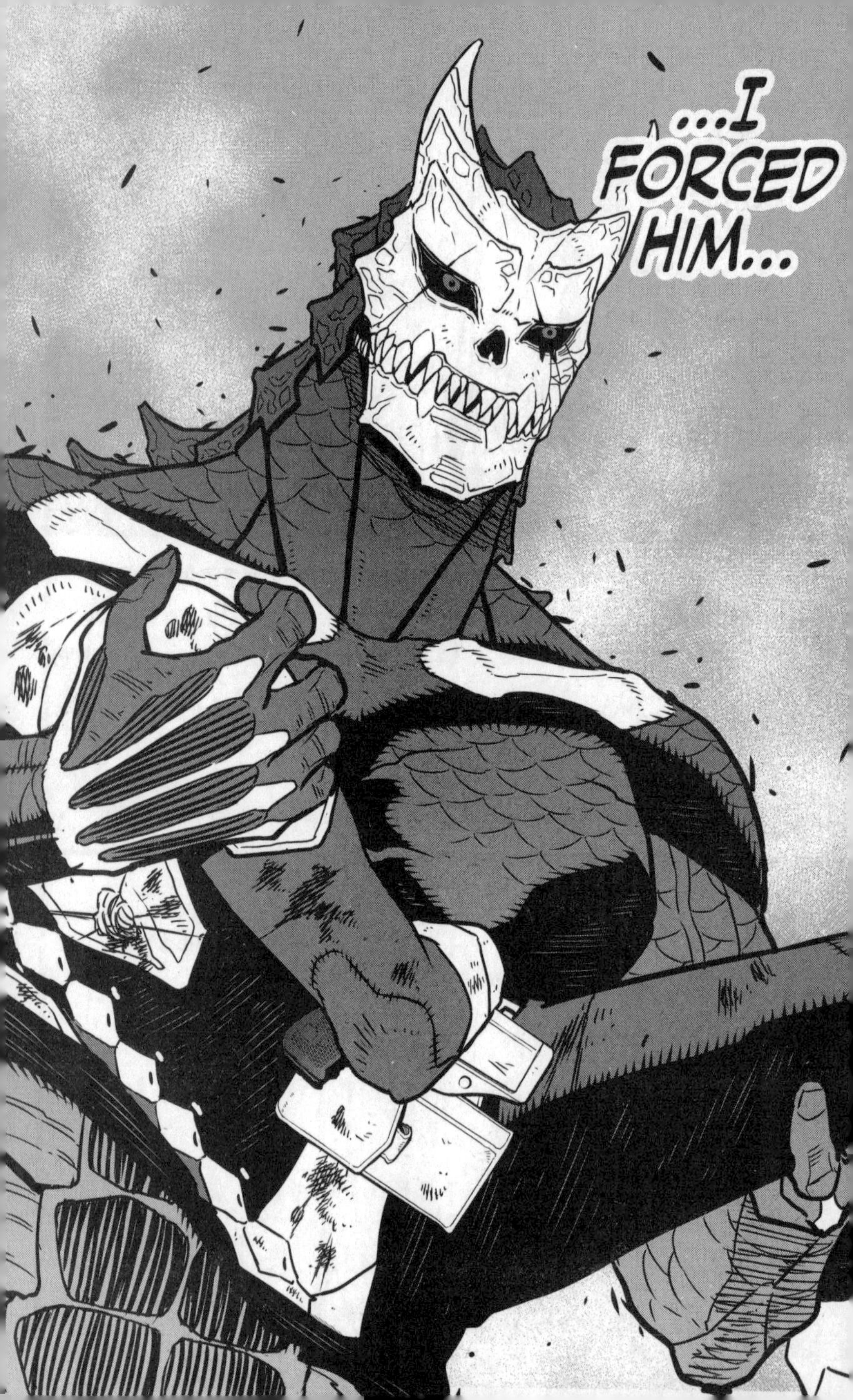
...I FORCED HIM...

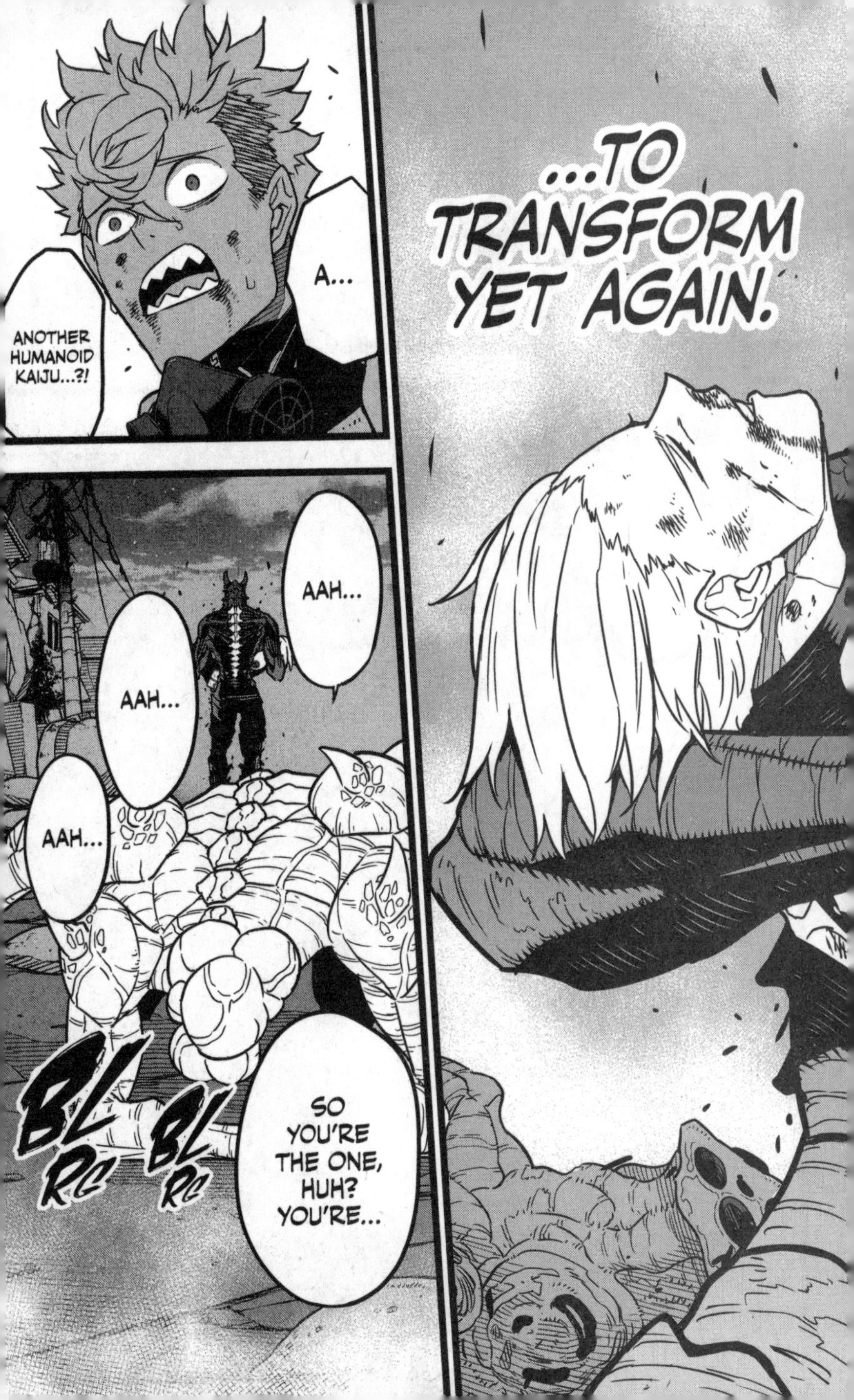
...TO TRANSFORM YET AGAIN.
A...
ANOTHER HUMANOID KAIJU...?!
AAH...
AAH...
AAH...
SO YOU'RE THE ONE, HUH? YOU'RE...
BLRG
BLRG

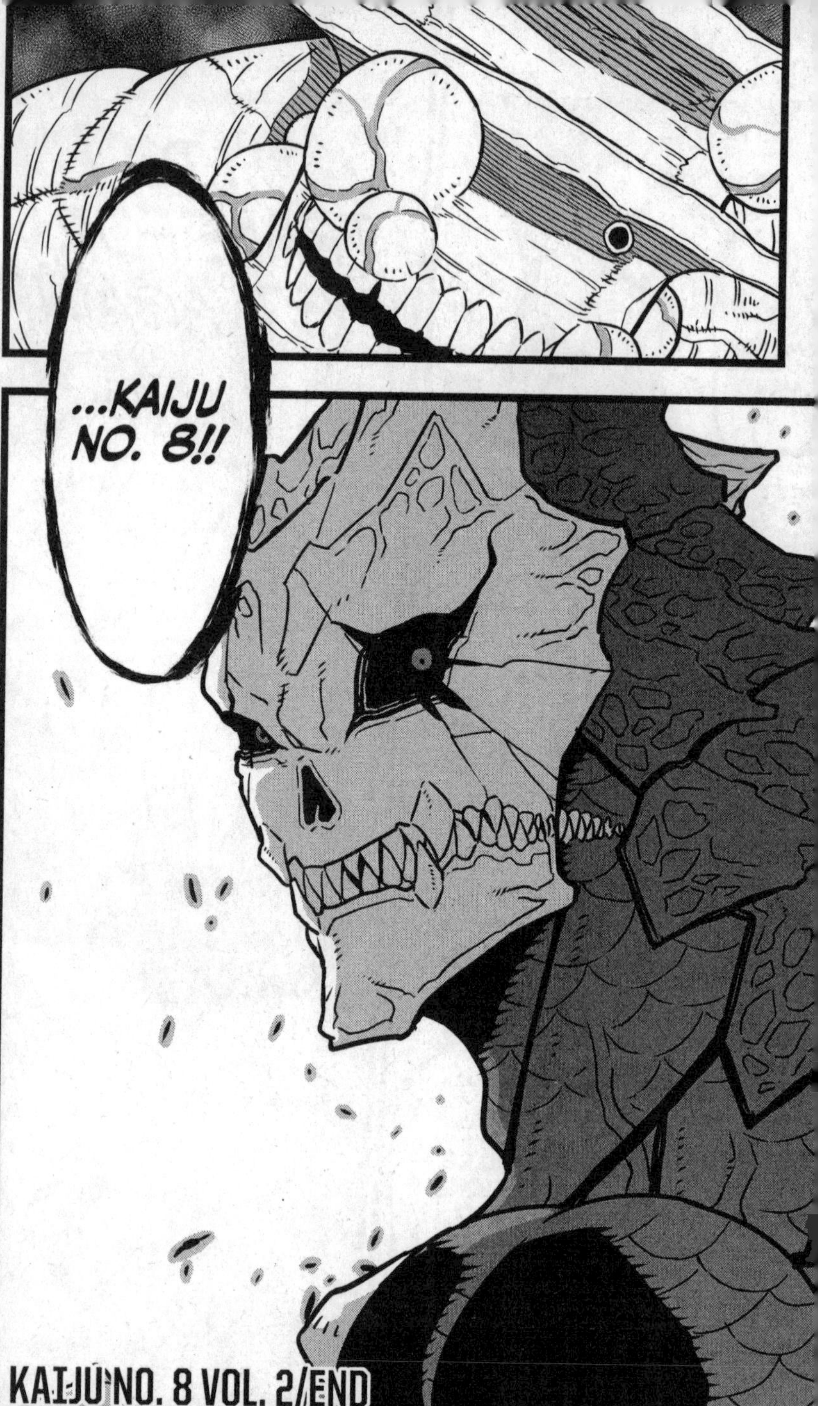
...KAIJU NO. 8!!
KAIJU NO. 8 VOL. 2/END

KAIJU NO. 8

2

STORY AND ART BY
NAOYA MATSUMOTO

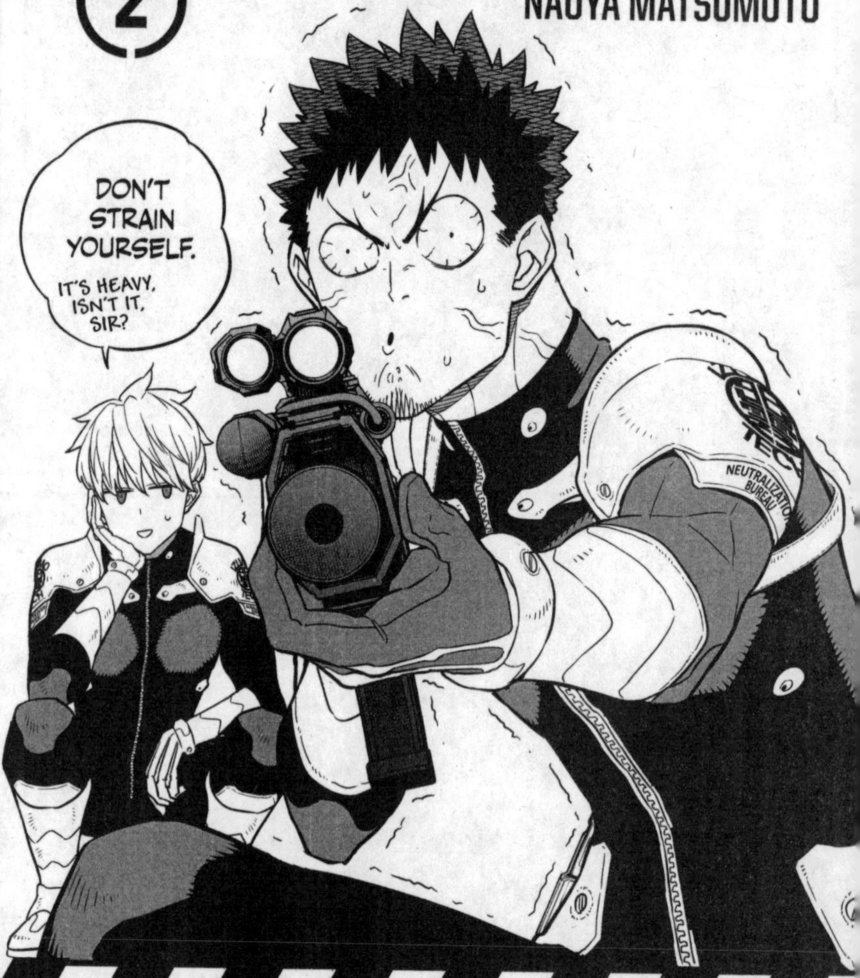
DON'T STRAIN YOURSELF.
IT'S HEAVY, ISN'T IT, SIR?
NEUTRALIZATION BUREAU

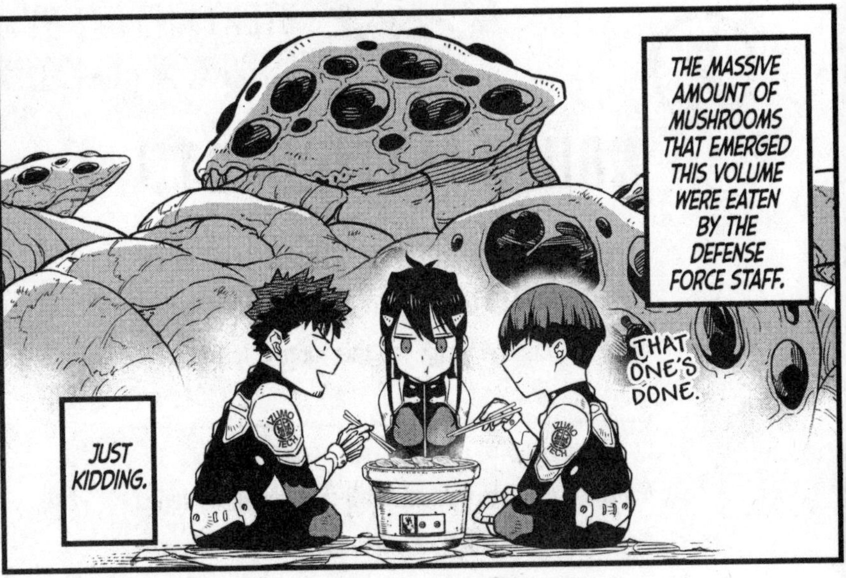
THE MASSIVE AMOUNT OF MUSHROOMS THAT EMERGED THIS VOLUME WERE EATEN BY THE DEFENSE FORCE STAFF.
THAT ONE'S DONE.
IZUMO TECH
JUST KIDDING.

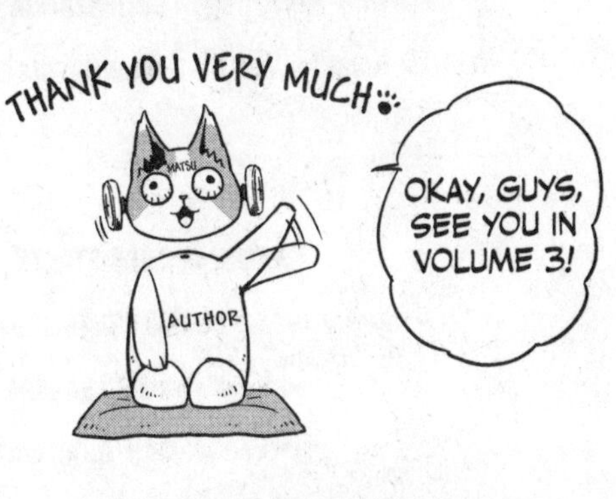
THANK YOU VERY MUCH
OKAY, GUYS, SEE YOU IN VOLUME 3!
MATSU
AUTHOR

NAOYA MATSUMOTO

I was able to put out volume 2 thanks to all of you.
I'll work hard to break my record and get to a fifth
volume! I hope you enjoyed this fungi-filled volume!

Naoya Matsumoto published his first serialized series,
Neko Wappa!, in *Weekly Shonen Jump* in 2009. His next
series, *Pochi Kuro*, began serialization in *Shonen Jump+*
in 2014. *Kaiju No. 8* is his follow-up series.

KAIJU NO. 8 ASSISTANTS

BACKGROUND ART **OSAMU KOIWAI (OSA PROD.)**

FINISHING WORK **JIRO SAKURA**

WEAPON DESIGN **MANTOHIHI BINTA**

KAIJU NO. 8 ②

SHONEN JUMP EDITION

STORY AND ART BY

NAOYA MATSUMOTO

TRANSLATION
DAVID EVELYN

TOUCH-UP ART & LETTERING
BRANDON BOVIA

DESIGN
JIMMY PRESLER

EDITOR
KARLA CLARK

First published in Japan in 2020 by SHUEISHA Inc., Tokyo.
English translation rights arranged by SHUEISHA Inc.

Printed in Canada

Published by VIZ Media, LLC
P.O. Box 77010
San Francisco, CA 94107

10 9 8 7 6 5 4 3 2 1
First printing, April 2022

ratings.viz.com RATED T TEEN

PARENTAL ADVISORY
KAIJU NO. 8 is rated T for Teen and is recommended for ages 13 and up. This volume contains crude humor and depictions of violence.

VIZ MEDIA

viz.com

SHONEN JUMP

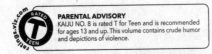

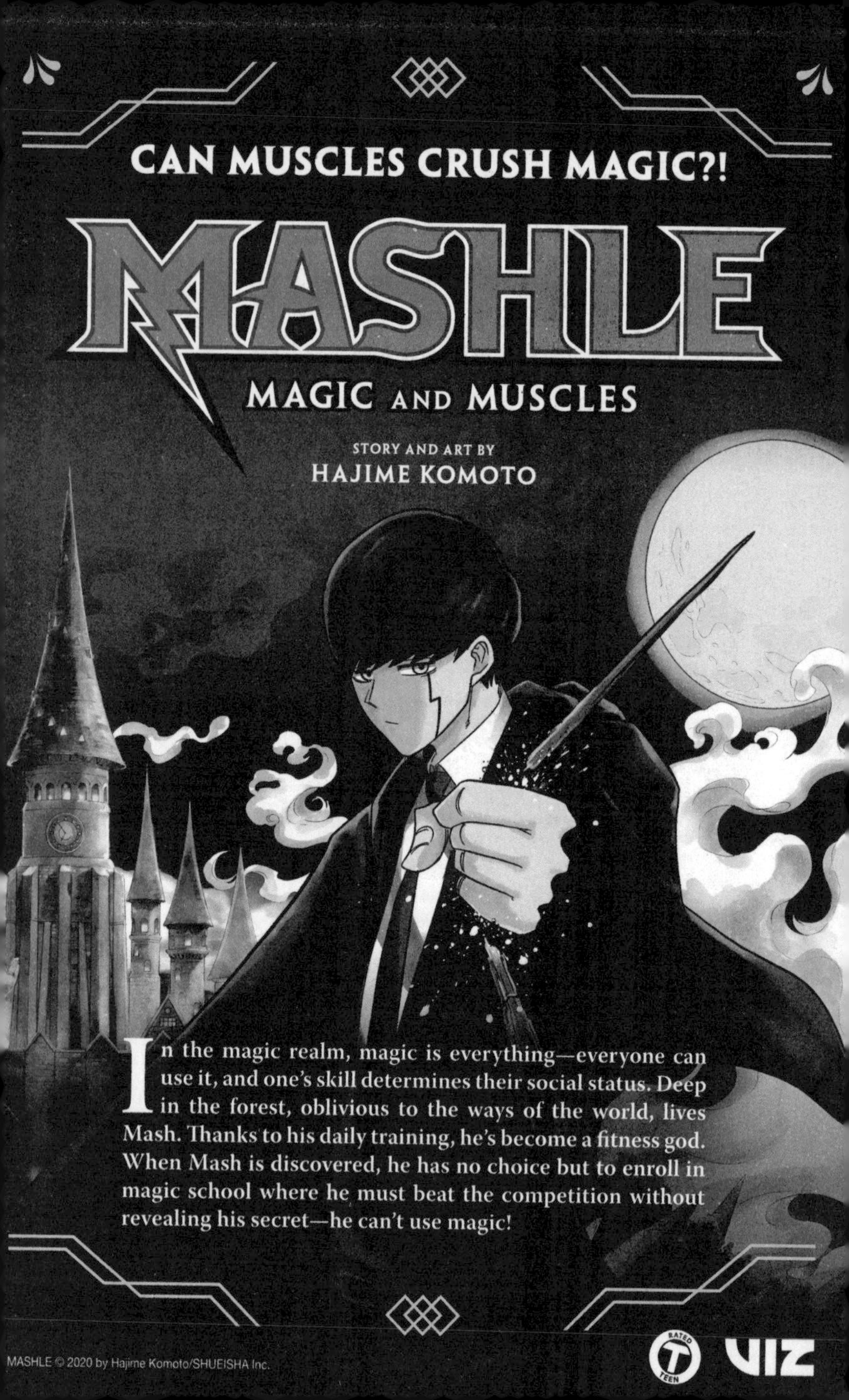
CAN MUSCLES CRUSH MAGIC?!
MASHLE
MAGIC AND MUSCLES
STORY AND ART BY
HAJIME KOMOTO
In the magic realm, magic is everything—everyone can use it, and one's skill determines their social status. Deep in the forest, oblivious to the ways of the world, lives Mash. Thanks to his daily training, he's become a fitness god. When Mash is discovered, he has no choice but to enroll in magic school where he must beat the competition without revealing his secret—he can't use magic!
RATED T TEEN
VIZ
MASHLE © 2020 by Hajime Komoto/SHUEISHA Inc.

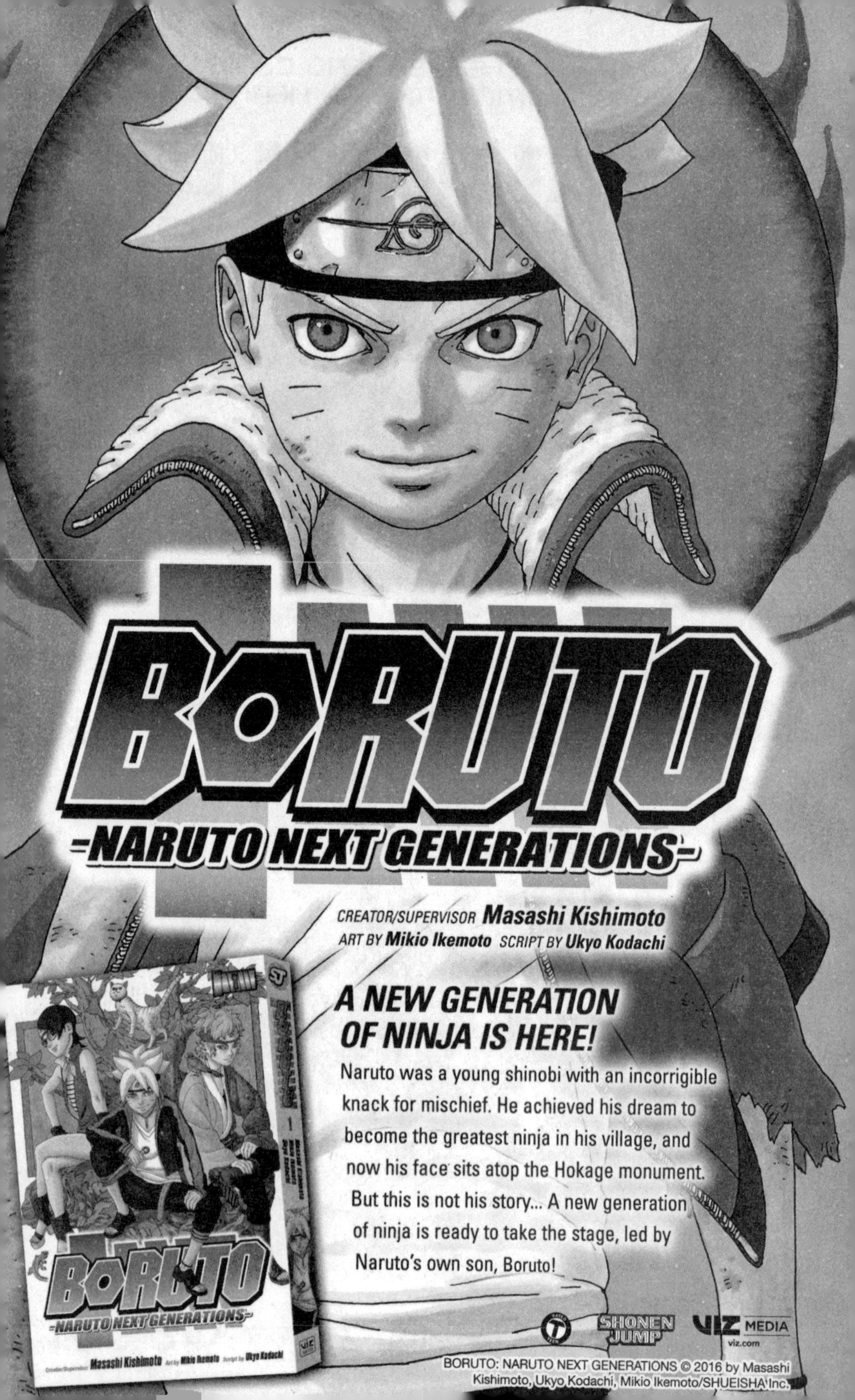
BORUTO
-NARUTO NEXT GENERATIONS-
CREATOR/SUPERVISOR Masashi Kishimoto
ART BY Mikio Ikemoto SCRIPT BY Ukyo Kodachi
A NEW GENERATION OF NINJA IS HERE!
Naruto was a young shinobi with an incorrigible knack for mischief. He achieved his dream to become the greatest ninja in his village, and now his face sits atop the Hokage monument. But this is not his story... A new generation of ninja is ready to take the stage, led by Naruto's own son, Boruto!
BORUTO
-NARUTO NEXT GENERATIONS-
SHONEN JUMP
VIZ MEDIA
viz.com
BORUTO: NARUTO NEXT GENERATIONS © 2016 by Masashi Kishimoto, Ukyo Kodachi, Mikio Ikemoto/SHUEISHA Inc.

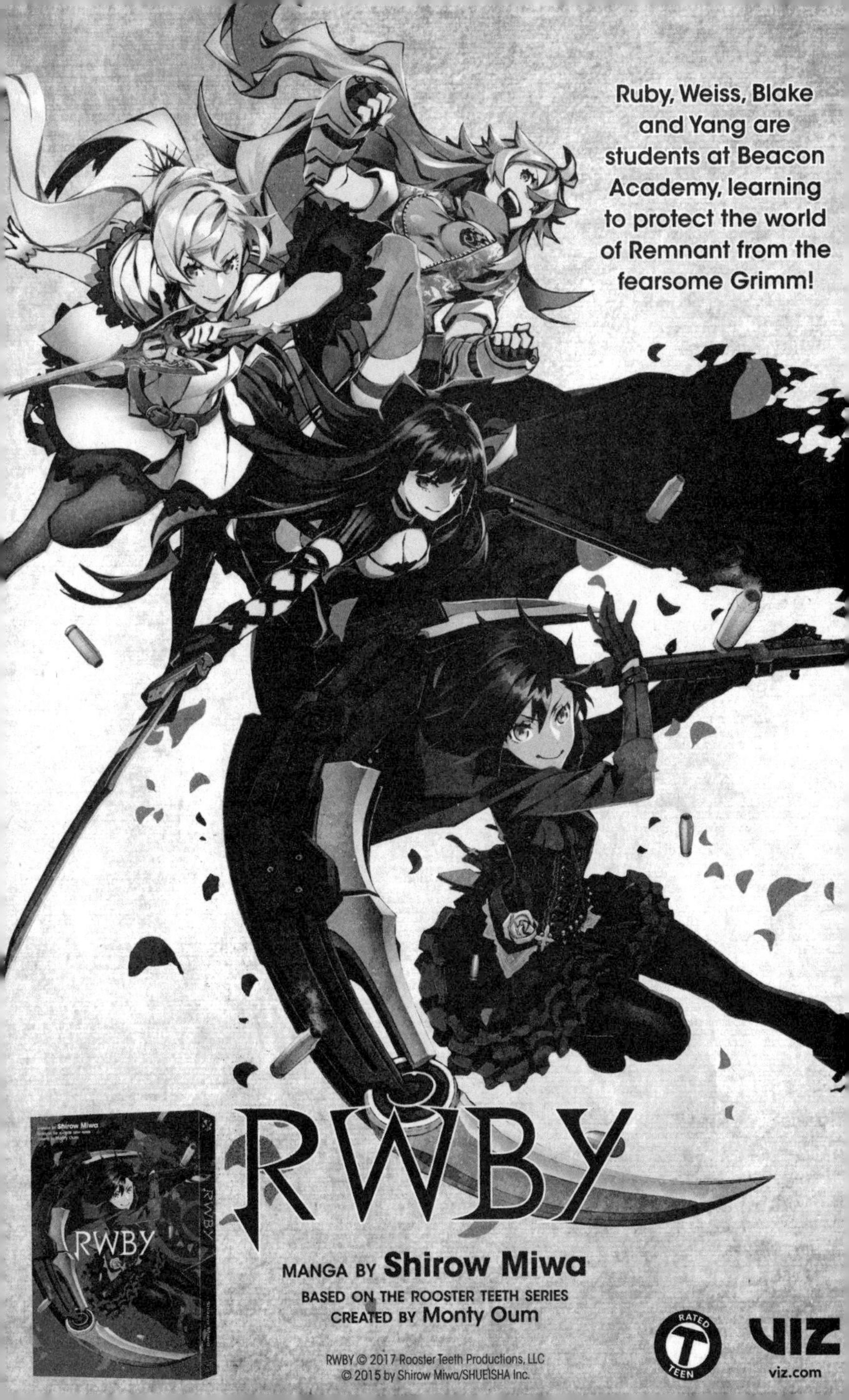
Ruby, Weiss, Blake and Yang are students at Beacon Academy, learning to protect the world of Remnant from the fearsome Grimm!
RWBY
RWBY
MANGA BY Shirow Miwa
BASED ON THE ROOSTER TEETH SERIES
CREATED BY Monty Oum
RATED T TEEN
VIZ
viz.com
RWBY © 2017 Rooster Teeth Productions, LLC
© 2015 by Shirow Miwa/SHUEISHA Inc.

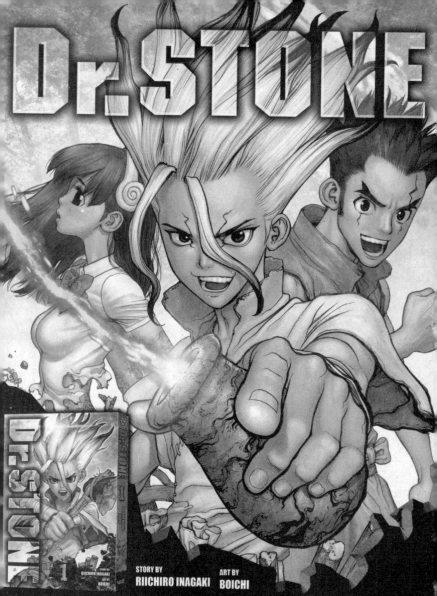

Dr.STONE

STORY BY
RIICHIRO INAGAKI

ART BY
BOICHI

One fateful day, all of humanity turned to stone. Many millennia later, Taiju frees himself from petrification and finds himself surrounded by statues. The situation looks grim—until he runs into his science-loving friend Senku! Together they plan to restart civilization with the power of science!

ALERT! EMERGENCY ALERT! EMER

YOU'RE READING THE WRONG WAY!

1
2
3
4
5
6
7
8
9
1
2
3
4
5
142

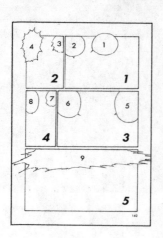

For your own protection, the last page of the book has been sealed off to prevent the ending from being spoiled. To safely consume the contents of *Kaiju No. 8* in their intended order, please flip the book over and start again.

Kaiju No. 8 reads from right to left, starting in the upper-right corner, to preserve the original Japanese orientation of the work. That means that the action, sound effects, and word-balloons are completely reversed from English order.

ENTER! DO NOT ENTER! DO NOT

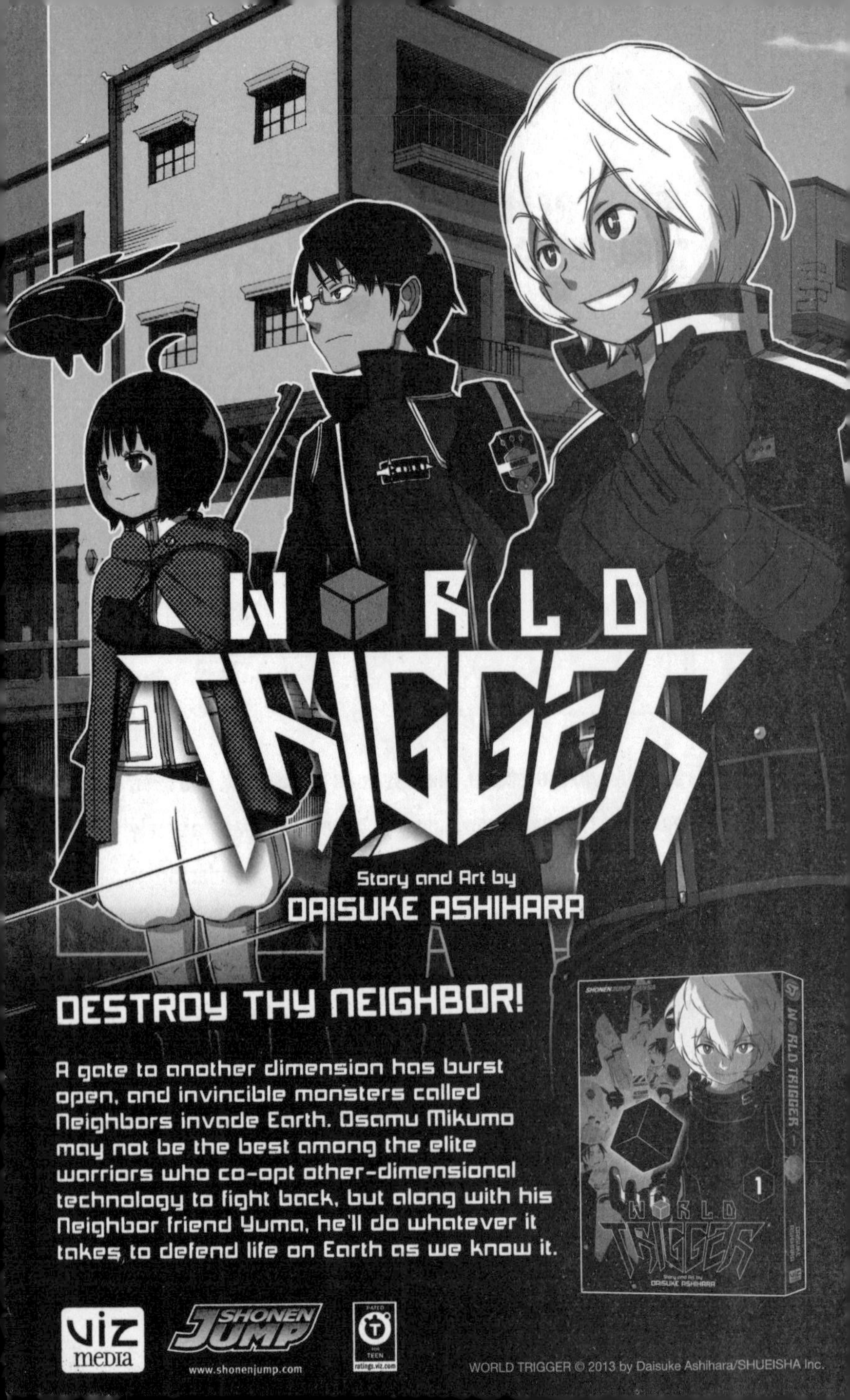

WORLD TRIGGER
Story and Art by
DAISUKE ASHIHARA
DESTROY THY NEIGHBOR!
A gate to another dimension has burst open, and invincible monsters called Neighbors invade Earth. Osamu Mikumo may not be the best among the elite warriors who co-opt other-dimensional technology to fight back, but along with his Neighbor friend Yuma, he'll do whatever it takes to defend life on Earth as we know it.
SHONEN JUMP MANGA
WORLD TRIGGER
1
WORLD TRIGGER
Story and Art by
DAISUKE ASHIHARA
viz media
SHONEN JUMP
www.shonenjump.com
RATED T FOR TEEN
ratings.viz.com
WORLD TRIGGER © 2013 by Daisuke Ashihara/SHUEISHA Inc.